Jonathan Bayley

The Divine Wisdom of the Word of God

Jonathan Bayley

The Divine Wisdom of the Word of God

ISBN/EAN: 9783742829054

Manufactured in Europe, USA, Canada, Australia, Japa

Cover: Foto ©Andreas Hilbeck / pixelio.de

Manufactured and distributed by brebook publishing software (www.brebook.com)

Jonathan Bayley

The Divine Wisdom of the Word of God

THE DIVINE WISDOM OF THE WORD OF GOD

AS SEEN IN THE SPIRITUAL SENSE OF THE

Histories of Samuel, Saul, David, Solomon, & Daniel

BY THE

REV. J. BAYLEY, A.M., Ph.D.

AUTHOR OF "THE DIVINE WORD OPENED;" "FROM EGYPT TO CANAAN," ETC., ETC.

JAMES SPEIRS
36 BLOOMSBURY STREET, LONDON
1892
[*Second Edition*]

PREFACE.

THESE discourses have been issued to illustrate the principle enunciated by the Apostle respecting the history of Abraham, "Which things are an allegory."

The Divine Word is an exhaustless fountain, and we have endeavoured to illustrate the method by which devout souls may draw with joy from the historic portions as well as the preceptive. Happy, indeed, shall we be, if we shall enable thoughtful readers of the Book of books to exclaim, when they perceive spiritual beauty in portions that were closed before, "When I found Thy words I did eat them, and they were the joy and rejoicing of my heart!"

J. BAYLEY.

CONTENTS.

		PAGE
I.	The Birth of Samuel,	1
II.	Hophni and Phinehas—Bad and Good Priests,	9
III.	Samuel and Eli,	17
IV.	The Ark taken by the Philistines,	25
V.	Dagon Fallen before the Ark,	33
VI.	Saul Anointed by Samuel to be King,	41
VII.	Saul's Victory over the Ammonites,	49
VIII.	Samuel's Charge in his Old Age,	57
IX.	Saul sparing Agag,	65
X.	David chosen by Samuel,	73
XI.	Goliath Slain by David,	81
XII.	Saul's Attempts to destroy David,	89
XIII.	Saul attempting to Kill Jonathan,	97
XIV.	Saul and the Witch of Endor,	105
XV.	David's Victory over the Amalekites,	113
XVI.	The Death of Saul,	121
XVII.	David made King at Hebron,	129
XVIII.	The House of David waxing Stronger, and the House of Saul Weaker,	137
XIX.	The Stronghold of the Jebusites at Jerusalem taken, and turned into the City of David,	145
XX.	The Sound of a Going in the tops of the Mulberry Trees the sign for overcoming the Philistines,	153
XXI.	David's Kindness to Jonathan's Lame Son,	161
XXII.	Nathan's Parable,	169
XXIII.	The Death of David's Child,	177
XXIV.	David driven out of Jerusalem by the Rebellion of Absalom,	185

CONTENTS.

		PAGE
XXV.	The Death of Absalom,	193
XXVI.	The Sin of David in Numbering the People,	201
XXVII.	David's Death, and Solomon's Reign,	209
XXVIII.	Solomon's Prayer,	217
XXIX.	The Judgment of Solomon respecting the Dead and the Living Child,	225
XXX.	Solomon's Temple Built without Axe or Hammer, or any tool of iron,	233
XXXI.	The Queen of Sheba's Visit to Solomon,	241
XXXII.	The Abundance of Gold in the Reign of Solomon,	249
XXXIII.	Solomon's Wives and Concubines,	257
XXXIV.	Solomon's Old Age, Declension from God, and Death,	265
XXXV.	Rehoboam's Bad Reign,	273
XXXVI.	The Kingdom divided into Judah and Israel,	281
XXXVII.	The Sun going back on the dial of Ahaz,	289
XXXVIII.	Hezekiah's Sickness and Recovery,	297
XXXIX.	The Destruction of Sennacherib's Army,	305
XL.	The Burning of the Temple and City of Jerusalem by Nebuchadnezzar, king of Babylon,	313
XLI.	Ezekiel's Vision of the Wheels,	321
XLII.	Jonah's Order to go to Nineveh, and his Disobedience,	329
XLIII.	Jonah's Penitence in the Fish,	337
XLIV.	The Repentance of Nineveh,	345
XLV.	Jonah and the Gourd,	353
XLVI.	Daniel and his three Companions in the Palace of Babylon,	361
XLVII.	Nebuchadnezzar's Dream,	369
XLVIII.	Nebuchadnezzar's Golden Image,	377
XLIX.	The Three Faithful Ones in the Fiery Furnace,	385
L.	Nebuchadnezzar's Vision of the Great Tree,	393
LI.	Belshazzar's Feast and Death,	401
LII.	The Restoration of Jerusalem.	409

SERMON I.

THE BIRTH OF SAMUEL.

"Wherefore it came to pass, when the time was come about, after Hannah had conceived, that she bare a son, and called his name Samuel, *saying*, Because I have asked him of the Lord."—1 SAM. i. 20.

SAMUEL was one of the great leaders of the Jewish nation. His life was long. His virtue was true and courageous. His influence was pure and powerful. His death was honoured with his nation's tears. All the Israelites were gathered together, and lamented him, and buried him at his house in Ramah.

The glory of the Word of God is that it discloses lessons of wisdom and importance in its outer, as well as in its inner meaning. The Bible, as that name implies, is the Book above all other books. "Thou hast magnified thy Word, above all thy name," is true of the literal sense, when devoutly and thoughtfully considered, as well as of the spirit: and tends to make a man who loves and meditates upon it, "thoroughly furnished to every good work." The period to which the divine history before us applies, was about three hundred years after the death of Joshua. The nation had passed through a long series of declensions, and sunk at last into a condition of lawless anarchy, division and impurity, but little better than that of the more ancient Sodom. The weakness of some judges, the wickedness of others, and the turbulence of the people, had brought the twelve tribes, formerly so wonderfully led from Egypt, to the brink of ruin; and a man was needed, who could once more introduce divine government among them, and be to them as the preserving "salt of the earth." God gave them such a man in answer to the pious Hannah's prayer. This gift of God was Samuel. The sacred narrative, in portraying the deep feeling of Hannah, —a prayer too deep for words—places strongly before us the inestimable value of a child. She was "in bitterness, and prayed unto the Lord, and wept sore," because she had no child. She vowed that if she were blessed by her heart's deep petition being granted, she would dedicate the child to the peculiar service of the Lord in the ministry; and in due time her prayer was granted. The birth of a child is so common an event that, like all our greatest blessings, which are common to all, it arrests but little attention. In parents and immediate friends a babe awakens feelings tender and affectionate, yet often much less deep than the wondrous occasion requires. What a lovely, what a mysterious, what an awful nature exists in that immortal little being! An unending life has begun! The germs of heaven, of earth, and of hell, are enclosed in its astonishing person. The power of increasingly enjoying the two worlds of sense and spirit is there, but the power also of perverting both! Humanity is a God-formed lyre to be played upon by the universe without, and the universe within, until every string thrills with the music of intelligence, wisdom, love, gratitude, beauty, and joy.

A child is an image of God Himself. All his infinite qualities are finitely shown in miniature, in the "heir of immortality." And the universe, the Deity's grander image, responds to humanity, even infantine humanity, because it issued from His Divine Humanity of love, justice, truth, order, use, and happiness. A wondrous, glorious thing is a child! After man fell, and the promise was given that the seed of the woman should bruise the serpent's head, an expectation filled the mothers of the Eastern world in that most ancient time that the child redeemer might be born of them. This surrounded babyhood with a peculiar glory, besides its intrinsic worth. This prevalent feeling is described by Virgil in his magnificent poem, "Pollio," and far more anciently still in the words of Eve respecting Cain: "I have gotten a man—the Lord." The word *from* in our translation is not in the original language. All over the East, the belief was spread and perpetuated that a divine child was to be born. That belief is referred to in the utterance by Zacharias, the father of the Baptist, when inspired by the Holy Spirit, and referring to the infant Redeemer, he said, "Blessed be the Lord God of Israel, for He hath visited and redeemed His people, and hath raised up a horn of salvation for us in the house of his servant David, as He spake by the mouth of His holy prophets, which have been since the world began." The expectation thus cherished and transmitted from generation to generation, gave rise to the allegories of Egypt, India, Babylon, and Greece, in which the incarnations of Deity hold a distinguished place, and at the same time, it imparted a holiness and depth to the desire for children, which is worthily cherished by the newly-married of our race, until the Babe of Bethlehem was born, and men could truly say, "Unto us a Child is born, unto us a Son is given, and the government shall be upon his shoulder, and His name shall be called WONDERFUL, COUNSELLOR, THE MIGHTY GOD, THE EVERLASTING FATHER, and THE PRINCE OF PEACE."

A child is a wondrous thing! Who knows what is wrapped up in its mysterious being? God helps men through men. When the infant Moses lay in his little ark, who could have surmised that in helpless innocence the deliverer of his people was there, the lawgiver, who would receive the laws of love afresh from heaven, and transmit them to untold myriads of the human race.

If mothers would feel like Hannah that their children were confided to them by the Lord, to be trained in gentleness, in purity, in principle, to become intelligent, pure and good, the world would soon be filled with nobler characters, and government, trade, commerce, and operations of every kind would feel the advent of a nobler Christianity, a living religion of integrity, light and love. If there were more Hannahs, there would be more Samuels.

Let us now penetrate into the divine page a little deeper.

We must ever bear in mind that the Word of God, like the works of God, contains a living inner meaning. "My words they are spirit and they are life" (John vi. 63), applies to all His words, precept, parable, and history alike.

The divine words must contain divine thoughts, and these are always on things higher than those of earth. It is written, "My thoughts are not as your thoughts, neither are your ways as my ways. For as the heavens are higher than the earth, so are my ways higher than your ways, and my thoughts than your thoughts" (Isa. lv. 8, 9).

The history of Israel, it is well known by spiritually-minded men, is a divine parable, as well as a real history. When the Psalmist was about to recite all the dealings of the Lord with his nation, from their life in Egypt onwards, he said, "I will open my mouth in a parable: I will utter dark sayings of old" (Ps. lxxviii. 2).

It is this spiritual meaning which constitutes the chief mark of the divinity of the Word. There is everywhere beneath its hallowed page, a stream of silvery wisdom, and yet another, and yet another, which reaches up to God. He has magnified His Word above all His name. These are the things the angels desire to look into (1 Pet. i. 12). In this respect the Law of the Lord is perfect, converting the soul (Ps. xix. 7).

To see the spiritual lessons involved in the divine history before us, we must notice the leading particulars related, and then apply the law of correspondences or analogy between the things of earth and those of heaven. We shall thus rise from the letter to the spirit.

Israel, under the judges, had sunk into all wickedness, lewdness, and lawlessness existed all over the land, and this was called doing "right in their own eyes."

The Jews, in the time of our Lord, had made the commandments of God of none effect by their traditions, and many Christians at the present day set the commandments of God aside by their traditions. These also do right in their own eyes. How many have the tradition that the commandments of God were never intended to be kept, and cannot be kept. These, therefore, do that which is right in their own eyes, restrained only by the law of the land, often far from righteous; or the custom of their trade, or of their associates, often far from moral or just.

How could the thousand knaveries of dishonest trade continue, unless in one way or another, by one tradition or another, the law of God were set aside, and laws were made by people for themselves, which are good in their own eyes? The moderate offend in a less violent way, the bold to the worst extreme; but each have the secret hope that he will take no eternal harm, for he has a tradition that by a priest or a prayer, he will make all right at last. He is doing that which is right in his own eyes, but forgetting the great truth that that which is highly esteemed among men is often an abomination in the sight of God (Luke xvi. 15).

For a society depraved and polluted by self and selfish maxims, there is no help but by a restoration of the Word of God. Divine light must penetrate the darkness. God must in some way give His mind again to the people. In man himself, there is no help. The way in which the Divine Mercy brings aid to man is the subject of the spiritual sense of the sacred narrative before us. Samuel was raised up, a seer, who received Divine Truth from the Most High, and imparted its pure lessons of life to the people. When the state of a church has become grossly dark and evil, so that a new beginning must be made, there are always a few, a remnant of good, whom the Lord can make a nucleus of better things. Noah, his wife, his sons, and their wives, were the remnant in the days of the flood. The Israelites in Egypt were the remnant in the days of Moses. Those who expected the coming of the Lord Jesus were the remnant by which Christianity was commenced, and to whom the Saviour said, "Fear not, little flock, it is your Father's good pleasure to give you the kingdom." Elkanah and his two wives represent the remnant in the days of the history we are now considering. They dwelt at Ramathaim Zophim, some heights, probably a day's journey from Shiloh, also in the country of Ephraim, where the tabernacle then was. Names and places in Scripture have a spiritual signification in the spiritual sense, which is indicated by the meaning of the terms. Ramathaim means heights, and Zophim, those who expect. *The heights* of the expecters, is expressive of the state of the few, in a corrupt time, who preserve themselves in high principles, the principles of virtue, charity, and love, and wait for better things. They are like the shepherds who kept watch over their flocks by night, and to whom the glory of the Lord was revealed. The "expectors" who yearn for a New Church when the old has become like "salt which has lost its savour," always spiritually keep watch over their flocks, or in other words, over those gentle affections which are grouped in their bosom, like flocks of sheep and lambs. They dwell spiritually in Ramathaim Zophim. They will not stoop to any practices which they feel assured are low, base, mean, or wicked. They expect the coming of the Lord, and they keep their lamps trimmed, so that when the Divine voice is heard, they may go forth to meet Him.

Elkanah, which in Hebrew means God the zealous, represents the Divine zeal, urging them to spiritual things—their conviction that God is zealous is implied, and that they should be zealous for him. The two wives, Peninnah and Hannah, represent the two affections which exist in the souls of the true servants of the Lord, the affection for outward truth, represented by Peninnah, and of inward truth, represented by Hannah. The word Peninnah signifies "a pearl," a precious stone, good, but of a low order, a product of the sea. Hannah means "grace," and refers to what is interior in religion. The same method of representing this interesting and important description of the Church, occurs often in the Holy Word. Lamech, with his two wives, is an early instance. Abraham, with Sarah and Hagar, which things are an allegory, as Paul said, is another instance. Jacob, with Leah and Rachel, really brings before us the same general subject; and the Prophet Isaiah, in the 54th chapter, uses the same divine symbols when he exclaims: "Sing, O barren, thou that didst not bear; break forth into singing, and cry aloud, thou that didst not travail with child: for more are the children of the desolate than the children of the married wife, saith the Lord" (ver. 1).

How very like is this triumphant burst of the prophet when he beheld in prophetic vision a spiritual church extending among men, to the joyful exultation of Hannah, when the Lord had granted her request. "The barren hath borne seven, and she that hath many children hath waxed feeble" (1 Sam. ii. 5). In the Gospel, the beautiful narrative of Lazarus, Martha, and Mary relates to the same interesting theme.

The Church, the bride and wife of the Lord Jesus, is represented by a woman, or rather by two women. Her first state is always external, like that represented by Hagar, Leah, Peninnah, Martha. While striving to obey the law of duty, whose reasons she can but faintly see, she is in servitude. She is a hired servant of our heavenly Father, in a good service, but yet one felt as somewhat of bondage. Religion in this external state has many sons before any are born again of inward truth. There are a far greater number of Marthas than of Marys. Many come into the state of obedience and do what they are commanded, and it is right they should. They are the sons of Peninnah. They find pearls, but pearls of the letter of the Word. The Lord loves them, encourages them, blesses them; but they are only in the outer courts of His kingdom. The truth has not yet made them free. The Lord is talking with them by the way, and their hearts often burn within them; but they do not yet exactly know who He is. The spirit of Truth is with them, but not yet in them. They are the children of obedience, but not the children of light, nor the children of love. Yet the inward church yearns to have children. She is a woman grieved and afflicted in spirit until some are born of her. The inward affection of truth yearns to bring forth, and to form a kingdom of heaven within. The truly spiritually-minded will not rest in the outside view of religion. Their yearning for inner wisdom is inexpressibly deep—too deep for words. They wish to know really the nature and character of the Lord, to know the laws of His kingdom; the spirit and life of His Word. The inward affection of such is represented by Hannah.

The outward church often, like Peninnah, make no account of those who wish to feel and to see something deeper, purer, and better than the common reiteration of the letter of divine things. They mock at those who seek "inner wisdom." They profess to think they **will have great deligh**t in seeing mysteries cleared up hereafter, **but have** no concern whatever to arise and receive the glory of the Lord now. Such are the Peninnahs. But Hannah, or those who are moved by inner grace, are in bitterness of soul. They pray and weep sore; they love truth and desire to have it now. They wish to know the Lord now. They desire to become heavenly now. Their aim is to have a new heart and a right spirit now. They know the Lord has promised the new birth, and they wish in humility to have it. They yearn to think as angels think, love as angels love, and enjoy a present heaven.

Eli observed Hannah in her prayer too deep for words, and did not understand her.

Those of the character of Eli, the good, easy ceremonialists, the formalists, the religious by trade, wonder at the emotion of such people. They believe them fanatical, enthusiastic, drunk, and are astonished that they cannot be quiet. But, on finding the case is too deep for them, they give it up, and let them go in peace. Such are the characters represented by the words of Hannah, and those of Eli. Hannah persevered with her prayer of faith, and the Lord heard her. Her manifest sincerity and earnestness impressed the high priest, and he said, "Go in peace; and the God of Israel grant thee thy petition that thou hast asked of Him" (v. 17). Hannah rose and was confident her prayer would be answered, and all would be well.

In due time Samuel was born, and the whole family was grateful, worshipped the Lord, and gave thanks. When the new-man, the babe in Christ, is born, he has been asked of the Lord, and he has been granted by the Lord. It is the new man yet a babe, but created in righteousness and true holiness (Eph. iv. 24), hungering and thirsting after righteousness, and with blessed aspirations. His mother, Hannah, the inward affection for interior truth, will nurse him well, and supply him with the sincere milk of the Word, as the apostle Peter says, "and in due time he will be weaned." (1 Pet. ii. 2).

Samuel appeared in the temple with three bullocks, an ephah

of fine flour, and a bottle of wine (v. 24). There will be inward meditation, inward devotion, and converse with the Lord, when the new birth has taken place, so that a full conscience, a goodly inner man is formed, and then he is presented visible to others in the Lord's church, with the offering of three bullocks, an ephah of flour, and a bottle of wine. These offerings represent the perfect obedience the child of the Lord desires to render; represented by the three bullocks by which the infant Samuel was accompanied to the temple: the one they slew is the acknowledgment that we should have no self-righteousness in this holy obedience we yield to our Heavenly Father and Friend, the contrite heart is truly his gift.

The ephah of flour means inward charity, called by our Lord the full corn in the ear (Mark iv. 28), and by the Divine Spirit in the Psalms the finest of wheat (lxxxi. 16), while the bottle of wine is the emblem of that cheering inner wisdom which gushes from the thankful heart when it is happy in conjunction with the Lord. New wine is put into the new bottle of a regenerated mind, the cup is felt to be running over, and the soul gratefully exclaims, Surely goodness and mercy shall follow me all the days of my life, and I will dwell in the house of the Lord for ever. The soul humbled in itself to the dust by a sense of grateful love, yet rejoicing in the divine mercy that has diffused into it a radiant glory full of heaven, exultingly exclaims with the words of Hannah's song, "He raiseth up the poor out of the dust, and lifteth up the beggar from the dunghill, to set them among princes, and to make them inherit the throne of glory." What a wondrous, what a glorious change is wrought in the soul when the new man is born! He who was poor indeed, becomes eternally rich. He who was a slave of sin, becomes divinely free. He who could look only to degradation and insanity, now knows that he will flourish in increasing wisdom and everlasting youth. He who was an incipient fiend becomes a beautiful angel. For the turbulence of a troubled mind, he attains the golden peace of heaven. O let us "give thanks unto the Lord, for He is good; for His mercy endureth for ever."

SERMON II.

BAD PRIESTS AND GOOD PRIESTS.

"And this shall be a sign unto thee, that shall come upon thy two sons, on Hophni and Phinehas; in one day they shall die both of them.
"And I will raise me up a faithful priest, that shall do according to that which is in my heart, and in my mind: and I will build him a sure house; and he shall walk before mine Anointed for ever."—1 SAM. ii. 34, 35.

THE Lord administers His blessings to men through the instrumentality of men. He is really the giver of all things, the all in all: but for man's happiness, and that man may receive somewhat of the Divine joy He has in giving, He imparts His gifts largely through the thousand offices of use for which He fits all human beings by their varied tastes, aptitudes, training, and circumstances. The labourer and the farmer, the mechanic and his employer, the seaman and the merchant, the artist and the scholar, the literary man and the philosopher, the legislator and the sovereign, all alike receive from the Divine Universal Father gifts in their daily callings to impart to their fellow-children of the Most High; and as each faithfully and lovingly does his duty in the vocation the Lord has given him, He imparts also His blessing in present peace and in continual progress. He who does his work well from love to the Lord is doing the work of religion, and contributing to the universal good.

The Lord gives the harvest through the farmer, the ploughman, and the sower. The Lord diffuses His blessings over the world by the merchant, the shipbuilder, and the seaman. He imparts the desire and the skill, and man co-operates in the execution. The Lord creates and multiplies objects of art and beauty; but the artist receives the impulse and the enlightenment, and develops these in the glorious picture, the lovely or the noble statue, or the brilliant gem. The Lord ministers to men by the appliances of machinery; but the engineer and the mechanic receive the skill, the power, and the patience which bring about the goodly results that facilitate human labour, and multiply the comforts of life for all. The Lord administers order and safety to a state by means of legislators and their officers, judges and expounders of justice and law; but these must first receive into themselves His good and perfect gifts, and thus become channels of blessing to their fellow-men.

The Lord blesses men through men in all the operations of life; and that men may be more perfect instruments of His Divine Love, yet in harmony with their freedom, He disposes some to devote themselves chiefly to one career of usefulness, and some to another. By thus devoting themselves pre-eminently and constantly to one class of avocation, universal experience has taught that greater usefulness, greater perfection, and greater success are attained. Hence have arisen the different ranks and arrangements of men in society, grades in government and literature, in trade, commerce, and business.

Among these the ministry of the Word is not the least important.

God gave His Word through men. He opens it and diffuses it through men. Hence He has appointed and continued in all ages a class of men who have been trained and set apart to administer the blessings of religion; and when they have been truly inspired by the Giver of all good, their influence has been deeply felt. The uses the Word of God has to accomplish among men are so great, varied, and important, that it has ever been felt that the office of the minister of religion is one whose faithful and worthy fulfilment is fraught with extensive blessings to mankind. Unworthy men are an affliction anywhere and in anything; but in the ministry they are intolerable.

The good minister is always presented in the Word itself as a great blessing. Thus we read, "And I will give you pastors according to mine heart, who shall feed you with knowledge and understanding" (Jer. iii. 15.) Our Lord called the good minister the good shepherd, who would know his sheep by name, and whose voice the sheep would hear and follow (John x. 3, 4.) The apostle Peter sets forth both the duties of a minister and his reward very clearly in his first epistle. "Feed the flock of God which is among you, taking the oversight thereof, not by constraint, but willingly; not for filthy lucre, but of a ready mind; neither as being lords over God's heritage, but being ensamples to the flock. And when the chief

Shepherd shall appear, ye shall receive a crown of glory that fadeth not away" (v. 2-4).

If we consider for a moment the rich harvest of blessings the truths of the Word of God have to diffuse among men, and reflect that it is only when those truths are explained and understood that their transcendent benefits can be fully experienced, we shall be impressed with the importance of the ministerial office, and the invaluable uses which are attendant on the labours of men who are called by the Lord, chosen, sincere, and faithful. They are watchmen who warn; they are soldiers who defend; they are shepherds who lead, guard, and feed the sheep and lambs; they are elder brothers who encourage; they are physicians under the Great Physician of souls; they are sowers of angel seed; they are standard bearers of heaven; they are ensamples of what they preach.

The truths of the Word which faithful apostles proclaim call men to repentance, and manifest to them the heinous nature of their sins. The truths of the Word have to evoke and strengthen love to the Lord, and charity to our neighbour, filling with the spirit of heaven every employment and office in which we are engaged. The truths of the Word are the means by which virtuous principles are formed and sustained; by them we are strengthened in the hour of trial, and consoled and encouraged in periods of darkness and distress. The truths of the Word impart freedom to men; they lead them in the regenerate life, and unfold in them beauty and order. The truths of the Word lighten up the gloom and aid us to bear the anguish of affliction, and they irradiate the scene of death with the dawn of eternal light and peace. "By the Word of the Lord are the heavens made, and all the host of them by the breath of his mouth" is as true of the Word as it operates in human souls, as it ever was of the Eternal Word or Wisdom by which the created universe was formed and is sustained. The work of the ministry is to exhibit and strengthen the foundations of human society, and irradiate the path of life with beams from heaven. Ministers of the Word are to raise up the golden candlestick, and diffuse over the dark pathways of existence a golden and a radiant gleam.

The faithful priest has been well described by Cowper, as—

> "Much-impressed
> Himself, as conscious of his awful charge,
> And anxious mainly that the flock he feeds
> May feel it too: affectionate in look,
> And tender in address, as well becomes
> A messenger of grace to guilty men."

But if we turn from the contemplation of what the ministry ought to be, to regard the account given of Hophni and Phinehas, what a spectacle of degradation do we find! Being sons of the high priest, their conduct was more than commonly disgraceful and nefarious. They oppressed the people; seizing with insolence more than their due, and taking by force what was intended to be the offering of willing hearts. They disgusted the people with divine worship, instead of commending it by their purity, their wisdom, and their holiness. "Wherefore the sin of the young men was very great before the Lord: for men abhorred the offering of the Lord" (ii. 17.) There is no greater harm that one man can do to another than to misrepresent religion to him by unfaithfulness, and dishearten him by a bad example.

But these unhappy priests went further. They degraded themselves by the most shameless conduct at the very door of the tabernacle. The evils most directly and interiorly opposed to the purity of heaven, they paraded in open defiance of the Lord, as if in mockery of their father, of their office, and of decency. The whole scene was that of an expiring church. The people wicked, the priests false to their vocation, the reins in the hands of feeble rulers, ruin at the door.

Such epochs of general decay always portend general disaster, and soon it certainly came. The Philistines invaded the country and carried all before them; the ark, the very centre of their worship and the glory of their dispensation, was taken; and the light of Israel was almost entirely extinguished. No more complete illustration can be afforded of what Cowper so justly described, than this period of the high-priesthood of Eli:—

> "When nations are to perish in their sins,
> 'Tis in the Church the leprosy begins.
> The priest whose office is with zeal sincere
> To watch the fountain, and preserve it clear,
> Carelessly nods, and sleeps upon the brink,
> While others poison what the flock must drink:
> Or, waking at the call of lust alone,
> Infuses lies and errors of his own.
> His unsuspecting flock believe it pure,
> And, tainted by the very means of cure,
> Catch from each other a contagious spot,
> The foul forerunner of a general rot."

The Church is the salt of the earth, when it is pure; it is the curse of the earth when it is depraved. Hence the Lord watches over the Church with jealous and tender care, and provides in every time of its decay the means of its restoration.

In the very house of Eli he placed a Samuel. Besides this, a prophet was sent to the feeble, miserable Eli, who spared the sins of his children, and ruined both them and his nation. The man of God came like a condemning conscience, unveiled the high-priest to himself, and announced to him the destruction of his family. "There shall not be an old man in thine house for ever" (v. 32.) There should be continued vexation and sorrow amongst his descendants when they ceased to be priests. "And the man of thine, whom I shall not cut off from mine altar, shall be to consume thine eyes, and to grieve thine heart; and all the increase of thine house shall die in the flower of their age" (xxxiii.)

What lesson is afforded here to over-indulgent and inconsiderate parents! They, like Eli, abstain from checking their children's faults, or only make a feeble remonstrance, and then close their eyes; not considering that each vice in a child is like a wolf, and will injure it more deeply than the bite of a wild beast. Hophni and Phinehas, the wicked sons who grew to be wicked priests, not only ruined themselves, but ruined their father, who died broken-hearted at their fall; and ruined their country, which, became by the battle they fell in, subject to the oppression of the Philistines. Had their father been faithful to his God, and to his duty to them, he might have lived for them to bless him, instead of dying amidst the ruin they had caused.

In one day they died both of them. And so will surely die spiritually all who are forgetful of the laws of truth and duty to our Heavenly Father, and a deeper death and a deeper condemnation must come to those depraved ministers who have profaned their office by their lusts, and have betrayed the holy cause of heaven among men which they were especially appointed to guard. "The soul that sinneth it shall die," is true of all. But priests who sin, as they have had more safe-guards and deeper responsibilities, sink more deeply when they fall, and doubtless are of those who are "beaten with many stripes."

Let us now turn to the second and more cheering portion of our text. In the description of what Samuel would be, we have the delineation of a real minister of the Lord Jesus Christ. "I will raise me up a faithful priest, that shall do according to that which is in mine heart, and in my mind". (v. 35.)

The Lord's heart is His Divine Love. The first characteristic of the true minister is to be in harmony with the Divine heart. The Lord desires to bless His children for ever in heaven, and to prepare them for this everlasting blessedness by regeneration. The true minister enters into the same spirit, he lives for this, and labours for this, among the people. That which is in the Lord's heart is in his heart also; and he rejoices in leading men to their Saviour, in elevating and strengthening in them all that is noble, pure, and good. He feels for the weak and the wicked, and pities them. He does not quench the smoking flax, nor break the bruised reed, but brings forth judgment unto victory. He tells men plainly of their sins, but also cheers them with the hope and faith which animate himself. He knows that whosoever seeks his Saviour truly and earnestly, receives power to turn away from his wickedness, and save his soul alive. The heart of the Lord Jesus is very merciful, very tender, and very patient; and the minister who knows the Lord does according to that which is in His heart.

"The sons of Eli," it is said, "knew not the Lord" (ver. 12), and so they did harsh, cruel, and vile things. True ministers of religion know the Lord, are in sympathy with Him, enter into the atmosphere of His Love, and delight in seeing Him giving sight to the blind, opening the ears of the deaf, causing the lame to walk, and raising the dead. One sinner that repents causes the angels who watch over him to rejoice, and to the good minister also there is a similar joy, when the lost sheep returns to the fold of the good again.

He does according to what is in the Lord's heart; but also according to what is in the Lord's mind. The mind of the Lord is infinitely wise. From the Divine Wisdom comes all truth, and without truth there is no progress. The faithful minister of the Lord is very zealous for the spread of truth.

One of the insidious dangers against which the Christian needs to be on his guard is slothfulness and unconcern in relation to truth. The feeling of indifference will creep over him at times; and when he sees people outwardly living a moral life, with many a form of erroneous doctrine and varied creed, the thought will sometimes come, "of what consequence can it be whether people have a false creed or a true creed, false doctrines or true, or if they know little or much of the truths of religion?" But this is an error as dangerous as it is unscriptural. We need truth daily to sustain us, to purify us, to strengthen and to elevate us. An outwardly becoming life may be induced by fashion, by fear, by desire of a good name, or by the dread of being singular or losing caste; and may cover a soul infested with selfish anxieties, dead to everything good and great. Such a one is a whited sepulchre, full of dead men's bones and all uncleanness. A lack of taste for truth is a mark of an evil state. The man who loves good, loves truth, and delights to speak about it, hear about it, and read about it.

When a person finds he has no pleasure in a good book abounding with truths, he may be certain he is spiritually unwell. He has a chronic, low, mental fever, and it deprives him of appetite. He should pray to the Lord as is done so often in the Psalms: "O send out thy light and THY TRUTH: let them lead me" (xliii. 3). "Thou desirest TRUTH in the inward parts, and in the hidden part thou shalt make me to know wisdom" (li. 6). "God shall send forth His mercy and His TRUTH" (lvii. 13). "O prepare mercy and TRUTH, which may preserve him" (lxi. 7).

From the inestimable value of the knowledge of truth, and because one leading duty of the true minister of the Lord is to diffuse it, we read, "For the priest's lips shall keep knowledge, and they should seek the law at his mouth, for he is the messenger of the Lord of hosts" (Mal. ii. 7). In like manner, in our text, the faithful priest is said not only to do according to what is in the Lord's heart, but also according to what is in His mind; or according to the Divine Truth. He is anxious that all around him should know the truth, and see it in its own light.

The bad priest is afraid of truth, and would rather that ignorance and superstition should continue to enslave mankind; that the multitude should be the tools and slaves of the few. The good priest, however, knows that truth is light, "the true light which enlighteneth every man that cometh into the world." He shudders to think of a world without light, and not the less does he dread to contemplate a soul without truth.

Without light no man can see the beauties either of earth or heaven. "He that walketh in darkness, knoweth not whither he goeth" (John xii. 35.) Error is the wrong road home. He who follows ignorantly may find his home at last, but not till after many a weary turn, and many a painful quagmire. Probably much more than half of the evils and sorrow under which men suffer, come from error and ignorance. People take the wrong road, believing it to be right. To be unconcerned and indifferent about this is to be heedless of lifelong and widespread suffering.

What were the famines and pestilences of the middle ages, but the results of that ignorance of divine laws which made men indifferent to districts of vile and festering vegetation, poisoning the atmosphere with vapours bearing on their horrid bosoms fever and death? What were the persecutions of past times, in which myriads suffered pains incredible, but the result of the ignorant persuasion that the God of Love would be pleased by fierce souls harassing to death those who thought differently from themselves? What has so long continued undiminished the terrible sufferings of innumerable diseases, but the false idea that afflictions come from God, instead of the truth, that they arise from the violations of God's laws, and indulging in self-will both in mind and body. The drunkard or the glutton dies of apoplexy, the immediate result of a last serious error; and disregarding the years and years during which he has violated the laws of health, people say he has died by the *visitation of God!* These false ideas are engendered by other and deeper errors which underlie them; and so vast strata sustain the mighty empire of wrong.

But the real messenger of heaven, the true minister of the Lord, unfolds the divine mind to the people. He unfurls the standard of truth. He opens the fountains of living water. "Arise, shine," he says, "for your light is come, and the glory of the Lord is risen upon you. Darkness hath covered the earth, and gross darkness the people; but the Lord shall arise upon you, and His glory shall be seen upon you" (Isa lx. 1, 2). Such a priest would Samuel be. Hence it is written, "He shall do according to that which is in mine heart, and IN MY MIND."

We read further, "I will build him a sure house; and he shall walk before mine anointed for ever" (ver. 35). To make Samuel a sure house would doubtless mean that he would be established as a prophet; that he would have a firm position in the esteem and reverence of the people. To walk before the anointed would be a prophecy that when a king, an anointed one, was chosen for Israel (they had no king then), Samuel would be his guide and director "for ever," that is, for his age or dispensation; for such is the import of the Hebrew term which is rendered "for ever."

But what is said of Samuel is still more deeply true of every real genuine minister of the Lord Jesus Christ, of every faithful and true priest. The Lord makes him a sure house. He is built up on the rock of ages; truths are the stones, and these are cemented with love. This is a sure house: neither death nor hell can shake it. He walks before the Anointed One. He lives on earth, and will hereafter live for ever in the Heavens, under the blessing and favour of the Lord Jesus Christ, who is King of kings, and Lord of lords.

SERMON III.

SAMUEL AND ELI.

> "And the child Samuel ministered unto the Lord before Eli. And the Word of the Lord was precious in those days; there was no open vision.
> "And it came to pass at that time, when Eli was laid down in his place, and his eyes began to wax dim, that he could not see;
> "And ere the lamp of God went out in the temple of the Lord, where the ark of God was, and Samuel was laid down to sleep;
> "That the Lord called Samuel: and he answered, Here am I."—1 SAM. iii. 1-4.

PERHAPS there is no period in the whole career of the Israelitish nation more sad to contemplate than that in which Eli was high priest. His feeble and heedless government suffered the elements of evil and decay to gather on every hand. It is true that he came to a position sunk in corruption, a land disordered, a people ignorant and degraded; a priesthood droning lazily a drowsy service, offering sacrifices not as offerings of the heart, but as their trade. All was mean, debased, and disorderly. But he made no real effort to stay the impending ruin, to restore that which was decayed, or to stand up for God and right among men. He was false to his vocation, faithless to his duty, permitting his children to mock at virtue, and to ruin the Church it was his supreme duty to preserve. In positions of great dignity and responsibility, neglect is treachery. Eli was a watchman, but he gave no warning. The wreck came, and the slothful heedless captain perished with the ship.

Before we proceed to the especial lessons of our text, it will be useful to notice the inference that presents itself from the statement that "the Word of the Lord was precious in those days; there was no open vision." It would seem to be suggested by that language, that open vision had preceded the Word of the Lord, that there had been a time when men consorted with angels, and saw the things of the eternal world.

The invisible world is not distant; it is only too refined for the coarse observations of natural life. The better world is as it were a soul to this—an inner universe; and when the eyes of our spirits are opened, it is visible all around us. When the Prophet Elisha prayed that his young man's eyes should be opened, we are informed, "And the Lord opened the eyes of the young man; and he saw: and, behold, the mountain was full of horses and chariots of fire round about Elisha" (2 Kings vi. 17). This was open vision. But when men became corrupt, they attracted to themselves impure and malignant spirits; and to prevent the influence of such spirits becoming all-powerful, Divine Providence veiled the one world from the other; so that spirits generally do not openly see men, nor men spirits, but the intercourse is only that of impulses and hints. There is no open vision.

The Word of the Lord is the teacher now, and it is indeed precious. It replaces all that angels taught, and discloses ever more and more. It contains divine thoughts. It is the ladder of communication on which the angels ascend and descend, and the Lord Himself is above it. The Word of the Lord is the refuge and strength of man, his very present help in trouble. The Word is the well of salvation, where we meet with the Saviour, who gives us the living water which springs up to everlasting life. The Word is the soul's armoury, from which he derives the sword, the shield, the spear, the bow and arrows of his spiritual battle. The Word is the divine table to furnish the soul's meat and drink. The Word is the meadow on which the flocks of the soul can feed, the pillow on which the shepherd can rest his weary head. The Word is precious for its uses, precious for its fulness, and most precious in that it unites the soul to the infinite Word, the Wisdom of the Lord Himself.

But we must not despise the uses of open vision. When vouchsafed by the Lord, at times whose necessities are observed by a merciful Providence, open vision has been the means of sustaining the faith of men, and restoring the light of immortality to a darkened world. The open visions of the patriarchs and prophets were gleams of glory from the inner world. The open vision of the shepherds of Bethlehem enabled them to see the messenger of heaven, and hear the heavenly multitude who sang to their descending and redeeming Lord, "Glory to God in the highest, and on earth peace; good-will towards men." The open visions of John unrolled to his prophetic gaze the whole history of the Church of the future;

and through superstitions and errors, persecutions, degradations, and struggles, its triumphant issue in universal light, love and peace. We must not disbelieve in visions as impossible, or imaginary, nor despise them as unworthy; but take their lessons as a blessing, when we have satisfactory evidence that they are truly given by the Lord. Of the decayed Jewish church at a later time it is said, as one of the sad signs of her degeneracy, "Her prophets also find no vision from the Lord" (Lam. ii. 9). "There was no open vision." Of the renewed times and better days of a restored church, we read, "And it shall come to pass in the last days, saith God, I will pour out of my spirit upon all flesh : and your sons and your daughters shall prophesy, and your young men shall see visions, and your old men shall dream dreams : and on my servants and on my handmaidens I will pour out in those days of my spirit" (Acts ii. 17, 18).

Let us now turn to the other intimations of the text, and we shall surely be impressed with the graphic portraiture of a church glimmering in a misty gloom, and tottering to its fall.

Of course the description is a literal portraiture of a night-scene at Shiloh. But it was selected and placed in the Word of God, as a picture of the Church at the time, and of the Church as it ever is at the end of a dispensation. The priests are sleepy, their eyes are dim, and they can hardly see. The lamp of God is going out in the temple of the Lord. Just regard the words again, "Eli was laid down in his place, and his eyes began to wax dim, that he could not see ; and ere the lamp of God went out in the temple of the Lord." The very words seem all full of drowsiness, dimness, and decay. And nothing could better describe a church nearing its doom. A drowsy priest, dim eyes, and a dying lamp.

Natural life, as compared to spiritual life, is as sleep to wakefulness. The intention of our Heavenly Father is that our existence in this world should be an alternation of natural blessings and spiritual blessings, like sleeping and waking, or night and day. Our duty at present is not to be always engaged on interior and spiritual subjects, but to change from the eagerness with which we pursue heavenly things, to the comparative rest and quiet of everyday life : then again, to awake with new interest to the acquisitions and the joys of interior wisdom and angelic delight. Hence it is written, "So He giveth His beloved sleep" (Ps. cxxvii. 2). The confidence and rest of healthy sleep are images of the inner rest of souls under the protection of the Lord, while the hands are busy with the engagements of daily duty. Such sleep is refreshing. We ought not to be always thinking on the same subjects, however exalted. The outer world of our Lord is His, and is full of beauty, and good, as well as the inner and higher world. We should love it for Him, and seek His wisdom in it. We should be earnest in our duties, as well as delighted to gaze on the angelic mountain. In describing our regeneration, the Lord said, "So is the kingdom of God, as if a man should cast seed into the ground; and should sleep, and rise night and day, and the seed should spring and grow up, he knoweth not how" (Mark iv. 26, 27).

That is true order, sleeping and waking, using both, and enjoying both. But where a person sleeps too much, when the sleep is unhealthy, and he is hardly ever properly awake; when the sleep is the result of narcotics, and is gloomy, full of horrid dreams; it is then the type of an evil state, a drowsiness to good. The wicked man, who never earnestly awakes to his eternal concerns, is like a pilgrim asleep in a dark valley, stupified by the fumes of the poppy. To such the Apostle cried, "Awake, thou that sleepest, and arise from the dead, and Christ shall give thee light" (Eph. v. 14). The sleep of Eli represented sleep of this kind, the "sleep of death" (Ps. xiii. 3).

How graphically does the Prophet Isaiah describe a priesthood of this kind. "His watchmen are all blind: they are all ignorant, they are all dumb dogs, they cannot bark; SLEEPING, LYING DOWN, LOVING TO SLUMBER. Yea, they are greedy dogs which can never have enough, and they are shepherds that cannot understand: they all look to their own way, every one for his gain, from his quarter. Come ye, say they, I will fetch wine, and we will fill ourselves with strong drink; and to-morrow shall be as this day, and much more abundant" (lvi. 10-12).

A power-loving and luxurious priesthood are the greatest curse of a church. Their minds are absorbed in their appetites. They are so greedy for gain that they are lynx-eyed for whatever will lead to pelf, but blink like owls at any ray of heavenly light. Their eyes are waxing dim, like Eli's, and they cannot see. They come at last to love mystery, and pride themselves in the darkness of their dogmas, hoping to keep power from the laity, under the plea of their being privileged guardians of impenetrable secrets, and awful, magical sanctities.

How simple is truth! "Cease to do evil, learn to do well."

"Do justly, love mercy, walk humbly with thy God." How simple is truth! Child of eternal love, live a heavenly life, and you shall go to heaven. Let heaven enter you, and diffuse itself around you here, and you will be prepared for the joys hereafter. How simple is truth! The Lord Jesus, your Heavenly Father, has given His Word to guide you; read its plain precepts, and practise them. Pray to Him for humility and strength; then walk on the path of life. You will rise as you are true to practice, and the higher you rise, the farther you will see. How simple is truth! Shun everything that is forbidden by the Lord, as sin against His Love and Truth, and hurtful to your fellow-immortals. "We know that we have passed from death unto life, because we love the brethren" (1 John iii. 14.) How simple is truth! By living a heavenly life, the spirit becomes more and more perfected in its spiritual body; it is an angel in its house on earth, and when the dust is laid aside, having done its work, the angel within goes to its fellow-angels in its house in heaven.

But these truths a corrupted and benighted priesthood cannot see; their eyes are dim to things really divine.

> "Then ceremony leads her bigots forth,
> Prepared to fight for trifles of no worth:
> While truths on which eternal things depend,
> Find not, or hardly find, a single friend."

A drowsy, dim priesthood stifle inquiry, dishearten research, warn against seeking to understand the truth. "The temple of the Lord, the temple of the Lord, are we!" is their cry, like the condemned priests in the time of Jeremiah. To them religion is a series of mysteries. These mysteries were settled and decided upon ages ago, and you must believe them. You cannot understand them; nobody can. Our eyes are dim, and we cannot see; and you must not think of opening your eyes; you must bow to our authority. O blind leaders of the blind! step out of the way. Remember Eli! Give way to your Master. The soul needs light. It does not need you, unless you are yourselves lovers of light. You should teach every disciple to pray: "Send out Thy light, and Thy truth; let them lead me; let them bring me unto Thy holy mountain, and to Thy tabernacles." "Lighten mine eyes, lest I sleep the sleep of death." Away, dull souls! ye are they who will not learn, and cannot teach.

The text continues: "Ere the lamp of God went out in the

temple of the Lord." The idea presented is that of a lamp, flickering, sinking, and dying out. The dimness of the eyes of Eli is the type, as we have seen, of the little understanding possessed by the priesthood of a decaying church. The lamp dying out represents the light of the Word almost extinguished in the Church.

A church, however much it has fallen from the truth, and however much it has hidden the light under the bushel of its own unwarranted dogmas, must keep up a professed reverence for the sacred volume. A few passages are believed to be the foundation of their authority; and to sustain that authority among the people, it must be understood to be supported by the word and will of the Almighty. The Word in the Church in such case is like a mysterious treasure, believed in, but seldom seen. Like the beast in the Revelation (xvii. 11), it is, and it is not. For the purposes of power and pelf, it is; for the illumination of the mind and the regeneration of the heart, it is not. For the aggrandizement of the clergy, it is; but for diffusing light in every home, in every soul, it is not. For the authorization of an awful power of benumbing the intellects of men, and scowling at science, it is; but for its own sacred work of diffusing spirit and life, of promoting the glorious liberty of the "children of light," it is not. And yet IT IS; for where the Word is, though only as a flickering lamp, there is the source of restoration, when the time comes, and the men are there. The Lord knows His own, and in due time He will call them.

Those who can form the centre of a New Dispensation are usually very few, humble people, who are, however, loving, thoughtful, faithful, and obedient. They are usually in Scripture called "a remnant." Here they are represented by young Samuel. They are the pith of the former church still remaining to give it life, when the lamp of Divine Light is flickering to its death: they are the handful of corn in the bushel of chaff which remains when a blighted harvest is ended; they are the gleaning grapes when the vintage is done. Anna, the prophetess, the aged Simeon, Zacharias, and the Apostles, were such a remnant at the end of the Jewish Church. "Fear not, little flock," the Lord said, "for it is your Father's good pleasure to give you the kingdom" (Luke xii. 32).

Such a remnant is alluded to in the Divine Word in terms so glorious as to form a comfort to humble souls who feel compelled to stand for truth and goodness amidst shallow and unthinking multitudes. The seven thousand who had not bowed their knees to Baal, were the remnant in the days of Elijah (1 Kings xix. 18). Indeed at all times of general sensuality and decay it may be said, "Except the Lord of hosts had left unto us a very small remnant, we should have been as Sodom, and we should have been like unto Gomorrah (Isa. i. 9). To be one of such a remnant, however despised by proud and haughty formalists, is the truest glory. "The remnant that is escaped of the house of Judah shall again take root downward, and bear fruit upward; for out of Jerusalem shall go forth a remnant, and they that escape out of Mount Zion: the zeal of the Lord of hosts shall do this" (Isa. xxxvii. 31, 32.) "And the remnant of Jacob shall be in the midst of many people, as a dew from the Lord, as the showers upon the grass, that tarrieth not for man, nor waiteth for the sons of men" (Mic. v. 7).

The mission of the remnant whose hearts are uplifted to the Most High in supreme affection is to bring down holy thoughts like celestial dew. In the inmost of their being, in the tranquil hours of meditation and devotion, the truths of peace descend like the zephyrs of a heavenly atmosphere. They are tranquillized, refreshed, encouraged and strengthened. They feel within themselves the assurances of Divine Love; thoughts of holy trust and glancing brightness fill the soul, like the calm dew of a new morning from the Lord, as the tender showers upon the grass.

Samuel represented such a remnant, especially among the priesthood; the Lord's voice ever comes to such. They are touched by the divine influence, and awakened. "The Lord called Samuel; and he said, here am I." In such tender souls as constitute the remnant there is a ready response to the voice of God in the conscience. "Here am I," is said in a moment. But although they have been aroused by a voice only heard by themselves, touched by an unseen hand, they always at first suppose they owe their new call to the old constituted order of things. Samuel ran to Eli, and supposed it was he who called him. The newly-awakened do not discriminate between the old and the new order of things. They suppose the church is as earnest as they are. They think the grand thoughts which are being unfolded within them, will be welcomed by the authorities, and they will be encouraged and cheered in the glorious visions opening before them. It is not, however, so; Eli had made no call. He had nothing to say, but "I called not, lie down again" (ver. 5.)

Nevertheless, the divine message does not rest; it is given

again, and a third time. Still it appeared to Samuel that the call was from Eli. "He did not yet know the Lord, nor was the Word of the Lord yet revealed to him" (ver. 7.) It is one thing *to know of the Lord*, and quite another TO KNOW THE LORD. To know the Lord is a thing of the heart, not of the head. We know the Lord in proportion as we are in sympathy with him. It is a deep and holy experience which comes from warm and inward affections. They who love God know God. "He that loveth not knoweth not God, for God is Love" (1 John iv. 8).

Those who are to lead great movements in a New Dispensation, know but little of the Divine purposes, or the meaning of the Divine Words. They are only conscious of a yearning after something higher, of a desire to be true to the inward voice that is stirring them up. They demand of their old teachers what they have to say in their wonderful circumstances. All that they can obtain in reply is, "We are compelled to believe for the moment there is something divine in this; wait and be obedient." Eli said unto Samuel, "Go, lie down; and it shall be, if He call thee, that thou shalt say, Speak, Lord; for thy servant heareth." Wise advice was this, though it made no difference to the giver of it. How many can give good counsel! how few follow it! The Samuels, however, hear and do. The name Samuel signifies "PLACED OF GOD." And those who are placed of God to be the seed of a new kingdom, are always they who pray for the divine guidance, who ask for the leading of Love and Mercy, affecting their minds, and touching their hearts. These are not content with following dull routine, having no convictions, no deep thoughts, no hallowed communings with the Lord in the silent depths of their being. To them the voice of a Divine Guide is a welcome voice; they are ready to follow it. They look around at so much that is "stale, flat, and unprofitable," that they rise above their prejudices and their fears, and with devout, yet trusting love exclaim: "Speak, Lord; thy servant heareth!"

In the changes and turmoils of to-day; in the indisposition to receive new light; in the confessions of multitudes that their eyes are dim and they cannot see, we may recognise a parallel to the time of Eli. Let us devoutly pray and strive that in the new unfoldings of the Word, and the new manifestations of Divine care from the Saviour God, we may ever preserve that humility of mind which bends down before the Mercy Seat, and says, "Speak, Lord; for thy servant heareth."

SERMON IV.

THE ARK TAKEN BY THE PHILISTINES.

"And the Philistines fought, and Israel was smitten, and they fled every man into his tent; and there was a very great slaughter: for there fell of Israel thirty thousand footmen.

"AND THE ARK OF GOD WAS TAKEN; and the two sons of Eli, Hophni and Phinehas, were slain."—1 SAM. iv. 10, 11.

THE loss of the Ark by the Israelites, when they had become quite unworthy of it, and its seizure by the Philistines to be paraded in their country, represented the loss of the Word by those who profess to revere the commandments of God but do not keep them, and its being taken possession of by those who neither profess to revere nor to keep the commandments of God, but expect to be saved by a scheme of their own devising, which they denominate THE SCHEME OF SALVATION.

The Ark represents the Word, and especially the divine commandments which are the centre of the Word. The Israelites represent the members of the church, at this time faithless, corrupt, vile, and unworthy; the Philistines those who make a religion of "faith alone," which they declare to be saving, but which leaves them quarrelsome, vindictive, self-indulgent, greedy of domination, eager for proselytism, unjust where it suits them, moderated only by what the society amongst whom they associate deem proper and allowable.

When we keep constantly before our minds, in reading the Bible, that its divine author intends its history as well as its precepts to be subservient to the regeneration of man, it magnifies the Word, and makes it honourable. "The law of the Lord is perfect, converting the soul" (Ps. xix. 7). We regard the literal history first; and our reverence makes us careful to acquaint ourselves fully with its facts and circumstances, that they may be a proper basis for the spiritual lessons we hope to receive. We study well and thoughtfully the divine record, and then we say with the apostle, "These things are an allegory" (Gal. iv. 24).

The Ark was the representative of the Word, because it contained within it the divine commandments on two tables of stone, and these are the essence of the Word. All the commandments may be regarded as comprised in two, "Love to the Lord, and Love to our neighbour;" and "on these two," as the Lord said, "hang all the Law and the Prophets" (Matt. xxii. 40). The Ark contained also the pot of manna, and Aaron's rod that budded. This signified that from the Word is all heavenly food, the "hidden manna" (Rev. ii. 17), and from it is all the power of spiritual growth in regeneration. We bear blossoms and fruit, as we receive life and power from the Word of the Lord. The chest formed of the precious cedar of Shittah, covered with gold within and without, represented the Word as it is received by the highest angels and the best of men. The precious gold of their inmost affections embraces the Word. It is impressed upon their inward parts, and written on their hearts (Jer. xxxi. 33).

The Israelites lost the Ark when they had long ceased to perform their part of the covenant of which the Ark was the abiding sign. It was about four hundred and fifty years from the death of Joshua to the death of Eli, and those years had been periods of great disorder and decay. The judges had ruled with a loose hand. The people had neglected the commandments and ordinances of the Lord. Virtue had gradually declined, and zeal for what is good was entirely lost.

The twelve tribes in their order, under the direction of Moses and Joshua, were the types of the Lord's true church. How grand they seemed when Balaam said of them, "How goodly are thy tents, O Jacob! and thy tabernacles, O Israel! As the valleys are they spread forth, as gardens by the river's side, as the trees of lign-aloes, which the Lord hath planted, and as cedar trees beside the waters" (Num. xxiv. 6). When they were zealous for God under their heroic leader Joshua, they were triumphant; and while he lived, they were faithful and true. They were then the proper representatives of the church, which the apostle calls "The Israel of God" (Gal. vi. 16).

More especially were Judah and Benjamin the types of the men of heavenly love, and the men of genuine faith. Those two great tribes were the centre and bulwark of the Israelitish power. Their lands were situated next to each other. Jerusalem was built at the joining of the two tribes.

Judah, large, fertile, beautiful, entrenched in glorious mountains, and populous in noble men, fulfilled the prophetic words of Jacob, "Judah, thou art he whom thy brethren shall praise: thy hand shall be in the neck of thine enemies; thy father's children shall bow down before thee. Judah is a lion's whelp: from the prey, my son, thou art gone up: he stooped down, he couched as a lion, and as an old lion; who shall rouse him up? The sceptre shall not depart from Judah, nor a lawgiver from between his feet, until Shiloh come; and unto him shall the gathering of the people be" (Gen. xlix. 8-10). The tribe of Judah was the largest and most influential, the sovereign tribe. Ultimately it gave its name to the whole nation, who from the name "Judah" were called "Jews." The tribe of Judah in its good and genuine state, represented those among Christians who are mainly animated by love to the Lord.' The name Judah means in Hebrew, "praise Jehovah." Those who love the Lord desire to do His will and to praise Him. They are those of whom the apostle says, "He is not a Jew who is one outwardly; neither is that circumcision which is outward in the flesh: but he is a Jew who is one inwardly; and circumcision is that of the heart, in the spirit, and not in the letter; whose praise is not of men, but of God" (Rom. ii. 28, 29).

The tribe of Benjamin was possessed also of a large, fertile, and beautiful country. Shiloh, where the Ark so long abode before going up to Jerusalem, was in their land. They were a noble people, and gave their first king, Saul, to the whole nation. They were also great archers, powerful with the bow, and exact in their aim. Their name, Benjamin, means "the son of the right hand;" and it indicates, prophetically, their skill and strength. Of them it is written, "The beloved of the Lord shall dwell in safety by him; the Lord shall cover him all the day long, and he shall dwell between his shoulders" (Deut. xxxiii. 12). In the spiritual sense, they are of the tribe of Benjamin who are animated by the faith which is grounded in love. These cultivate their intellect, they abound in divine truths because they love them. They are keen and powerful against wrong. The Lord is with them and covers them all the day long. The Lord dwells between their shoulders. He is the source and fulcrum of their power.

Jerusalem, the true church of the Lord, is formed of the combination of both, of men of affection, and men of intellect; and in each person of love in the heart and truth in the understanding, and hence the earthly Jerusalem, the type of the church, was placed where the lands of the two tribes met.

But let us now turn to consider the Philistines, who for a great part of their history were prominent as enemies of Judah and Benjamin, and who inhabited the country between those two tribes and the Mediterranean Sea. They were originally from Egypt; and after having inhabited Caphtor (most likely the island which is now called Crete), they settled in the land of Canaan. They would no doubt take with them the learning of the Egyptians, and their habit of expressing their ideas in personifications and hieroglyphical forms. In the days of Abraham and Isaac, they appear to have possessed a true knowledge of God: for when those patriarchs resided among them they expressed themselves most reverently concerning the Lord, spoke of their seeing that the patriarchs were blessed of the Lord, and were very desirous of doing His will (Gen. xxi. xxvi.).

They must have been familiar with the science of correspondences, for this was well known in Egypt, from whence they came; and the same fact appears from the measures they took in returning the Ark when they dared not longer retain it amongst them. They would know, therefore, that a fish corresponded to a disposition which delights in knowledge, as the fish delights in water. The ocean of truth in its lowest form is the object of scientific investigation; and those who pursue this are as fishes who swim about and so enjoy themselves. The water of the heavenly river which the prophet Ezekiel saw in vision, would, it is said, "cause all the fishes TO LIVE, whithersoever the river came" (Ezek. xlvii. 9); because, when wisdom from heaven fills all the scientific ideas we have, it animates them with angelic life. One of the most ancient accounts of the impartation of knowledge to mankind was the story among the Babylonians related by a very early writer, Berosus, "that a creature from the sea, with the head and hands of a man, but the body of a fish, came and taught them agriculture, literature, arts, law, and religion;" no doubt an ancient allegory describing the fact that scientific thought, derived from the vast domains of knowledge, gave them all the intelligence which nurtures and embellishes human life.

Pharaoh, as the representative of Egypt, the land of science, is described by the prophet Ezekiel when he says, "Thou art as a great fish in the seas: and thou camest forth with thy rivers, and troublest the waters with thy feet, and fouledst their rivers" (xxxii. 2). And again, "Pharaoh, king of Egypt, the great dragon that lieth in the midst of his rivers, which hath said, My river is mine own, and I have made it for myself" (Ezek. xxix. 3). When a scientific man boasts himself in his attainments, and believes that his knowledge is supremely great, supremely valuable, self-derived, and the means only of self-exaltation, he is just like Pharaoh. He is saying " My river is my own, and I have made it for myself."

The Philistines had great stores of knowledge; they were enterprising traders; they made an image of a fish with human head and hands, and they worshipped it. This was their famous god Dagon; " Dag,' in their language, meaning " fish." It was the symbol of their character and state of mind. Their intellect was their deity. They made their own scheme of life, and they worshipped that. Their hearts remained what their natural impure selfishness made them. They regarded thought as everything. With them it was religious thought, for all ancient nations were religious. They worked out the views of God and man which seemed to them the truest and the best. Their hearts, the great sources whence issue life or death, being overlooked and unpurified, the Philistines became restless, quarrelsome, impure, and cruel. They are generally denominated in Scripture the "uncircumcised Philistines," a phrase no doubt literally true, but also indicating that impurity of heart which ever exists where religion does not perform its daily work of resisting sin, and promoting chastity and justice. The Philistines, when they took possession of that part of Canaan which they afterwards made their own, exterminated the Avims, a terrible race distinguished for violence and cruelty (Deut. ii. 23), formed a regulated and powerful nation, and became of so much importance by their trade and commercial activity, that by their name the whole country became chiefly known, as it is to the present day; for Canaan is even now best known as "Palestine."

The Philistines, then, were learned even in divine things; they had much knowledge of God; they lived in Canaan; they were skilful and energetic; they were well-ordered and well-trained; but they were corrupt, self-seeking, quarrelsome, and restless. Their minds were clever, but their hearts were bad. The fish with human head and hands was their most sacred symbol; as if they would indicate that the science of things human and divine was the supreme object of their regard. As they had a true knowledge of God in their early days, they probably used the fish at first only as a symbol of the Divine Intelligence, that attribute of God which they chiefly revered; but it became to them latterly a mere idol. They worshipped the sign, and lost sight of the thing signified. Thus had Egypt also degenerated from her early reverent knowledge of God and heavenly wisdom, and thus all idolatry had its rise.

We have now all the elements for forming a clear idea of those at the present day who are Philistines in Christendom, and who war against the Israelites. They are the religious by memory and by thought. All religious people have first to learn religion as a sacred science. They go down, as it were, into Egypt. They must know what religion teaches before they can embrace it. They next form some plan of religious doctrine which constitutes them a section of the professing church in an island of their own, as the Philistines went from Egypt to Crete or Caphtor. A religious denomination is like an island in the world's great sea. They then expel from themselves those rude evils which constitute a lawless life, signified by giant Avims whom the Philistines drove out, and take upon themselves the outward form and demeanour of religion. They have their particular symbol of religious creed, and unhappily they stop there. They set up Dagon. Their scheme of doctrine they call their *faith*, prostituting that beautiful word, which means LOVING TRUST, to mean a formula of certain views. They talk much of their doctrines and of faith; they meditate upon their doctrines, they dream of their doctrines, they push their doctrines forward in season and out of season. They think little of humility, piety, patience, gentleness, charity, faithfulness to duty, love for truth, order and virtue. Their scheme of thought, or their "faith" as they call it, or it may be, their particular form of church government, their shibboleth, is their one chief thought, their Dagon. They who admit their especial creed, are the church of Christ; they who do not, are no Christians. The Bible is their book of passages to prove their scheme correct, not their law of love and goodness. They know where to find their favourite passages, but are little versed in the divine truth which teaches self-denial. They sneer at justice, mercy, devotion to the good of others, struggle against interior evils, and a heavenly life of usefulness, from love to God and man. They are swift to mark, and harsh to denounce, those who differ from the scheme they have set up. They are "bitterly" good, meaning by goodness their particular form of church life; but when some selfish end is to be sought in business, or political conduct, they are reckless of all true justice, real right, or divine religion, as though no divine law existed. THESE ARE THE PHILISTINES.

They are uncircumcised in heart. "O Jerusalem, wash thine heart from wickedness, that thou mayest be saved" (Jer. iv. 14). "Cast away from you all your transgressions whereby ye have transgressed; and make you a new heart and a new spirit: for why will ye die, O house of Israel?" (Ezek. xviii. 31.) "Why call ye me, Lord, Lord, and do not the things that I say?" are the words of the Lord Jesus (Luke vi. 46). "Put off the old man, which is corrupt according to the deceitful lusts, and be renewed in the spirit of your mind" (Eph. iv. 22). Circumcision is nothing, and uncircumcision is nothing, but the keeping of the commandments of God" (1 Cor. vii. 19). Such are the teachings of divine wisdom by prophets, apostles, and the Lord Himself, but the Philistines maintain it is faith, faith alone, which saves; faith in five minutes, faith at the moment of death, although a life-time has been spent in desecrating the whole man by lust and passion. The Philistines are bigots; severe about jots and tittles, fastidious about any deviations from their dogmas, harsh in temper, bitter and persecuting, but ready to excuse very grave faults indeed in a sound believer. Such are the Philistines. They are fond of contention, and come up often to assail the Israelites. They respect the Word, as the Philistines did the Ark (ver. 6, 7, 8), but only as a means of power, not for its humbling or regenerating influence.

The Israelites, on the occasion of the battle mentioned in our text, were smitten and overcome by the Philistines. And we are taught by this divine lesson that having true principles will avail nothing, unless we are true to them. The men who say they believe that the Lord should rule in their hearts, but who still permit selfish pride to reign there, who declare God's commandments should be done, but who dispense with them at their will, who are for everything good, so far as professions go, but in practice are as avaricious, impatient, violent, impure, or untrustworthy as others, cannot stand against the Philistines. They believe and they do not believe. Theoretically they believe in charity, goodness, and obedience; practically, they believe as the Philistines do, that these are of no importance or cannot be done. These are the corrupt Israelites, who are overcome of the Philistines. Sooner or later, their intellects become darkened by the evils of their hearts. They love darkness rather than light, because their deeds are evil. Their candlestick is taken out of its place (Rev. ii. 7). Their lamp has received no oil, and their light has been hidden under a bushel, until it has gone out. Philistia has triumphed, and the false and corrupt Israel has fallen.

Thirty thousand footmen fell that day. Footmen, as distinguished from horsemen, spiritually represent the principles which affect the details of daily life. Life in this world is like the movement of the feet of the immortal man. Hence there is so much in the Divine Word of the foot slipping, of the necessity of washing the feet, of cutting off the offending foot, and of the feet walking in the way of the Lord's commandments. Thirty, like three, represents that which is full. By thirty thousand footmen are meant, spiritually, all the truths of daily life. They fell, signifying that in such minds they become inactive, dead, and extinct.

Thirty thousand footmen fell; that is, all the religion of daily life is lost: the Ark of God is taken, all true reverence for the Word of God has expired, and the two sons of Eli, Hophni and Phinehas, are slain. The destruction of these two signify the death both of intellect and heart, which complete the moral ruin of a church or of a man, when death triumphs over life, when corruption has done its awful work. Israel is confounded and hushed in mourning and defeat. Philistia triumphs and carries off the Ark. How sad is such a consummation! How different all might have been!

> "But if thou slight the King of kings,
> Behold Him here disclose,
> How surely disobedience brings
> A thousand thousand woes."

How much is it otherwise when the soul is an Israelite indeed! Then the heart becomes purified by the Lord Jesus, while repentance amends the life. Then a life of holiness acquires greater and greater power within, as regeneration proceeds. No enemy triumphs over the obedient soul. The Ark of God gleams with a richer and a brighter glory; and no Philistines can approach, or live in its radiant atmosphere. O let us this day again resolve that we will be faithful, sincere, and true. Let us, my brethren, pray that the divine words may ever be realized in us: "Happy art thou, O Israel: who is like unto thee, O people saved by the Lord, the shield of thy help, and who is the sword of thy excellency! And thine enemies shall be found liars unto thee; and thou shalt tread upon their high places" (Deut. xxxiii. 29).

SERMON V.

DAGON FALLEN BEFORE THE ARK.

"And when they arose early on the morrow morning, behold, Dagon was fallen upon his face to the ground before the ark of the Lord; and the head of Dagon, and both the palms of his hands, were cut off upon the threshold; only the stump of Dagon was left to him."—1 SAM. v. 4.

WHAT a beautiful thing is religion! It is the spirit of meekness, gentleness, charity, goodwill, uprightness, and devotion. It is the spirit of heaven upon earth. Its truths are truths of love. It never envies, is never puffed up; it suffers long and is kind. It rejoices not in iniquity, it rejoices in the truth. When presented in its true nature, it wins the admiration of all who have not lost their reverence for goodness. It sanctifies and sweetens human life, and diffuses a gentle grace around, like the modest perfume of the violet; while, at the same time, it hallows the dignity of the greatest, and gives to all human nobleness a charm derived from heaven. Religion is that gracious spirit which ever ascribes glory to God in the highest, and on earth seeks peace, and goodwill towards men. "Above all these things," says the apostle, "put on charity, which is the bond of perfectness" (Col. iii. 14).

Religion has a humble but entire faith in the Lord as our heavenly Father and Saviour. It confides in His will and in His providence. It has no anxiety for the things it cannot have. It is content in God and has peace. True religion is diligent in doing its duty. It is true to all that is just. It delights in God's commandments. It values them far above gold and rubies. To do the least thing for the Lord is a great joy. Religion is faithful in little things, and thus ensures faithfulness in much. "Whatsoever things are true, whatsoever things are honest, whatsoever things are just, whatsoever things are pure, whatsoever things are lovely" (Phil. iv. 8), these are dear to true religion.

Those who are in this spirit fear sin; they have no other fear. They love the Lord Jesus and keep His commandments; if they err from weakness they humble themselves very deeply before Him, and pray for strength. He lays his right hand upon them, and says, "Fear not, I am the First and the Last." They are full of loving hope; they trust their Lord in tribulation, sickness, and sorrow; their faith burns brightly in the hour of death. They see the world beyond.

> "See smiling patience smooth his brow,
> See kindred angels downward bow
>   To raise his soul on high,
> While, eager for the blest abode,
> He joins with them to praise his God,
>   Who taught him how to die!"

But now, having noticed what religion truly is, and what is realized by a few here and there, we are obliged to confess that a great multitude in Christian lands fail to exhibit this lovely character of heaven-born practical religion. Multitudes of professing Christians are unscrupulous in word and deed, greedy, thoughtless of others, proud, vain, untrustworthy. Multitudes with the Christian name are keen, anxious, disquieted, fretful, exacting, impatient, and severe. The affairs of a nation calling itself Christian will often be seen to be as little just, as much tainted with selfish and fraudulent characteristics, as if the whole religion of the country had been brought out to be aired on Sundays, and was laid by for the rest of the week. Protestant lands have as many prisons as Romanist or Mohammedan ones, and as many criminals to fill them. Professing Christians figure in the annals of fraud, if not as much as non-professors, yet with alarming frequency, while it is often remarked that zealots in religion are very unpleasant to live with. When professing Christian nations come into contact with uncivilized tribes, the latter, as a rule, are deceived, betrayed, debased by their so called religious neighbours, roused to revengeful and despairing resistance, and ultimately perish. Christian nations agree very little among themselves. Their wars, full of havoc, desolation, and cruelty, are the very landmarks of history.

The true and thoughtful Christian must blush at these sad illustrations of Christianity in its professors. But is it really the religion of the Prince of Peace which is exhibited to us in this deplorable picture? Has the hallowing influence of heaven upon earth really impressed itself in such harrowing lines upon the records of human life? God forbid. No! It is Philistinism, that seized the ark of God, and took it into the temple of Dagon. It is self-love, by means of an acute intellect, making a style of religion of its own, decorating it with the Christian name, and saying, "The temple of the Lord, the temple of the Lord are we!" There are idols of the heart and of the intellect as well as of wood and stone, and Philistinism has made an idol of "faith alone," and set it up to be worshipped. This is its Dagon.

Let us observe Philistia at work. The object of that frame of mind is to have a religion, and secure heaven, but not to interfere with its lust of power and pre-eminence, nor seriously to depress or renounce self-indulgence. It supposes that God made the world from the love of his own glory, as a selfish man would have done. God with them, indeed, is an infinitely selfish man. Taking the account of man in Eden literally, it regards Adam and Eve as having by their disobedience incurred infinite wrath, and brought eternal condemnation, not only upon themselves, but on their unborn posterity through all time. It enlarges upon this, and reasons upon the assumption of infinite wrath. It labours and expands these ideas. That the Lord is love itself and mercy itself, never enters into its calculation. It works away at the wrath of the Almighty, and the condemnation and misery of the doomed race, until it has framed some sort of head for its Dagon.

As this, however, would merely bury themselves and all mankind in ruthless and eternal despair and ruin, the Philistines must invent again; and they assume another, a second, divine person, very different from the first, who is not wrathful and vindictive, but who offers to sustain all the fury the first designs to inflict, and thus to pay His demand. As His reward, He is to have a certain number of souls, who are to go to heaven, notwithstanding any sins they may commit. At some time in their life or death, they will have faith given them, without any effort of their own, and a third divine person is assumed to give this faith. This is the head of Dagon. It is an artificial image altogether. There is neither Scripture nor sound wisdom for a line of it. Yet it is cunningly contrived. It looks like a human head. As it opens a way to heaven, without a daily keeping of the Lord's commands, numbers of those who have an aversion to humility, obedience, self-sacrifice in temper, and a spirit of love, are induced to accept it.

Others, too, are won by its having an imposing appearance in words, of humiliating man, and exalting the grandeur and omnipotence of God. Many souls will abase themselves before anything that is powerful. They cannot perceive the greatness of goodness, the glory of wisdom, the attractive beauty of all angelic excellence: the worth of virtue, patience, uprightness, faithfulness; but *power* fills them with awful dread. The head of Dagon is skilfully contrived to work upon their fears, and has a strange attractiveness for them.

There are allusions in Scripture to the manner in which idols are made, which illustrate the contrivances of the mind while framing an intellectual idol. "The carpenter stretcheth out his rule; he marketh it out with a line; he fitteth it with planes; and he marketh it out with the compass, and maketh it after the figure of a man; that it may remain in the house, . . . He falleth down unto it, and worshippeth it, and prayeth unto it, and saith, Deliver me; for thou art my God" (Isa. xliv. 13, 17). The intellectual carpenters, in making Dagon, have stretched their rule, and marked it with their line, so as to make it suit thoroughly well the selfishness of the natural man. He is appalled by fear, and can easily imagine a Being like himself, but infinite. He can conceive how unsparing *he* would be, if any one touched *his* apples, when he forbade them to do so; provided he had infinite skill to detect, and infinite power to crush. He can easily conceive of the infinite anger of one whose majesty and dignity are offended. He conceives that God is altogether such a one as himself (Psa. l. 21).

The head must not, however, be made too rough. It must be planed a little, and rounded according to the compasses. It would drive people to despair, and the whole scheme be finally rejected, if the terrors of infinite vengeance were described alone; so the mercy of a Saviour must be introduced, not the Lord Jesus according as Scripture manifests Him, one who forgives from His own mercy and regenerates from His own spirit and power, but one who shall sustain the vials of divine wrath, and pay our debt. Thus shaped, it has the beauty of a man; it looks rational and very wise: it is only the premises that are wrong. It begins from self, and not from love. So fair, however, to many minds, does the "scheme" of salvation, thus imagined, seem, that they consider it the perfection of spiritual beauty, a fine human head. Nay, in the book of Revelation, the dragon, the symbol of the same system, is said to have seven heads. It appears to its votaries to be superhumanly wise. Yet, what is it but just caricaturing the Lord as one who is almighty, but without mercy (although He is love itself), and then as so weak that He will be quite satisfied if He punish somebody, it matters not whom, guilty or innocent; so that He is content to punish with more than infernal tortures His own divine and spotless Son.

We have noticed how the head of Dagon is formed; let us proceed with the inspection of the body, the fish part. This is composed of a few of the prophecies respecting the coming of the Lord, and of the facts of the Gospel, especially of our blessed Saviour's death and resurrection. It is said, whoever believes these, and that these events took place to pacify the wrath of the Father against the sinner, all condemnation against him is wiped out, done away with, and obliterated. By that belief he is saved, by that belief he is justified, by that belief he is sanctified, by that belief justice is arrested, and he is absolved. Adulterer, murderer, or however great a villain he may have been all his life, and up to the hour of death, by that belief he enters heaven. If this idol be gilded a little with gold, or, in other words, covered over with holy phrases, and hung with a few chains of silver, or a few spiritual truths put about it, the Philistine nature is satisfied and delighted. "The workman melteth a graven image, and the goldsmith spreadeth it over with gold, and casteth silver chains" (Isa. xl. 19). He makes it as firm as he possibly can, "he chooseth a tree that will not rot; he seeketh unto him a cunning workman to prepare a graven image, that shall not be moved" (ver. 20).

We have got at present, however, only a head and a stump: there must be hands also. It is true this religion asserts that salvation is by "faith alone," and therefore works are unnecessary. Yet there is so much said in the Bible about *doing* what the Lord commands to prepare for heaven, and that is so firmly fixed in the minds of the common people, that in some way we must have good works connected with our faith. Dagon must have hands. We will make him artificial hands. Our good works shall be building places of worship for proselytism, and plenty of meetings for excitement; good works of worship, not of life. We will declare that good works follow necessarily from our faith, and so our hands will appear proper human hands. When good is done by humble souls amongst us, whose hearts are given to love and goodness, we will say, it is the result of our faith. When evil is done, we will say, it does not condemn; faith, faith alone, saves.

Here is a religion that interferes very little with bitter tempers, greedy impulses, or ambitious schemes. It makes heaven certain, however unheavenly we may be. We shall doubtless have time enough to utter the cry for mercy, and make the claim that our debt was paid on the cross, and our "scheme" of salvation makes us safe. Everything was finished eighteen hundred years ago, and we have only to believe.

No need of charity, no need of divine commandments, no need of love, no need of doing justly, no need of doing anything, Dagon suffices for all. Great is Dagon of the Philistines!

But now the Ark of the Lord is brought into the house of Dagon. The Word of God and Dagon come face to face. During the night, nothing was observed. "When they arose early on the morrow," however, "behold, Dagon was fallen on his face, before the Ark of the Lord" (ver. 3).

What consternation must have seized the priests, as their idol lay helpless and prostrate! But nothing less could happen. The Ark contained the commandments of God, the laws and the centre of all holiness. These precepts the Philistines denied, but they are quick and powerful. "Is not my Word like a hammer that breaketh the rock in pieces?" (Jer. xxiii. 29).

They discovered the prostration of Dagon early in the morning, because this period of the day denotes a new state, with some degree of enlightenment. That degree of illumination reveals the contrariety of "faith alone" to the Word of God, and ensures the downfall of Dagon.

Very early in the morning Dagon fell. But in the course of the day, the priests set him up again. The mind is a wonderful and complicated object. When a truthful impression has been made upon it, and it has been manifested in the clearest light, that a certain view is erroneous, the cherished phantasy has been dethroned; but very soon prejudice and old associations rally round, and set Dagon up again.

> "And they believe him!—Oh! the lover may
> Distrust that look which steals his soul away;
> The babe may cease to think that it can play
> With heaven's rainbow; alchemists may doubt
> The shining gold their crucibles give out:
> But Faith, fanatic Faith, once wedded fast
> To some dear falsehood, hugs it to the last."

The Ark, however, was still there, and judgment went on. So will it be with our judgment. The Word will judge us, and every Dagon will be overthrown. Another morning came, and they arose early. Behold, Dagon was again fallen upon his face to the ground, before the Ark of the Lord. Now, he was worse injured: "the head of Dagon and both the palms of his hands were cut off upon the threshold; only the stump of Dagon was left to him."

This is a still more vivid illustration of what takes place in a mind where the Word of the Lord and the system of "faith alone" come face to face, and new light has broken in. The head of Dagon is seen to have nothing to do with the body. The body consists of a knowledge of the facts of the Lord's death and resurrection. These are historically true. But the "scheme" of salvation, the supposed covenant between three separate divine persons, the supposition that one divine person was infinitely angry, and another divine person was infinitely merciful, and undertook to appease him by his own punishment and death; this head of Dagon is altogether artificial and altogether false. It rolls off on the floor, while from the Holy Word, the Holy Ark of the Lord, come the divine assurances: "The Lord is good to all: and His tender mercies are over all His works" (Psa. cxlv. 9). "I, even I, am He that blotteth out thy transgressions for mine own sake, and will not remember thy sins" (Isa. xliii. 25). God is Love! The life and death of our Lord were not to satisfy any wrath of a vindictive Deity, but to satisfy His own Divine Love and desire for man's salvation. Our Heavenly Father Himself became our Redeemer and Saviour. "Thou, O Jehovah, art our Father, our Redeemer; Thy name is from everlasting" (Isa. lxiii. 16). "I, even I, am Jehovah; and beside Me there is no Saviour" (Isa. xliii. 11).

Our Heavenly Father became in His humanity our Saviour, to redeem us from the power of hell (Hos. xiii. 14; Luke i. 74; Heb. ii. 14); to bruise the head of the serpent (Gen. iii. 15); to save His people from their sins (Matt. i. 21); to purify them (Mal. iii. 3); to reconcile them to Himself (2 Cor. v. 19). Salvation is effected by believing, loving, and doing the will of God in keeping His commandments (1 Cor. vii. 19; Rev. xxii. 14). That head of Dagon is a thing of nought; let it roll upon the floor. It has nothing to do with the facts of the gospel: they are the stump of Dagon, they can remain, but they must not be made into an idol.

Those hands, too, are not the true hands of a living religion; they are only artificial hands. The true service of God is doing right in our daily life, and repentance from all evil, especially that to which we are most prone. Our blessed

Saviour demands, "Why call ye me, Lord, Lord, and do not the things which I say?" (Luke vi. 46).

The three cities of the Philistines, to which the ark was taken, and whose inhabitants were severely punished, represent three varieties of those whose religion is resolutely that of faith only, and who despise love and obedience to the Lord as being concerned in the work of salvation.

Ashdod, where Dagon was set up and adored, and whose name signifies "the fire of affection," represented the love of evil in which those are who, notwithstanding their acknowledgment of some of the truths of religion, exhibit none of its spirit in their hearts or its power in their lives. They will not obey where their lusts are strong, and they defiantly maintain that belief alone is saving.

Gath, whose name means "a press," represented those who sustain salvation by faith alone, chiefly by reasoning, for the rational faculty is a species of intellectual press, and when it is worked by cunning it gives great intellectual power. Goliath the giant was of Gath.

Ekron, where Beelzebub, the god of flies, was worshipped (2 Kings i. 2), and whose name signifies "torn away," represented such as trust to faith only, because they lead a frivolous and heedless life, separated from all that is noble and good.

The emerods, or hæmorrhoids, which are painfully swollen veins at the lower parts of the body, gorged with impure blood, when the liver only sluggishly performs its duty, inducing severe inflammation, and sometimes death, exhibited the misery caused by impure influences in the soul, when there is an unwillingness to self-examination, and none of the work of repentance. When the presence of the Word of the Lord presses upon them, such as are hardened in these states, swell with hate, agony, and defiance, and perish in spiritual death. They will not repent, and they will not submit. Suffering, they struggle in daring and desperate defiance.

Let us, my beloved friends, fly from the fate of the Philistines, and so purify our hearts and lives that our Lord may say, Ye are Israelites indeed, in whom is no guile.

SERMON VI.

SAUL ANOINTED BY SAMUEL TO BE KING.

"Then Samuel took a vial of oil, and poured it upon his head, and kissed him, and said, Is it not because the Lord hath anointed thee to be captain over his inheritance?"— 1 SAM. X. 1.

THE introduction of kingly government amongst the Israelitish people marks a great change in their constitution and history. They had been ruled by the high priests and judges, at first wisely, but afterwards feebly. The result had been, to a great extent, anarchy and weakness. They had much disorder among themselves, and they fell often under the yoke of strangers. Since men lost their early infantile nature, order and happiness can only be nourished and preserved under a government whose laws are just, and also uprightly executed. A nation without a firm government is a rope of sand, a circumference without a centre, a body without a head. This the Israelites felt, and they therefore cried out for a king. Their request was not granted at first, and their prayer for a monarch was condemned; but when they persevered their request was granted, and the appointment of Saul, with the sanction of heaven, took place.

The kingly office has often been objected to, as exalting one human being too high above others to be consistent with human dignity, and that freedom for the people which is essential to true manhood, and the birthright of every human being. But where there are no slaves there will be no tyrants. The true king is only the first citizen of a true nation, whose sacred duty it is to yield perfect obedience to the law, and whose high charge it is to guard the enactments of the legislature, and to be responsible for obedience to them throughout the kingdom. For the sake of the nation he must be surrounded with splendour and dignity, to attract obedience, and invested with power to enforce it in all ranks of society from the highest subject to the lowliest workman. The king is surrounded with respect, and made wealthy and powerful, that he may, as the representative of the law, overawe the powerful and protect the weak, and thus preserve the reign of law and the public good. Where law rules God rules; for law, freely and thoughtfully enacted, is as much of God's wisdom as the justice and judgment of the law-makers can receive and embody for the nation. If the laws which are passed in a legislature freely chosen are not the very best, they are the best possible at the time, and should be faithfully carried out by prince and people. "Justice and judgment are the habitation of Thy throne; mercy and truth shall go before Thy face. Blessed is the people that know the joyful sound: they shall walk, O Lord, in the light of Thy countenance" (Psa. lxxxix. 14, 15). It is well said by a great writer: "He is a wise king who considers the law as his superior, and he is an unwise king who considers himself as superior to the law. The king who considers the law as his superior annexes royalty to the law, and makes himself subject thereto, because he knows that the law is justice, and all justice as such is divine. But the king who considers himself as superior to the law annexes royalty to himself, and fancies either that he himself is the law, or that the law, which is justice, is derived from himself. In this case he claims to himself that which is in its nature divine, and unto which he ought to be subject. He is a true king who lives in obedience to the laws of his kingdom, and thus sets an example to his subjects. The king ought to be obeyed according to the laws of the realm, nor in anywise to be injured by word or deed, for on this depends the public safety. An absolute monarch, who fancies that his subjects are his slaves, and that he has a right to their lives and properties, and exercises such a power, is not a king but a tyrant."

It may, however, be very properly demanded, if the kingly office be of such essential value to mankind, how it happened that the proposition to have a king was received with repugnance by Samuel, and was condemned by the Lord. It is written: "The thing displeased Samuel, when they said, Give us a king to judge us. And Samuel prayed unto the Lord. And the Lord said unto Samuel, Hearken unto the voice of the people in all that they say unto thee: for they have not rejected thee, but they have rejected me, that I should not reign over them" (1 Sam. viii. 6, 7). The Lord directed Samuel also to explain to the people the disadvantages of kingly rule, its expense, and the possible tyranny of monarchs, yet with the direction that, if they persisted, a king should be granted and anointed, and thus the divine sanction be given to what was not the best thing in itself, but what was best for them under the circumstances. When men were in a heavenly state, and were ruled interiorly by the Lord, their tendencies and their lives were loving, good, and wise; they needed no other government. They loved right and they did it. They needed no outward king: the Lord was their king. The patriarchal government was sufficient, and they enjoyed a simple and a happy life. They had no outward king, nor any outward law. They were innocent in their wishes, simple in their tastes, and orderly, useful, and peaceful in their daily conduct. The impulses of the Spirit of the Lord in their consciences guided them to all that was right; the law was written upon their hearts. But as men declined in spirit, and self-love grew more and more audacious, filling them with lusts destructive of peace and contentment, and passions destructive of property and at length of life, they rejected the Lord, and His government within them, and unless an outward law and an outward rule had been introduced, everything would have become lawless, and the human race would have perished. Hence, then, we may say that though outward law is not so good as inward law, it is far better than no law at all. And, in like manner, though the government of a king is not so good as the government of the Lord in the conscience, in a state of innocence, yet it is immeasurably to be preferred to the reign of anarchy, disorder, and wild confusion. Even a bad government, in the evil interior state in which men now are, is better than no government, on the principle that one tyrant is better than a million. Hence we may understand how it was that the wish of the Israelites to have a king was a declension for them, who had been governed by the Divine King, and yet it was permitted when they had forsaken the Lord, to save them from still severer evils, even the worst of all, the intolerable mischiefs of wild confusion, and the carnival of villany which results to a land when "order, heaven's first law, is utterly contemned." Nay, we may go further, and say that an efficient enforcement of order in a state by outward government, and a conscientious and firm rule by the monarch and the officers of state, high and low, are the first great prerequisites to form "a wise and understanding nation." When order prevails, peace prevails; and with peace the arts flourish, education spreads, literature expands, industry is requited, religion unfolds her virtues, and national wellbeing presents on earth a faint image of heaven.

As it was with the Israelitish nation, so is it with an individual. The human mind in an unregenerate condition is a kingdom in disorder, often in insurrection. It has long been separated from the Lord and lived in wayward folly, in dull uncertainty or wild disorder. It gratifies itself with rude pleasures, it is true; but these are followed by pangs of heart, by losses, and suffering and strange dreads of a terrible future. The sweet days of early childhood have long passed. The ponderings of youthful faith, the young heart's dedication of itself to its Saviour, the ingenuous hopes of a frank and unperverted spirit, have all been long laid aside or indrawn, and the soul tossed about by the disorderly impulses which contact with the world has drawn out, and an undisciplined character has very feebly restrained, has sown the seeds of misery, and begun to reap in many a sorrow and many a pain the sad fruits of impiety and folly. "He has sown the wind and reaped the whirlwind." The tares which have been planted have come up, and the fair show of earlier days has been blighted by many a sin. Hearts and homes which had once glistened brightly with hope and joyous anticipations have become grave with sorrow.

> "When ranting round in pleasure's ring
>   Religion may be blinded,
> Or if she give a random sting
>   It may be little minded;
> But, when on life we're tempest driven,
>   A conscience but a canker,
> A correspondence fixed wi' heaven,
>   Is sure a noble anchor."

Happy is it when there comes to the soul in which sorrow has excited reflection, a yearning after help, after principle, after salvation. A sense of its weakness and folly induces the desire for a better governed mind. This is to ask for a king. To consult Samuel, spiritually is to consult the Word of God; and this induces meditation. The unwillingness of Samuel to permit the nation to have a king, represents meditation in the soul, during a state of repentance, on the innocence and happiness of its early days, of the blessedness of a state where nothing reigns but Divine Love. It sees this, and feels this; but it knows how far it is from that pure and holy state, and recognizes the necessity of having a king, or, in other words, a definite ruling fixed principle of outward religion, to which its whole conduct must conform. Those who are brought into this state are made sensible that religion at first will be a yoke, but they are convinced they need a yoke. They will be curbed in many of their desires, but they know they need curbing. They will have to take up a cross; but they resolve to bear the cross that they may wear the crown. The freedom of sin they had found to be a horrid slavery, full of captivity, full of misery, and full of alarm; and they resolve to place themselves under a healthy discipline, which, though binding at first, will lead to celestial freedom. The fear of eternal ruin is pressing hard upon them, as the fear of their enemies round about filled the Israelites with consternation, and they must have a defender.

Samuel was becoming old; and his two sons, Joel and Abiah, though they were judges in Beersheba, took bribes, and were easily turned aside from the way of right. Samuel the prophet represents the Word of God to us; for this is our grand prophet. This prophet grows old, when its teachings are little regarded. The two sons represent the two faculties, the will and understanding, in an unconverted man. They are bribed by pleasure or gain, which turns them aside from the path of wisdom and good sense, and allows vice to triumph over virtue. The intentions of the evil are well known to be vigorous enough in sentiment, before there has been any real conversion of the soul; but they are easily warped by self-indulgence. Like Samuel's sons, they have no practical value. They rather betray and ruin, than help and save. The soul that knows its weakness and its sorrows perseveres, and must have a king.

Divine Providence had prepared in a wonderful way to meet this want of the Israelites, and also in every particular case He prepares a remedy for ours. A young man, Saul, a Benjamite, the son of Kish, a choice young man, noble in stature, capable of reigning, was already on a journey which would bring him to Samuel. The asses of his father's farm had gone astray, and Kish had sent Saul forth to recover them. This young man was apparently on a trivial errand; yet what is trivial in which an immortal soul engages? This young man was Israel's future king. He was, without knowing it, being guided by Divine Providence to Samuel, who would open to him his advancement and his future career. Our steps also are guided or overruled in every event of life; and out of seeming small circumstances come results of the weightiest consequence, that we may know that the Most High rules over the affairs of men, and even out of seeming evil elaborates eternal good. Afterwards, a solemn assembly was called by Samuel, and a trial by lot was taken to ascertain, after sacrifice and burnt-offerings, who should be the chosen sovereign. Saul was elected. His modesty kept him in retirement; but he was brought forth, and his goodly appearance and bearing won the hearts of the people, and they exulted in the new monarch, crying out in one grand acclaim, "God save the King!"

We have already seen that the demand of Israel for a king was not only a literal fact, but was representative of the soul's demand for an outward religion to rule it, to be its king. All the particulars in this point of view are most interesting. The asses which had gone astray were the symbols of the natural thoughts and affairs of man which go far astray, when there is no religious conviction to guide them. Horses represent the intellect in its power of progress in spiritual things; hence it is written, "The Lord of hosts hath visited His flock, the house of Judah, and hath made them as His GOODLY HORSE in the battle" (Zech. x. 3). The true Christian is said to ride on a WHITE HORSE, and to have a bow in his hand and receive a crown, going forth conquering and to conquer (Rev. vi. 2). The natural intellect, as compared to the spiritual intellect in a man, is as the ass compared to the horse. Issachar is said to be a STRONG ASS couching down between two burdens (Gen. xlix. 14); because he represented those whose religion is that of the letter and servitude, not that of interior spiritual intelligence, which is "the glorious liberty of the children of light." Our Lord rode on an ass to Jerusalem, to represent religion guiding all the natural affairs of life, so as to bring them into harmony with the spirit of heaven. Saul seeking for the lost asses, therefore, represents the soul yearning after true principles in its business, its household affairs, and its daily life, so that it may return to order again, as it had been in earlier years.

Saul was a Benjamite, and taller by head and shoulders than any other Israelite (ver. 23). The tribe of Benjamin was the intellectual tribe of Israel, and Saul's being of that tribe indicated that all intelligence assents to the truth that religion should be king in the mind. The conviction that we should live for heaven in all our ways on earth, is the highest and noblest conviction of the mind. It is, like Saul, head and shoulders above everything else. We have family relations, with their cares and interests; we have business ties, with their many concerns; we have the connections of citizenship, of art, science and enjoyment; but that which is supreme above all other is the one thing needful, to live for heaven; this is Saul, higher than all the rest of the people. "What shall it profit a man, if he shall gain the whole world, and lose his own soul?"

Saul was anointed by Samuel, to teach that this conviction of the supremacy of religion is in full harmony with the Word of God. The anointing oil is the symbol of heavenly love, called in Scripture the oil of joy (Isa. lxi. 3), and indicates that our religion must ever be filled with the Spirit of love. "Above all things, put on charity, which is the bond of perfectness" (Col. iii. 14). The kiss of Samuel represented the DIVINE BLESSING, and the interior joy that is experienced when a soul resolves that religion shall henceforth be its regal influence.

Samuel informed Saul that now he would soon find two men by Rachel's sepulchre, who would tell him that the asses were found. These two men by Rachel's sepulchre represent the experiences of faith and love associated with the Church of the past, which would assure him that now all is in true order; earthly things, the asses, are in their places, as well as heavenly things. Saul was to go on further, and he would meet three men, bearing three kids, three loaves, and a bottle of wine. As the soul advances in its new life it will receive a full faith in all holy things (the three kids); goodness, the bread of life, to support and strengthen the heart in all its purposes of good, (the three loaves); and a bottle of wine, or such encouraging truth as will cheer and animate it in its heavenly course,—the new wine of the kingdom. The two loaves which he should receive represent the good which would strengthen love and faith, to be followed in due time by the good of life. In his further progress, he was to come to the hill or mountain of God; and there he should meet with a company of prophets, with a psaltery, a tabret, a pipe, and a harp, before them: "and they shall prophesy, and the Spirit of the Lord will come upon thee, and thou shalt prophesy with them, and thou shalt be turned into another man." This coming to the mountain of God represents the newly converted entering into a state of adoration and gratitude. We praise the Lord, when we feel that we have indeed been accepted and saved by Him. The company of prophets represent all the hopes and grateful feelings that descend into the soul. Angels too are joined with us, and stimulate us to joy and praise. The heart and mind send up the grateful music of exulting thankfulness, like the psaltery and the tabret, the pipe and the harp, while the penitent feels he is another man. "The Lord upholdeth all that fall, and raiseth up all them that be bowed down. My mouth shall speak the praise of the Lord; and let all flesh bless His holy name for ever and ever" (Ps. cxlv. 14, 21).

— Saul having been chosen from the tribe of Benjamin, represented that man must become religious by truths which reach him through the intellect. He must be intelligently good, not stupidly good.

— One other incident in the installation of Saul we must not overlook. When the lot had indicated that he was to be king, he was not to be found. This hiding of himself was a sign of humility, the essence of every virtue. There is no religion without humility. "Blessed are the poor in spirit, for theirs is the kingdom of heaven." Saul felt at the time that he was least of all. So will every principle of true religion in a man feel when he is truly converted, and enabled to reign by the power of truth, in the little kingdom of his own soul. It was revealed that Saul had hid himself among the stuff. This circumstance readily reminds us, that our Lord Himself was born in a manger, and the truth represented is very much of the same character in both cases. The manger where horses are fed, is an emblem of the memory, in which truth is stored up, and which supplies the understanding with its food. The memory, as a storehouse, is the magazine where the stuff is laid up for future use, and among that stuff is the grand principle stored up from childhood, though yet hidden from view, that we were born for heaven, and should live for heaven. When this principle is brought out, animated with new life and placed to govern the soul, thenceforth it is indeed seen to be a noble thing. The edifice of the soul is crowned. This is worthier than aught of time, or talent, or science, or philosophy. "There is none like him among all the people." With religion everything is gain; without it, all is loss.' If we have not chosen this principle for our guide, external though it may be at first, we are yet grovelling in the shades of night. We need a faith which, like Moses, or like Saul, shall be a leader for us, and then a king will reign in righteousness within us, and princes rule in judgment. "He shall be as a hiding-place from the wind, and a covert from the tempest; as rivers of water in a dry place; as the shadow of a great rock in a weary land" (Isa. xxxii. 2).

SERMON VII.

SAUL'S VICTORY OVER THE AMMONITES.

"'Then Nahash the Ammonite came up, and encamped against Jabesh-Gilead; and all the men of Jabesh said unto Nahash, Make a covenant with us, and we will serve thee.

"And Nahash the Ammonite answered them, On this condition will I make a covenant with you, that I may thrust out all your right eyes, and lay it for a reproach upon all Israel."—1 SAM. xi. 1, 2.

ONE of the general signs of the superiority of the present age over the barbarous periods of the past, is its horror at such cruelties as that proposed by the Ammonite in our text. Yet they were common in the gloomy days gone by, before our Lord's coming into the world. And when, after His coming, the overwhelming crowds of rude barbarians were baptized by command of their conquerors, and received into the Church with all their coarse passions, their dark and cruel minds unchanged, similar revolting crimes were commonly committed in the middle ages by so-called Christians. The proceedings of those ages of rude uproar were rather the conversion of the names, forms, and doctrines of the Church to the purposes of selfishness, greed, and wickedness, than (as was fondly dreamed) the conversion of savage nations to the faith of the Lord Jesus. The celebrated Emperor Constantine himself (whose conversion was the subject of endless exultation by the then leaders of the Church), even after he had presided at the famous Council of Nice, not only put his son to death in a wild fit of anger, but caused his wife to be burnt alive.

The Christianity of the middle ages was chiefly heathenism in a Christian dress, and was quite as cruel as heathenism had previously been. What have been called religious wars, the crimes of the Inquisition, the pains and penalties inflicted for the sake of opinions, and the burning of so-called heretics in the name of the divinely merciful Prince of Peace, all arose from brutality being conjoined with superstition. "The dark places of the earth are full of the habitations of cruelty" (Psa. lxxiv. 20). Hence the effort of us all should be to diffuse by every means in our power the light that leads to a good life, the wisdom that comes from above, and which is so beautifully described by the Apostle James as "first pure, then peaceable, gentle, and easy to be entreated, full of mercy and good fruits, without partiality, and without hypocrisy" (James iii. 17).

Again may we congratulate ourselves on the advance of the new age of love towards the Lord, and love to our neighbour, so far in the way of good, that anything so revolting as the horrid proposal of Nahash the king of the Ammonites in our text would be now impossible in civilized and Christian communities. But whether something mental, quite as cruel and quite as detrimental to human progress, is not even now too prevalent, let us proceed very patiently to inquire.

The eyes correspond to the understanding in the mind. The bodily eyes are formed to perceive objects in earthly light; the eyes of the intellect are formed to see mental objects in heavenly light. Such is the constitution of things, and it is everywhere recognised in Scripture. Hence the apostle says, "The eyes of your understanding being enlightened; that ye may know what is the hope of his calling, and what the riches of the glory of his inheritance in the saints" (Eph. i. 18).

Light corresponds to truth; not so much to truth in statement as to interior truth, which shines in the mind, and enables it spiritually to see. This light shines from the Lord Jesus, the Heavenly Sun; and to receive it, and to comprehend all things important to our wellbeing, and to enrich us with mental beauty, He has given, and He sustains in us, THE EYES OF THE MIND.

He teaches us to pray—"Open Thou mine eyes, that I may behold wondrous things out of Thy law" (Psa. cxix. 18). Again we read: "Mine eyes have seen Thy salvation" (Luke ii. 30). "I am the Light of the world; he that followeth me shall not walk in darkness, but shall have the light of life" (John viii. 12).

These, and other frequently recurring passages of Holy Writ, demonstrate the recognition in the Word of God of the correspondence of natural light and natural eyes with spiritual light and spiritual eyes. From common conversation, also, it is perfectly clear that the analogy between the body and the mind, in this respect, is universally perceived and understood. When a person is ignorant upon a certain subject, he is described as being in the dark; when true thoughts upon it are entering his mind, he is said to be getting a little light, and when he fully understands it, he is said to see clearly. This ordinary form of speech, familiar to every one, indicates that some portion of the analogy between the outward world of matter and the inner world of mind is generally seen, and taken for granted.

But this consideration may well be pondered over; for if inner truth is like light, and the understanding eyes to the mind, how immensely important both must be to our real well-being, will be suggested by a few reflections on the value of light, and the inestimable blessings we realize from the use of our eyes.

It is to LIGHT we owe all the fertility, as well as all the beauty, of the glorious universe of which we form a part. Without light no forest-trees would ever have waved their majestic heads or risen upwards to the sun; no fertile fields would have abounded with grateful harvests; not a flower, not a leaf, not a blade of grass would have grown. The earth without light would have been bare, hard, arid, bleak, and dead. No sun would have poured over the world his morning splendour or his evening glory. The myriad stars and starry systems, with all their varying shades and multiform magnificence, the silvery moon with her mild beauties, would, without light, all alike have been to us hidden and unperceived. Without light there is no colour. All the hues of nature, all the varied loveliness of flowers, all the varying aspects of the sky, nay, the very changes of the human face expressive of the shades of joy and grief, of human thought and feeling, are revealed to us by light.

> "Prime cheerer, Light !
> Of all ethereal beings first and last !
> Efflux divine ! Nature's resplendent robe !
> Without whose vesting beauty all were wrapt
> In unessential gloom ! and thou, O Sun !
> Soul of surrounding worlds, in whom, best seen,
> Shines out thy Maker !"

But grand beyond description as light is for the outer world, still grander is TRUTH, which is the light of eternity, of heaven, of angels, of sages, the light of the mind, the "true light which enlighteneth every man that cometh into the world." It is the manifestation of Divine Love, the splendour of God. From truths flowing out of love, come all the blessings of life, all true joys, all progress, all victory, all purity, all glory, in time and in eternity. Truth is the Word of God, the King of kings, the Lord of lords, adorned with many crowns. If the thought of nature without light is appalling, still more dreadful is it to think of the soul, with no truth to light its path to wisdom; of the inner universe, of heaven, without truth to reveal their supernal splendours. Here, indeed, must one say with Milton, who knew by his privations the unspeakable worth of light,—

> "Hail, holy light, offspring of heaven first-born,
> Or of the eternal co-eternal beam,
> May I express thee unblamed? Since God is Light,
> And never but in unapproached light
> Dwelt from eternity, dwelt then in thee,
> Bright effluence of bright essence uncreate."

Oh yes! light for the outer world, and light for the mental and spiritual worlds are divine gifts, for which all praise must ever fall far short: so great are their excellences that our warmest thanksgivings must needs be inadequate, poor and weak!

Yet, worthy as they are, they would have been as nothing to us, if we had not been furnished with eyes! Grandeur and loveliness would have been above and around us as at present; but without eyes we could not have perceived a single ray. Hence we perceive how accordant with the Divine Wisdom it is to have given us eyes so curiously and wonderfully formed, and so guarded that it is difficult to hurt them. Mark how they are placed in the front of the head, best for observation, best also for protection. They are placed in bony fortresses, projecting beyond them on every side. There are the eyelids ever nervously alive to cover and protect. There is then the thick outer coat of the eye, very difficult to injure. Within, there is the IRIS, ever opening and contracting, so that an injurious amount of light even may not destroy the delicate tissues which constitute the inner chambers of the eye. Then there are the three humours, the aqueous, the crystalline, and the vitreous, which attemper and refract the light, so that by the lens, and these delicate substances, in proper order, perfect vision is secured.

And what an amazing marvel is that! The world around, countless objects with their shades and varied proportions, stars at incalculable distances, minute forms and diverse hues, all pass their images through a small aperture of about the eighth of an inch, and are reproduced on the exquisite membrane at the back of the eye, the retina, that finest of all network, and there inform the soul of the world around. By the same wondrous organ, the soul flashes out its intelligence, and utters in burning glances the glowing fervours of the immortal being within. Oh wondrous door of thought! oh wondrous window through which the radiant splendours of the spirit shine! Oh wonderful photographic power which transfers the universe, and with God-given appliances fixes all the pictures! What malicious being would dare or desire to injure an organ so guarded and so prized by Providence Divine?

Yet in such cases as the one in our text, wretched cruel tyrants have sought ruthlessly to destroy what the skill of all the philosophers who ever lived could never make. We shudder to think what a monster Nahash the Ammonite must have been! He proposed to put out the right eyes of the inhabitants of this city. Appalling crime! Yet how many there are who, from lust of power, or from an unguarded acquiescence in blind traditions, are constantly seeking to induce spiritual blindness. Have we quite as vivid a dread of these? "You must not dare to think for yourself. Religion is a collection of dark mysteries, of which we have the keeping. You are not to think, but to heed what we say, in blind obedience to what we call faith." Yet to darken the soul is more mischievous than to darken the body. "You must sacrifice your intellect," say these blindness makers. "The greater the mystery, the greater the faith." "I believe because it is impossible." "The more impossible, the more certain." These are of the tribe of Nahash the Ammonite. His name signifies "serpent;" many such serpents there have been in the past, and many such there are at the present day. They long for a blind people, especially in relation to THE RIGHT EYE. The *right* eye corresponds to the intellect which is directed chiefly to notice things of *love;* the *left* eye to that part of the understanding which is directed to things of *faith.* The mental right eye, when it looks up to the Lord, sees that He is good to all, that His tender mercies are over all His works. When it looks to heaven, it beholds the realms of bliss a kingdom of love; when it looks to religion, it regards charity as chief; when it looks to human conduct, it rejoices when it sees a loving heart and a good life.

What is there in all this to offend Nahash the Ammonite? Let us see.

Jabesh-Gilead was situated in the portion of the Israelitish possessions beyond the Jordan. They had a beautiful country, rich in fruits and flowers, surrounded by glorious mountains, part of the territory granted to the two tribes and a half, Reuben, Gad, and the half tribe of Manasseh. They represented good,

simple people, who are upright, but who do not think deeply
or care for much beyond the letter of the Word. The name
Jabesh, which signifies *dryness*, is expressive of their state;
there is but little of sap in them, but in external life they conform themselves to the teaching of the divine commandments.
Gilead means a "heap of testimony." It was the place where
Jacob and Laban made a covenant. It signifies such a state
of religion as a Gentile would admit, and to which he would
conform. The Ammonites were the descendants of Lot from
one of the two sons who were the result of his unhappy proceedings in a cave: Moab was the other.

Ammon represented a religion of perverted truth originating
from evil, and an obscure state of mind, a mind like a cave.
Moab represents a religion of ceremony, with a similar origin,
Both are superstitious, and hate the light.

Lot was the cousin of Abraham, and was in a certain state
of good, but a very low one. After he was saved from Sodom,
he declined, and he represented those who have dispositions
towards religion, but whose gloomy minds are like a cave.
They invent a religion of their own, but a religion of grimness.
They take some parts of the letter of the Bible, but never enter
into its loving, broad, and genial spirit. They have no love,
and they don't think God has any. They magnify what they
esteem to be duties, and these must be attended to, whatever
becomes of the weightier matters of the law. They would
neglect their families to attend a prayer meeting; they would
grind down their workpeople to build a place of prayer. They
would multiply services of worship and profession; but the services of justice, uprightness to all men, goodness, real virtue,
and gentleness are, in their code, of no account. They will,
like the Pharisees of old, move heaven and earth to make a
proselyte, but it is a convert to their party, not to wisdom, to
loving-kindness, or to God. They make much of a few things
in the letter of religion, and call it FAITH to believe in these;
but all the loving part of religion they despise. This is the
reason of their being represented by Nahash desiring to put out
the right eyes of the men of Jabesh-Gilead. These latter,
being simple people, had not sufficient power to drive their
foes thoroughly away, but they held them at bay for a time.
They desired a truce of seven days.

Seven is the sacred number, and the truce for seven days implied that in the loving religion of the Heavenly Father there
would be found help for them.

In the meantime Saul had been chosen king, and had taken the responsibility of government. Messengers came to him, whose tidings spread sorrow around. The Spirit of God came upon Saul and filled him with courage and wisdom. He took his two oxen and hewed them in pieces, sending the pieces by messengers in every direction, requiring all the able-bodied men to assemble with him, and denouncing the destruction of the oxen of all who failed to attend.

Oxen correspond to obedience, the plodding spirit of duty; the two oxen imply the acknowledgment of duty to God and duty to man; and Saul sent pieces of the oxen around, inviting thus the aid of all who sympathized with him in the conviction that the one indispensable principle is obedience to the commandments of God, to obey God in using rightly the faculties He has given, and to repel all who in His name are "blind leaders of the blind." This is the true duty implied in Saul's invitation to come up to the help of the men of Jabesh-Gilead. Religion is a thing of light, not of darkness; of seeing, not of blindness.

The thirty thousand men of Judah and the three hundred thousand men of Israel who came, represented all the teachings of love and all the powers of faith; for three, which is the chief number concerned, is used in Scripture when fulness of truth is intended to be expressed. They sent messengers to Jabesh-Gilead to assure them of help on the morrow, when the sun should be hot. When the soul has marshalled its powers as carefully as if all depended upon itself, and stands ready to do its best for the Lord, it will soon have a glorious morrow; the sun will soon be hot, and victory will soon be achieved. The Lord is the Sun of the soul, the Sun of righteousness; and when we prepare ourselves in devout and loving trust in Him, He will soon rise in the warm glow of love, with healing in His wings. The soul burning with zeal and courage will chase as "chaff before the wind" all who love darkness rather than light. The agents of man-made mystery must then fly like detected owls. Divine mysteries indeed there are, but they are hidden wisdom, which we are invited to fathom (1 Cor. ii. 7). "Unto you it is given to know the mysteries of the kingdom of heaven," said the Lord to His disciples (Matt. xiii. 11), and He says the same in every age.

"Let there be light" was His original charter for mankind. It is His charter now. Conspiracy demands secrecy and darkness; innocence, virtue, and progress rejoice in the light. They are of the tribe of Nahash the Ammonite, who seek to put out the right eyes of mankind, who say, "Don't pry into divine things, don't examine, don't think, you are sure to be either infidel or insane if you venture to use your mental powers." It was well said by an ancient sage, "The wise man's eyes are in his head, but the fool walketh in darkness" (Eccles. ii. 14). When poor Caspar Hauser, who had been confined from childhood in a dark cellar, first saw the brilliant sky on a splendid star-light night, all radiant with magnificent loveliness, he burst into tears, and exclaimed, "Oh what have I ever done that I should not have been permitted to see this wondrous sight before!"

Look further at a beautiful sunrise. See how the glorious light diffuses its splendours over the east, and gilds the mountain tops. As the sunbeams spread down, and lighten up the plains, fields, forests, gardens, towns, and towers, the soul exclaims, rejoicing at the beauties bursting into view on every side, "These are Thy glorious works, parent of Good! Thine this universal frame!" Just so it is with the splendours of truth when they enter the mind. Fields of thought, landscapes of mind, expand before you. Heaven opens its bright lights irradiated with golden hopes, and the Lord shows you the path of life. Mysteries give place to holy beauties, and you rise above the mists and fogs of ignorance and error to lovelier and still lovelier things, until your thoughts settle on the Lord Jesus in His glorified beauty for ever. "Your sun shall no more go down, nor your moon withdraw itself: for the Lord shall be your everlasting light, and your God your glory."

Dread, as a sacred duty, the efforts of all who would substitute dreamy darkness for the light of holy truth that commends itself by being spiritual, rational, and scientific at the same time. When the superstitious would call you down to gloom and contradiction, do you rise to the glorious liberty of the children of light; and in the spirit of charity invite the sleepy sons of superstition to awake, in the divine words of the prophet, "Arise, shine; for thy light is come, and the glory of the Lord is risen upon thee" (Isa. lx. 1).

SERMON VIII.

SAMUEL'S CHARGE IN HIS OLD AGE.

"Moreover, as or me, God forbid that I should sin against the Lord in ceasing to pray for you: but I will teach you the good and the right way.
"Only fear the Lord, and serve him in truth with all your heart: for consider how great things he hath done for you."—1 SAM. xii. 23, 24.

THE prophet Samuel's life was really a noble one. The characters of Joseph and Samuel stand out far beyond all others in the Israelitish history, as having from childhood to old age been singularly stainless. We have their whole history before us; and by Divine Mercy their lives were so pure that no one could lay anything to their charge. The blessings of a well-spent life gathered round their declining years; and while they were grateful to Him whose shield had protected them as they went in and out before them, they felt they could claim in the sight of their people to have been absolutely blameless.

It was a grand time for Samuel when, having surrendered the government of the nation at their request to a young and valiant king, he could appeal to them in full assembly, and say, "I am old and grey-headed; and, behold, my sons are with you: and I have walked before you *from my childhood* unto this day. Behold, here I am: witness against me, before the Lord, and before His anointed. Whose ox have I taken? or whose ass have I taken? or whom have I defrauded? or whom have I oppressed? or of whose hands have I received any bribe to blind mine eyes therewith? and I will restore it you." It must have been delightful to the grand old man to hear the reply of the assembled people: "Thou hast not defrauded us, nor oppressed us, neither hast thou taken aught of any man's hand." Though the good man has in his own conscience the testimony that he has faithfully done his duty, it is a pleasure as well as a right to receive from those who have been the objects of his care the assurance that they entirely acknowledge his service and his faithfulness. The approbation of the Lord in the conscience is the testimony the good man values highest; but next to that, the testimony of those he has loved and aided, is music to his ears.

Samuel had passed through great vicissitudes. In childhood, he had waited on Eli, and must have witnessed with horror the disorders of the priests and the people. He had heard of the capture of the ark, seen the flying multitudes who brought the tidings of defeat; probably was near when the aged high priest Eli, stunned by the astounding intelligence, fell from his seat on the wayside, broke his neck, and died. What bitter grief must have been suffered by the faithful among the priests, while the ark, the symbol of the Divine Presence among them, was in captivity amongst the wicked Philistines! In the interval of seven months, during which the sacred chest was lost to Israel, it must have been a consolation to hear, from time to time, that it was no gain to Israel's foes; but we can only faintly picture the bereavement of such as Samuel, while the golden cherubim, the tables of the commandments, the pot of manna, and the rod of Aaron, with the golden covered ark itself, were in the hands of the uncircumcised. That must have been a mournful period; but after a while the Ark, the palladium of Israel's strength and safety, was brought within the precincts of the country once more. It was not, however, returned to Shiloh. For twenty years it remained at Kirjath-jearim, in the house of Abinadab, on a hill; until, by king David, it was removed to Jerusalem.

Israel bitterly lamented the disorganized state of things they had fallen into; and then the conscientious character of Samuel acquired new lustre. He pointed out to the people their idolatries and pollutions, which had been the sources of their sorrows. He called an assembly of the nation at their council-city, Mizpeh, where they had often met in former days for advice and encouragement. A solemn confession of sin was made, and a renunciation of idolatry; and thus a basis was formed for the return of prosperity.

At this indication of the commencement of a better life, their fierce foes, the Philistines, put themselves in motion. They were determined to destroy the new movement in the bud. Before the assembly had broken up, the hosts of Philistia appeared, and filled the timid with consternation. But Samuel, equally great in the eloquence that sustains an assembly and animates to deeds of daring, and in the piety that looks to

Divine Providence for help, cheered and encouraged the people. A thunder-storm was a sign to the Israelites that the Lord was once more with them since their repentance. It spread panic among their enemies. The result was, that the Philistines received such a discomfiture that they left Israel in peace all the days of Samuel. He was now recognised as the chief man of his nation; the prophet, hero, and judge of his people. He set up a monument of stone, and called it Ebenezer, "the Lord our help;" saying, "Hitherto the Lord hath helped us."

Samuel went on circuit, from year to year, to judge the people at Mizpeh, Gilgal, and Bethel. Whatever his integrity and wisdom decided, seems to have been satisfactory; while the land was restored, under his benign administration, to order, confidence, and prosperity.

After a life so long, so active, and so eventful, it would not have been wonderful if, in his old age, some one had felt himself aggrieved, and had made some charge of imaginary if not real wrong against him. But, no; his integrity no one impugned; no man raised his voice with a word of complaint. He laid down his power as free from the imputation of wrong as when he took it up. He remained, by universal consent, the tried and trusted counsellor of king and people. The advice he gave to both is contained in the words of our text, which we will now proceed to consider.

He first assured the assembly of his constant affection for them, and declared he would never forget to ask, in his daily prayers, for the divine blessing to guide and preserve them. Indeed he intimates that, if he should fall away from this labour of brotherly love, it would be a sin against the Lord. "God forbid that I should sin against the Lord, in ceasing to pray for you."

The practice of intercessory prayer does not commend itself to all; but it was clearly a duty deeply and affectionately fixed in the mind of the prophet Samuel. Indeed, a little examination will show that prayer for others pervades all prayer as authorized in the Holy Word. To pray only for self, is SELFISHNESS IN PRAYER; the very opposite of the state which prepares us for divine blessings. Solomon's prayer consists almost entirely of petitions for Israel, in the changing circumstances through which their national life would take them. He prays for them when they trespass individually or generally, and entreats pardon for them when they are penitent. He prays for them in sorrow, and in captivity; and entreats the divine support and comfort for them in every coming need. The Lord's prayer itself is an intercessory prayer. We say "Our Father," and in every petition we are led to ask for others all that we ask for ourselves.

It may be said, But why pray for others? Does not the Lord love them as much as He loves you? and will He not care for their good, and their salvation, as much as He cares for yours? Is it not presumptuous for you to dictate to Him what He shall do in relation to others of His children, who are as much under the inspection of His Infinite Goodness and Wisdom, as you can possibly be?

To these objections we may justly reply—Prayer in our own cases is not offered up to change the Divine Being, but only to prepare us to receive those mercies He is wishful to bestow. He waiteth to be gracious. He suggests the prayer when we are in a humble frame of mind; and what we ask when thus prompted is assuredly bestowed. When we abide in Him, and His words abide in us, we ask what we will, and it is done unto us (John xv. 7).

> "Not that our prayers make heaven more prompt to give,
> But they make us more worthy to receive:
> There is in that celestial treasury
> Wealth inexhaustible, admission free:
> But he that never prays rejects the golden key."

We do well to pray, then, and to pray fervently, as if the divine blessings altogether depended upon our prayers; and then to work earnestly to earn success, as if the gracious result entirely depended upon our earnest and skilful labour.

So in our prayer for others, there is no more reason to think we shall not do them good, than there is to imagine that any other service we can render them would not be truly useful. Prayer is the desire of the heart uttering itself in words; or, too deep for words, but ascending as an incense to heaven. A response is often given in the way of a suggestion of something for their benefit, that has not occurred to us before. Prayer is a kind of converse with the Lord. When our souls are opened to Him in a spirit of love and wise devotion, we are like the high priest with his breastplate of precious stones; and divine flashes of light will prompt us in reply, if WE DO NOT ASK AMISS. (James iv. 3.) We are wonderfully bound together with others, not by outward relations only, but by inward spheres; and just as our aid outwardly is needed to help a brother or sister on in some external position or circumstance of life, so may it well be that our prayers may be the inward help that is needed, as the channel for some hope, some consolation, some strength, that would lift another soul from trouble, and carry comfort where it is sorely wanted.

There is a remarkable incident illustrative of this, related in the Acts of the Apostles. Cornelius prayed at Cæsarea, the Roman capital of Palestine; and in a vision an angel directed him to send Peter to Joppa, thirty-five miles away. In the meantime, while the messengers were on their journey, Peter, during his devotions in the middle of the day, had a vision in which he was taught that these men were coming; that he must return with them to Cæsarea, and introduce Christianity to Cornelius, and regard him as the first-fruits of those who in every nation would be gathered in and compose the glorious fold of the Christian Church. Such was the answer to fervent prayer.

Let us then learn with Samuel to pray for humility, for integrity, for loving-kindness, for wisdom, for ourselves; but let us never forget also to pray for our families, for our friends, for our enemies, for the advancement of every good object we are striving to realize, and for the progress and happiness of mankind all over the world. All men form one vast humanity on earth; and the whole will prosper in proportion to the fervour and the loving service of every individual alone. Let us regard all human beings as our brethren, and say with the prophet, "God forbid that I should sin against the Lord in ceasing to pray for you." We shall be irradiated by the Spirit from on high, which will prepare us better to serve those whom we earnestly remember in prayer; and they will be touched with a loving influence which will dispose them to receive our efforts, and give them full success. Those whom we pray for we shall tenderly regard, and love will find a thousand ways of watching over them for good.

To prayer, however, Samuel adds, there must be teaching. "I will teach you the good and the right way." Prayer furnishes impulses from within; but teaching must be added from without, or there will be no satisfactory progress. Man is an intellectual being, and must never be left to sentiment alone. He must be taught, and well taught. It must be line upon line, and precept upon precept, until he rationally grasps "the good and the right way," or he will be feeble in the day of trial. Even the simplest things of religion should be often illustrated and often enforced. Only when truths have been abundantly supplied, arranged in order, and bound together with the cement of love, is there a wall round the soul, which is impregnable. "Jerusalem is a city that is compact together." Nothing is more simple than the good and the right way, when it is properly taught; yet simplicity comes at last, not at first. All converging colours blending together form white. All the truths of religion as they apply to heaven and earth, to the soul and the Lord, in His characters as Creator, Father, Redeemer, Saviour, and Regenerator, enable us to be strong, when we have lovingly learned, and been well taught, that the Lord Jesus is God, who is Love itself, our All in all; and that to love Him, to have faith in Him, to shun all that is evil in His sight, and to keep His commandments, is the good and the right way. "What doth the Lord require of thee but to do justly, love mercy, and walk humbly with thy God?"

The prophet proceeds, "Only fear the Lord, and serve Him in truth with all your heart."

There are two kinds of fear, which we must learn carefully to distinguish; the fear of love, and the fear of terror. When we dread a being who has the power to injure us, and is not, we surmise, unwilling to do so, we suffer from the fear of terror. This fear excites pain in proportion as we believe the power we dread to be terrible. This fear we ought never to harbour in regard to the Lord, who is unchangeably good, and loves all His immortal creatures with more than a father's, more than a mother's love; nay, with an affection exceeding that of all the fathers and all the mothers since time began, if the whole were concentrated into one breast. The fear that we ought to entertain for the Lord, is the fear that resembles that of an affectionate child towards a good parent; a fear to do that of which the good parent would not approve. This is the fear of love. It is the fear of doing anything of which the Lord would not approve; of doing anything which is not right. The more we have of true love, the more we shall have of this tender fear. "The fear of the Lord," the wise man wrote, "is to hate evil" (Prov. viii. 13). In this sense, the aged Samuel wrote, "Only fear the Lord."

> "Fear Him, ye saints, and you will then
> Have nothing else to fear:
> Make you His service your delight;
> He'll make your souls His care."

The prophet continues—"Serve Him in truth." And the sentence not only indicates the importance of a religious and just life, but of the principles of our lives being true. "Serve Him in TRUTH." A want of truth is not so fatal to our spiritual wellbeing as a want of good; because with good, if we persevere, the Lord will sooner or later bring us to the truth. Granting this, however, it must yet be acknowledged that the want of truth entails immense detriment, multiplied fears and sorrows. Life without truth is life in a fog. Life without truth is taking the wrong way home. It is attempting to work out the problems of human conduct with erroneous rules. The soul without truth is a ship without a compass or a guiding star. The world without truth is a wild sea without a lighthouse. Multitudes walk in superstitious fears and glooms for years, for want of the divine truth which assures us our Heavenly Father is the Father of lights, the Father of love, in whom there is no variableness nor shadow of turning.

For want of truth, the religion of many is not the loving service of cheerfully doing right in all the relations of life; but pilgrimages, superstitious observances, and protracted and often repeated joyless prayers. They think to be heard for their much speaking; and when they uselessly afflict themselves, they imagine they are doing what is highly pleasing in the sight of God. This life often sours man and severs him from the Lord, whose yoke is easy, and whose burden is light. On the contrary, the life of religion is a service in the cheerful performance of duty. It is doing everything in the truest and best manner. It is, from love to our neighbour, to do right to him in all the relations of life. It is a life of justice and judgment in all our works, like the Divine life of the Lord Himself. We must serve the Lord in truth; and for that object we must learn and understand the truth, rejoice in finding the truth, distinguish the truth from error in all things with which we have to do; certain that truth is one of our best friends, both for time and eternity.

"Dare to be true: nothing can need a lie:
A fault which needs it most grows two thereby."

The joy of exercising our faculties to acquire the truth is an exalted felicity. It is called in Scripture "seeking for goodly pearls," "coming to the light," "the truth setting us free." Let us then joyfully yield the Lord a willing service; but let us never forget that the Lord's will and our wellbeing incessantly require the bright service of an intelligent performance of real useful duties, performed in accordance with TRUTH.

Lastly, the prophet Samuel urges that we should serve the Lord with all the *heart*. The heart means the will. The voluntary faculty, or will, is to the soul what the heart is to the body, THE CENTRE OF ENERGY AND ACTIVE LIFE. THE MAN IS WHAT HIS HEART IS. The heart is a little house of four chambers, brim-full of vigour; and, by the blood it sends down the arteries, it is present in every portion of the body, and sustains the uses and gives a character to the activities of every part. As the blood returns from the various parts of the body, the heart sends it into the lungs to be purified; and only when it has been brightened and returned is it sent round the body again. THE WILL, in true order, has similar functions to perform for the soul. A firm will, with a virtuous ruling love, sends its sentiments out with power throughout the mind. It infuses life into everything. But it is also ever watchful to purify its aims and purposes by the understanding, THE LUNGS OF THE SOUL, rejecting from them whatever is not in accordance with the spirit— the atmosphere—of heaven. Let us do our duty, then, in the sight of the Lord with all the heart; and pray that our hearts may ever be made newer and purer, so that our heart and mind and all our powers may be consecrated to His glory, whose service is perfect freedom, perfect happiness, and a real heaven.

For, as the prophet Samuel said, "Consider what great things the Lord hath done for you." These latter words were indeed especially applicable to the Israelites. Samuel had just reminded them of their marvellous history. And when they remembered the wonders of Egypt, of the Red Sea, and of the desert, to say nothing of the astonishing deliverances from Philistia in Samuel's own time, well might the adoring exclamation arise from every heart, "What hath God wrought!" "Consider what good things the Lord hath done for you."

And in concluding our meditation of to-day on this important charge of Samuel, let us each glance at the no less wonderful mercies of the Divine Goodness in our individual cases. In the amazing gift of life and health, in the marvellous construction of our bodies, so fearfully and wonderfully made, in the formation and support of this beautiful world redolent with variety, loveliness, abundance, and blessing, alike calculated to support and embellish our being while we live here, and to prepare us for our higher being in our everlasting home, well may these words sink into our tenderest affections, and inspire us with the deepest gratitude to that Father, Saviour, and King, the Lord Jesus Christ, "who is, and who was, and who is to come, the Almighty." "Consider what great things the Lord hath done for you." "Oh that men would praise the Lord for His goodness, and for His wonderful works to the children of men!"

SERMON IX.

SAUL SPARING AGAG.

"Then said Samuel, Bring ye hither to me Agag the king of the Amalekites. And Agag came unto him delicately. And Agag said, Surely the bitterness of death is past.
"And Samuel said, As thy sword hath made women childless, so shall thy mother be childless among women. And Samuel hewed Agag in pieces before the Lord in Gilgal."
1 SAM. xv. 32, 33.

THE Amalekites are represented in Scripture as a powerful, deceitful, treacherous, and cruel people. They dwelt in the habitable part of Arabia extending from the Red Sea to the Salt or Dead Sea, a district probably three hundred miles in length. They were dreaded alike for their malice and their subtlety. They appeared in battle array against the Israelites, in the early part of that people's march into the wilderness; and by a most obstinate conflict with them, while they were yet poorly armed and unaccustomed to self-dependence, sought to extinguish them altogether. Having failed in that, they hung round them on their march; and like deadly but wily savages, they slew any who from weakness or weariness fell behind the main body. They never spared where they were able to destroy (Deut. xxv. 17-19). Sometimes the Amalekites joined with other nations in invading and destroying Israel (Num. xiv. 43-45). They never seem to have missed an opportunity of infesting the Israelites, and doing them all the harm they could. They had a bitter aversion to the sons of Israel; and while with other nations there was sometimes peace and sometimes war, with Amalek there was a constant life-and-death struggle. Hence it is written, "Because his hand is against the throne of the Lord, the Lord shall have war with Amalek from generation to generation" (for such is the true rendering of the words in Ex. xvii. 16).

The name Amalek, *He who licks up*, or *He who takes away all*, is very expressive of the malignant character of this people, and of the utter destruction they sought to inflict upon the objects of their ferocious hatred. Agag signifies *the roof*, and was probably the title of all their rulers, as we find an Agag in the time of Balaam (Num. xxiv. 7), as well as at the period referred to in our text. It probably imported *the crown, the head*, and was used as "Pharaoh" by the Egyptians, and "Abimelech" by the Philistines, and as "cæsar" or "czar," "king," "emperor," and "sultan" are at the present day. The Amalekites were very powerful in the time of Balaam. He calls them "the head of the nations" (Num. xxiv. 20); although he announces at the same time that their final lot will be "that they will perish for ever."

The long, bitter, and powerful enmity of Amalek afforded a sufficient reason for the command to Saul to go and extirpate this terrible foe. The power of Israel was now placed in one firm hand; and if it were wielded faithfully, vigorously, and prudently, this old and fearful foe would cease to harass or to destroy. Saul's want of perfect obedience in carrying out the direction of Samuel, lost his family the kingdom, and himself at last his life; for while he lay sorely wounded, the finishing stroke which dealt death to him was inflicted by a man of Amalek (2 Sam. i. 8, 13).

But it is not as a record of outward broil and battle that the conflicts narrated in the Bible have their chief interest; it is as a mirror of the conflicts in the soul. There are enemies in the kingdom within each man far more terrible than any outward foe; and it is with their destruction, and with spiritual victory, that the Word has really to do in all those narratives which outwardly relate to the military exploits of Israel. The spiritually-minded man says with the Apostle Paul, "We wrestle not against flesh and blood; but against principalities, against powers, against the rulers of the darkness of this world, against spiritual wickedness in high (that is, interior) places" (Eph. vi. 12).

The evils which are the enemies of the soul are as numerous and as varied as the enemies of Israel were. Some are more deadly, some are less so. Some are external, some are internal. Some are palpable, and disdain covering; some are subtle, and hidden under smooth pretences and pious professions. Some are the results of light-hearted heedlessness; some, of inward aversion to everything pure, holy, and true. Some evils are from ignorance, from false teaching, and from the circumstances in which a person has lived and been trained; others are from malice, and in spite of the clearest instructions. Some people grope in the dark because they cannot yet help it; some love darkness rather than light, because their deeds are evil. There are, as the Apostle John says, sins unto death, and there are sins not unto death. All unrighteousness is sin (1 John v. 16, 17).

The differences between crime and crime in the sight of men, are chiefly estimated by the damage they cause; and in this point of view, it is quite right to regard more sternly the plunderer of thousands of pounds than the pilferer who filches sixpence. But the leading difference in the sight of God between sin and sin is the ground from which they flow. The untruthful exaggeration which is uttered to raise a laugh, though always to be avoided, is a very different thing from the falsehood which is intended to take away virtue, or character, or life; and still more from the deep malignant falseness which makes the whole life a lie, however fair or however smooth. This inner malignity which constitutes the essence of evil, which is ready to rush in whenever the soul is weary, or weak, or lagging, to betray it to despair or goad it to sin, is Amalek.

Amalek is aversion to heaven. It has no misgivings. It says, with Milton's Satan, "Evil, be thou my good." It hates truth, because truth leads to good. It will, however, sometimes cover itself with forms of piety and religion, will enter into religious functions and seek the highest places, conforming itself to sanctimoniousness for the greater part of a life; like Gobet, archbishop of Paris, who, though he had passed most of his lifetime in apparent devotion, renounced and caricatured religion at the time of the French Revolution; or like many a vile pope in the middle ages: and yet have underneath neither gratitude, love, nor reverence to the Lord; neither respect nor regard for anything tending to the virtue or the good of mankind. Such is Amalek; *it takes away all:* and such an Amalek lies hidden in every unregenerate heart. The work of every one is to beware of it, and have war with it, from stage to stage, until it is destroyed.

This hidden evil is so covered over by the courtesies of society and the discipline of social life, that few suspect anything so malignant to be really contained under the fair appearances of youthful and polite life. Like Hazael, when the aged prophet told him what enormities he would commit, we are ready to say, "Is thy servant a dog, that he should do this great thing?" (2 Kings viii. 13.) But alas, when the changes of time have taken the gloss from men, and the wear and tear of actual struggle in society have revealed them to themselves, and the circles of family and business existence, what revelations are often made! The warm-hearted, genial, courteous youth frequently becomes the bloated, brutal, sensual man, who would fain absorb in selfish indulgence all upon which he can lay his hands. He has often stopped in his career and made resolutions for the future; he has seemed for a short period to be reclaimed, and there has been joy with all who loved him; but he has become weary and lagged behind; old yearnings have come over him, and down came Amalek and made him a brute again. The giant was stunned, but not slain. The volcano had smouldered under the covering, not been cleared out. And again, and again, the hidden horrors burst forth, until the poor soul is a blighted wreck, an object piteous to men and angels. Oh how often should we pray in the language of the Psalmist, "Search me, O God, and know my heart: try me, and know my thoughts; and see if there be any wicked way in me, and lead me in the way everlasting" (Ps. cxxxix. 23, 24).

The army of two hundred thousand footmen and ten thousand men of Judah, which composed the force of Saul, represented a state of soul fully furnished for spiritual victory. The two hosts, or two hundred thousand footmen, indicate a complete equipment of goodness and truth in daily life; the ten thousand men of Judah represent interior principles of praise and worship in fulness. Telaim, where they were assembled (1 Sam. xv. 4), which was a small city of Judah, and whose name signifies *their humility*, is expressive of the humble spirit in which alone any spiritual combat ought to be undertaken. In the state of soul meant, all is ready; only faithfulness and perseverance are needed now.

The charge to Saul was; "Now go and smite Amalek, and utterly destroy all that they have, and spare them not: but slay both man and woman, infant and suckling, ox and sheep, camel and ass:" which implies that the interior malice which is opposed to heavenly things, with all belonging to it, ought to be extirpated. Man and woman, in the spiritual sense, signify intellect and affection; infant and suckling represent the first beginnings of evil desire, and every disposition to suck in nourishment or confirmation of it. The sheep and ox are the symbols of good affections of charity and obedience perverted to cover inward sin and make it courteous and agreeable; while the camel and the ass represent science and natural thought which have also been pressed into the service of wickedness. To smite the whole is to renounce the evil state in which we have been, both in essence and in act, in thought and in word, in association and in conduct, in confirmation and in persuasion. All that is at enmity with God must be dangerous for us, and should be resolutely declined and repressed.

There is a noble decision of character, a sacred bluntness, that every true servant of the Lord has to learn. It is a blessed thing to say "No!" boldly to those who are still in the sin we have learned to dread. Rudeness for right is better far than obsequiousness to wrong. Evil is never overcome by half measures. Repentance requires that we should shun the company of the vicious, turn our minds away from their wiles, their smiles, their very modes of thinking and of speech. Gilded sin is far more to be dreaded than open vice. "The tender mercies of the wicked are cruel" (Prov. xii. 10). The smooth tongue, the sleek caress, the artful speciousness which decorates vice with the semblances of friendship, virtue, and courtesy, these are the insidious snares that, Judas-like, betray the soul with a kiss. The Word of God, our Samuel, ever says, then, smite all belonging to Amalek. Everything is tainted and dangerous. "Arise ye, and depart; for this is not your rest; because it is polluted, it shall destroy you, even with a sore destruction" (Micah ii. 10). Such is the import of the charge to Saul; and every true penitent must often use that portion of the Divine Prayer which says, "Lead us not into temptation." The danger of open vice is slight; it is in the concealed approach that treason lurks and ruins. The poison is in the poppy, although it looks bright and pleasant. Dread the first step, and you will never make the second. Shun the siren, whose alluring smiles seek to win you to wrong, and whose steps leads down to hell.

Saul was successful against all opposition. "He smote the Amalekites from Havilah until thou comest to Shur" (1 Sam. xv. 7); that is, from the western border of Judah to the site of the present Suez. He smote the common people of that part of the land of Amalek, but he "spared Agag, and the best of the sheep, and of the oxen, and of the fatlings, and the lambs, and all that was good, and would not utterly destroy them: but everything vile and refuse, that they destroyed utterly." This tampering with the divine command, and saving the king, shewed a heart not right with God. The whole statement represents the condition of those who war against the effects of evil, but RETAIN THE CAUSE. There are many people who lament the misery which sin occasions, but never mount up to the source, and abhor sin as sin in the sight of God. They reject sin when it is vile and refuse; but when it is respectable, and, like Agag, comes forward delicately, they do not see that there is very much amiss. Such may see somewhat of the evil of sin, but they do not perceive the sinfulness of evil. If wickedness could always be successful, they would know no difference between it and goodness. They do not look below the surface. They reject rough sins because they are rough, not because they are sins. The smooth and treacherous vices, though immeasurably more deadly and far-reaching in the ruin they induce, they pass by, or perhaps support. These are they who take what they call the good things of Amalek, and spare Agag, making a deceitful peace where there is no real peace.

He who spares the Agag of sin in spirit, is sparing his deadliest foe. He may go on smoothly for a time, but only for a time. The traitor in his heart will surely ruin him. He may think, like Saul, he has done well; but when Samuel comes, or when the Divine Word is truly seen by him, he will find his conduct to be utterly condemned.

The excuse of Saul, that the best of the sheep and the oxen had been preserved to sacrifice to the Lord, was wholly unsatisfactory. To do evil in conduct, that we may worship more daintily, is an ancient, but grave self-deception. We are not to do evil that good may come. How weighty is the reproof of Samuel in this respect. "Hath the Lord as great delight in burnt-offerings and sacrifices, as in obeying the voice of the Lord? Behold, to obey is better than sacrifice, and to hearken than the fat of rams" (1 Sam. xv. 22). Prayer without obedience, piety without justice, are of no value in the divine sight, although the error of Saul has been the error of ages. Obedience first, and worship afterwards, is divine order. It is on obedience to the commands of the Lord, and especially on resisting by His grace every sin against them to which we are prone, that regeneration proceeds, and blessings come down to us from heaven.

Saul was for the time convinced of his sin, yet not so deeply as to lead to real interior change. He set up an excuse, a false plea. He said he had done wrong out of fear of the people. There is no intimation of this before, and probably it was a mere afterthought. The true penitent always condemns himself, the false one always blames others. "God be merciful to me a sinner," is the cry of the man of sincere and lowly heart; he does not justify himself, but humbles himself in the dust, and owns himself wholly without vindication or apology. Saul seems soon to have ceased to trouble himself about his sin, but craved to be honoured in the sight of the people. A genuine penitence would never have thought about estimation before the people, but would have sought the one thing needful, acceptance with the Lord.

Samuel proceeded to say, "Bring forth Agag the king of the Amalekites." Samuel, as we have said, represents the Word of God; and his judgment on the present occasion represents the judgment of the Word at all times. Our Lord said, "The Word which I have spoken unto you, the same shall judge you at the last day" (John xii. 48). The Word is always directed against sin itself, interior sin. "The Lord seeth not as man seeth; for man looketh upon the outward appearance (the eyes), but the Lord looketh upon the heart" (1 Sam. xvi. 7). This sin of the heart is represented by Agag, the king of the Amalekites. Too many, when reading the Word, read it as if it spoke of the Lord Jesus taking their punishment away from them. They cry out in the hour of danger, and in the dread of death, to be forgiven their sins; meaning that they do not want to be punished. But the Word says far more about sin than about punishment. Let sin be removed, and sorrow will die of itself. Hence we read, "Repent, and turn from all your transgressions; so iniquity shall not be your ruin" (Ezek. xviii. 30). "Thou shalt call His name Jesus, for He shall save His people from their sins" (Matt. i. 21). "Behold the Lamb of God, which taketh away the sin of the world" (John i. 29). Well will it be for us, if we listen to the voice of Divine Truth to-day, when it says, Bring out Agag, the king of the evil world within you, that he may be judged and destroyed now, and not wait for the disclosures of the eternal world.

What is our Agag? Is it the pride that disdains aught but its own self-will; that despises the laws of truth and goodness, and cannot tolerate the least contradiction either to our wishes or our views? Are we bitter, violent, passionate, if our caprices are contravened? Is our Agag vanity, the desire to dazzle the world, and win its applause by vain show? Do we spend our time in devising fresh means of attracting the admiration of those who are as light and frivolous as ourselves, and who repay our efforts by insincere applause and secret envious scandal? Is our Agag sensual pleasure? Do we indulge our appetites at the expense of all the noble aims of human life? Has Agag destroyed in us all the yearning after wisdom, virtue, and the public good? Has he made us deaf to generous impulses, blind to all exalted truths, and buried us in the sordid gratification of coarse and brutal appetites? Bring forth Agag and let him be seen.

Agag is said to have come forth "delicately," or, as it might be rendered, "as a man of delights." The ruling love always seems delightful to the man. A wicked love seems full of delights, until it brings its wretched results in ruin and misery.

The exclamation, "Surely the bitterness of death is past," expresses the expectation of evil in one who has spared it long, that it will still be spared. But the utterance of Samuel exhibits its real nature and its proper treatment. "As thy sword hath made women childless, so shall thy mother be childless among women." The cruel character of this man Agag was expressed literally; but in the spiritual sense it unveils the ferocious character of inward sin. It always makes women childless; that is, destroys all the sweet germs of innocence, hope, and joy. The affections in the soul, like the Graces of the ancients, were intended to fill their little world with all that is lovely, pure, and good. Sin blights this fair promise, and fills the soul with hates, impurities, and miseries.

Happy is it when we take the sword of truth and hew it in pieces before the Lord. We should rejoice in making its mother, that is, THE LOVE OF IT, childless. To extinguish sin in ourselves is to destroy a brood of serpents. It is to dry up the source of a thousand sorrows. It is to root out the vilest of tares. It is to extinguish the issues of death, and to open the way for a new Eden of life, beauty, and blessing.

To do it before the Lord is to do it *sincerely;* and it was done in Gilgal, because this word signifies *a revolution;* and when we destroy our Agag, the grandest possible revolution is effected; the revolution which breaks the fetters of the soul, transforms one who has been the bond-slave of the vilest of tyrants into an angelic freeman, a partaker of the glorious liberty of the children of light. If this great work yet remain to be done in us, let us take the sword of the Spirit, which is the Word of God, and hew our Agag in pieces before the Lord in Gilgal.

SERMON X.

DAVID CHOSEN BY SAMUEL.

"And Samuel said unto Jesse, Are here all thy children? And he said, There remaineth yet the youngest: and, behold, he keepeth the sheep. And Samuel said unto Jesse, Send and fetch him: for we will not sit down till he come hither.

"And he sent and brought him in. Now he was ruddy, and withal of a beautiful countenance, and goodly to look to. And the Lord said, Arise, anoint him; for this is he.

"Then Samuel took the horn of oil, and anointed him in the midst of his brethren: and the Spirit of the Lord came upon David from that day forward. So Samuel rose up, and went to Ramah."—1 SAM. xvi. 11-13.

DAVID was undoubtedly Israel's greatest warrior, greatest king, and greatest poet. His wonderful rise from the condition of a young shepherd, the valiant guard of his father's sheep, to become the victorious king of the twelve tribes, and the singer of those divine psalms which have, ever since his day, formed the principal vehicle of praises and thanksgivings, not only for Israel but for the multitudes of the Christian Church, will make David's an ever-interesting career. But that which most endears his history to the Christian is that he is the type of the higher king of the grander Israel, the King of kings, the Lord Jesus Christ. Being the type of the Lord Jesus, he is also the type of every spiritually-minded man; for the Christian is a follower of the Lord Jesus in the work of regeneration. What the Lord did for the great world, the Christian has to do, by the Lord's help, in the little world of his own mind. David, therefore, represented the Lord; and he represented the Christian. In both these respects his character will afford us lessons of the deepest significance, as we read it in the Word of God, and yield us themes of wise direction and of heavenly comfort, as we consider them in the light of heaven.

We must not, however, confound the character of David as a man, with that of David as a type. David was not a *pattern* for a Christian, although he was the TYPE of one. The Christian's only pattern is the Lord Jesus Christ. We are to follow Him, learn of Him, derive our life from Him, lean upon Him. He is the Vine, we are the branches; without Him we can do nothing. David was a great Jew, with great qualities, and with great failings. He was great in government, brave, and tender; but his polygamy, his adultery, and the murder of a faithful soldier, by which he sought to cover his crime, his cruelty to his enemies, and the revenge he breathed out in his dying moments, all place him, as a man, far below the Christian standard; and eternal right was right to him, as it is right to all men. As a man, there is much to condemn. It is not in this respect that he was a man after God's own heart, but as the typical king of a typical nation. He was faithful to that office; he was obedient to all the divine requirements in that respect. His sins even typified the evils of the heart, as they present themselves in the Christian's soul, in the hour of temptation; and as our Saviour saw them in the nature He assumed. His real character would be explored in the eternal world, and we have nothing in the way of judgment to do, but to leave him to the Judge of all the earth, who ever does right. What we are concerned with is the accurate representation afforded by his circumstances, condition, and history, of the Lord Jesus, and of His spiritual servants.

The fact of David's father being Jesse, and Jesse meaning the same as Jehovah, "He who is," or "He who will be," is itself a striking circumstance. For David being the type of the Lord Jesus as to Humanity, the father Jesse represents the origin of the Humanity of our Lord to have been, as all the Scriptures declare, the Divine Love, Jehovah, the Father. The Humanity was called the Son of God, because God's love produced it by means of the Virgin Mary. Thus the angel said, "The Holy Spirit shall come upon thee, and the power of the highest shall overshadow thee: therefore also that Holy One which shall be born of thee shall be called the Son of God" (Luke i. 35). David, with his father Jesse, was in this respect the type of Jesus, the Son of the Divine Love, the Father, within Him. The father of David was called the Bethlehemite (ver. 1); and when we remember that the Lord was providentially born in Bethlehem, and that Bethlehem means *the House of Bread*, we shall perceive the type to be strikingly obvious in this respect. In giving the Lord Jesus, the Divine Love was giving to the world Him who is the Bread of Life: and was therefore represented by Jesse the Bethlehemite. The Lord Himself said, "I am the living bread who came down from heaven; if any man eat of this bread, he shall live for ever; and the bread that I will give is my flesh, which I will give for the life of the world" (John vi. 51).

But let us regard the other particulars expressed in the text, not omitting that seven sons had been brought before Samuel, and passed on without being chosen, so that David was the eighth; the number eight being indicative of a new principle, or of regeneration, from its being the commencement of a new series. Seven, in Scripture, is used when what is complete is represented, and the word "seven" and the word "perfect" are the same. The seven previous represented the good things of a previous dispensation, a series finished, now no longer operative, no longer influential. They were fair to look upon, but not satisfactory within. David being the eighth and the youngest, represented the new spiritual life introduced by the Lord Jesus to mankind, and which would make old things pass away and all things become new.

It is not without meaning that it is said, "and, behold, *he keepeth the sheep;*" for it was for the sake of the sheep, and to preserve the sheep, that the Saviour came into the world. Those who are gentle, kind, obedient, and charitable, are called the Lord's sheep. He is the Good Shepherd. Jehovah, in the Old Testament, is the Divine Shepherd, and He declared He would come to seek and save His sheep. It is written, "For thus saith the Lord God; behold, I, even I, will both search my sheep and seek them out. As a shepherd seeketh out his flock in the day that he is among his sheep that are scattered; so will I seek out my sheep, and will deliver them out of all places where they have been scattered in the cloudy and dark day" (Ezek. xxxiv. 11, 12). In the Gospel, the Lord, who had come into the world to fulfil this prophecy, says, "I am the Good Shepherd, and know my sheep, and am known of mine. As the Father knoweth me, even so know I the Father: and I lay down my life for the sheep" (John x. 14, 15). Surely, then, we can see the reason why it is said of David, the type, "Behold, he keepeth the sheep."

Samuel the prophet replied to Jesse, "Send and fetch him: for we will not sit down till he come hither." This saying of the prophet implies that, according to the Divine Word, it was imperative that the Divine Humanity should be king. There would be no settled peace for the universe, until God should become our Redeemer. The "Queller of Satan," the Lord of both worlds, must "on His glorious work now enter and redeem mankind." "Send and fetch him, for we will not sit down till he come hither."

When David appeared, the following description of him is given. "He was ruddy, and withal of a beautiful countenance, and goodly to look to." David was, no doubt, a beautiful youth; but it is with the diviner beauty of the Redeemer, for the sake of whom his history is given, that we have chiefly to do. The second clause, "withal of a beautiful countenance," should be rendered, "with beautiful eyes" (in Hebrew, beautiful of eyes). Thus, he was ruddy, with beautiful eyes, and goodly. The ruddiness expresses the love of the Lord in His Humanity. The glow of healthy warmth in youth is the fitting symbol of that divine warmth of love which is the heat of heaven, the heat of the good man's heart, and the divine fire in the bosom of the Eternal Father from whom all things come. The beauty of the eyes is expressive of the loveliness of the Divine Wisdom; for wisdom is as eyes to Him who sees all things. "His eyes were as a flame of fire," said John (Rev. i. 14); because the wisdom of the Lord is full of love. The goodliness, which was the third quality mentioned of David, represents, in the Lord Jesus, the union of love and wisdom in his whole life. He was "the chief among ten thousand, and the altogether lovely" (Cant. v. 10, 16). He went about doing good. Grace was on His lips. Mercy beamed from His countenance. Virtue went out in every motion; so that spiritual wisdom was taught, the infirm became healthy, the lame walked, the deaf heard, the dumb spake, the blind received sight, and the hungry were fed. He was altogether goodly.

The text proceeds to say, "The Lord said, Arise, anoint him: for this is he." The anointing was the type of that descent of the Divine Love into the Humanity, which is described in Ps. xlv. 6, 7 : "Thy throne, O God, is for ever and ever: the sceptre of Thy kingdom is a right sceptre. Thou lovest righteousness, and hatest wickedness: therefore God, Thy God, hath anointed Thee with the oil of gladness above Thy fellows." The Divine Love, like oil soothing and blessing, descended into the Lord's Humanity, as it became purified and prepared, anointing it with gentleness and joy. As He came out of the waters of Jordan, it is said, "the heavens were opened to Him" (Matt. iii. 16). He received "the oil of joy for mourning, the garment of praise for the spirit of heaviness" (Isa. lxi. 3). The anointing of the priests, kings, and sacred objects in olden times represented the sanctification of the soul which love gives when it enters into any object, principle, or character, and makes it the abode of its own sweet and sacred virtues. David, thus selected and anointed, became therefore the appropriate type of the Lord Jesus, especially as the Redeemer of mankind from hell. He was pre-eminently the Jewish conqueror. He was the type of the Divine Conqueror of the powers of darkness. "The Spirit of the Lord came upon David from that day forward." The name "David," or "the beloved one," forms another feature in the resemblance to Him who is so often called the well-beloved Son, whom all the world should hear (Matt. xvii. 5; Deut. xviii. 15, 18, 19; Acts iii. 22, 23).

Very soon had David to enter upon his warlike career. He is distinguished subsequently as a man of war (1 Sam. xvi. 18; 2 Sam. xvii. 8). He was forbidden to build the Temple, because his reign had been a reign of war (1 Chron. xxviii. 3). Any one who takes a superficial view of the Lord's history as it was seen by men in the world only, might be led to suppose that there was but little resemblance between the Jewish warrior and the peaceable Redeemer. Yet in the prophets, the psalms, and the gospels (when closely considered), it will be seen that the Lord Jesus was engaged in awful conflicts with the powers of darkness from time to time, and overthrowing them. By a narrow school of teachers the Lord's work has been so confined to the cross that *this* dreadful part of his sacred labours for us has been greatly obscured, and our gratitude has been comparatively dimmed. Yet, from the first prophecy of the coming of a Saviour, we learn that his object was, "to bruise the serpent's head" (Gen. iii. 15). The head of the serpent of selfishness was that infernal power which is congregated in the inner world, where those terrible masses of the evil exist which we call hell. They were in insurrection when redemption became indispensable. They had long crowded the intermediate world, and gathered in such vast hosts around men's minds, that human liberty was all but lost. No power could remove them but that of a DIVINE MAN: of man, that He could approach without destroying them; of a Divine Man, that His power might be sufficient to accomplish His wonderful work. The Philistines, the Amalekites, the Moabites, the Ammonites, against whom David fought, and over whom he was victorious, were the symbols of the hosts of hell, and the varied classes of their abominable legions, over whom Jesus, the Divine David, triumphed.

Let us read a few of the descriptions of His redeeming labours as they occur in the prophets and the gospels, remembering that the especial scene of them is the inner world, intermediate between heaven and hell, with which our minds are associated while, as to our bodies, we live in this. "For every battle of the warrior is with confused noise, and garments rolled in blood; but this shall be with burning and fuel of fire. For unto us a Child is born, unto us a Son is given, and the government shall be upon His shoulder, and His name shall be called Wonderful, Counsellor, the Mighty God, the Everlasting Father, the Prince of Peace" (Isa. ix. 5, 6). That this prophecy related to the redeeming work of our Saviour, is evident from the description of His birth into the world. Nothing, however, like the terrible struggle it describes took place in the outer world of nature; it must, therefore, have been realized in the inner world. "The Mighty God," too, in the titles of the Redeemer recited, has a peculiar significance, for it might strictly be rendered, "God, the Hero."

Read Isaiah lix., and especially ver. 19, 20: "When the enemy shall come in like a flood, the spirit of the Lord shall lift up a standard against him: and the Redeemer shall come to Zion." The representation here is that of the assaults of a raging flood against human nature: and such it was. The infernal power, like a surging sea, beat against conscience and the remains of goodness and health in the soul; and if the Redeemer had not come to aid, all would have been lost, the world itself becoming a second hell. The storm on the Sea of Galilee was a symbol in nature of the same thing. This is strongly expressed in a previous verse: "And He saw that there was no man, and wondered that there was no intercessor; therefore His arm brought salvation unto Him; and His righteousness, it sustained Him" (ver. 16). A similar passage exists in the sixty-third chapter; "I have trodden the winepress alone, and of the people there was none with me: for I will tread them in mine anger, and trample them in my fury: and their blood shall be sprinkled upon my garments, and I will stain all my raiment. For the day of vengeance is in mine heart, and the year of my redeemed is come" (ver. 3, 4). The intermediate state is denominated the winepress, because there a man's inner character is separated from its surroundings, as the juice from the husk of the grape. The divine influx of the Saviour God was necessarily felt by the wicked as anger and fury. From the large amount of prophetic testimony, we will notice one other passage, " I will ransom them from the power of hell;[1] I will redeem them from death: O death, I will be thy plagues: O hell, I will be thy destruction; repentance shall be hid from mine eyes" (Hosea xiii. 14).

In the Gospels the work of the Redeemer in conquering the powers of darkness, and clearing the world of spirits, so that human minds could be free, is set forth with terrible distinctness. "He that cometh after me is mightier than I, whose shoes I am not worthy to bear; He shall baptize you with the Holy Ghost and with fire: Whose fan is in His hand, and He will throughly purge His floor, and gather His wheat into the garner: but He will burn up the chaff with unquenchable fire" (Matt. iii. 11, 12). The intermediate state, the world of judgment, is called the barn-floor, because the wheat is taken there after being cut down in the field, and the husk is removed from the grain, and its real condition made known. The Lord Himself gives a glimpse of His divine labours in this respect on various occasions. Thus, "I beheld Satan as lightning fall from heaven. Behold, I give unto you power to tread on serpents and scorpions, and over all the power of the enemy, and nothing shall by any means hurt you" (Luke x. 18, 19). Again, "Now is the judgment of this world: now shall the prince of this world be cast out" (John xii. 31).

In the garden of Gethsemane, and at the Lord's last suffering, the death of the Cross, it was the presence and assaults of legions of infernals which constituted the chief feature in the mysterious agony of the Redeemer. In the garden, when He was seized, He said, "This is your hour, and the power of darkness" (Luke xxii. 53). And the apostle declared, that "through death He destroyed him that had the power of death, that is, the devil" (Heb. ii. 14). The awful gathering around Him while on the Cross is described in the twenty-second psalm, which serves the twofold purpose of more fully opening to us some of the scenes only briefly disclosed in the New Testament, and at the same time demonstrating that in the person of David the Lord Jesus was represented. The psalmist speaks as if of himself; but in the gospels we have it distinctly applied to the Lord. See, then, the crucifixion as described in this psalm, which commences with the words used by the Saviour on the Cross: "My God, my God, why hast Thou forsaken me?" Here the inner horrors of the Lord's sufferings are

---

[1] The word "grave" in our English version obscures the passage; it ought to be rendered hell.

unveiled. The multitudes of infernals crowding round, and described by correspondences, as bulls, lions, dogs, swords, threatening the inner life of the Lord's Humanity, must to His purity, upon which the redemption of mankind then and to all future ages depended, have been unspeakably loathsome and horrible. His victories over them are what the victories of David represented. They were various, as the enemies of David were various. They assailed Him probably in the order in which David was assailed, the Philistines (the bitter maintainers of the sufficiency of a false faith) first.

The throne of David, when established, would represent the Lord's government in heaven and the church, when every enemy was put down. And thus we shall understand the magnificent language which is employed in connection with the name of David (Luke i. 31-33; Isa. ix. 7; Jer. xxiii. 5, 6). When we think of the vast hosts of the blessed which form the multitudes of heaven, which no man can number, who are under the government of the Lord Jesus, the Divine David, at once David's Son and David's Lord, how amazingly our ideas expand! The little throne and state of Israel and Judah become to us the symbols of the sway of the Saviour's love and wisdom, ever increasing and ever to increase, until earth in all her climes with heaven in all its realms shall crown Him Lord of all.

In conclusion, let us once more be reminded that David is also the type of the Christian. He must, like David, be a keeper of sheep. He must watch over the little flock of good affections within him. He has, like David, to be a man of war. The Lord says to him, "I come not to send peace, but a sword" (Matt. x. 34). He must strive against his evils like so many nations of foes. And as he overcomes, the Lord will bless him with the joys of victory and peace. The Christian must be "ruddy" with the love of heaven, "beautiful of eyes," or full of intelligence and faith, and "goodly" with all the virtues of integrity and benevolence. Samuel, or the Word, will then anoint his head with the holy oil of the divine blessing; and he will be enabled to say, "Surely goodness and mercy shall follow me all the days of my life; and I shall dwell in the house of the Lord for ever" (Ps. xxiii. 6).

SERMON XI.

GOLIATH SLAIN BY DAVID.

"David said moreover, The Lord that delivered me out of the paw of the lion, and out of the paw of the bear, he will deliver me out of the hand of this Philistine. And Saul said unto David, Go, and the Lord be with thee."—1 SAM. xvii. 37.

THAT the Christian life is in part a warfare, is the experience of every true follower of the Lord. There is much of peace, and much of blessing, attendant upon one who walks in the path that leads to life; but there is also much of struggle. Hence we may see the reason of the history of Israel, of which the old Testament mainly consists, being so much taken up with narratives of military affairs, which would be distasteful to the spiritually minded man, were it not that, either dimly or clearly, he can perceive that they are types of internal conflicts. He must fight against the lusts, passions and practices which are in his lower nature, if his soul is to become a kingdom of peace, and if the palm of victory is to enable him to say with the apostle; "I have fought a good fight, I have finished my course, I have kept the faith; henceforth there is laid up for me a crown of righteousness" (2 Tim. iv. 7, 8.)

Nor is the battle of spiritual life a single struggle. It consists of many campaigns. There are foes manifold and various, which are to be resisted and conquered. The Word of God is said to have many crowns. The apostle said, "I die daily" (1 Cor. xv. 31); and so it will be with every Christian. His first struggles will be of a comparatively external kind. He will have to decide to break off from the vices and the company of bad men, and commence a new life. This is a great achievement at the time, and requires courage; prayer, faith and determination for its accomplishment. It is with some a hard battle; but it is one which leads to a great victory. We usually rest a while after this early effort; but find, as life continues, that other enemies assail us, some under one form and some under another; and we need all our vigilance, and all our faithfulness, to come off on all occasions completely victorious. We shall be wounded, sometimes, and half dead (Luke x. 30); but, blessed be the Divine Mercy, if we are but faithful, we shall never fail to come out at length more than conquerors through Him who loves us, and is able to save all those who trust in Him.

Three classes of conflict are referred to in our text. David alludes to his conflict with a lion, and also with a bear; and every Christian must not only be like David, spiritually a keeper of sheep, or in other words a preserver of the affections of innocence and charity in the fold of his heart, but he must also fight against the lion and the bear, when these would take and devour a lamb out of his mental flock.

The lion comes in the form of a spirit of opposition to all religion. A raging spirit of contempt for all that is good, infused by evil spirits, is a furious lion, daring and destructive. "The devil, as a roaring lion, walketh about, seeking whom he may devour" (1 Pet. v. 8). David speaks of his trials in this respect on several occasions. "My soul is among lions; and I lie among them that are set on fire, the sons of men, whose teeth are spears and arrows, and their tongue a sharp sword" (Ps. lvii. 4). "Break their teeth, O God, in their mouth; break out the great teeth of the young lions, O Lord" (Ps. lviii. 6). To break their great teeth is to scatter by truth their pretended facts and false statements. In the ninety-first Psalm it is said to the man who loves the Lord, "Thou shalt tread upon the lion and adder; the young lion and the dragon shalt thou trample under feet" (ver. 13). Every spiritual David has to fight against the lion; and if he be faithful and true, he will be able to say, like David, "The Lord delivered me out of the paw of the lion."

But, in due time, he will have a visit from the bear. This heavy, lobbing inhabitant of the forest and the cave, is the type of an absorbing love of the world. It is an animal of strong affections, but low, clumsy, and coarse. It seems all appetite; it pants and longs, and is full of restlessness. It is like the love of the world, never at ease. The bear's eagerness, the bear's growl, the bear's coarseness, all symbolize the impatient, hankering, surly disposition of one who only cares for earthly things. Some men who have resisted the lion, yet succumb to the spirit of the bear. They wish to be suddenly rich. They clutch and hug the possessions of earth; they pant for more with unceasing eagerness, and never have enough. It is as if a man fled from a lion, and a bear met him; or leaned his hand upon the wall, and a serpent bit him (Amos v. 19). If they fail in their overweening desires for carnal delights and pleasures, their deep and bitter mourning realizes the words of the prophet: "We roar all like bears" (Isa. lix. 11). If, however, we are faithful to our high calling, and set our hearts upon the treasures of heaven first, and desire only so much of other things as the good Providence of the Lord awards to us while we are living in accordance with His Divine Will, we shall be able to say like David, "The Lord hath delivered me also out of the paw of the bear."

But these two deliverances not only afford matter for grateful recollection, as mercies past, but also serve as a foundation for confidence in the Divine protection in the severer conflict that lies before us, the conflict with the terrible giant of Philistia. "He will deliver me out of the hand of this Philistine."

We have endeavoured, in previous discourses, to make it apparent that the Philistines represent those who adhere to the phantasy of salvation by faith alone; which is their idol, their Dagon, their all in all. These people will write, wrangle, fight, and pray, for what they call faith: while love and charity, justice, mercy, and humility are ruthlessly trampled under feet. Formerly, the Philistines in the Church would rush eagerly to plunder and destroy the property of those who differed in creed from themselves; and were quite reckless if thousands fell of those who in their estimation did not rightly believe. Happily this extreme is now seldom experienced; but even yet there is far more regard for those of the same creed, and dislike for others, than justice or true religion would sanction. Goliath is the type of these. He was proud, boastful, and lifted up in his own conceit. His name signifies "'lifted up."

Goliath was of Gath. The name "Gath" means "wine-press," and the wine-press corresponds to the rational faculty, whose office is to press out the essences of things, so as to get at their hidden meanings. Goliath, the giant of Gath, represented those of the present day who are bold and strong in their announcement that the way to heaven is not a heavenly life from love to God and man, strengthened by faith in the Holy Word, but that belief only in the death of Christ to pay the penalty of their sins is the one thing needful. No need of repentance, no need of God's commandments, no need of doing anything; "only believe."

This is so remarkable a contradiction to the plain statements of the Bible, that of itself it would sink by its own weakness. But, to give it strength, resort is had to reasoning; and the unregenerate heart readily favours the arguments which are to "make the commandments of God of none effect" (Matt. xv. 6).

"God is so perfectly, so infinitely pure," they say, "that no one can obey Him to the extent which His purity requires. The smallest failing even in thought must vitiate all we do, and make it sinful in the Divine sight." As if our Heavenly Father were like a parent who required a young child to do things far beyond its power, and punished it for what it was unable to perform. The Lord says, "My yoke is easy, and my burden is light" (Matt. xi. 30). But these reasoners say, "The Lord's yoke is infinitely difficult, and His burden it is quite impossible to carry." The Philistines reason again: "Man was upright at first; but he has lost his ability by sin: and therefore it is impossible now to obey the will of God, and our virtues themselves are sins." As if the Lord had not set forth our works of obedience done from love and faith, as GOOD WORKS. "Let your light so shine before men, that they may see your GOOD WORKS, and glorify your Father who is in heaven" (Matt. v. 16). The same reasoners declare that if a true penitent were to be faithful all the rest of his life, he would yet be as far from salvation as ever, because the Divine wrath would be against him for past sins, which he could never atone for, inasmuch as every good act of every day is already due to God, and therefore there is no merit left to set against sins gone by. As if the Lord had ever said that for so much sin there must be so much merit. As if the Lord had not declared: "If the wicked will turn from all his sins that he hath committed, and keep all my statutes, and do that which is lawful and right, he shall surely live; he shall not die. All his transgressions that he hath committed, they shall not be mentioned unto him; in his righteousness that he hath done he shall live" (Ezek. xviii. 21, 22). Men do not go to heaven, because of merit, or payment of any kind; but because of the Lord's goodness and mercy, and their preparedness. "They that were ready went in with Him, to the marriage; and the door was shut" (Matt. xxv. 10). "I, even I, am He that blotteth out thy transgressions for MINE OWN SAKE, and will not remember thy sins" (Isa. xliii. 25). "Again," say these reasoners, "to make salvation dependent on what any man does, is to take the glory from the Lord Jesus Christ, whose all-sufficient Atonement on the Cross paid the Father for all man's sins past, present and to come. But where do we read in Scripture of the sorrows of the Saviour being paid to the Father? He was the Father in the Son. "God was in Christ, reconciling the world unto Himself, not imputing their trespasses unto them" (2 Cor. v. 19). "Our Saviour Jesus Christ, who gave Himself for us, that He might redeem us from all iniquity; and purify unto Himself a peculiar people, zealous of good works" (Tit. ii. 13, 14). When men who were his debtors had nothing to pay, whether they owed five hundred pence or fifty, He "frankly forgave them both" (Luke vii. 42).

These and such like reasonings, then, have in reality no foundation in the Divine Wisdom, nor in the Written Word. Yet by these means, and the secret inclinations of our depraved nature, the system of salvation by FAITH ONLY has become a giant, and has long boastfully defied the armies of the living God. It has filled thousands of pulpits with far more exhortations not to think of pleasing our Heavenly Father by keeping His commandments, than with those encouragements to do His holy will which our weaknesses so much require. A good life seems, in the estimation of many, to be more dangerous, as leading to self-righteousness, than a bad life as unfitting us for heaven.

The height of Goliath, six cubits and a span, represents the imposing character of this system in its own esteem. It is far above the measure of a man. Six is used in Scripture in reference to the labours and states of the regenerate life; thus, there are six days in which we are to labour, before we attain the sabbath of rest. The six cubits and a span spiritually intimate that, in the estimation of the mental Philistines, their system is a full substitute for the whole of the regenerate life, and something more. They claim our Lord's righteousness to be imputed to them. We might as well claim His Omnipotence, His Godhead. But, of course, if it could be had, it would be equivalent to all our spiritual attainments, and something more.

Goliath was well armed. "He had a helmet of brass upon his head, and he was armed with a coat of mail: and the weight of the coat was five thousand shekels of brass. And he had greaves of brass upon his legs, and a target of brass between his shoulders" (ver. 5, 6). This abundance of armour in other parts, while the feet were comparatively exposed, would seem to imply the possession of abundant knowledge of religion, and acquaintance with the Word of God, except such parts as relate to obedience and righteousness in daily life. It is written, "Thy shoes shall be iron and brass: and as thy days, so shall thy strength be" (Deut. xxxiii 25). That is, thy daily walk, all thy actions, shall be guarded by truth and goodness: and help shall be given as thy daily needs require. Goliath had nothing for his feet. The system of BELIEVING ONLY takes little notice of the feet. And yet the Lord says, "He that is washed needeth not save to wash his feet, but is clean every whit" (John xiii, 10). True religion never forgets the head; but it also never forgets the feet. "If thy foot offend thee, cut it off" (Mark ix. 45). If there be anything in thy business or thy daily doings contrary to the spirit of Christian virtue, reject it, and see that thy feet, as well as thy head, go in harmony with true religion. "Our feet shall stand within thy gates, O Jerusalem" (Ps. cxxii. 2). The apostle Paul, in describing the Christian's spiritual armour, did not forget the necessity of having the "feet shod with the preparation of the gospel of peace" (Eph. vi. 15.)

Goliath's challenge and boasting are indicative of the vaingloriousness of an unpurified heart. Pride and self-confidence are always found where innocence and heavenly charity have not yet been allowed to enter.

But let us now return to David. He represents the spiritually minded man; the man who has already overcome the opposition to religion from falsity, and the carnal-mindedness which would animalize our nature. He has slain the lion and the bear; and is now equally ready to oppose a vain semblance of religion which is not obedience, nor charity, nor love; however confidently proposed or defiantly proclaimed. He trusts in the Lord with simple love and faith. Saul's armour is offered and declined. It is not outward arguments that are needed. Nothing in which the external man trusts will suffice.

He takes his staff in his hand. The staff corresponds to those promises of the Word which encourage and support. David says in another place: "Though I walk through the valley of the shadow of death, I will fear no evil: for thou art with me; thy rod and thy staff they comfort me" (Ps. xxiii. 4).

He takes five smooth stones out of the brook, and puts them in a shepherd's bag. Stones correspond to truths; smooth stones to truths of love. The brook signifies the "living waters" of the Word, as then known and present to the soul. "God is Love" is the *first* of these smooth stones. "The Lord is good to all: and his tender mercies are over all his works" (Psa. cxlv. 9). This is a beautiful stone, as well as a smooth one. It is a "pearl of great price." (Matt. xiii. 46). The *second* of these smooth stones is the first and great commandment: "Thou shalt love the Lord thy God with all thy heart, and with all thy soul, and with all thy mind." (Deut. vi. 5; Matt. xxii. 37). How smooth and delightful is the truth that we should love Him who has infinitely loved us, and done such wonders of mercy and love for us. The *third* is that for the Lord's sake we should love our neighbour as ourselves. "We know that we have passed from death unto life, because we love the brethren" (1 John iii. 14). The *fourth* smooth stone to take from the brook of the Word is that from love we should obey the Lord's precepts. "If ye love me, keep my commandments" (John xiv. 15). "I love thy commandments above gold; yea, above fine gold" (Ps. cxix. 127). "O how I love thy law! it is my meditation all the day" (ver. 97). The *fifth* smooth stone is the assurance that we are ever in the Lord's hands. His care is over us, and His love works within us, wherever we are, and whatever we do. In health and in sickness, in life and in death, THE LORD WILL PROVIDE. "The steps of a good man are ordered by the Lord; and He delighteth in His way. Though he fall, he shall not be utterly cast down; for the Lord upholdeth him with His hand" (Ps. xxxvii. 23, 24).

David's placing these stones in the shepherd's bag represented our placing truths in the memory. This is a spiritual bag, for containing what we need; and it is the most capacious and the most convenient of all bags. It is of this the Lord speaks; "Provide yourselves bags which wax not old" (Luke xii. 33).

The sling is that which gives direction to the stone, as the bow is the director of the arrow; and like the bow, it corresponds to doctrine: for this teaches how to apply the truths of the Word, so as to be effective. The victorious Christian is represented in the Book of Revelation as riding on a white horse, with a bow in his hand, and going forth conquering and to conquer (vi. 2). David's sling gave the proper direction to his stone: the Christian's doctrine teaches how to apply his truths, so as to repress any evil against which their power is brought.

David aimed at the giant, and struck him in the forehead. He fell vanquished at once. The forehead corresponds to the will, as to its motives or intentions. The forehead is above the eyes: the intentions are above the eyes of the intellect or understanding. The saints in heaven are said to have the

Father's name written on their foreheads (Rev. xiv. 1): not that they have a *word* written there; but that the Divine Love, the *nature* of the Father, is expressed in all their aims and in their every motive. The forehead of Goliath, however, signifies the motive of those who love and sustain a religion which rejects obedience and love as essential to salvation. It is not love that rejects love; for love is the life of the Lord, the life of heaven, the life of every virtue; "love is the fulfilling of the law" (Rom. xiii. 10). What is it, then, which despises charity, and rejects justice as an essential of true piety? What is it that dares to scorn the commandments of God as the essential laws of the life of a Christian? What is it that has separated religion from life, and made zealots who are bitter, ill-natured, peevish, and who yet think they are true followers of the lovely Prince of Peace? What is it that swells up bombastically, and disdains humble and sincere Christians who diligently follow their Saviour, but who cannot follow them? It is self, self-conceit, pride of intellect. This is the moving cause, the head and front of their offending. The stone of God's truth sinks deeply into this forehead, and the giant is overthrown. The spiritual Christian sees they who are of such a defiant, insolent spirit, "love darkness rather than light, because their deeds are evil" (John iii. 19). The Lord is love; they are self. Whosoever does not deny himself cannot be the Lord's disciple. He who denies love and obedience, denies the whole Word of God; for on the two grand commandments hang all the law and the prophets (Matt. xxii. 40). Without Christian love there is no faith; for "with the *heart* man believeth unto righteousness" (Rom. x. 10). It is love that believes all things, says the apostle (1 Cor. xiii. 7): and without love there is no church, no good works, no heaven.

The giant reels, and falls: and David rushes forward, and cuts off his head with his own sword; or, in other words, shews that the whole aim and end of such a system, which professes to defend itself by the letter of the Bible, is condemned by the letter of the Bible: for every part of the sacred book is full of exhortations to the effect of the Lord's own declarations. "If thou wilt enter into life, keep the commandments" (Matt. xix. 17). "Whosoever shall break one of these least commandments, and shall teach men so, he shall be called the least in the kingdom of heaven: but whosoever shall do and teach them, the same shall be called great in the kingdom of heaven" (Matt. v. 19).

SERMON XII.

SAUL'S ATTEMPTS TO DESTROY DAVID.

" And it came to pass on the morrow, that the evil spirit from God came upon Saul, and he prophesied in the midst of the house: and David played with his hand as at other times: and there was a javelin in Saul's hand.
" And Saul cast the javelin; for he said, I will smite David even to the wall. And David avoided out of his presence twice."—1 SAM. xviii. 10, 11.

WHEN the Apostle Paul, in his Epistle to the Galatians, referred to the history of Abraham, and his two wives, and their children, he said: "Which things are an allegory: for these are the two covenants." He did not mean that they were not true history; but that the history is recorded in the Word of God for the sake of the spiritual lessons to be taught by it. What the two women with their sons represented in general, and, according to the Apostle, in his time in particular, was the old covenant from Sinai, with its outbirth, the religion of the Jews, and the new covenant from the Lord Jesus Christ, with its offspring, the religion of Christianity. The one was bondage, the other was freedom: the one was of the letter, the other of the Spirit. "For this Hagar," he says, "is Mount Sinai in Arabia, and answereth to Jerusalem which now is, and is in bondage with her children. But Jerusalem which is above is free, which is the mother of us all. . . . Now we, brethren, as Isaac was, are the children of promise. But as then he that was born after the flesh persecuted him that was born after the Spirit, even so it is now" (Gal. iv. 24-29).

As it was said in that case, so may it be said in the one of Saul and David now before us. These things are an allegory equally with the narrative of Abraham: and the general lesson is the same. It describes those who receive religion externally, and go no farther; who are represented by Saul: and those who go on and become men of the Spirit, men of internal religion, "children of light;" who are represented by David. The one class are comparatively in bondage; the other in glorious liberty. As he that is born of the flesh persecuted him that was born of the Spirit, as the Apostle says, so did Saul persecute David. A great part of Scripture is in reality taken up with the descriptions of the similarities, diversities and changes of state of these two classes of men; or, as it may be, with the states and activities of the two classes of feelings in the mind of one man; for in each mind there is an outer man and an inner man, a natural mind and a spiritual mind, a Saul and a David. These divine subjects are treated of in the histories of Abraham and Lot, of Rachel and Leah, of Israel out of Canaan and Israel in Canaan, of the disciples before their conversion when Jesus was *with* them, and the disciples after their conversion when Jesus was *in* them (John xiv. 17).

The character of a very considerable portion of the religion of the present day is such that its possessors go but little beyond the external religion represented by Saul; the religion of moderated selfishness. They have the religion of fear and of hope: but very slightly the religion of wisdom and peace; of delight in truth for the sake of truth, and in goodness for its own sweet sake.

It is a grand thing, indeed, to come on the Lord's side at all. It is a wonderful thing when a man ceases to do evil and learns to do well. To be a hired servant of the King of kings is of course infinitely better than to be a bond-slave of hell. But great as this new beginning is, in relation to a state reckless, careless, and rebellious against God, it is only a very external state, compared to the further attainments of spiritual and celestial men. It is a grand first step, but it is only a first step.

It was a great day when Saul was chosen King of Israel, and the people made the air ring with their acclamations of joy, and shouted "God save the King!" But what troubles revealed themselves afterwards; and how sad was the monarch's end on the mountains of Gilboa! So, how often it is that one who began his religious career well, was full of joy at his deliverance, and for a time ran cheerfully in the religious path, at length has paused, become half-hearted, vacillated, exhibited failings that have saddened all who loved him, sunk from bad to worse, and perished in his sins. This is a state like Saul's. We must never forget that it is well to begin with the letter of the Word and religious life in its plainest, simplest form; but we must not stop there. We must mount up in truth and love into angelic states; never pausing or turning back until the kingdom of the Lord has been fully formed and the glory of the Lord revealed in us, and dwelling in the spirit of love, we know that we are dwelling in God, for God is Love (1 John iv. 16).

We will endeavour to point out some of the characteristics of the Saul-state and of the David-state: by which we may with greater clearness discern the failings of the one and the excellencies of the other. And may the Divine David from His eternal throne guide us, and grant in His light to see light that will lead to the mountain of His holiness.

First, then, the Saul-state of the religious man is one in which self-love has been but little subdued, and he is soon puffed up and easily offended. How jealous Saul was of David! how envious at his success! Although he could not have slain the giant himself, yet when the women sang, "Saul hath slain his thousands, and David his ten thousands," Saul was very wroth, and the saying displeased him (xviii. 8). David was confident in the Lord, but perfectly unassuming. When questioned by the king as to who he was, he did not even refer to his great service not long before, in having healed the troubled spirit of the king by the music of his harp; but simply replied, "I am the son of thy servant Jesse the Bethlehemite" (xvii. 58). Interior religion in the spiritually-minded man is that love which the Apostle describes: which "envieth not, vaunteth not itself, is not puffed up: doth not behave itself unseemly, seeketh not her own (but the Lord's will), is not easily provoked; thinketh no evil" (1 Cor. xiii. 4, 5). This spirit, as it entirely destroys the elation of self-love, cannot be borne at first by the external Christian; he takes the javelin of his hatred, and would fain destroy it. He wants to be great in religion, and he is told he must be humble. He resists hard, and would fain away with it again and again; but it is nevertheless eternal truth, and must prevail. The Pharisees hated our Lord, because they were in this very state. They wanted a Messiah that would lift them up above all nations; and when they were taught: "Blessed are the poor in spirit, for theirs is the kingdom of heaven" (Matt. v. 3); "He that is greatest among you shall be your servant" (xxiii. 11); "Except ye be converted, and become as little children, ye shall not enter into the kingdom of heaven" (xviii. 3); Saul-like they strove to put the Lord to death. Happy would it have been for Saul had he conquered this spirit in himself! Let us take this blessed course; and follow Him who, though the Highest of all, said,

"Learn of me: for I am meek and lowly in heart; and ye shall find rest unto your souls" (Matt. xi. 29).

The second characteristic of the external man is that he thinks much of outward glory: he likes a popular religion, a great show. He would not think much of heaven itself, if it were not for the crowns, thrones, robes, and external glories which he associates with the angels. It inflates his self-love to dream of sitting like a Sultan, and having celestial beings passing to and fro to do his bidding. When internal religion comes, and says, "All these things must be spiritually understood: the crowns are wisdom; the thrones are fixed principles of heavenly judgment; the robes are robes of intelligence and righteousness; the joys, the blessedness of doing good, the delights of ever-increasing progress in all celestial and spiritual graces: 'The kingdom of God cometh not with observation; neither shall they say, lo here! or lo there! for the kingdom of God is within you:'" he is startled as from a fond dream, and at first he would fain destroy the unwelcome herald, and cling to his fond delusion. He persecutes David, until he finds it is entirely useless, and in fact that David is really his best friend. He then grieves at his ungrateful conduct and hardness of heart, and acknowledges that David must be King.

The third feature in the character of the externally religious man is that he is vacillating, and easily drawn aside. Saul's whole life was one of sinning and repenting, and falling again. How many failings the Lord's disciples had when in their external state! What murmurings, what jealousies, what disputings, terminating with an entire forsaking of their Master in his hour of direst trouble! How conspicuous was this in the case of Peter! No one was so ready as he in confident declarations and professions of attachment: yet when trial and danger came, he vacillated and fell, sunk most dismally and disgracefully into cursing and swearing, and the denial of his Divine Benefactor and Friend (Matt. xxvi. 74). Such is the external Christian. But when these same men became internal men, and entered into the spirit of Divine things, they became true, firm, and faithful unto death.

Fourthly, the externally religious man cares little for spiritual truth. He may have been charmed and soothed with the sweet revealings of heaven, as Saul was in earlier times with the music of David's harp; but the flesh has been strong with him again, and now he dreads and hates what before was like

"The faint exquisite music of a dream."

To raise the soul to the eternal kingdom to contemplate its laws, its glories, and its felicities; to see, as it were, heaven opened and its celestial splendours realized to the soul, until earth fades, and becomes in comparison dim and of little worth; this is the music which comes from David's harp:

> "Lo! the Psalmist strikes the lyre,
> And with holy transport sings!
> His, the Spirit's sacred fire,
> And his theme the King of Kings,
>
> How should we delight to hear
> Strains that hope and love impart;
> Strains that chase away our fear,
> Strains that elevate the heart."

But Saul is heavy with the evil spirit, which his own evil state has attracted to him, and which Divine Providence has permitted, that he may be cured by the strokes of his own rod: and so the divine music does not elevate him. He detests it, and strikes at David with his javelin; or, in other words, repels the spiritual state with distaste and dislike.

Lastly, the external man is in the religion of fear. He fears death. He fears loss. He has no certainty in anything. Only "perfect love casteth out fear" (1 John iv. 18). Saul was afraid of David: afraid for his family: afraid of the Philistines: afraid of death. The spiritual man knows he will never die: that what is called death is only an elevation to higher life.

One of the many merciful objects for which our Lord came was to free us from [the bondage of the fear of death (Heb. ii. 15). But the natural man still fears it with a great fear; and casts his javelin at the spiritual man, when he perceives his influence becoming powerful over him. Oh how we should pray to have this fear of death removed! but it can only be in proportion as the spiritual man in us is fully opened by truths of heavenly wisdom rendered familiar by being thought upon and followed out from day to day; and that perfect love perseveringly sought, which casteth out fear.

It seems very astonishing to observe the perseverance of Saul in his attempts to destroy David. Seven times are recorded in which, under various circumstances, he sought to accomplish this unhappy purpose. The first time on the occasion mentioned in the text; the second in his palace, after David had slain the Philistines (xix. 10): the third time in Michal's house by night (xix. 11, 12): the fourth time at the feast of the new moon, when he was saved by Jonathan (xx. 33): the fifth among the Ziphites (xxiii. 19-26): the sixth in the cave of Engedi, when he confessed his sin (xxiv. 17): and the seventh near the hill of Hachilah, when he confessed his sin again, and finally gave up the pursuit (xxvi. 25.) We will notice these varied efforts, or some of them; for they are the reflex of our own states. We let the natural man prevail over the spiritual man again and again.

When satisfied with the success of our earthly affairs, we are enjoying ourselves like a king in his palace. We don't wish to be intruded upon; we are pleased with things as they are, and we don't want to be reminded that we are mortal. We wish our mentor to be gone.

Again, after David has slain the Philistines, and we find there is no foundation at all for thinking that a religion of the head only will do, we confess that the truth is so, but we do not want to be troubled with it now. We think there is time enough. We will do it all by and by; and in the meantime we wish to be let alone. We can't bear the sight of David sitting there always. Eternal things will do very well when we are sick and old, and have finished the very important matters that concern us now. As if the matters for our bodies for a few years could for a moment be compared with those of life for ever: or as if any harm could come to any just temporal interests by seeking first the kingdom of God, and His righteousness who has promised that if we do this, all other things shall be added unto us (Matt. vi. 33).

The most peculiar of these attempts of Saul was that when he sought to seize David in his own house: on which occasion he was saved by a curious stratagem, devised by Michal his wife, the king's daughter. The attempt to slay David by night represents the repugnance to the spiritual man which is cherished by the natural man when in a very dark state; when the soul is benighted, and we repel everything but the trouble with which we are then engaged. Michal, the king's daughter, who had become David's wife, is the representative of that glorious principle, the affection for truth. She was given to David after his victory, to teach us that when we have overcome the tendency to a religion of faith only, we are gifted by the Lord with a holy earnestness for those truths which will teach us how to live. This affection is the king's daughter who is "all glorious within: her clothing is of wrought gold" (Ps. xlv. 13). The name Michal signifies "who has all," or "who is perfect;"

and this sacred principle, the love of truth, is that which leads to everything sacred and good; it leads constantly from state to state, until it conjoins us to the All-Good, the Only Perfect, after whom it constantly yearns. By truths sought in the love of truth, we obtain justice, order, goodness, piety, innocence, heaven, all. It is interesting to notice, by the way, that Merab was the daughter that Saul promised (xviii. 17), but that Michal was the one who loved David, and whom he took. The name Merab signifies, "She who disputes," and would indicate a more external affection; one that loves arguing and controversy for victory, rather than inquiry after truth for truth's sake and goodness' sake, which is expressively represented by Michal. The latter preserved David, and presented an image of him to her father, supported by a pillow of goat's hair (xix. 13). It seems an innocent wife's stratagem to preserve her husband from the jealous and vindictive father; but it yields a spiritual lesson also. The goat's hair represents the truths of faith. Men who delight in expatiating on the great truths of religion are represented by the goat, which leaps from rock to rock on the mountain side. The Lord condemns the goats when he is exercising judgment; because they represent such as had gone through life without uniting to their attainments in faith the love and the duties of charity (Matt. xxv. 32, 33). The goat-spirit, however, is good if it be combined with the spirit of love. A young one of the goats might be offered in the paschal supper as well as a lamb (Exod. xii. 5). The spirit of faith has glorious things to do, to cheer, to brighten and to sustain us. To preserve what is spiritual with us, and to assert its pre-eminence, is the special work of faith. "Faith," says the apostle, "is the evidence of things not seen" (Heb. xi. 1). That the spiritual man must not be destroyed, and that if he were, all truth would die, and nothing but calamity would follow, is signified by the image of David being supported by the pillow of goat's hair, and by Michal's speech to her father (xix. 17).

At the feast of the new moon, David ought to have been in his place, and would have been if Saul had been rightly minded|; for the new moon represents faith in clearness, a new light on the understanding diffusing brightness over the mind. But what avails this, if the heart is rankling with envy? No real interior life can be developed there. All is empty, dark and miserable, when malice has usurped the place of loving-kindness in the will. So again Saul was disappointed, and David was not there.

The remaining attempts of Saul, and the manner in which David baffled him, and repaid jealousy and malice by kindness and forgiveness, represent the spiritual man gradually overcoming the natural man by returning good for evil. At last the spiritual becomes entirely the stronger; and the natural man confesses that the government will pass to David, and that every blessing will come from its doing so. All that is intimated in the tender words of Saul, when he saw and confessed his wickedness and folly (xxiv. 16-22).

How beautiful and happy would all things be, if true order were only properly maintained! The natural man fears that his delights will be lost, if he submit himself to the spiritual. But in reality true delight only then begins. Let the natural mind be purified from evil, and the spiritual rule in all things; and then, like Egypt under Joseph's rule, peace would flow like a river, and righteousness like the waves of the sea (Isa. xlviii. 18). Confidence and goodwill would then soon be restored among men, and the roses of life would be divested of their thorns. The world would soon re-echo the order of heaven, and the reality would be what has long been promised: "The tabernacle of God is with men, and He will dwell with them, and they shall be His people, and God Himself shall be with them, and be their God" (Rev. xxi. 3). All this, and much more, is included in Saul's ceasing from his attempts to injure David; and submitting to the divine will that David should take the throne to which he has been appointed.

So, if we take the whole world as the kingdom of Saul, and notice its injurious efforts to resist the rising government of the kingdom of the greater David, the Lord Jesus Christ, how sad, how self-tormenting, how self-destructive does it seem! But oh may it speedily pass away! It cannot always last. The days are coming, and will surely come, and let us pray that they may speedily come in us, that the Lord Jesus shall take the throne of His father David, and "He shall reign over the house of Jacob for ever; and of His kingdom there shall be no end" (Luke i. 33).

SERMON XIII.

SAUL ATTEMPTING TO KILL JONATHAN.

"And Jonathan answered Saul his father, and said unto him, Wherefore shall he be slain? what hath he done?
"And Saul cast a javelin at him, to smite him: whereby Jonathan knew that it was determined of his father to slay David."—1 SAM. xx. 32, 33.

THERE is no character in the Jewish history that leaves a pleasanter impression on the mind than that of Jonathan. His heroism appears from the first scene in which he is presented to us in the sacred narrative, until he dies on the fatal field of Gilboa by the side of his father. "In their death they were not divided" (2 Sam. i. 23).

Jonathan's nobility of mind was particularly displayed in his faithful and disinterested attachment to the young hero who had slain Goliath. The recollection of his love is presented in the affecting words of David's lamentation on the occasion of his death (2 Sam. i. 26, 27). Their mutual attachment was founded on the virtues which they possessed in common. Their souls were knit together when young men. "The soul of Jonathan was knit with the soul of David, and Jonathan loved him as his own soul" (1 Sam. xviii. 1). And whatever might be the lot of his friend, Jonathan remained true to him, and comforted and succoured him, even when his exasperated father threatened to destroy Jonathan himself as well as his hated friend.

Jonathan felt how unworthy was the jealous aversion of the king his father to the brave and modest young man who had wrought so great a deliverance for Israel; and through the eight years of their companionship he never swerved,—but in the palace spoke for him, in the field sent him information, and in the wilderness secretly consoled him. When he knew that it was the will of the Divine Being that David should be king in the room of his father, his piety made not the least complaint. He was perfectly satisfied that, in the government of God, all would be for the best. He asked only that David's friendship might repay to his children the love he had received from their father: a request which in David's prosperity obtained an ample fulfilment.

In the princely Jonathan, then, we have a model of a virtuous life; of superiority to prejudice, jealousy, and narrow unjust family influence: we have friendship constant and true in adversity as in prosperity, and valour faithful to death. All these admirable qualities constitute a character which will ever be respected by those who esteem the worth of a loving heart, of integrity, of genuine sympathy, of tried and enduring self-sacrifice, which makes it sweet to offer up our all, even life itself, for the good of our country.

Let us now endeavour to look a little deeper than the letter of the Word, for the spiritual lessons which are available and salutary in every stage and condition of human life: alike to the civilian and the warrior, the simple and the sage.

Israel under Saul represented the church as it is at its early stage, and as it continues for a time, before it has been able to realize the true spiritual character to which the Lord intends to bring it, that it may become his heaven upon earth. Jonathan signifies the good life which the best members of the church realize at that time. Saul and the people with him were weak, wayward, jealous, and selfish. Jonathan was consistent and upright. Saul represents the external church in general, with a little good and much evil. Jonathan the best portion of that church, with much good and little evil. Saul made outward profession of esteem for David, but inwardly regarded him with aversion. David is the type of the Lord Jesus, and spiritual-mindedness from Him. Jonathan had a deep affection for David; representing the sincere members of the church, who love the Lord Jesus from their very hearts, and do not dread but hail his kingdom over themselves and over all. The Word of the Lord is full of emblems and illustrations of this distinction between the external church and the internal church: and in all cases the external dies, that the internal may fully reign; as Saul died to make way for the reign of David.

Moses leading the people out of Egypt, and directing them during the forty years in the wilderness, during which the first generation died, represented the same general state of the external church as Saul and the people under him. Moses dying, and, being succeeded by Joshua, had the same general lesson to teach (but with interesting differences) as Saul dying, and being succeeded by David. Jonathan, like Caleb, was a true and faithful heart, that always maintained integrity, and stood by the right. Jonathan, then, is the type of the really good in the external church. He was the son of Saul, and his name means the "GIFT OF JEHOVAH." He signifies the new external man, the new nature or character in a man, which is acquired by repentance and reformation.

For religion in a man to have any worth at all, it must have a son. "Except a man be born again (or *born from above*), he cannot see the kingdom of God" (John iii. 3). In this new man, the gift of Jehovah, the friend of Jesus in the soul, we have, then, that which Jonathan represented, and which will always make his character a profitable and delightful study to the thoughtful Christian. In his strength and in his weakness, every sincere Christian claims kindred with Jonathan. Every Christian must have the new birth; and though we must earnestly and willingly receive it, yet it is the "gift of Jehovah." We must be born from above, of water and the spirit (that is, of truth and love), or we cannot enter into the kingdom of God (John iii. 5). Religion must be in deed as well as in word, revealed in new conduct and new tempers, visible to men and inspired by God, or our profession is vain as sounding brass or a tinkling cymbal. "Be renewed in the spirit of your mind" is the essence of apostolic teaching. Eph. iv. 23-25; Col. iii. 9-14.

Jonathan, then, is the type of those in the church who really have a new and genuine character; doing justly, loving mercy, and walking humbly with their God: and in an individual, of that new nature which genuine religion has formed in his character. His conquest over the Philistines in Gibeah of Benjamin represented the victory of those who are sincere and true, over all such as would lead them to a profession of religion without real change (xiii. 2, 3). To do this *in the hill*, which Geba means, is to act according to the truth from the high feeling of love for it. This gives earnestness, courage and success.

The easy victory of Jonathan and his armour-bearer over the formidable host of the Philistines, when they were invited to come on, represented the vanishing away of the supposed difficulties of keeping the Lord's commandments, when those difficulties are confronted with a simple heart and an earnest mind. Terrible in aspect as the cloudy giants of the Hartze mountains of Germany, are the difficulties conjured up by those who ask, threateningly, "Can you pretend to keep the commandments of God? Do you pretend that any one can go to heaven by doing right? Do you believe in salvation by good works?" Yet frail as those monsters of vapour are such difficulties, when met by an humble faith which says, "I can do all things through Christ which strengtheneth me" (Phil. iv. 13). Of the chimeras that frighten us from a new life, and from doing good, it may truly be declared:

> "Like the leaves of the forest when summer is green,
> That host with their banners at sunset were seen;
> Like the leaves of the forest when autumn hath blown,
> That host on the morrow lay withered and strown."

Jonathan's devotion to David represents the new man's devotion to the Lord Jesus: and although in his old nature, represented by his father, with his enmity and envy, the Lord is repelled from the soul; yet the better nature, represented by Jonathan, always yearns after him, goes to him in the wilderness, is conjoined to him soul to soul, and will not let him go. The mysterious states and working of the principles of good and evil in the little world of man's mental constitution, are represented in the meetings and conversations of David and Jonathan.

Saul's anxiety to have David present at the feast of the new moon, that he might take the opportunity to kill him, represents the radical aversion of merely external religion, full as it is of selfishness, even in its worship, to the spiritual kingdom of the Lord. A proud man is proud in his worship, proud in his prayer, proud in his singing, proud in his pew. He cannot bear pure truth. Self-abasement, humility, a tenderness for the feelings of others; the love of truth for truth's sake, and of goodness and innocence as the greatest of treasures, the conviction that the humblest will be greatest in heaven, be he a cottager or a king;—these are things of the internal man, and Saul hates them all. He hates them in teaching, and he hates them in his worship. David's non-appearance indicates that there is no communion possible between the spiritual kingdom in the mind, and such a selfish and evil state of heart.

Jonathan's disbelief in the depth of his father's malice being so great as really to destroy David, indicates that the better nature in the soul cannot conceive the depth and depravity of the unregenerate part of us. Yet so it is. Fair as we seem to ourselves, "from within, out of the heart of men, proceed evil thoughts, adulteries, fornications, murders" (Mark vii. 21).

And Jonathan found himself compelled to believe that, rather than have David reign, his father would not only destroy David, but destroy him too. Terrible revelation of the states of all those who have not steadily pursued the work of heart-conflict, who have not "died daily" by struggling against self in all its forms, and not least against self in the forms of religion!

> "From charity its living root,
> True faith produces holy fruit;
> But they who only leaves can show
> Still on the stock of nature grow.
>
> Lord, let Thy word effectual prove
> To work in us obedient love;
> And teach our wandering hearts to dread
> A name to live, where life is dead!"

It is wonderful to contemplate the mercy of the Lord Jesus in dealing with the human soul! Before the work of religion truly begins, although there is in it an embryo of heaven from our blessed Creator, it is a mass of iniquity, a "body of sin" (Rom. vi. 6), a "body of death" (vii. 24), "a vile body" (Phil. iii. 21), as the apostolic phrases are. How is this mass of impurity, vanity and selfishness, to be transformed into an angel? We are selfish in our audacious crimes, self-seeking in our virtues. How can we be so changed as that reverence for Divine Love and Wisdom, reverence for innocence, purity, goodness and truth, shall so entirely govern us that all selfish considerations shall be an abomination to us, and at length entirely silent for ever; and the Lord and heaven reign supreme within us? How can the wolf be made to dwell with the lamb, the leopard to lie down with the kid, the calf and the young lion and the fatling together, and the little child to lead them (Isa. xi. 6). How can these miracles be wrought? With men this is impossible, but "with God all things are possible" (Mark x. 27).

The Lord appeals to men's hopes and fears, to their joys and sorrows. They are shaken with dread, they are excited by the hopes of everlasting reward. A host of favouring circumstances are by the Divine Providence gathered round to aid, and unless an utter resistance and aversion from persistent and continuous malice exist, so that no tenderness can melt, and nothing less than the destruction of free will (that is, the destruction of manhood altogether) can move, the sinner becomes a penitent, and owns his Saviour. "The bruised reed is not broken, nor the smoking flax quenched; but judgment is brought forth to victory." The soul to be saved is taken into the rough ark covered with pitch, and preserved from the flood that would have drowned it; but what a motley cargo has entered along with it! Saul is among the prophets; but what a Saul! What enmities, what hates, what ostentations, what vanities, what meannesses are enclosed in his complex nature, before it becomes a palace of purity, peace and joy! But, blessed be the Divine Mercy, when the spirit of obedience is engrafted in the soul, a new nature is gradually implanted: and though a large and complicated mass of evil remains, which appears from time to time, which is really opposed to the Lord as Saul was to David,—on the other hand there is now a Jonathan there who is his friend. What amazing condescension it is of the Spirit of the Lord, that He will permit Himself to be treated in man as David was treated by Saul! He mourns in us,—He is driven out, struck at again and again, must disappear and reappear, watch and wander, and even in some states be crucified and put to open shame, and Jonathan His friend be reviled. And He submits to all this! The Divine Helper has to fly from our perversities, and wander as a stranger within us, and say: "Thou hast not called upon me, O Jacob; but thou hast been weary of me, O Israel. Thou hast bought me no sweet cane with money, neither hast thou filled me with the fat of thy sacrifices: but thou hast made me to serve with thy sins, thou hast wearied me with thine iniquities" (Isa. xliii. 22, 24). Yet, notwithstanding this, the unutterable goodness of our Lord is such that He continues His wonder-working operations within us. In all our afflictions He is afflicted, and the angel of His presence saves us. In His love and in His pity He redeems us. He bears and carries us all our days (Isa. lxiii. 9).

When Jonathan and David were in the field together, it was determined that information should be conveyed respecting Saul's state of mind by means of three arrows. After three days waiting, David was to take his stand by a stone, called Ezel. Jonathan would fire three arrows, and would cause a youth to look for them. If they were made to fall short of the stone, so that Jonathan should say, "The arrows are on this side of thee, take them;" then David would know that there was no danger, and return with Jonathan to the presence of his father. But if the arrows went beyond the stone Ezel, and beyond where the lad had reached, then it was a sign that Saul was purposing to destroy David; and the latter must, for the safety of his life, go away (ver. 19-22.) This appears a curious arrangement; but it was carried out, and accomplished the end. Jonathan, as we learn from a later portion of the chapter, gave the information by means of an arrow shot beyond the stone and the youth; by means of which David knew that his life was in danger; and after an affecting parting with his faithful and loving friend, David departed, and Jonathan returned to the city (ver. 42).

In considering the spiritual lesson involved in the arrangement thus made between the two friends, it will be well to notice the curious fact that David was to take his stand by the prominent stone or rock Ezel. A rock corresponds to truth, especially to firm foundation truths. "He set my feet upon a rock, and established my goings" (Psa. xl. 2), evidently means, He has set me firmly on the truth, and enabled me steadily to walk in a new life. "When my heart is overwhelmed, lead me to the rock that is higher than I" (Psa. lxi. 2), means obviously, when I am in sore trouble, lead me to the truth, and the God of truth, who will comfort and console me. The stone here also corresponds to the truth; and Ezel, which is Hebrew for "walk," means truth of life. When David stood by the stone Ezel, and it was to be ascertained whether Saul's designs against him were deadly or not, it is intimated that the truth which determines a man's lot is the truth he lives, it is not the truth he has in his memory, but what he has in his walk; what he loves and does. He must stand by the stone Ezel.

The boy with the arrows signifies the memory which contains the knowledge which we may use for good or evil. He is said to know nothing of higher matters. The mere memory does not. It serves, and does not meddle further.

The arrows which Jonathan was to shoot represent bitter thoughts and bitter words. These, when employed against the good, are like cruel arrows, stinging and piercing; arrows aimed at the breast represent cruel assaults destructive of charity (Psa. lvii. 4; lxiv. 3, 4). The arrows of bitter, spiteful, malicious words are amongst the most terrible instruments of mischief ever used by violent souls; the wounds they make rankle for years and years, and often inflict fatal injury. We can never be too careful of our words, nor of the thoughts which inspire them. The arrows fired by Jonathan were to be indicators of Saul's state. If they fell short of the stone Ezel, there was no danger. If they went as far, or beyond, they indicated a deadly state in Saul. They went beyond; and

David took the warning. The only solace was the warm love of his friend Jonathan, who came and wept with him when he could do no more (ver. 41).

In spiritual matters, the arrows that fall on this side the stone Ezel represent the objections that people may oppose to matters of theory or of intellect, but which do not strike against the religion of life. These objections come from ignorance, from circumstances, from mistakes of education, these do no fatal harm to any one. They do not arise from malice or the love of evil. They intend no harm to David. The Lord can conjoin those to Himself who are in many errors, and who have opposed Him unwittingly, thinking they were doing Him service. Jonathan, when he has to give an account of these, will make his arrows fall short of the stone Ezel, and no harm will be meant against David.

In indicating Saul's state, however, Jonathan made the arrows go beyond, importing opposition to what is good, not only in doctrine but in life. He hated David altogether. There are souls who love darkness rather than light, because their deeds are evil (John iii. 19). They mean deadly harm to David. They hate the Lord's kingdom; they hate the Lord Himself. They burn to make themselves greater than the Most High. They will not have this man to reign over them. These are they who are described by Saul's state, indicated by the arrow going to the stone Ezel, and beyond.

There may be a Saul in us who opposes the reign of David, and, when we would do good, makes evil present with us; and in such case we should be utterly condemned,—there would be no hope for us; but, happily, Jonathan may be in the same breast; and when David comes out of a place towards the south (as expressed in ver. 41), Jonathan will be ready to meet him, and they will kiss one another, and from love weep one with the other. The south is the direction of the sun at noonday when light is great, and in spiritual things it signifies a state of intelligence. While there may be much to deplore in us, represented by Saul, there may also be much for gratitude, for hope, for trust and joy, represented by Jonathan, and David in communion with him. These and the offsprings of these blessed conditions in the soul will form a new world of light and love and peace. Good within from the Lord, and good without, also previously from the Lord, will unite together, kiss one another, and prepare us for the blessing pronounced by Jonathan: "Go in peace" (ver. 42).

SERMON XIV.

SAUL AND THE WITCH OF ENDOR.

"And when Saul enquired of the Lord, the Lord answered him not, neither by dreams, nor by Urim, nor by prophets.
"Then said Saul unto his servants, Seek me a woman that hath a familiar spirit, that I may go to her, and enquire of her. And his servants said to him, Behold, there is a woman that hath a familiar spirit at Endor."—1 Sam. xxviii. 6, 7.

ONE of the promises most delightful to the Christian is the declaration that there will always be a reply to him when he seeks counsel from his Heavenly Father. "Because he hath set his love upon me," it is written, "therefore will I deliver him : I will set him on high, because he hath known my name. He shall call upon me, and I will answer him; I will be with him in trouble; I will deliver him, and honour him" (Psa. xci. 14, 15). The Lord is a strong habitation; a Divine Friend, to whom we may continually resort, and obtain answers of wisdom and peace, so long as we are humbly desirous of being guided aright. How sad then is it when wilful, obstinate and persistent disobedience has brought about the reverse of this gracious promise, and heaven is closed to us, as in the case of Saul. We call, and there is no answer. "When Saul enquired of the Lord, the Lord answered him not, neither by dreams, nor by Urim, nor by prophets."

The three methods of heavenly communications enumerated are calculated to open to us very interesting considerations; and we will notice them as they are presented to us in the text: dreams,—Urim,—and prophets.

That the Lord conveys instruction sometimes by dreams is not only corroborated by the remarkable dreams recorded in Scripture, but in all ages there have been confirmations which history has not disdained to preserve. When we remember how considerable a portion of our lives we spend in sleep, and how largely many people dream, we may rationally conclude that we are not overlooked by Divine Mercy in these hours of our helplessness; but that intimations for our good are given in the night, as well as in the day. "God speaketh once, yea twice, yet man perceiveth it not. In a dream, in a vision of the night, when deep sleep falleth upon men, in slumberings upon the bed; then He openeth the ears of men, and sealeth their instruction, that he may withdraw man from his purpose, and hide pride from man" (Job xxxiii. 14-17). The Lord refreshes us and restores our strength during sleep, thus bestowing blessings of incalculable value to both the weary body and the wearied mind, when "He giveth His beloved sleep:" and why not impart instruction? Not that we are to suppose that every wild vagary occurring during dreams is to be taken as a guide, or as a revelation, or as a disclosure of fact. This cannot be truly said indeed of what is spoken and shewn to us when we are awake; much less should we expect it when we are asleep. But when any weighty matter is delivered to a person in a dream, there is usually some peculiar impressiveness, some solemnity which the spirit feels and cannot shake off, which imparts a conviction that Providence has spoken in the dream. The dreams of Joseph and of Pharaoh were of this character. Of such it is said: "Hear now my words: If there be a prophet among you, I the Lord will make myself known unto him in a vision, and will speak unto him in a dream" (Num. xii. 6).

Dreams however have uses, and important uses, for all: they intimate clearly how completely the soul can live in its own world, quite independent of the body. The soul can enjoy pleasure, suffer pain, go, return, communicate with others in a state of life and being, while the body is unconscious and at rest. Dream-life, then, is a revelation to every one of the capability of spirit-life independent of the body and the outward world, and therefore of its certainty: since the Divine Being makes nothing in vain. Dreams shew us, too, that the mental world is as real to the spirit and as full of objects as the material world is to the body. But dreams do more than this. They should be interpreted by correspondence or analogy; and then they inform us of what quality the spirits are who are near us. Pleasant dreams, pure, innocent and lovely objects, are indications that angels are near, and we are inbreathing somewhat of the atmosphere of heaven. Horrid dreams, "making night hideous," full of fantastic, monstrous things, loathsome and painful, are emblems to warn us that subtle and vile spirits are near, seeking to influence us by "blasts from hell," stimulating whatever in us leads to impurity, or to rage. Such dreams, it may be said, are occasioned by indigestion, heavy suppers, diseased states of body, and anxieties. Be it so. These are the disorderly conditions in us, into which evil spirits can and do pour their influences. Our bodies are at such times in bad states; the spheres of bad spirits are in accord with these vitiated conditions of body, flow in with their foul phantasies, and fill our minds with terrible pictures, reeking from their own foul dens.

Dreams, then, are a species of revelation. They warn when they are unpleasant, to turn the soul to the Fountain of Purity, and to look well to our habits both of mind and body; and to one who has been agitated by hideous scenes in the night, it may be said, in the words of the poet Burton:

> "Take them home to thyself: and if unto thyself
> The answers the same should be,—
> Then beware of thyself, and take care of thyself,
> Or so much the worse for thee."

Heavenly dreams are visions which strengthen hope; which charm us with lovely pictures of the distant and the future, by which the sorrowful soul is for a little time bathed in bliss, and lifted above its cares, so that it feels like the prophet who had been gladdened with the view of his country purified and raised to more than its ancient glory. "Upon this I awaked, and beheld; and my sleep was sweet unto me" (Jer. xxxi. 26).

Saul had now, we are informed, no revelation from the Lord in dreams. He inquired, and there was no response. Yet surely this was reply enough. He was of those who say and do not. He had sinned, and sinned until the door was shut. The closure of the inner door of the soul ought to have led him to repentance. But instead of taking that simple straightforward course, he is ready to try every thing but that. Astonishing infatuation! And yet how common it is! How many persons there are who have a strange facility of hardening and blinding themselves against the plainest teachings of experience. Their whole lives are repetitions of the same blunders. They learn nothing, and they forget nothing. In their early youth they are headstrong, silly and vain. They scorn all the cautions of the wise, and the teachings of the Word of God. They come to grief, and in loss of fortune, health or prospects, or all together, they get their first great lesson as to the iniquity of their conduct, and a great call to repent. There are a few sighs, it may be, a few prayers, and a few promises; but the danger passes away, they begin afresh, and with a fatal fatuity they are found forgetful of their chastisement, speeding again downhill to another fall and then another, notwithstanding the repeated warnings they have received. Their whole career is a long chain of blunders and misery, and they die unchanged. The self-love of such men is really self-hate, and takes them round the same dull circle of blunder and pain, until the sad scene is closed, in a sadder catastrophe. And yet how simple is the way of heaven! We have done wrong; let us do right. We have suffered; let us repent. We have been foolish; let us be wise. The goodness of God leads us to repentance. Our Saviour lends His divine hand; and He is Omnipotent to aid. The angels will rejoice over us. Every good awaits us. Let us arise, and go to our Father. Oh how easy this is, when we are sincere, faithful to God, and faithful to ourselves! With it all is well. Without it, without an honest change of heart and life, the Divine Voice will become fainter and fainter to us. We may continue worship; but our worship will be a heartless mockery when there is no worship in our *lives*. We may pray and enquire of the Lord. The Lord answers the heart, not the mouth. There will at length be a final, fatal close; and no reply either by dreams, or by Urim, or by prophets.

The reply by Urim, or by lights, was the gleam that came upon the high priest's breast, when he went into the Holy of Holies with the breastplate of precious stones placed upon his heart, and prayed for divine direction. The breastplate of precious stones represented the inner truths and virtues of religion. When we have full faith in these, and love them, they are like a golden breastplate sustaining precious stones, and borne upon the heart. Let a genuine soul present itself before the Lord with its petitions for strength, for counsel and for cheer; and divine lights will brighten up the troubled spirit, and shadows and sorrows will pass away. "Light is sown for the righteous, and gladness for the upright in heart" (Psa. xcvii. 11). In the Lord's light we shall see light. It may have seemed to us that life has become a desert; but when the glory of the Lord has shone round about us, the weary shades pass off, and in the bright lights of the inner Urim shining about our hearts, our wilderness will become like Eden, and our desert like the garden of the Lord (Isa. li. 3). But to such as Saul; to those who cling to the old man with his lusts, when, with a sense of dark foreboding of coming ruin, there is a shrinking from the gloomy future, but even yet no real repentance,—a dread of pain, but not a dread of sin, though there may be a loud prayer; there is no reply by Urim; no heavenly lights pour their blessed radiance into the soul. All is voiceless; the soul is a dark vault, where nothing answers but the echo of one's own voice, the heavy sound of one's own foot.

There is no reply by prophets. The Word of God, which is a company of prophets, has no reply of comfort for the soul that will not repent. There is every hopeful promise for the penitent. All is forgiven to those who feel they have nothing to pay. "Lord, save me, or I perish," from a sincere soul, has always the response: "Come unto me!"

But the Sauls of the world are still not made wise. They still blunder on, and sink from bad to worse. Finding no help from heaven, Saul sought for aid and information from those familiar spirits, as they were called, who, though they had quitted the body, yet hankered after earth and the things of the earth, and were the source among the corrupt nations of Canaan of the foulest abominations; which was, indeed, the reason why the Israelites had to overthrow and extirpate them.

That we are associated spiritually with angels and spirits, is a truth declared alike by the Word of God and by universal experience in all ages. This communion is the work of Divine Providence, and renders us blessed help in the ministry of angels and good spirits. He giveth His angels charge concerning us, to keep us in all our ways (Psa. xci. 11). Besides guardian angels, who are to watch over us, and perceive all our emotions and tendencies, that they may continually protect us, and ever elevate our motives and ends to the Lord and His kingdom, we are associated with spirits good and evil, good with the good, evil with the evil: these spirits being such as are in each case nearest to the spiritual states of those with whom they are associated. Men could not live and breathe in the world in a vacuum; nor could the spirits of men think and act mentally in utter separation from the spheres of other spiritual beings like themselves. Hence thoughts from good spirits flow into the minds of good men, and thoughts from evil spirits flow into the minds of evil men. Hence the crowds of sympathies and sensations which press upon us on all sides and stimulate us, and often, as we say, strike us in unexpected directions. Sometimes a bright idea will enter the mind like a new star, and open the way to brilliant disclosures of real magnificence; sometimes fiendish suggestions will press into an evil mind with an intensity of villany shocking even to one who has been long familiar with sin. So long as these influences come only as influences, they may be attractive and seductive, but they do not take away a man's liberty. He can accept or he can repel them. Only with his own consent, and by the instrumentality of his own lust, can a bad man be made the slave of devils worse than himself.

The Lord keeps men free, by preserving them from open intercourse with spirits. For this merciful and imperative reason it is that, although we are constantly in communion with spirits, from the necessity of our being, yet they do not know with whom they are allied and associated, and we do not know them. The Lord preserves, varies, and changes these connections, and adjusts them by ways of wisdom and mercy known in all their fulness only to Himself. It is true the Infinite Goodness of our Heavenly Father has occasionally permitted angels to be seen, and intimations and revelations to be given to men from the inner world; to preserve among men the knowledge that they were born for heaven, and to keep fresh and green within them the invaluable impression: "There is another and a better world: death is but the dark lattice that shrouds from the good the glories of eternal day." When the Lord does this, it is well. He selects the persons, and guards the circumstances, so that no harm can come.

If man, however, unbidden, from curiosity alone, and careless of the consequences, seek open intercourse with spirits, it is fraught with peril; he is doing a forbidden thing. The only spirits who will aid him in this are evil spirits, and good cannot come of it. Hence it is forbidden both in the Old Testament and in the New, and in the case of Saul before us, we have an illustration of the sad consequences of seeking to commune with FAMILIAR SPIRITS. Saul knew he was entering on forbidden ground. He was aware of the Divine Laws against it. He had himself been most severe in the execution of those laws (ver. 9). Yet he was so blinded as to do a plain and well-known evil, in the vain hope that good might come to him.

When a person has, from curiosity, or from the desire to become famous, sought by yearning, entreaty and perseverance, to become a medium for open intercourse with spirits, until it has been obtained, the spirit or spirits become consciously familiar with his thoughts, purposes, aims and circumstances, and are therefore called familiar spirits. These familiar spirits become conscious of his mental tendencies, his weakest points of character, and play upon his lusts and passions, leading ultimately to abominations of which he himself would never have dreamed. Hence the divine laws are so imperative against them. "Regard not them that have familiar spirits, neither seek after wizards, to be defiled by them: I am the Lord your God" (Lev. xix. 31). "And the soul that turneth after such as have familiar spirits, and after wizards, to go after them, I will even set my face against that soul, and will cut him off from among his people" (Lev. xx. 6). "There shall not be found among you any one that maketh his son or his daughter to pass through the fire, or that useth divination, a sorcerer, an enchanter, or a witch, or a charmer, or a CONSULTER WITH FAMILIAR SPIRITS, or a wizard, or ONE WHO ENQUIRES OF THE DEAD. For all these things are an abomination unto the Lord; and because of these abominations the Lord thy God doth drive them out from before thee" (Deut. xviii. 10-12). Saul despised these clear divine warnings. He had shut the Word of the Lord and the influences of heaven from himself; and now, instead of humbling himself at that late period and repenting even then, he sought by forbidden arts to obtain from below the succour he had wilfully disabled himself from receiving from the only true source, the fountain of salvation.

The woman was quite as conscious of the guilty work in which she was engaged as the king himself; but being pressed she proceeded. And soon an old man came up, covered with a mantle, and apparently having the figure of Samuel; for Saul recognised him, and bowed himself before him (ver. 14).

Endor, the place where this woman lived, was a village in Manasseh. The name is in Hebrew THE EYE OF THE GENERATION, and she is the symbol of a superstitious religion, a perversion of truth, to suit an adulterous generation. Such a state of religion introduces to spirits, but they are evil spirits; and to a prophet, but a false prophet. The woman said: "I see gods ascending from the earth." It would have been better rendered "god," as the word used in the original (Elohim), though plural, usually only means one person, and evidently does so here: for Saul said, "What form is *he* of?" And she said "An old man cometh up." That it was not Samuel is evident, for he came up as if *out of the earth*. In the spiritual world, which is seen when the sight of the spirit is opened, there appears an earth as in this world. Above is the heaven of angels; below is the world of infernals. This spirit *came up*, yet he professed to be Samuel. It was in fact an evil spirit who assumed the form and spoke in the character of Samuel. It is one of the chief arts of evil spirits to personate and to deceive. "Beloved," said St. John, "believe not every spirit, but try the spirits whether they are of God" (1 John iv. 1). "Satan himself," said another apostle, "is transformed into an angel of light" (2 Cor. xi. 14). Hence we may discern with perfect clearness the reason for the absolute prohibition of all seeking for intercourse with spirits, or, as it has been strongly, but not too strongly called, spirit-hunting. "When they shall say unto you, Seek unto them that have familiar spirits, and unto wizards that peep and that mutter: should not a people seek unto their God? for the living to the dead? To the Law and to the Testimony: if they speak not according to this word, it is because their is no light in them;" or, as in the Hebrew, "because there is for them no morning" (Isa. viii. 19, 20).

Saul, however, still seeking to avoid the one honest remedy—repentance, and finding no help from heaven on any other terms, clutched around for unlawful aid, and was introduced to a false and terrible Samuel, a prophet only of despair and death. Just so has it ever been with a carnal unrepentant world. When men, by persisting in evil, have closed heaven against themselves, and can get no answers to their appeals for aid and comfort, they turn to superstition; which, like this weird woman of Endor, is in league with the powers of darkness. For the brightness of joy there then comes the gloom of despair, a settled melancholy, a fearful looking forward to judgment and sorrow.

Had they but the genuine wisdom to cease to do evil and learn to do well, to turn away from their transgressions and lead a new life, heaven would be opened to them. They would see the Lord's church, the bride, the Lamb's wife, ready to welcome them. There would be no need to have recourse to witches, wizards, or familiar spirits of any kind; but light, comfort, consolation and blessing would stream in. There would be answers from the Lord by dreams, by Urim and by prophets. There would not be a false Samuel to denounce against them the dark horrors of despair, but the true Samuel, the Holy Word, with its finger ever pointing upwards to the glorious land, the home of the blessed, where the wicked cease from troubling, and the weary are at rest.

SERMON XV.

DAVID'S VICTORY OVER THE AMALEKITES.

"Then said David, Ye shall not do so, my brethren, with that which the Lord hath given us, who hath preserved us, and delivered the company that came against us into our hand.

"For who will hearken to you in this matter? but as his part is that goeth down to the battle, so shall his part be that tarrieth by the stuff: they shall part alike."—1 SAM. xxx. 23, 24.

It is one of the errors of inexperience to suppose that the work of religion is one struggle; that with a sharp bitter agony and effort of the soul the work of regeneration is accomplished, and full victory attained. This is only very partially true. There is a period, doubtless, when a soul decides to forsake sin and live for heaven. With more or less of struggle, with more or less of humiliation and of sorrow, and in some cases of deep wretchedness of soul, a person determines to turn away from his wickedness and do that which is lawful and right, that he may save his soul alive, just as the Israelites suffered and marched out of Egypt. The step is a great one. It is virtually a stride from slavery to liberty, from hell to heaven. The Lord blesses it; angels rejoice over it; the person feels happy. The work, however, is only begun, it is not completed. Outward evils are reformed, but inward ones are only concealed, and kept down by the Lord's mercy until the penitent becomes stronger, and by little and little can overcome, and finally silence them for ever.

All this is represented in the Word by the dealings with the Amalekites recorded there from time to time. Amalek represented that inward opposition to heavenly things that loves darkness rather than light. It is often conquered, but it appears again and again. It is that malicious vile self, which manifests its virulence in various ways, sometimes creeping, sometimes defiant, but always covertly or openly seeking to betray and ruin the soul. Amalek is always opposed to the

H

throne of the Lord in the soul, and the Lord has war with Amalek from generation to generation (Exod. xvii. 16).

When the Israelites had marched but a little way on their journey to Canaan, there was Amalek in the Valley of Rephidim determined to arrest and destroy them. This subtle and powerful people, which Balaam called "the head of the nations," (Num. xxiv. 20), never seemed done with. They were powerful in the days of Saul, who spared the king when he ought to have exterminated him and all within his power; and here, in the chapter before us, we read that they had made another irruption, burnt Ziklag where David lived, and carried away captive the women and children.

When we think of the spiritual sense of these warlike transactions recorded in the Word, how surely they illustrate the fact that the struggle between good and evil, heaven and hell within us, is a life-and-death struggle. We must destroy sin, our especial sin, the sin which most readily besets us, which is that in which our evil self-hood displays its malignity, or it will destroy us. Saul failed, because he was unfaithful against Amalek: David wept, until he had no more power to weep, when he saw what Amalek had done, and instantly sought help and counsel from the Lord, followed it out, and triumphed.

We ought not to enter with feeble and vacillating heart on the campaign against sin in ourselves, the holy war of bringing the whole of our being into purity and peace; but resolutely do the Lord's work within us, subduing every affection, thought, imagination, habit, way and work to the spirit of the Lord Jesus, the benign sway of the Prince of Peace. We should joyously labour on in this holy work of self-conquest, taking rest when the Divine Mercy and Providence afford it, but always ready to resist every instigation and impulse to evil, saying with exulting courage, "Blessed be the Lord my strength, who teacheth my hands to war, and my fingers to fight: my Goodness, my High Tower, and my Deliverer; my Shield and He in whom I trust; who subdueth my people under me."

But before we proceed further to contemplate this portion of the Word, in its bearing upon the individual warfare of the Christian against the sins which present themselves in the course of his regeneration, let us regard it in its more general and grander aspect, as the record of the Wars of Jehovah in His work of Redemption. The Lord Jesus was not only Jehovah the Creator, but Jehovah the Redeemer, "Jehovah mighty in battle" (Psa. xxiv. 8). "For thy Maker is thine Husband,

Jehovah of hosts is His name : and thy Redeemer the Holy One of Israel; the God of the whole earth shall He be called" (Isa. liv. 6). Redemption was the deliverance of mankind from the powers of darkness, and thus winning for mankind again the "glorious liberty of the children of light." Jesus, our Lord, Jehovah in the flesh, wrought out this Redemption by vanquishing the infernal hosts again and again, until they were entirely subdued, and new power was given to men to work out their salvation with fear and trembling, but gratefully and resolutely, in all their daily walk. "I will ransom them from the power of hell (not *the grave*); I will redeem them from death : O death, I will be thy plagues! O hell, I will be thy destruction!" such was the promise of God the Redeemer, when about to come into the world : and when He was in the world, and carrying out His glorious work, Jesus said, "I beheld Satan like lightning fall from heaven. Behold I give you power to tread on serpents and scorpions, and over all the power of the enemy: and nothing shall by any means hurt you" (Luke x. 18, 19).

David was the type of the Lord Jesus, thus redeeming man from the direful slavery of evil spirits. In this respect, the Redeemer was like David, a Man of War. He the Prince of Peace, at first came not to send peace upon earth, but a sword. He was a Divine David in His redeeming work : He became a Divine Solomon in His Glorified Humanity; the King of kings and Lord of lords.

How wonderful is the Word of God, which in the same narrative gives the history of David, the spiritual experience of the Christian, and a description of the Divine Work of the Lord Jesus in redeeming the world! Yet so it is. Every incident in the sacred narrative before us has its proper place and bearing in all these respects. Hence it has been the conviction of the spiritually minded in all the Christian ages that not only in the well-known instances quoted in the gospels, where the words of David are quoted and said to be fulfilled in the Lord Jesus, but everywhere the Psalms, though spoken of David, have their grandest application to Jesus, David's acknowledged Lord.

This is taught clearly by the Lord Jesus Himself. "He said unto them, These are the words which I spake unto you, while I was yet with you, that all things must be fulfilled which were written in the law of Moses, and in the prophets, and in the Psalms concerning Me. Then opened He their understanding, that they might understand the Scriptures" (Luke xxiv. 44, 45). Let us pray, my beloved brethren, that the same gracious aid may be afforded to us, that our hearts may burn within us while the Lord speaks to us in His Word, and our eyes may be opened to behold wondrous things out of His law.

Ziklag, which was a small town in the south of Judah, David's dwelling-place, and whose name signifies "a pressed measure," represented the few truly good, called often in Scripture "a remnant," who were faithful to the Lord and waiting for His coming, when the world was buried in sin and darkness.

The rush of the Amalekites on Ziklag and its destruction by fire, while they carried the women with their sons and daughters captive, including David's two wives, represented the overflow of the powers of hell, enslaving the last of the good among the human race, and bringing into bondage the church, internal and external, figured by the two wives of David. In the fifty-ninth chapter of Isaiah the state of mankind just before the Lord Jesus came into the world is vividly described, and it is represented here by Ziklag in flames, and the inhabitants a prey to the plunderers. "Yea, truth faileth, and he that departeth from evil maketh himself a prey; and the Lord saw it, and it displeased Him that there was no judgment. And He saw that there was no man, and wondered that there was no intercessor; therefore His arm brought salvation, and His righteousness it sustained Him" (ver. 15, 16). Again, "when the enemy shall come in like a flood, the Spirit of the Lord shall lift up a standard against him" (ver. 19). The infernals poured out their terrible influences upon and around the remaining good among the human race, and with inflamed passions those horrid fires of the soul seemed about to have everything their own way. But the eye of Divine Love was upon them.

> "His creatures fell, no pitying eye,
> No mighty arm to save was nigh,
> Or aid our feeble powers:
> He saw, He came, He fought alone,
> And conquered evils not His own
> That we might conquer ours."

The grief of David and the men who were with him, at the devastation they beheld, represented the sorrow of the Lord and His angels at the calamities of mankind. "Then David and the people that were with him lifted up their voice and wept, until they had no more power to weep" (ver 4). The sorrow of the Redeemer at human folly and its wretched results, is described in those affecting words of the prophet which seem the condensation of tender lamentation. "Behold, and see if there be any sorrow like unto my sorrow." Jesus wept at Lazarus dead and bound in grave clothes, the symbol of humanity then dead to all the purer joys, and holier virtues, bound in the grave clothes of narrow and corrupt superstitions. He wept again over Jerusalem, and gave expression to His divine sorrow in the tender words; "If thou hadst known, even thou, at least in this thy day, the things which belong unto thy peace."

By David encouraging himself in the Lord his God, is meant that all the courage and impulse to redeem, in the Human Nature of the Lord, was derived from the Father within. "As the Father had life in Himself, so hath He given to the Son to have life in Himself" (John v. 26). David called for the ephod, the linen garment for the chest worn by the priesthood. "And Abiathar brought thither the ephod to David." The ephod was the symbol of the heavenly truths of charity, of that charity which "hopeth all things, believeth all things, and endureth all things." The inquiry by David from the Lord, "Shall I pursue and shall I overtake them?" with its answer, is again an intimation that all things that the Redeemer did, He did from the Father within Him.

The six hundred men represented all things requisite for the labours of Redemption. Six is used in the spiritual sense when labour and toil are connected with the subject referred to, derived from the six days preceding the Sabbath.

They came to the brook Besor; the name of this brook signifies evangelization or gospel. When the Lord had commenced the work of redeeming man from the powers of darkness, those Amalekites of the soul, He also came to a fresh era in the progress of humanity, the era in which the glad tidings of great joy could be published for all people." This was coming to the brook Besor. Two hundred men were faint, and could not go over the brook, and four hundred passed on with David. Some have not the vigour to become internal men. They are good to a certain extent, but they have little desire for the deep truths of the gospel. They are faint, and cannot pass on. Four hundred, however, go forward, and are conducted to complete victory.

And now a very singular incident occurred. They met an Egyptian in the field. David questioned him, and said; "To whom belongest thou? and whence art thou?" He said, "I am a young man of Egypt, servant to an Amalekite, and my master left me, because three days agone I fell sick." This mention of a young

Egyptian will remind us that Israel was in Egypt, the land of science, before going into Canaan, and the infant Redeemer was taken down into Egypt, and this because it was needful to fulfil the prophecy, "I called my son out of Egypt." It is an interesting fact in the ways of Divine Providence, that whenever a new dispensation of religion is given, there is also a new outpouring of science. Grecian and Egyptian literature were opened out in the Roman world at the publication of the gospel, so as in this respect to offer a beautiful auxiliary to religion. The young Egyptian was in the field. At the present day, when the Lord is revealing a still larger amount of heavenly wisdom, a still deeper effulgence of the gospel, what a cornucopia of scientific truths has been poured into the world! Who that looks around and contemplates in this new age the wonders of astronomy, the marvels of steam, the discoveries in light, in printing, in improved roads, in navigation, in telegraphs, in all the departments of science, but must confess that the young Egyptian is again in the field?

The Amalekite takes possession of the young Egyptian, but he always falls sick in his hands. The emissaries of evil try to use science against religion; but it always becomes sick in their hands.

"The undevout astronomer is mad."

Science is only in a healthy state when it is the servant of religion, and is carrying out the behests of benevolence and wisdom. David gave the young Egyptian bread and water, and he ate and drank; and this is mentioned in the Word to teach that Goodness and Truth, which are heavenly bread and the water of life, are as it were the soul and the support of all true science. The figs and the raisins which were also given represent the outward virtues which proceed from goodness and truth within.

The Egyptian guiding David to the Amalekites, and making it a condition that he should not be delivered to his former master, is a sign that science is repugnant to evil, and in the hands of religion is one of the most effectual means to its overthrow. Science is from God equally with religion, and speaks with reverence of her Maker. "The heavens declare the glory of God, and the firmament sheweth His handiwork. Day unto day uttereth speech, and night unto night sheweth knowledge. There is no speech nor language in which their voice is not heard" (Ps. xix. 1-3). Whatever religion forbids, every breach of the divine commandments, science also brands as mischievous. Science in a thousand ways deplores an evil, but cannot put it down. Over-toil, violences of temper, unchastity with its myriad pollutions and degradations, science can point out, but she cannot cure. But when the young Egyptian shews them to David, he will smite them from the twilight even unto the evening of the next day: or in other words, the divine Redeemer who broke down the power of hell, and instituted purity of heart and life as the law for Christians, was powerful to bruise the serpent's head, to condemn and root out sin until night began to cover His Church again, until the evening of the next day.

The spoil that was recovered, and which is called David's spoil, his two wives, the sons and daughters of the people, the flocks and herds, represented the good in the spiritual world, who had been waiting for redemption to be completed before they could ascend to heaven:—the captivity which the great Redeemer led captive when the everlasting doors were opened to receive Him. (Ps. xxiv.; Eph. iv. 8.) The presents which were sent by David to the inhabitants of the various cities of Judah represented the joys and blessings experienced by the angelic hosts when the Lord had finished His Divine Work. Heaven was happier, for men were saved. Glory to God was sung in the highest (heavens), while there was peace and good-will towards men. The glorious proclamation echoed through the eternal regions: "Sing, O ye heavens; for the Lord hath done it: shout, ye lower parts of the earth; break forth into singing, ye mountains, O forest, and every tree therein: for the Lord hath redeemed Jacob, and glorified Himself in Israel" (Isa. xliv. 23).

We have taken this general view of the Divine Work, as shadowed forth in the history of David, when we view the Jewish hero as a type of the Divine Hero, the Lord Jesus, the Conqueror of death and hell. Let us now briefly notice the application to the Christian as a spiritual warrior, and in one of those temptations by which he is from time to time beset. Ziklag would represent the state of religion in the soul, when it is yet feeble and weak. The Amalekites would represent the crowd of evil impulses that at such times rush into the soul, and inflame its lusts, and carry away for a season its good affections, so that they seem distant and in captivity. This state is described when it is written, "My soul is among lions, and I lie among them that are set on fire" (Ps. lvii. 4). Ziklag is burned, and the soul is in prison. The Lord's truth comes into us, and fills us with a sense of His sorrow for us, of His mercy towards us, and of His power. The Egyptian which in the quality of guide shews David where our foes are, represents scientific knowledge, which, under the name of common sense, rejects evil and denounces it equally as do the teachings of Divine Wisdom. We cry mightily to the Lord for help. The Lord lives in us, walks in us (2 Cor. vi. 16), fights in us, and conquers in us. David destroys our Amalekites, and sets free the church in us, and all our new-born better principles, which, like sons and daughters, have peopled the little kingdom of the soul. The hopes, joys, consolations, and blessings which are diffused throughout the soul, with the grateful confession that they are all from the Lord, are David's spoil sent to all the places around. The whole soul is filled with delight. The divine joy is in our joy, and our joy is full. Our head is anointed with oil, and our cup runneth over.

Yet in our best states some imperfections appear. This is represented in the complaint of the wicked men adverted to in our text, and the words of the previous verse. They expressed disdain for their weaker brethren, and sought to have all the spoil for themselves. We are often so delighted with new acquisitions in religion, that we think lightly of the states which have gone before. But this is a serious error. Past good should be retained, as well as new excellences acquired. The men who stayed at the brook Besor guarded the stores of the host; or, as David said, tarried by the stuff. The virtues of everyday life, the common duties of home, the business and ministrations of this lower world, the moral obligations and courtesies of society, are neither to be forsaken nor despised by those who have conquered in spiritual warfare, and are triumphing in spiritual bliss. "As his part is that goeth down to the battle," said the triumphant David, "so shall his part be that tarrieth by the stuff. They shall part alike."

With perfect obedience to this divine law, more perfect Christian characters would be attained. The purest hearts are thoroughly compatible with the gentlest manners. The most delicate conscience may be surrounded by the greatest capacity for successful trade. The external man and the internal man should both be in true order, each in its own sphere; then the divine blessing will be upon both. They shall part alike. Only conquer the inner Amalekites, and seek first the kingdom of God and His righteousness; and all other things will be added unto you.

SERMON XVI.

THE DEATH OF SAUL.

"And, when his armour-bearer saw that Saul was dead, he fell likewise upon his sword, and died with him. So Saul died, and his three sons, and his armour-bearer and all his men, that same day together."—1 SAM. xxxi. 5, 6.

LIFE is full of contrasts. Youth and age, prosperity and adversity, sickness and health, strength and weakness, poverty and riches, success and defeat, alternate before us with strange vicissitude. But when we would contemplate this wonderful variety in human affairs in its most remarkable conditions, we need only turn to meditate upon the career of Saul. How wonderful was the elevation of his youth! Raised at Mizpeh from the farm to the throne; the whole multitude which thronged the plain crying out, God save the King. Thenceforward victory waited on his banners. He overthrew the Ammonites, he overthrew the Philistines in many a hard fought field; and his kingdom seemed firmly established. But see him in the history before us, his army slain or scattered, his sons fallen one after another, flying before the swiftly pursuing archers, sorely wounded, bleeding, despairing, asking for death from a friendly hand as a favour. What can be more sad! Once so high, and now so low! Yet such is the experience of life. Such is the frailty of human hopes. By such contrasts are we taught that our abiding place is not here; that our true and stable treasures are not position, not treasures, and not fame, but goodness, wisdom, faith, hope, virtue, spiritual treasures all derived from heaven, all looking to and leading to our everlasting home. Change is the law of this lower world. Health is to us uncertain, riches are often fleeting and temporary. "There's nothing true but heaven." "Labour not for the meat that perisheth, but for that meat which endureth unto everlasting life." "Sell that ye have, and give alms; provide yourselves bags which wax not old, a treasure in the heavens that faileth not, where no thief approacheth, neither moth corrupteth:" "for where your treasure is, there will your heart be also." Of things that happen in time, the only certainty is death. That is sure to come in sunshine or in storm, and hence the supreme wisdom, the imperative duty of living daily for heaven, so that in the hour of nature's dissolution death may be to us the crown of life. We then should feel as described by Dr. Young:

> "Death wounds to cure: we fall, we rise, we reign;
> Spring from our fetters ; fasten on the skies
> Where blooming Eden withers in our sight,
> Death gives us more than was in Eden lost:
> The king of terrors is the Prince of Peace.
> When shall I die to vanity, pain, death?
> When shall I die? When shall I live for ever?

Saul is not presented in Scripture as a bad man in his ordinary life. He is rather described as in general a good man with two grievous drawbacks—he was imperfectly obedient to God, and he was envious towards David. In David's lamentation over the destruction of the royal house by the slaughter on Mount Gilboa we read, "Saul and Jonathan were lovely and pleasant in their lives, and in their death they were not divided." Saul was brave, simple, self-denying, virtuous in social life, up to the Israelitish standard of virtue. He was no tyrant, and had the confidence of his people to the end. He was for the greater part of his reign strict in rendering and maintaining obedience to the Divine Law. From the absence of anything to the contrary, and from the deep attachment of a large portion of Israel to his house, though only very feebly represented, we may conclude that he was acknowledged and loved as a good father and a good king. His sons were true to him to the last, even to death; and for seven years and six months, though David was anointed king over Judah in Hebron, Israel clung to the house of Saul, and only at the end of that time did David become king over the whole land.

These observations are, however, not only true in relation to Saul, but they suggest reflections of great importance to us all. We are apt roughly to class mankind into good and bad. We often forget that characters are blended of varied materials in every kind of proportion. The good are seldom so good as to have no fault of any kind; the bad are seldom so bad as to have no redeeming quality. Besides, there is variety in good as there is variety in trees. All trees are not olives, or vines, or figs, though the fruits of all these are good, some for one valuable quality, and some for another. Of bad trees all are not bad alike; some bear one kind of poisonous juice or mischievous thorn, and some another. So is it with men. And from this circumstance a frequent cause of self-deception is, that a man overlooks a very grievous fault in himself, because it is not the fault which is manifest in a notorious neighbour or a troublesome acquaintance.

All men are prone to evil, but all are not prone to the same evils. John seems to have had no propensity to push himself forward before his Lord, which was the weakness of Peter; neither of them seemed to have been troubled with avarice, which was the besetting sin of Judas. The Pharisee in the temple gave thanks to God that he was not as other men, not even as the publican; yet it was manifest he was self-righteous, sanctimonious and boastful.

A covetous man will give himself credit that no one can charge him with disorderly habits, of which he only grudges the expense. A prodigal will often glorify himself because he is not a miser. A steady man of business will deem himself faultless, or not seriously wrong, although a bitter temper may be the secret curse of home. Thousands will give themselves credit for not giving way to drunkenness, to which they have little proneness and therefore slight temptation, who are nevertheless, in other respects, grievously forgetful of the Lord, and grievously unjust, unkind, and offensive to their fellow-men. We are faithful to our Heavenly Father, not in proportion to the smoothness of our demeanour as to those sins to which we have slight tendencies, and are never deeply tried, but in proportion to our resistance to evils when our natural inclinations are strong, and our trials severe. The true Christian is one who places himself under the light of heaven, not that he may notice the defects of others, but that he may see his own. He gives himself no quarter, but condemns his shortcomings and his evils, and prays to the Lord constantly for help against them. He treads upon the lion and the asp, the young lion and the dragon in himself. He is filled with a humble fear of himself, and always acts in the spirit of the words:

> "Thou tread'st upon deceitful ground;
> Perils and snares beset thee round:
> Beware of all! guard every part!
> But most the traitor in thy heart!"

He will not repeat the words, "Lord, have mercy upon us, miserable sinners," and then be surprised and indignant if any one charges him with a fault. He knows he has sins; he seeks honestly to see them in the light of truth, and to struggle against them at all times, but especially when he is strongly tempted to commit them. Then by the help of the Lord Jesus, the Divine Saviour, he obtains victories, and finally can bless his Divine Helper that the sinful propensity has been succeeded by a loathing of what he used to love, by strength where he was weak; he has fought again and again the good fight, and the Lord has given unto him "beauty for ashes, the oil of joy for mourning, the garment of praise for the spirit of heaviness."

How different would it have been with Saul if he had thus been faithful. If he had simply obeyed the Lord's command by the mouth of Samuel and rooted out the Amalekites, instead of picking and choosing, and thinking it would be as well to spare the king, he would never have fallen from his crown and dignity, and sunk faint and weary on the field of Gilboa, to receive the last thrust from the hands of an Amalekite. "Lord Jesus, what wouldst thou have me to do?" is the language of faithful obedience, and when we see the right, with loving earnestness we should obey. "What doth the Lord thy God require of thee, but to do justly, love mercy, and walk humbly with thy God?" Saul failed from a vacillating, hesitating, imperfect obedience. The real Christian spirit is to say from love and faith with the apostle Paul, "Circumcision is nothing, and uncircumcision is nothing, but keeping the commandments of God." Had Saul done this, heaven would not have been closed against him, he would not have had to fly before his enemies and sunk down to die, while Philistia triumphed over him, and the shield of the mighty was vilely cast away.

Saul's other fault, envy, was also a very grievous one. He was jealous of David, even when the young hero had freed the whole army from the boastful wrath of the giant of Philistia. In the triumphal procession the women played their tabrets and sang, "Saul hath slain his thousands, and David his ten thousands," which was perfectly true; for although Saul had watched over and preserved the host, yet had David really been blest by Divine Providence to achieve the victory. But "Saul was very wroth, and the saying displeased him, and he said, They have ascribed unto David ten thousands, and to me they have ascribed but thousands; and what can he have more but the kingdom? And Saul eyed David from that day and forward." Although David had conferred the greatest possible benefit upon both king and kingdom, and in every charge committed to him behaved justly, wisely, and modestly, yet the envy of Saul was busy, first secretly contriving against his life, and afterwards openly assailing him and hunting him over the land as if he were a wild beast, instead of being his own son-in-law, and the country's best and most capable friend.

Such is the character of envy. It tortures its possessor with gall, distilled drop by drop, and corroding with a constant pain all that is valuable in the soul. It is ever maligning the object of its hate. It sees everything from malice. When others are rejoicing, it is gnawing itself with anguish. It is the opposite of that charity which envieth not, and is not puffed up. It is a mental jaundice, which discolours all it looks upon, and forms in the breast of its possessor a pandemonium in which self-torture, and the desire to torture others are incessantly at work.

How wonderful it is that, for such a thing as this, a man will often, as Saul did, forfeit his peace, his wellbeing, even his life precisely as, in ancient times, all was offered up to Moloch. Yet so it is. Lord, save us from this horrid idol, and give us that holy love derived from love to Thee, which will animate us always with the desire to bless others, which will even return good for evil, and rejoice over all the gifts Thou bestowest on all Thy children, as much as if they were bestowed on us, delighting in the joy around, and saying, "We know that we have passed from death to life, because we love the brethren." Give us grace, Lord Jesus, to think less and less of ourselves, and feel that whatever good we have or whatever we are, it is by Thy mercy, and not by our merit. "Blessed are the poor in spirit; for theirs is the kingdom of heaven."

Having considered the individual character of Saul, and such reflections as appeared to arise out of that consideration, let us now turn to his representative character. We need not dwell upon the fact that, in preparing our souls for heaven, we have all to become kings and priests (Rev. i. 6). They who receive abundance of grace and the gift of righteousness shall reign in life by One, Jesus Christ (Rom. v. 17). The little kingdom of the soul has to be brought into order and governed by the spirit of religion derived from the Word of God. But religion at first is only external with us, it is the kingdom of Saul. It is a great advance upon the loose condition in which no virtuous principle governs us, but it has serious defects. These defects are represented by the failings of Saul. We are earnest, it may be, but there is much of self mixed up with our religion while it is in this external state. The disciples of the Lord before the day of Pentecost were just of this character: they were modified, but they were not really converted. Hence, what disputings they had about who should be the greatest; how often their faith failed, and how completely they were disappointed when the Saviour's crucifixion extinguished all hope of a grand earthly kingdom in which they would be lords and chiefs. If it were not for the goodness of the Most High condescending to take us at first just as we are, it would be impossible for any man to be saved at all. By nature, man is a mass of evil, with seeds of good, it is true, but with evil so organized in his spiritual body that in Scripture it is often called a body of sin, a body of death, a vile body. Yet the Lord takes a man as he is, allows him to come influenced by hope of reward and fear of everlasting punishment, and makes him one of his hired servants. Far better it is, indeed, for a man to be a hired servant of the Best of beings, than a bond-slave of hell. The hired servants of our Heavenly Father have bread enough and to spare. Yet this is the lowest state of religion—it is the Saul-state. It has its usefulness for a time, and is indispensable for the early period of religious life; but as the kingdom of the Lord advances in the soul, the David-state must come, and Saul must die.

The Jewish religion at its best was represented by Saul; it was a religion of the letter and of reward. The Christian religion is properly a religion of the spirit, in which the Lord seeks for men to worship Him in spirit and in truth, not for reward but for purity and truth. The LOVE OF THE TRUTH is the proper Christian motive. The apostle complains of some because they received not the love of the truth, that they might be saved (2 Thess. ii. 10). As the love of truth leads the soul to enter more deeply into angelic graces, truths become loved for their own sakes; they are seen and felt to be pearls of great price. The spirit and life of the Word are now the treasures which are sought for their own sakes. Reward as a motive becomes odious, the Lord Himself is followed as the Way, the Truth, and the Life, and the possession of internal treasures the all-sufficient reward. Now it is this revolution of state in the soul which is meant by the death of Saul, and the advent of David to the throne. Jesus as seen outwardly, the rewarder, gives place to Jesus as seen inwardly, the enlightener, the imparter of spiritual gifts, the author and bestower of a present heaven.

To represent this entire change in the soul, Saul fell down and died at Mount Gilboa, for the name Gilboa signifies *the revolution of inquiry*. In the Saul-state, there is little inquiry, the soul is satisfied with little; but in the David-state, the soul hungers and thirsts after righteousness, and first learns what it is to be filled. That Saul was slain by the Philistines will not be difficult to understand when we bear in mind that the Philistines represent such as are in some knowledge of religion, and believe it to be enough to depend upon faith in the few things they know, and which they declare to be sufficient for salvation. The Philistines are called uncircumcised, because they represent those whose heads are somewhat engaged about heavenly things, but who declare that the heart cannot be purified, and that it is not necessary to try, there is a better way. The Philistines were very quarrelsome, they were ever attacking. Those of the true Philistine class now are very disputatious, very zealous, very bitter, and very selfish. There is an outside of religion, but the heart and life receive very secondary attention, and the spirit of charity is almost entirely absent.

The Philistines make Saul die, because they shew that essentially his state is the same as theirs. The external Christian, though he acknowledges he ought to obey the Lord Jesus in all things, is so weak, and so often fails, that his state and the Philistine state are very nearly alike, with the exception that the Philistine does not profess to care for charity and a good life as essentials of salvation, and the true Israelite in heart does. The attack of the Philistines represented a severe temptation in the Christian soul, in which its defects are clearly and strongly manifested. The bitter thoughts which pain and distress the mind in such a condition of anguish are the arrows which hit Saul and sorely wounded him.

The death of Saul and his three sons represents a perception of the inadequate character of the whole state. A feeling of condemnation presses with agony before us; we condemn ourselves, we reject ourselves; our whole state, our faith, our love, our obedience, seem little better than self in a disguise. We see the Word condemns such a state as ours has been. This is like taking the sword and falling upon it. We border on despair, the anguish of the soul is awful. We pour out our sorrow, we are in darkness and see no light. We cry, Enter not into judgment with thy servant, for in Thy sight shall no man living be justified; for the enemy hath persecuted my soul; he hath smitten my life down to the ground; he hath made me to dwell in darkness, as those that have been long dead.

When the surging of temptation is at its height, and the anguish so bitter, the spirit dies as it were in the soul, it seems as if all its efforts had been without any saving efficacy. The Philistines triumph and deride: "This is the man who declared we must keep God's commandments; and see what it has all come to! See how he has fallen; see how hopeless he is, how prostrate, how sunk!" They cut off Saul's head; that is, they declared there was neither intelligence, sense, nor power in such a state. The severe depression in which he was, shewed the utter fallacy of all effort to walk according to God's holy will. It was published in the house of their idols; that is, it was exultingly proclaimed to be a confirmation of their fallacies, a triumph for their delusions, as the Pharisees thought when the Saviour was crucified. But the steps of a good man are ordered by the Lord, and He delighteth in his way. Though he fall, he shall not be utterly cast down, for the Lord upholdeth him with his hand. Jesus was crucified, but He rose glorified. Saul died, but David took his place. External religion expires; but internal religion rises, conquers the Philistines completely, and reigns. They put Saul's armour in the temple of Ashtaroth, the moon-goddess, and fastened his body to the wall of Bethshan. Bethshan was about six miles from Gilboa, and its name signifies the house of the tooth, or the sharp rock. The significance of this bestowal of Saul's armour and his body, it is not difficult to perceive. When a good man is dejected in temptation the Philistines regard it as a tribute to their idol of faith alone, the moon-goddess. The moon is the symbol of faith, and when made an idol it represents faith alone, faith not with love and good works, but a substitute for them.

The men of Jabesh-Gilead came and took away the bodies, and buried them respectfully under a tree. They remembered how Saul had saved them in his early days (1 Sam. xi.). Jabesh Gilead was outside the Jordan, a part of Manasseh. The name signifies the *mourners of the covenant*, and they represent such as know and feel the immense difference between those who live and labour for heaven, though they stumble, and those who make it a dogma that struggling with sins has no saving efficacy at all. These mourn, but they are comforted. They mournfully bury Saul, then hopefully turn to David. They rise above the letter of religion, and pass now for ever to its spirit and its life.

SERMON XVII.

DAVID MADE KING AT HEBRON.

"And his men that were with him did David bring up, every man with his household: and they dwelt in the cities of Hebron.
"And the men of Judah came, and there they anointed David king over the house of Judah. And they told David, saying, That the men of Jabesh-gilead were they that buried Saul."—2 SAM. ii. 3, 4.

IN the midst of the mountains of Judah, surrounded by magnificent scenery and by fertile lands, about eighteen miles from Jerusalem, is the ancient city of Hebron. Poor as this city is now, perhaps no spot in the world is more distinguished for its associations, than is this old capital of Judah. It is said to have been built before Zoan, the capital of Lower Egypt (Num. xiii. 22). It was in the neighbourhood of Hebron that Abraham, Isaac and Jacob chiefly lived; and there is the cave of Machpelah, where their remains were buried, and where their tombs are preserved and jealously guarded even to the present day.

The country is dotted with ruined towns, which had been famous in their days of vigour, and where successive churches had flourished and decayed. About ten miles from Hebron was Debir, whose name signifies "the Oracle," and whose still earlier name, Kirjath-Sepher, meant the METROPOLIS OF THE BOOK, intimating in a most significant manner that it had been the centre of a former divine revelation. Right and left of Hebron, before and behind, were rich slopes covered with vineyards and oliveyards, fields of corn and magnificent prospects, all forming a rich reminder of that heavenly Father and Friend, from whom descend all the glories of earth, as well as all the perfections of heaven.

The first time Hebron is mentioned in the Word is in the history of Abraham (Gen. xxiii. 2). It is there called Kirjath-Arba, or the chief city of Arba; for Kirjath means metropolis or chief city. Arba is described as the father of a race of giants, the Anakim (Josh. xiv. 15; xxi. 11). The inhabitants seem to have been very kind and gentle in the time of Abraham; afterwards they partook of the corruption of the Canaanites in general, and, being strongly intrenched, they presented a formidable obstacle to Joshua when he was completing the settlement of the Promised Land. He gave it into the hands of the noble Caleb, who drove out the three sons of Anak, and with the assistance of the brave Othniel, secured for the tribe of Judah not only Hebron, but also Kirjath-Sepher, with its highly valued upper and lower springs of water (Josh. xv. 13-19).

Hebron, then, rich in its sacred recollections, rich in its prospects and productions, rich in being the very centre, the very metropolis, of the great tribe of Judah, became the seat of David's sovereignty; and for seven years and a half his rule extended but little beyond.

In its early associations, in its subsequent possession by giants, and in its adoption of David for its king, Hebron was the representative of the centre of the church among the Jews when the Lord Jesus came into the world, and their becoming the nucleus of the new, the Christian Church. In an individual soul, Hebron, whose name signifies *friendship*, represents the good dispositions implanted in our voluntary nature, their enslavement to lusts for a time, and their ultimate reception of the Lord as king within, although there is much unsubdued and unsanctified in us, which can only gradually be brought into the order of heaven.

The centre, the best part of a church, in the sight of God, is often very different from the chief part as it would appear in the sight of men. The humble, the pure in heart, the good and the true, whether among the poor or the rich, are the centre of the Church in the sight of the Lord. "The Lord seeth not as man seeth: for man looketh on the outward appearance, but the Lord looketh on the heart" (1 Sam. xvi. 7). Those genuine and sincere souls who had been waiting for deliverance by a coming Saviour were such as Anna the prophetess, Simeon, the parents of John the Baptist, Nathanael, Zaccheus, Joseph of Arimathea, and the disciples of the Redeemer generally. These felt that Jesus, the divine David, was their true king, and they exalted Him and enthroned Him in their hearts. They were Jews spiritually as well as naturally, and they made Him King of Judah in Hebron.

To be king of this spiritual kingdom the Lord Jesus came into the world. Hence, when Pilate demanded of Him, Art thou a king then? "Jesus answered, Thou sayest that I am a king. To this end was I born, and for this cause came I into the world, that I should bear witness unto the truth. Every one that is of the truth heareth my voice" (John xviii. 37). We know that He was not a literal king; no earthly diadem encircled His brow, no earthly sceptre was the symbol of His royalty. He came, however, to be the King of the wise and the good. And this kingdom was far more extensive and enduring than the kingdom of any earthly monarch. It is a kingdom embracing heaven as well as earth: it is everlasting; for truth and goodness, the bases of this kingdom, never perish, and have no limits either of time or space. They take in all worlds and all ages. He who is King in these respects, is King of kings, and Lord of lords. David, then, crowned king at Hebron, was the type of Jesus as Divine Truth, enthroned in the hearts of angels and men. It was that which He Himself announced, when He declared, "All power is given unto me, in heaven and on earth" (Matt. xxviii. 18).

This Kingship of the great Redeemer forms a prominent feature in all the prophecies respecting Him, and is only compatible with His being Divine Wisdom in human form, God Himself incarnate, and thus justly the Supreme Ruler of the wise and the good. The Jews expected their Messiah to be a king, but a king with the pomp, the power, the trappings of earthly splendour. It is true that He was to be a king; but a king with attributes truly divine, not encumbered with things so poor as those. An earthly monarch passes by in grand parade, and is greeted by the acclamations of the multitude; but ere the roar of applause dies away, the sneer of envy shows how superficial it all was. The hosannas of to-day are often turned into the "Crucify Him" of to-morrow. But when Wisdom becomes King of the hearts of the truly humble, the penitent, the spiritual, that is a kingdom that lives and grows and blesses for ever. This was the kingdom of the Lord Jesus. This was meant by David, in the representative Israel, becoming King at Hebron.

When we take this interior view of the Lord's kingdom, the grand terms of the prophecies can be truly understood. Thus, when Isaiah has proclaimed the future Redeemer to be the Child once born, the Son once given, the Mighty God, the Everlasting Father, and the Prince of Peace, he adds, "Of the increase of His government and peace there shall be NO END: upon the throne of DAVID, and upon His kingdom, to order it, and to establish it with judgment and with justice from henceforth, even for ever" (Isa. ix. 7). How plain is it that the throne of David which was in Jesus to exist for ever was the throne of justice and judgment, or goodness and truth, which are everlasting. In Jeremiah we have the same grand lesson. "Behold, the days come, saith the Lord, that I will raise unto David a righteous Branch, and a King shall reign and prosper: and shall execute judgment and justice in the earth. In His days Judah shall be saved, and Israel shall dwell safely; and this is His name whereby He shall be called, THE LORD (OR, JEHOVAH) OUR RIGHTEOUSNESS" (Jer. xxiii. 5, 6). Viewed as an outward fulfilment of this sublime prophecy, nothing could be more unlike than the life of the Lord Jesus; but regarded in its spirit, what fulfilment more precise can be thought of, than that reign of the Lord in the hearts first of a few, then of an increasing number, in nation after nation, in age after age, of those who are truly Judah, because Jews inwardly, as the apostle Paul says, and truly Israel, in whose hearts are no guile, and whom He saves and governs because He is Jehovah our Righteousness. This reign will never cease. It will ebb and flow; but through ages and dispensations it will widen and deepen and spread, until one Lord shall be king over all the earth. "In that day there shall be one Lord (Jehovah), and His name One" (Zech. xiv. 9).

> "Till o'er our ransomed nature,
> The Lamb for sinners slain,
> Redeemer, King, Creator,
> On earth shall fully reign."

The vicissitudes of earth will all conspire to bring in that great consummation of which it is written, "The seventh angel sounded; and there were great voices in heaven, saying, The kingdoms of this world are become the kingdoms of our Lord, and of His Christ; and He shall reign for ever and ever" (Rev. xi. 15).

But Hebron, and David's entering upon His kingdom there, form an equally suggestive theme if we regard it as an emblem of the heart, and of the Spirit of the Lord Jesus acquiring its inner sovereignty therein. Hebron in its early days will represent the heart, especially as to the good the Lord implants there, and which is so beautiful and attractive in the days of childhood. Hebron was said to be built before Zoan in Egypt. Before there is any science in the mind, there are loving emotions, traits of heaven, smiles of sweetest tenderness, embraces in which soft arms entwine around our necks, soft fingers touch us, and holy gleams from the glistening eyes speak of innocence and happy joys within. The Saviour said, "Of such is the kingdom of heaven."

Heaven lies about us in our infancy, and certainly it lies very deeply and very sweetly within us. "Their angels do always behold the face of my Father in the heavens" (Matt. xviii. 10). As we grow in stature, however, we often decline in innocence. Other thoughts and impulses which belong to a lower grade of our nature, the carnal part, derived from our human ancestry and depraved by human faults, shew themselves. The coarse and corrupt ways of the world around us call out in us states of evil, and habits very different from the sweet purity of childhood. The giddy girl, and the rough boy, shew that the Hebron within is not what it once was. Three giants now live there, sons of Anak, and they have strongly entrenched themselves (Josh. xv. 14). Only by a grand struggle can they be driven out. These three giants are, the LUST OF THE FLESH (*polluted pleasure*), the LUST OF THE EYES (the love of show), and the PRIDE OF LIFE. They are hard to overcome, and many flinch from the struggle through cowardice. These monsters got in when they were little, but have now become great. They tyrannize over everything, and defile everything. Every one knows that they produce abundance of misery, but faint-hearted ones flinch from facing them. Yet without their destruction there can be no peace.

See what ruin POLLUTED PLEASURE has caused; what disease, what sorrow, what loss of character, what loss of health, what horrid experiences of body and soul, what insane follies are the inflictions of this giant who has long cursed Hebron with his vile presence. The myriads of drunkards are his work, the myriads of gluttons, the foul army of those who are the deadliest foes of the purities of home are all his followers. It is full time he should be cast out, with all belonging to him.

Then his brother, LUST OF THE EYES, is little better than he. What thousands have been ruined for vain show! The restless spirit of vanity, which is ever striving to deck itself out with some new gewgaw, and to procure a little more gilding, a little more finery, suffers integrity to be utterly lost, and the great aims of life utterly to fail before the tinsel of to-day. This senseless giant induces his poor victims to imagine they are exciting admiration by their silly expenditure, when they are only inducing sorrow in the judicious, and provoking sneers in such as are like themselves: sneers at their vanity in their elevation, and mockery at their ruin when they fall.

And lastly, PRIDE. He is an awful giant, the eldest son of the terrible Anak of self-love. What ruin has he not caused! Pride in the despot has cried "havock and let slip the dogs of war." What devastated lands and ruined cities, what burning houses, slaughtered brothers, husbands, and fathers, abused maidens, sisters, mothers, mangled and mutilated bodies, and brutalized minds! These are thy works, O Pride. Who should spare thee? Then see in the disdainful walk, the insolent haughty silence, the supercilious look, the bitter taunt, the insulting gibe, the factitious separations between the children of the same Heavenly Father induced by thee, the neglect of the humble, and the swelling jauntiness of the high; how thy gall embitters all the ways of private life, and makes the sweet intercourse of life, intended to multiply all our blessings, a constant struggling through thorns. With many, life is a long agony, mainly, O Pride, through thee. But Joshua has given orders that both thou and thy terrible brothers shall be cast out of Hebron. Down, down, all of you! Why should poor souls be vexed, harassed, cursed and destroyed by you any longer, either in time or in eternity?

The faint-hearted fear these giants, and are afraid they will never overcome them. But those who have true courage and trust in the Lord, are always victorious. These were represented by Caleb, who took Hebron, and drove out the giants. He and Joshua were the two faithful ones who were firm for the Lord and for right, when the timid spies disheartened the people by their discouraging report. To the brave Caleb, whose name signifies AS THE HEART, and who represents a firm affection in the heart for the Lord and for religion, it was given to take Hebron, and introduce into it peace and rest. He said to Joshua, "As yet I am as strong this day as I was in the day that Moses sent me: as my strength was then, even so is my strength now, for war, both to go out, and to come in. Now therefore give me this mountain, whereof the Lord spake in that day: for thou heardest in that day, how the Anakim were there, and that the cities were great and fenced: if so be the Lord will be with me, then I shall be able to drive them out, as the Lord said. Hebron therefore became the inheritance of Caleb the son of Jephunneh the Kenezite unto this day, because that he wholly followed the Lord God of Israel" (Josh. xiv. 11, 12, 14). If we were all single-hearted and courageous like Caleb, what mighty giants would fall before us! The sins of the heart are strong in our fears and timidity, much more than in any power of their own. Let a man resolve with the help of the Lord, that he will overcome the evil he hates, and persevere, and he will assuredly triumph, and that soon. The giants will fall and fade, and he will be astonished how soon. Oh how sad it is to see a man bewailing his sin, despising himself, and bemoaning himself, and going again, as if drawn by a cart rope, to the old lust and the old misery. What a terrible hold an evil has, when a man is ashamed of himself, and feels he is ruining himself, and yet, as if drawn by a strong magnet, goes to the same unhappy slavery again.

> "Oh, where's the slave so lowly,
> Bound fast by chains unholy,
> Who, could he burst
> His chains at first,
> Would pine beneath them slowly?"

If we were all true Calebs, and acted from religion in the heart, our exulting faith would cheerfully exclaim, "I can do all things through Christ that strengtheneth me" (Phil. iv. 13). Our giants would soon perish, and the Hebron of our hearts would be taken possession of first by Caleb and his family, or in other words by the desire to be conformed to the Lord, and then by the Lord Himself, our Divine David, coming to be King at Hebron.

Caleb was not satisfied with taking Hebron; he determined also to take Kirjath Sepher, the neighbouring city, whose name signifies the Metropolis of the Book. He acquired it by the aid of the brave Othniel, to whom he gave his daughter in marriage, and as a dowry the upper and lower springs. The taking of the city of Kirjath Sepher, represents the removal of the Word from those who had made it of none effect, to be honoured, loved, and obeyed by those who regarded it as abounding with truths for heart and life, the upper and the nether springs. They who have expelled giant lusts from the heart, by the power of true love for God and their neighbour, go to the Word with earnest yearning, and draw from it with joy holy water as from the wells of salvation (Isa. xii. 3). The waters of life from the upper springs refresh and purify the inner man: the waters of life from the lower springs wash the feet of the soul, and make the daily conduct pure. Stimulated and gladdened by the sacred and pellucid waters of the sanctuary, they run and are not weary, they walk and never faint (Isa xl. 31).

The blessing of David being anointed king in Hebron, or,

in application to the progress of our regeneration, making the Lord the ruler of our inner man, is unspeakable. When religion has become embedded in the heart, and exists there as a fountain of hopes and aspirations, the heaven within begins to be felt, and becomes a focus of new powers and new joys. There may yet be many a conflict to reduce the outer man to order, but the power is there that can do it. David will need to stay seven years and six months at Hebron (ver. 11), or in other words, he must acquire a full sanctity of state in the inner man (signified by the seven years), and a full faith that by steady untiring labour the outer man will be regenerated also (for this is meant by the six months); and then he will become king over the whole land. We shall find still that in the outer man there is much sin working death; but we delight in the law of God after the inward man (Rom. vii. 22, 23). David is king in Hebron. What we would, often we cannot do; what we would not sometimes unhappily is done. When we would do good, evil is present with us; but we will neither despair nor cease our efforts, until the whole soul becomes the embodiment of virtues and thoughts of wisdom. We are cleansing the inside of the cup and the platter, and the outside will become clean also (Matt. xxiii. 26).

Our text adds, "They told David, saying, the men of Jabesh Gilead were they that buried Saul." The respectful burial of Saul signifies the respectful remembrance of the good of a former state. Saul had done good service, though his day of government was over. So is it with us in the progress of our regenerate life. We come into states of experience in which we discern how inadequate and how poor were the thoughts, sentiments, and affections of our early religious life. Yet they were everything to us then. We should bury them with a grateful confession of their worth, like the men of Jabesh Gilead. They buried the remains of Saul under an oak-tree; which, in spiritual things, represented the perception by the soul of the help the religion of the letter of the Word had been in our early childlike states. This is accompanied with sadness, which Jabesh signifies, but with gratitude. We enter on a new career, laying aside the former with the feeling:

> "He who has helped us hitherto,
> Will help us all our journey through:
> And give us daily cause to raise
> A new and grateful song of praise."

SERMON XVIII.

THE HOUSE OF DAVID WAXING STRONGER, AND THE HOUSE OF SAUL WEAKER.

"Now there was long war between the house of Saul and the house of David: but David waxed stronger and stronger, and the house of Saul waxed weaker and weaker."—2 SAM. iii. 1.

EVERYTHING changes by degrees. The spring glides into summer, the summer into autumn, the autumn into winter. This is done so gradually that it is difficult to say when the one ends and the other begins. So when the morning breaks, how slowly does darkness give way to dawn! Like a dissolving view the light gradually blends with shade, and the day emerges; but by such faint changes that all flows peacefully on, and nature sustains no shock. With the first faint streaks of light you hear the first chirps of the early birds, and these with the increase of day pour forth a livelier song; but only when the sun appears, in all its splendour, does the full gush of harmony salute the ear. It is so with all growth, natural and spiritual. By little and little does Divine Providence work out its benign operations, whether in robing the earth with beauty, or in restoring and regenerating the soul. It is "first the blade, then the ear, after that the full corn in the ear" (Mark iv. 28). What amazing love there is in this! what adorable wisdom! A man to whom religion is yet a stranger, is little better than a savage, covered more or less completely with a superficial polish, and frequently disclosing the vicious nature underneath. For this unhallowed soul to become a full image and likeness of God, one who loves everything good and true purely for the sake of goodness and truth, what a vast change must be effected! All the aims of life need to be transformed. He must learn to love what he once hated, and hate what he once loved. Pride, power, fame, applause, pleasure, those deities which allure and attract the worldly, must cease to be objects of concern and attachment, and give place to humility, charity, piety, wisdom, and the love of use. How can it be done? By what strange and wonderful process can the fiend be transformed into the angel, the hell of a vile heart be changed into the heaven of a breast beating only with sentiments of purity, integrity and peace? With men this is impossible, but with God—God who desires the salvation of every one of His children—all things are possible. The gradual mode by which Divine mercy accomplishes this, is the subject treated of in the inner sense of that part of the Word which describes the warfare between the house of Saul and the house of David.

It will be well, however, at the outset, to consider the wonderful arrangement of the mind, by which the Lord has provided, in our fallen nature, for the regeneration of every soul which is not obstinately bent on rebellion. The lower animals have instincts which are their affections for objects proper to their nature; and they cannot go against them. Upon some of them a certain discipline in obedience to man can be induced; but this makes no radical change: and when the authority of their trainer is absent, the cultivation vanishes, and their own instincts invariably triumph. Their intellectual parts and their voluntary or will parts are indissolubly united. What they will and desire they must think and do. No real inward change is possible. The tiger, the wolf, the hawk, the shark, must lust for their prey. No conscience, no sense of right can be formed to check them. They are inevitably what they ever will be. They may be extirpated, but not changed. It is quite otherwise with man, and with every man. Even the idiot has the human part slumbering beneath his tangled and imperfect nervous system, preserved for the future. Man has, in his fallen voluntary part, impulses far more terrible than those of any wild beast; a "heart that is deceitful above all things, and desperately wicked." A beast of prey destroys for food: but the man who has not checked but pandered to his worst propensities will destroy for caprice, for malice, for sport, to glut a depraved imagination. Swine are by nature filthy; but there are men who blend the fiend and the swine together, and gorge themselves with brutality and impurity. Such horrid impulses are contained in the fallen heart, out of which are the ISSUES OF DEATH.

If the intellectual part of man had been closely joined with his voluntary part, as in animals, he never could have thought otherwise than he lusted. His mind would have been totally taken up with schemes to secure the gratification of his propensities; and he must invariably have gone, like the devil-possessed swine of old, headlong into the deep. But, with infinite mercy, and inscrutable skill, the Lord has provided for man's salvation. He has separated the intellect from the heart. We can learn the truth, and delight in its beauty and order, as if we had nothing in us that loved darkness rather than light. The imagination, the head in a man, may glow with sublime sentiments, while his habits, the result of his lower voluntary nature, are degraded below those of the beast. The higher part of his mind may be like a golden harp, often touched by angelic fingers, and filling the air with music fresh from heaven; while the real man, the voluntary and actual conduct-making man, is mean, sordid, heartless, brutal. The whole being in that case is like those fabled creatures of old, the centaurs, half-man, half-beast, and probably to convey this truth the ancients so pictured, sculptured and described them. But how great is the mercy, that to the human beast is adjoined the man, and that the man may not only acquire the mastery, but transform the beast into a man! In nature there are many marvellous changes; the ugly seed becomes a glorious flower, the grub becomes a moth, the caterpillar a butterfly: but these are faint and shadowy transformations compared to that most wonderful one in which the world-in-ruins of the human soul, full of horrid monsters, is changed by the wonder-working power of the merciful Saviour, into a new heaven and a new earth, full of celestial affections, thoughts and virtues; the desert made like Eden, and the wilderness like the garden of God, with an angel to tenant and enjoy it.

The first part of this divine operation is the implantation of truth into the memory. The memory is a wonderful storehouse, capable of containing great stores, and into this treasure-house, among other knowledge, can be received the knowledge of the Word of God. At first it is little prized; but by circumstances and the leadings of Divine Providence the intellect is awakened. The rational faculty is more or less stirred up. Immortality, and man's relations to his Maker, and his future life, startle and awaken him. Unless he resist obstinately, he begins to feel the vast concerns of everlasting life, and he cries, "What must I do to be saved?" The Spirit of the Lord Jesus visits him, as He visited the world, and new hopes dawn within him. He feels himself a lost sheep, but the Good Shepherd has come, and carries him home rejoicing. He feels himself a prodigal; but his Father has seen his penitence, and his yearning to return, and while he is yet very far off, has run and fallen on his neck and kissed him. He who was lost is found; he who was dead is alive again. He is placed under government now; but it is the government of Saul, or the religion of the letter of the Word. He is yet only a child in divine things, and he thinks as a child, and speaks as a child. His is the religion of fear, but it is also the religion of hope. He has repented earnestly, and changed his conduct, and saved his soul alive. He obeys the law of God from the spirit of obedience. "Thus saith the Lord" is enough for him. He shuns whatever he understands to be forbidden; but he does not understand very much. He delights in being saved, and in anticipating the glories of heaven; but he has not much conception of heaven except as a grand reward, or of hell except as a horrible and everlasting punishment.

There is much of self mixed with this state; much of self-complacency and self-conceit. Although there is often zeal and joy connected with it, there is not much deep insight either into the soul or into divine things. The law is a burden; and at times a burden very grievous to be borne. When the experience of life brings severe trials, when the revealings of the soul unfold evil impulses which were mercifully concealed from view at first, the joyous confidence felt in days gone by becomes dim, and the soul sad. Various tossings and troubles come, a sense of defects, sins of thought and feeling, and gradually that rigid sense of obedience connected with the religion of fear becomes less firm and vigorous, and revelations are made of the worthlessness of outward obedience, if defiled by self-righteousness and destitute of love. There are glimpses now and then of a higher state, of a religion of the spirit of the Word, of light and of pure affection; but this only at fitful intervals, like the appearances of David in the history of Saul. His religion of exact observance, the Christian begins to learn, is of no value if it does not yield him heavenly light and heavenly charity. God is not a God of terror, but of light and love. He should not obey from fear, but from perceiving that the Lord's commandments are essentially right, are the laws of happiness, and therefore the laws of heaven. The spirit of the Word grows upon him, and the letter becomes more and more subordinate. He comes into the delight of truth, and he sees the Lord Jesus as the Way, the Truth, and the Life. There is awakened in him quite a- new series of heavenly states, quickening a thousand affections that lay dormant before, and giving him meat to eat, of which before he knew not.

This is the state in which David reigns; and as Divine Truth becomes more and more effulgent in the soul, the house of David becomes stronger and stronger, and the house of Saul, or the external and imperfect condition of religion, becomes weaker and weaker. The religion of fear must precede, for the wicked man can form little conception indeed of the blessedness of being true and being good. He must fear, when he cannot restrain himself except from dread of the eternal consequences of disobedience; but happy is it when the time shall come that perfect love will cast out fear. The house of Saul will become weaker and weaker, and the house of David will become stronger and stronger.

When we are in the external states of our early religion, the letter of the Bible is everything. If we have heard of the spirit, it has been as of something distant, vague, and mysterious. We must have everything literal, nothing but the letter. We know there are many things hard to comprehend, but we would rather take everything as we find it, and ask no questions. We have a vague sort of notion that the Lord will be better pleased if we take it unhesitatingly, although we may take it wrongly. But when the Spirit of the Gospel opens in us, we become "merchantmen seeking goodly pearls" (Matt. xiii. 45). We prize the Word not less, but more. We dig deep and find the jewels. We view the letter as the lowest step of the ladder to heaven, which enables us to place our feet on another and another. We hunger and thirst after righteousness. We already see a bright heaven of delight in the grand truths which, like streams from the light of the blessed, teach us to think as angels think, and love the truths of heaven for their own dear sakes. Thus, the house of Saul waxes weaker and weaker, and the house of David waxes stronger and stronger.

In the days of our Saul-state, when our duties were brought before us, we thought only of the letter of the law; and if we had done no wrong against that, many a bitter taunt and many an inconsiderate act escaped us. We were strong for our sect, but weak for our loving-kindness. We let the faults or failings of others form often the subjects of conversation: we were more ready to blame than to palliate or to excuse. We were hard, like Saul. Now, however, when the Spirit of the Lord Jesus has entered into us, we look very strictly upon our own shortcomings, but very tenderly on the weaknesses of others. We hope for the best. "Charity never faileth." We love and labour on. We look at the spirit that pervades the acts of others, and accept a well-meant endeavour, even if the performance has been much short of what might have been wished. For ourselves we do not ask what the letter commands that we should do, but what the spirit and intention of the Divine Law require; for we see that he who knows to do good, and has the talent, and doeth it not, to him it is sin. In this respect the house of Saul waxeth weaker and weaker, and the house of David waxeth stronger and stronger.

In the Saul-state we dread evil, but it has for us a strong attraction. If sin had been allowed, it would have been our delight. There is a secret yearning for the forbidden fruit, though we restrain ourselves with a strong hand and many a struggling prayer. The tradesman is strongly induced to think it would be useful to lie; but conscience forbids. To take what belongs to another, seems to many a greedy soul delightful if he durst. There are evils called pleasant sins, which stir the natural man with strangely tempting influences, although the strong redeeming power of truth from the Saviour binds and restrains the fiend within. In this sense there is a skeleton in every house, a weak place in every mind. But when the David-state, when the spirit of religion has begun, sin comes to be more and more regarded as detestable in itself. We come to regard dishonesty in word or deed as the necessary destroyer of confidence, the corrupter of mind and life, the treacherous betrayer of commerce, the murderer of sympathy, the bane of peace. We find growing in ourselves a loathing of impurity in all its phases. We know it is forbidden, but we begin to see and to feel why it is forbidden. We see the impure man sinking lower and lower into a defiled abyss tainting his whole soul, destroying all the sweet sympathies, delicacies, purities, and sanctities of higher humanity, and filling soul and body with curse and corruption. We begin faintly to see sin as the Lord sees it, and to groan, as the apostle did, "Who shall deliver me from the body of this death?" (Rom. vii. 24.) It is not the punishment we fear, now; but the iniquity itself. We now dread not that we shall be found out in our wrong-doing; but we dread to do wrong. We do not complain that perhaps the Lord will condemn us after all; but we lament that we do not love Him enough, that we are ever cold to Him who loads us with benefits. We want to bless Him, who has always blessed us; to praise Him with our whole being. A holy tenderness comes over us, a gush of love, a perception of ever-increasing splendour in our communion with the Lord. His face shines as the sun shining in its strength; and His garments are white as the light. The old shades are dying away, the new splendours are ever brightening. "The house of Saul is becoming weaker and weaker, the house of David waxing stronger and stronger."

This dying and rising again was strongly exemplified in the case of Paul. "I die," he said, "daily." He was also rising daily. Yet, though he wrote his epistle to the Romans 25 years after his conversion, he still describes the struggle within him of two classes of feelings and sentiments. "I find then," he says, "a law, that, when I would do good, EVIL IS PRESENT with me. For I delight in the law of God after the inward man: but I see another law in my members warring against the law of my mind, and bringing me into captivity to the law of sin which is in my members. . . . So then with the (higher) mind I myself serve the law of God; but with the flesh (the lower mind) the law of sin" (Rom. vii. 21-23). This is precisely the war between Saul and David. Four years later, when he wrote to the Philippians, we find still the same struggle not yet completed. "I count all things but loss for the excellency of the knowledge of Christ Jesus my Lord: for whom I have suffered the loss of all things, and do count them but dung, that I may win Christ, and be found in Him, not having mine own righteousness, which is of the law, but that which is through the faith of Christ, the righteousness which is of God by faith: that I may know Him, and the power of His resurrection, and the fellowship of His sufferings, being made conformable to His death; if by any means I might attain unto the resurrection of the dead. Not as though I had already attained, either were already perfect. . . . Brethren, I count not myself to have apprehended; but this one thing I do, forgetting those things which are behind, and reaching forth unto those which are before, I press toward the mark for the prize of the high calling of God in Christ Jesus" (iv. 8-14). Here we have not only a description of the same struggle, and by struggle, progress; but also an intimation of the real cause of it. The interiors of the soul are in harmony and communion with heaven; the exterior or body of the soul, is a vile body, all tangled and disordered by sin, ugly and evil, full of "wounds and bruises and putrifying sores" (Isaiah i. 6). It is the change of this spiritual body—a change as great, or we may even say far greater, than the change of a natural body full of disease, saturated with leprous ulcers, into a renovated and lovely form, all joyous and beautiful, radiant with health and joy, which correctly illustrates the transformation which religion has to effect. Die unto sin, live unto righteousness. Glorious words! Change priceless, unspeakably great! By little and little the defilement disappears, and by little and little the angelic nature discloses its glorious beauty. The old man dies, and dies hard. His deeds, his dreams, and his lusts, by the wonder-working power of the Lord Jesus working within us, are subdued and removed; while the new man is put on, which after God and from God is created in righteousness and true holiness (Eph. iv. 22-24).

What, then, are the heavenly lessons we may gather from the teachings of our text concerning the long war of the house of Saul and the house of David? Are they not these? Firstly, The work of regeneration is vast, complicated, and momentous. It involves toils and triumphs, it requires faithfulness and perseverance; but the Lord is our Great Saviour and Helper; and if we are humble and obedient, He will transform us into the image of Himself. We may begin more or less suddenly, and having set out, we are on His side, and so far all safe. But only by walking on, and working steadily, do we enter into our grand inheritance thoroughly, and realize the heights and depths and blessings of the inner spiritual life. Secondly, Let us not be surprised if our progress occasionally appears slow. We know not the depth and the number of the ulcers in our spiritual being which need to be probed and healed. Through changes like the chilly days and the warm bright days of spring, through storm and sunshine, through pain and peace, the Divine work in us is achieved, and he who was blind and lame and leprous, is brought to the feet of Jesus, healed and lovely and in his right mind, a child of the King of kings, clothed with the garments of salvation. Lastly, Let us never tire, or lack faith and loving trust in the Lord Jesus. Confide in Him. He will finish His work. The fears and weaknesses of your early states, the dim gropings of your early days, and the shades of the letter of the Word, so needful to you then, may cling to you long; but the house of Saul will become weaker and weaker, and the house of David will become stronger and stronger, until He altogether reigns over you who said, "I am the Root and the Offspring of David, and the Bright and the Morning Star." Even so, come, Lord Jesus.

SERMON XIX.

THE STRONGHOLD OF THE JEBUSITES AT JERUSALEM TAKEN, AND TURNED INTO THE CITY OF DAVID.

"And the king and his men went to Jerusalem unto the Jebusites, the inhabitants of the land; which spake unto David, saying, Except thou take away the blind and the lame, thou shalt not come in hither: thinking, David cannot come in hither. Nevertheless David took the stronghold of Zion: the same is the city of David.
"And David said on that day, Whosoever getteth up to the gutter, and smiteth the Jebusites, and the lame and the blind, that are hated of David's soul, *he shall be chief and captain*. Wherefore they said, The blind and the lame shall not come into the house."—2 SAM. v. 6, 7, 8.

As soon as the conviction that there is a correspondence between the world of matter and the world of mind has been fully established in the soul, the universe around has acquired a new value, and the Word of the Lord a new and living glory. Every object is instructive as a symbol as well as a fact. The incidents of human life are tokens and illustrations of the workings of the world within us, and teem with wisdom. The changes of everyday life, the movements of the seasons, all the events which form history, reflect before the eyes of mankind important truths associated with our mental progress, and flash light from time to time over heart and home.

The historical parts of the Word are divinely arranged as illustrations of this grand principle. Of all of them we may truly say with the apostle, "Which things are an allegory" (Gal. iv. 24): and of none more clearly than of the striking circumstances related in our text: the taking of Jebus, and transforming it into the city of David. David had been king at Hebron, the chief city of the tribe of Judah, and the ancient capital of Canaan, for seven years and six months (ver. 5). He had reigned over the noblest of the tribes peacefully and happily, but the remainder of the land still rejected his sway. The Jebusites were so strongly posted, so firmly entrenched and fortified, that they treated with disdain the idea of David's being able to take possession of their city: they posted blind and lame men as defenders, and defied him to remove them. For seven years and a half David was not strong enough to make the attempt, but at length the time came when he could safely undertake the arduous work, and obtain the triumph reported in the words before us.

The partial conquest of Canaan represented the partial regeneration of the soul. Hebron was the ancient capital of the country; it had been the seat and centre of a former religion, and its name signified "amity" or "friendship." It was the type of that brotherly love or charity which is the very essence of religion. "We know that we have passed from death to life, because we love the brethren." For a person to become spiritually-minded, and of the Lord's church at all, he must open his heart to this spirit of charity. And thus David comes to reign at Hebron. An inner state of spiritual life is developed and held sacred as a holy thing within. Sacred sentiments are experienced and enjoyed, delight in worship is felt again and again; we feel an assurance that we have the Lord's blessing, and really love the divine will and the things of heaven. This state of heart becomes matured and perfected, and thus attains to the condition signified by seven years, and capable of making further advancement, signified by the half-year or six months.

When internal religion gets a footing in the soul, the gladdened heart hails it, welcomes it, and rejoices in it. For a while it looks but little beyond this great attainment: it knows there are conditions of family or business or social position that are not exactly what they ought to be, but these are little thought of. They are regarded as things which cannot be set right, and must be endured. They are our stronghold of the Jebusites, and we say David cannot come in hither. With some the stronghold of the Jebusites will be the fiery faults of temper, which are supposed to have been born with them, and must remain with them to their grave. With some it is a particular position in life which entails habits which religion cannot approve, and which they do not see their way to alter. By some a trade is pursued or a calling exercised which conscience condemns, but which is too lucrative to be set aside; on which they seem almost exclusively to depend, and without which, their future seems to be doubtful. These and many other phases of life, where change entails difficulties which seem to the anxious Christian to be insurmountable, are strongholds which it is thought cannot be overcome, and of which we say, "David cannot come in hither."

The Jebusites were so satisfied of the strength of their fortress, that they exhibited and paraded their weakness so far as to shew that many of their defenders were blind and lame. In ordinary cases, commanders rather make a show of strength greater than they possess, to deter and dishearten their assaillants by the appearance of great numbers or great ability in the defenders. The Jebusite troops were many of them blind and many lame, but David was challenged to get at them, and overcome them if he could. And it is said, these blind and lame were hated of David's soul. David represented the spirit of the Lord Jesus in us, disclosing our evils of various kinds, and resolutely inducing us to overcome them.

That David was a type of the Lord Jesus is very evident from the prophets, from the gospels, and from the teaching of the apostles. In Ezekiel, for instance, we read, "I will set up one shepherd over them, and He shall feed them, even my servant David; He shall feed them, and He shall be their shepherd. And I the Lord will be their God; and my servant David a prince among them" (Ezek. xxxiv. 23, 24). Those who regard the Lord Jesus as the One Grand Shepherd of His whole spiritual flock, will have no difficulty in accepting Him as represented here under the type of David. His Humanity is David, His interior Divinity is Jehovah, who would still be their God.

The words, "They pierced my hands and my feet;" again, "They parted my garments among them, and for my vesture they did cast lots;" and the cry of bitter suffering on the cross, "My God, my God, why hast thou forsaken me," are taken from the twenty-second Psalm. It is difficult to see how they could be applied to David himself, but to the Lord Jesus they are expressly applied in the Gospel, and in Him they were manifestly fulfilled. The apostle Peter quotes other Psalms, and especially a great portion of the sixteenth. After citing, among others, the words, "Thou wilt not leave my soul in hell (hades), neither wilt thou suffer thine Holy One to see corruption," he says expressly, "Men and brethren, let me freely speak unto you of the patriarch David, that he is both dead and buried, and his sepulchre is with us unto this day. Therefore being a prophet, and knowing that God had sworn with an oath to him, that of the fruit of his loins, according to the flesh, He would raise up CHRIST to sit upon his throne; he, seeing this before, spake of the resurrection of CHRIST, that his soul was not left in hades, neither his flesh did see corruption" (Acts ii. 27, 29-31). There is, then, abundant evidence that David was the type of our Lord as the Redeemer from the powers of darkness. He conquered the evil dominion as a whole, the serpent's head, in the days of His sojourn in the world, and he has now the keys of Hell and of Death (Rev. i. 18). He conquers sin in us, when he enables us to see, to fight against, and to overcome our various evils, and step by step to work out our salvation. "I give you power," He said to His disciples, and He says the same to every one of us, "to tread upon serpents and scorpions, and over all the power of the enemy, and nothing shall by any means hurt you" (Luke x. 18).

David, therefore, represents the Divine David, the spirit of the Lord Jesus when He has been born in us, and has acquired strength and settlement in our affections as our Lord, the King of our Israel, the source of purity, holiness, and blessing. For a considerable time after we have chosen the Lord Jesus for our inward king, there is a state of peace and quiet vouchsafed to us; we have much of interior consolation and heartfelt joy. A time comes, however, when some great department of our lives has divine light thrown over it, and we see it in many respects contrary to the Divine Will, and to the spirit of heaven. The King and His men, the Lord Jesus and His angels, draw near to us, and having an increase of light, and a fuller enjoyment of the atmosphere of heaven, the opposite states of falsity and evil are revealed to us.

We perceive the blind and the lame, which we have but slightly observed before, and we see how opposite they have been, and are, to the spirit of the Lord. The blind are those who are in false principles; the lame those who are more or less in evil, and hence walk imperfectly in the way of truth. We are all blind in so far as we do not appreciate divine truth in its beauty, worth, and practical character.

> "O blind to truth, and God's whole scheme below,
> Who fancy bliss to vice, to virtue woe."

Some, however, are blind from ignorance and want of reflection, not from an obstinate preference to wickedness. Others love darkness rather than light, because their deeds are evil. The blind and the lame in our text occur in that order to indicate probably that the imperfections of those who can be regenerated, and who can be transferred from the side of evil into the kingdom of the Lord, arise from insufficiency of light.

They do not see fully, and in its true character, the wrong in which they are. They are blind, and therefore lame. Let their eyes be opened to a clear perception of the nefarious character of what they do, and they are astonished at themselves, and rise to a higher life. Many pursue trades which are injurious to the community; many carry on, in the businesses in which they are engaged, practices which are vicious and unjust, but which they justify because they are commonly done. Many enter upon the most solemn relations of life from external considerations alone: they readily contract marriage with the worthless, if only there be outward attractions or plenty of money, and thus lame their progress and their peace in this world, and seriously imperil their everlasting state. Some have habits of petty deception, of fashionable untruths, or of small hypocrisies to their children, and are only shocked at length when they find unhappily that small insincerities lead to large miseries. All these things are hated of David's soul, or in other words, are abominable in the sight of the Lord, because they are contrary to His purity and to His kingdom. "All His works are done in truth." "Justice and judgment are the habitation of His throne." "The Lord is righteous in all His ways, and holy in all His works."

Our faults are said to be hated of David's soul, when we discern their hateful character. We abhor them, and we abhor ourselves for the weaknesses by which we have suffered these evils so long to infest our souls. We say with the Psalmist, "Search me, O God, and know my heart: try me, and know my thoughts: and see if there be any wicked way in me, and lead me in the way everlasting." And when we recognise the baneful character of principles in which we have lived because they were the practice of our class, but which now manifest themselves to us in their true unworthy nature, we look up to the Lord and add, "Do not I hate them, O Lord, that hate Thee, and am not I grieved with those that rise up against Thee? I hate them with perfect hatred: I count them mine enemies." The inhabitants of the land said, "Except thou take away the blind and the lame, thou shalt not come in hither:" thinking David, cannot come in hither.

How often do we say we *cannot* do this or that: the secret cause being that WE WILL NOT. Our self-will desires not to be disturbed, or not to be disturbed now, and suggests that though certain practices are bad, though they are blind and lame, yet they cannot be altered or amended. What blindness can be greater than such an infatuation!—Not alter a state of things which we discern and admit to be wrong? why not? How can wrong be right? How can wrong lead to right? The Lord and His Providence are on the side of justice and virtue; and They will make the crooked straight, and the rough places plain, for those who love and who seek the good and the true. You must, you think, go on with a course that you condemn a little further. "Not yet, not yet. Wait a little longer." Oh throw away the flimsy pretext! That which you see to be wrong has already done mischief enough, and too much. Cast it away, ere it be too late. If slavery had been abolished in America fifty years ago, what blood and treasure, what sighs and tears, would have been saved! When we fully see an evil, the time to alter it has come. Spare it not. Hew it down as Samuel did Agag, rather than spare it as Saul did, to lose crown, kingdom, and life. But you think, perhaps, as the Jebusites said, "David cannot come in hither." The Lord cannot do this thing. Was ever anything so childish? The Lord, the Conqueror of all hell, cannot conquer this small matter in you! The Lord, the Sustainer of all worlds, cannot sustain you! Rather take up the language of the apostle, and say, "I can do all things through Christ that strengtheneth me." Depend upon it, the Lord has all power in heaven and on earth. Be faithful to Him, and fear nothing. Commit thy way unto the Lord: trust also in Him, and He shall bring it to pass: and He shall bring forth thy righteousness as the light, and thy judgment as the noon-day. But let us remark the reply of David, and gather the divine wisdom it is intended to convey.

Allow me, however, to direct your notice to the italics which compose a more than usually large portion of ver. 8, and which indicate that the translators felt considerable difficulty in the rendering. The meaning of the original is not that he who got up to the gutter should be chief and captain, but that *every one* should get up by the gutter, and get into the place at the back of the defenders, and thus obtain full possession. The gutter was no doubt a secret sluice, down which the drainage of the fortress descended. By discovering this covered and neglected passage, we may easily conceive how the defences might be turned, and the guards surprised and defeated. And when we suppose that some evil course of ours cannot be rectified, is it not that there is some impure and secret influence within us, that is at the bottom of the difficulty? We declare such and such things cannot be done. Why not? Because we idolize our money, and we think we should gain less, or we have some secret self-indulgence that lies in the background, and is like a gutter down which the impure influences of our hearts, as secret defiled streams, flow forth. The Lord, the Divine David, says, "let every one get up to the gutter." Explore in this thing your hidden desire, and see if it will bear the light. Oh "the heart is deceitful above all things and desperately wicked." But the Lord looks upon the heart. Do you look upon it also, and do not spare what is selfish and impure. Lay bare the secret sins of your soul, and dare to look upon yourself, as ere long you will be seen in the light of eternity. Wrestle with the principalities and powers within, which are opposed to the Lord. Thus smite your Jebusites, and the blind and the lame. Remember in this respect the words of the Lord, "I am not come to send peace upon earth, but a sword." Fight the good fight of faith, until you have overcome again and again, and you will be able often to say, while rejoicing in many a victory, "Blessed be the Lord my strength, which teacheth my hands to war, and my fingers to fight: my goodness, and my fortress; my high tower and my deliverer: my shield, and He in whom I trust; who subdueth my people under me" (Ps. cxliv. 1, 2).

The last portion of the text announces a proverb which arose in Israel from the circumstance of the blind and the lame having been derisively set up to insult and oppose David. "Wherefore they said, the blind and the lame shall not come into the house." When we consider heaven as represented by David's house, after he had got possession of Jebus, and turned it into the Zion of the Holy One of Israel, we shall not fail to perceive the spiritual meaning of the divine words before us. Blindness is a grievous loss. The glorious lights and beauties of the universe all shut out. The lovely hues of flowers, the expressive changes of the human face, all unperceived, and the magnificent panorama of the skies displayed around us in vain. One inestimable sense paralyzed, and grandeurs unutterable, all shut out. Such is the lot of the blind. But pitiable as bodily blindness is, mental blindness is worse. Life in the dark is, to be deprived of the consolations of heavenly wisdom. The bright gleams of divine truth pass by the soul that will not open its eyes. We can easily imagine that the condition of a blind person would be greatly aggravated if he laboured under the delusion that he was seeing all the while, and persisted in describing and acting upon everything wrongly. Yet with many of the mentally blind, this is actually the case. Wrong they call right, sweet they call bitter, darkness they call light, mystery they say is better than clearness. They stumble and hurt themselves again and again, but again go blundering on, until at last they fall finally, and are only of use as spectacles of warning. They were blind, but they obstinately said "we see," therefore their sin remained (John ix. 41). Yet it is an eternal truth, the blind do not come into the house. The Lord is light. Truth is light. Heaven is the land of light. They who love light, though they are dim at present, can be cured of their blindness, and will rejoice as the blind man in the Gospel did when he said, "One thing I know; whereas I was blind, now I see" (John ix. 25).

Let us never forget we have to receive the truth before we enter heaven. The blind man does not come into that house. And we can receive the truth best now. The mind is less hardened and more susceptible of truth now, than it will be if we continue wilfully in darkness when the light is pressing to enter. The Lord urges, "Bring forth the blind people that have eyes, and the deaf that have ears" (Isa. xliii. 8). Do not refuse His invitation. He has promised:—"I will bring the blind by a way that they knew not: I will lead them in paths they have not known: I will make darkness light before them, and crooked things straight. These things will I do unto them, and not forsake them" (Isa. xlii. 16). Nor do the lame come into the house. We must put away our faults, or we do not enter heaven. We must walk uprightly. We must cease to do evil and learn to do well sincerely, or our faith is vain, and our knowledge vain. Repentance improves our walk. The Lord Jesus will give us strength, if we wait upon Him, not only to walk, but to run. We shall not only do His will, but do it with a delighted mind. When He comes into the soul, "Then shall the lame man leap as an hart, and the tongue of the dumb sing" (Isa. xxxv. 6).

Once more, let me say, "the lame and the blind do not come into the house." Let us press, then, to the light, let us seek for the Saviour's strength, and we shall lovingly keep His commandments, for they are not grievous" (1 John v. 3). "Arise, shine, for thy light is come, and the glory of the Lord hath risen upon thee." Never, oh never forget, "THE BLIND AND THE LAME DO NOT COME INTO THE LORD'S HOUSE."

SERMON XX.

THE SOUND OF A GOING IN THE TOPS OF THE MULBERRY-TREES THE SIGN FOR OVERCOMING THE PHILISTINES.

"And the Philistines came up yet again, and spread themselves in the valley of Rephaim.

"And when David enquired of the Lord, he said, Thou shalt not go up; but fetch a compass behind them, and come upon them over against the mulberry-trees.

"And let it be, when thou hearest the sound of a going in the tops of the mulberry-trees, that then thou shalt bestir thyself: for then shall the Lord go out before thee, to smite the host of the Philistines."—2 SAM. v. 22-24.

THE frequency with which we meet with the Philistines imports that they are intended to represent principles which largely trouble the spiritual Israel. The Philistines were the foes which infested the twelve tribes in the days of Samuel. If we read a chapter of the history of Saul, it is still the Philistines who mainly harass and vex the Israelites: and in the history of David, it is again the Philistines who appear, and turn the fair abodes of a peaceful land into a theatre for the horrid scenes of war. When we recollect that the divine history, though a record of what really took place among the nations of Palestine, is representative of Christian life, we cannot fail to perceive that the Philistines must represent states and feelings which are extremely troublesome to the Christian. And indeed, though a quarrelsome Christian is a contradiction in terms, yet there is in every one so much of what is selfish, that it engenders incessantly states of vexation and trouble, states of envy and animosity, states of spiritual pride, which take pleasure in the faults of others, and view their feelings with ill-concealed satisfaction. These states, when they are indulged and allowed to go forth, make the unpleasant neighbour and troublesome man: when they are resisted and overcome, they still give so much of worry and anxiety as to induce at times in the sincere Christian the deeply-felt exclamation, "O wretched man that I am, who shall deliver me from the body of this death!"

The true Christian is a man of love, of meekness; never unkind, never condemnatory, considerate to human weakness, though a firm upholder of the right, true to virtue, but gentle and amiable in mind and manner, slow to believe ill of any one, a friend of reconciliation, a man of usefulness and peace. The beautiful definition of charity by the apostle is the definition of the genuine Christian, the Israelite indeed. "Charity suffereth long and is kind: charity vaunteth not itself, is not puffed up, doth not behave itself unseemly, seeketh not her own, is not easily provoked, thinketh no evil: rejoiceth not in iniquity, but rejoiceth in the truth: beareth all things, believeth all things, hopeth all things, endureth all things: charity never faileth." He who is in charity is a Christian—one of the Israel of God. He who is not in charity is not a Christian, but if he has Christian knowledge and is quarrelsome, he is a Philistine, an enemy of God, and a foe to Israel. Yet how much of the Philistine there is in all! How often will swarms of unkind thoughts and fault-finding dispositions spread themselves in the mind. We may abhor them, and repel them from time to time, but they come again, and again seek to possess us with hard thoughts of others, and a depreciation of all around us. We know this is wrong, yet instead of lifting ourselves to high and holy themes by supplying our minds with wholesome reading and solid reflection, we are often oppressed by our Philistines once more. These are the states represented by the Philistines coming and spreading themselves out in the valley of Rephaim.

The valley of Rephaim was so-called from its having been the abode of a race of terrible giants in ancient times. These are alluded to in Deuteronomy; "The Emims dwelt therein in times past, a people great and many, and tall as the Anakim, who also were accounted giants (Rephaim) as the Anakim: but the Moabites called them Emim (ii. 10, 11). The Rephaim are also alluded to in several places of Scripture, the word being, in the common view, translated "the dead." As in Isaiah, "Hell from beneath is moved for thee, to meet thee at thy coming: it stirreth up the dead (Rephaim) for thee, even all the chief ones of the earth; it hath raised up from their thrones all the kings of the nations. All they shall speak and say unto thee, Art thou also become weak as we? art thou become like unto us?" (xiv. 9, 10). Again, "They are dead, they shall not live, they are deceased (Rephaim), they shall not rise; therefore hast thou visited and destroyed them, and made all their memory to perish (xxvi. 14). The valley of the Rephaim, then, was the former abode of the old gigantic races, who were terrible alike for their wickedness and their size.

Spiritually considered, the valley of the Rephaim would represent that region of the soul where old lusts had their abode. The passions which ruled in former times are, of course, when a man has become religious, put down by repentance, and thus, like slain giants, are dead and buried. But is there not something solemnly suggestive in the intimation that the Philistines spread themselves out in the valley of the Rephaim? May it not be that a man who was once notorious for outward violence, and who has renounced this at the voice of religion, may in his later career have a tendency to vex and harass others by mental strife? He no longer afflicts men's bodies, but he has a tendency wofully to afflict their souls. His Philistines spread themselves out in the valley of Rephaim. May it not be that the man, once greedy of unlawful gain, when this is no longer considered allowable, may have a tendency to be greedy of knowledge, or of applause, not from the love of usefulness, but from the love of self? His Philistines would spread themselves out in the valley of Rephaim. We should ever be aware of the possibility of having still to deal with the old man, only under a new face. The Philistines will spread themselves out, if they can, in the valley of Rephaim.

David's hearing of the invasion by the Philistines, and inquiring of the Lord, represents the perception and anxiety of the spiritual man at the presence of evil feelings. The Lord's answer, "Thou shalt not go up, but go round, and come behind them, over against the mulberry trees," represents the teaching of Divine Wisdom as to how these worrying and offensive feelings may best be overcome. Generally, when we are harassed by the presence of evil thoughts and impulses, we are wishful to exterminate them at once. We would like to make short work of them. We are of the same mind as Luther, when he said, if sin were in his coat, he would soon change it, if it were in his hat, he would quickly get a new one: but the change of soul is not thus rapidly to be made. We do not know our inner constitutions, nor our mysterious connections with other spiritual beings, in this wondrous framework of the universe. The Lord, who knows all things, works wonderfully within us, when we are obedient to His Divine counsels; He requires of us patience and submissive waiting, and then all will be well. This was exemplified in His directions to the Israelites when they left Egypt. "He led them about, He instructed them, He kept them as the apple of his eye" (Deut. xxxii. 10). It is ever so. If we wait patiently on the Lord, He inclines to us, and hears our cry, and brings us out of the horrible pit (Psa. xl. 1, 2). But we must not go as we wish, straight up. We must enter into reflections, and meditate upon the subject and come round it, over against what is meant by the mulberry trees.

To appreciate the Divine lesson intended by their coming out over against the mulberry trees, we must bear in mind that trees are symbols of principles of thought and perception, grown up and expanded in the mind. The seeds of all true principles on religious subjects are contained in the knowledge stored up in the Word. "The seed," our Lord said, "is the Word of God" (Luke viii. 11). The seeds of Divine instruction are as varied and as multiplied as the seeds of earthly plants. Some are seeds of herbs, some of flowers, some of timber-trees, and some of fruit-trees. There are principles of greater and of less importance to furnish and complete our spiritual state; but the Lord's will is that the soul should become a little paradise, or as expressed in Isaiah, a watered garden. "And the Lord shall guide thee continually; and satisfy thy soul in drought, and make fat thy bones: and thou shalt be like a watered garden, and like a spring of water, whose waters fail not" (lviii. 11). The parable of the trees (Judges ix.) is a lesson of Divine Wisdom leading us to understand the excellency of different principles, according to their specific qualities. The olive represents the highest celestial wisdom, and that tree's refusal to leave its oil and reign, expresses the quality of that exalted principle, which is TO BLESS, but not to rule. The vine represents the principle of faith, and its animating teachings are the wine which cheers both God and man. These strengthen and direct, but also have no desire to rule. The fig-tree represents the principle which teaches the natural good that ought to be done, and done to benefit others, not to acquire selfish influence, or to gratify the lust of ruling. Each of these trees, with its specific nature, represents a specific principle, and so it is with the mulberry tree.

The mulberry tree seems to have an especial reference to the heart. Its leaves are heart-shaped. Its fruit seems like a little heart, and made up of still smaller hearts. The ripe mulberry is a delicious fruit, and the leaf supplies the proper food of the silk-worm, from which that soft and splendid article of dress, so esteemed in the world, is obtained. The mulberry tree, then, would seem to be the tree of tender sentiment: the principle that teaches the infinite pity of Divine Mercy, and would lead us to be very pitiful to others.

The tree is, as it were, full of hearts, leaf and fruit. And if we have learned how the Divine Tenderness of the Lord regards us, and spares, excuses, forgives, helps, and perfects us by love, we are induced to be kind and tender too. Mulberry trees grow up within us. It had a sad influence in the world, when men in the Middle Ages, owing to the Gospel being gradually laid aside for human tradition, taught once more the doctrine of a stern and dreadful God. Then came wars in the name of Christ. Persecutions and crusades for their Christ, no longer the All-Merciful Saviour, but a God their own dark fancies had made, like themselves. There were few mulberry trees grown then. But since the Word has happily again been set free, and multiplied by millions, and studied and loved, the trees of righteousness, the branches of the planting of Jehovah, (Isa. lxi. 3) are plenteously to be met with again.

Again, we have learned that the Divine Love pities and forgives, without money and without price. "The Lord is good to all, and His tender mercies are over all His works" (Ps. cxlv. 9). "O give thanks unto the Lord, for He is good: for His mercy endureth for ever (Ps. cxxxvi. 1). In His love and in His pity He redeemed us (Isa. lxiii. 9). The Divine Creditor had two debtors; one owed Him five hundred pence, and the other fifty; and when they had nothing to pay, He freely forgave them both (Luke vii. 41, 42). The Lord's mercy extends from the highest heaven to the lowest hell, and our mercy should go out to all. What are we, that we should be strict to mark, and keen to punish, we to whom the Lord has been so tender and so sparing? Peter asked of the Saviour how often he should forgive his brother, until seven times? And Jesus replied, "I say unto thee not until seven times, but until seventy times seven." Our mulberry trees should be well grown both in leaf and fruit; or in other words, our thoughts should be full of tenderness of heart, and our deeds full of tenderness of heart. We should have a full grove of them, and then when the Philistines show themselves, and we are tempted to think hardly of others, to worry and to vex them, to be disputatious and quarrelsome, ready to reprobate and condemn, swift to discover, and apt to magnify faults in all around us, the Lord will say to us, "Just come round, and come out over against the mulberry trees, and listen." All around amongst the mulberry trees the air will seem to be full of lessons of peace and pity. The leaves will tremble with tenderness, and seem to say,

> "O be kind to each other,
> The night's coming on:
> When friend and when brother
> Perchance may be gone."

But many another lesson will be there, all breathing consideration and kindness. The evil are objects of pity, for they always injure and pain themselves more than they can affect any one else. Others they can injure temporarily, but they eternally injure themselves. The temporary injuries, too, which the evil are permitted to inflict, are overruled to the real welfare of the good. Joseph was sent to Egypt in bitter circumstances, but it was the means of elevation to highest dignity, and uses of the widest character.

To return then good for evil is not only most Christian but most rational. It may benefit the evil-doer; but it will certainly benefit the doer of good. Besides, we know very little. Much of what seems evil to us may be only the result of misconception and mistake. We see a person limp, but we do not know how the shoe pinches his foot. The proper course is therefore to strive for the best, to make every allowance, and to hope for the best. When we act, if there be good within the object of our care, it will be drawn forth; if there be not, we shall not have injured ourselves by harsh feeling. When therefore the Philistines of harsh feeling, of animosities and condemnations come out and spread themselves out in the Valley of Rephaim, do not go right at them, and begin to quarrel, by quarrelling with the quarrelsome, in the vain hope of wrangling them out of their quarrelsomeness, but quietly get behind the whole state, and come out over against the mulberry trees of calm charity and loving gentleness, and listen for the going forth of the Lord.

> "Did we the sighs we vainly spend,
> To heaven in supplications send;
> Our cheerful song would oftener be,
> 'Hear what the Lord hath done for me.'"

The sound of a going in the tops of the mulberry trees means illustration and influx from the Lord. When we seek the divine guidance, in a spirit of charity, there is a sweet flowing in from the Lord, full of mercy and full of peace.

Nor must we forget the last use of the mulberry leaves; their transformation by passing through the bodies of the little worms which feed upon them, into that glossy silk which furnishes robes of soft and delicate beauty. They are not wrought gold, but they are little behind it in splendour or in worth. Those silken robes are the emblems of the robes of righteousness the spiritually-minded wear, when they have brought the sweet sentiments of charity through the humble uses of daily practical life to become entirely their own. They have lived the life of angels, they have clothed themselves with the thoughts of angels, and they will shine with the blessed beauty of angels, in which hope, love, gentleness, and intelligence will be the symbols in the raiment they wear of the graces possessed within.

But we must also bestir ourselves, when we feel the divine influx directing and impelling. The Lord is operating, we must co-operate. All that is externally required we must supply. The Lord supplies the power, we must supply the means. The favouring breeze has come, we must guide the ship, and so divine aid and human freedom will go hand in hand together.

All harsh blame, all ill-feeling, uncharitableness and enmities, those Philistines of the soul, then fade away and perish. The whole scene alters from top to bottom, from Geba to Gazer. It is like sunshine dispersing a mass of thunder-clouds. It is the descent of heaven into the soul. The Lord has dissolved and driven out the host of the Philistines, and all is well. David had very little trouble with the Philistines after this. And if the Christian would always so act, very soon all jarring discord would cease among brethren, and a thousand charities would replace the clangour of quarrel.

One of the most lamentable traits of a shallow Christianity is the tendency to quarrel about trifles. Not only do nominal Christians differ about differing views of doctrine, or differing modes of expressing the same doctrine, but about things far less serious, about slight changes of form, seeking change when it is known that it would lead to strife for no important end, and for looks, and trifles light as air. But this is Philistinism, it is not Christianity. The Lord Jesus is the Prince of Peace. Of His dominion and peace there should be no end. Heaven is the habitation of peace. The true Christian will make for peace; and if he must fight, he will fight against the tendencies to quarrel in himself. The calmest man will have many a severe battle within, but the results alone will be observed by others, in steady and courteous tranquillity. When he feels himself assailed, he will wait, if need be, until he is perfectly calm. He will never reply in anger. He will come round by the mulberry trees, and regard everything in the most charitable spirit, co-operating in all things with the Lord. Thus the Philistines will cease to harass, and his soul will be at rest.

Let us constantly take this lesson home, and strive against strife. Let us copy the example of the Lord Jesus, and never speak, however taunted, when to speak would increase anger. He was led as a lamb to the slaughter, and as the sheep before the shearers was dumb, so He opened not His mouth. So shall we, by this heavenly discipline of mind, attain that inestimable blessing—tranquillity of soul; and though in the world we may still have tribulation, in the Lord Jesus we shall have peace. Thus will all the Philistines be driven out of our souls, and though we may have other work to do, and other blessings to attain, these wicked ones will cease from troubling, and David in us will have a tranquil land. Sometimes we suffer ourselves to enter into quarrels and excitement, because we fear if we do not speak then, our cause, and the cause of right, we assume, will be lost or suffer disadvantage. But this is a mistake. A good cause is always endangered by hurry and anger. The Lord will Himself sustain His righteous cause, and does not need our fretfulness and impatience to aid Him. Fret not thyself because of evil-doers, neither be thou envious against the workers of iniquity: for they shall soon be cut down like the grass, and wither as the green herb. Trust in the Lord, and do good, and thou shalt feed upon the truth. Delight thyself in the Lord, and He shall give thee the desires of thine heart. Thus will the Philistines perish, and David reign in peace.

SERMON XXI.

DAVID'S KINDNESS TO JONATHAN'S LAME SON.

"And the king said, Is there not yet any of the house of Saul, that I may shew the kindness of God unto him? And Ziba said unto the king, Jonathan hath yet a son, who is lame on his feet."—2 SAM. ix, 3.

THE divine declaration, "the law of the Lord is perfect converting the soul," is felt by the thoughtful mind to describe truly the purpose of the whole Word of God. The ways of the Lord are not our ways, nor His thoughts our thoughts. We are too much concerned with our earthly cares, our buying and selling, our marrying and giving in marriage; whereas with the Lord, but one thing is needful, the good part which Mary chose, to learn and live for heaven.

When holy men of old then wrote, what the Spirit of Christ, as Peter said, in them did signify (1 Pet. i. 11), we may rest assured that the great aim of everything they wrote was the regeneration and salvation of the soul. The histories, as well as the Law and the Prophets, will be full of the spirit and life which our Lord said His words always contained. Let us see how this will appear in the Divine history before us.

We might readily doubt if much of an edifying character could be obtained by studying the treatment of the young prince with the lame feet, if we did not bear in mind how much there is in Scripture of what may properly be called THE RELIGION OF THE FEET. The whole body corresponds to the whole mind, and each portion of the body corresponds to some answering part of the mind. The soul is a spiritual body, having of course its interior principles, and its external forms, as the natural body has its inner and its outer parts. There is a supreme region of the soul, or head, of whose interior activities, though they are most wonderful, we know little. This is represented by the head of the body. There is the middle portion, containing the heart and the lungs, of whose movements we are more conscious. And, in the Divine Word, there is much said of the heart, and the spirit, or breathing part of the soul, and the necessity of their being purified and made new (Ezek. xviii.). But, we can only contribute to this indirectly, by prayer to the Lord, and by obedience to His commands. The actual change of the heart and the intellect is done by the Lord Himself, while man has faith in him, and obeys Him. THE FEET, however, are visible to man; he can absolutely control them; hence they correspond to man's life in the world, his daily life, and to those powers of thought and affection which produce his works.

A man stands upon his feet: he rests upon his daily deeds. All a man's inner and higher powers, views and states, ultimately rest upon his life and position in the world. Hence, the feet, the lowest part of the body, correspond to the lowest part of the soul; the degree of the soul engaged in our earthly doings, and the performance of our duty from principles of justice and judgment, is called walking uprightly. From a perception of this correspondence of feet, a large number of passages of Scripture previously obscure become at once lucid, and many a declaration that seemed mysterious teems with practical wisdom. There is a curious passage in Psalm xlix. 5, "Wherefore should I fear in the days of evil, when the iniquity of my heels shall compass me about?" What can be meant, a person might say, who thought only of the letter of Scripture, what can be meant by the iniquity of my heels? But, when we regard the feet as corresponding to the natural mind, the feet of the soul; and remember that our hereditary evils are imbedded in that portion of the soul, we see the application of the words, and feel their force. Why should we fear in the hour of temptation when our evil tendencies rise up and harass us, for the inner mind, the angels and the Lord are for us. The heels are against us, the head is on our side. "My feet were almost gone; my steps were well-nigh slipped, for I was envious at the foolish when I saw the prosperity of the wicked" (Psa. lxxiii. 2, 3). Again, "For Thou hast delivered my soul from death; wilt not Thou deliver my FEET from falling, that I may walk before God in the light of the living" (Psa. lvi. 13). "O bless our God ye people, and make the voice of His praise to be heard, who holdeth our soul in life, and suffereth not our FOOT to be moved" (Psa. lxvi. 8, 9). In all these cases, when we understand the feet to mean the mind which is employed in our daily life, we see clearly what is meant. We almost give way to evil feelings, when we suffer envy to influence us. We pray that the Lord will keep us from evils of conduct; and we praise Him that so far we have been preserved in the path of right.

In Isaiah it is said, "If thou wilt turn away thy foot from the Sabbath, from doing thy pleasure on My holy day; and call the Sabbath a delight; the holy of the Lord, honourable, and shalt honour Him: not doing thine own ways, nor finding thine own pleasure, nor speaking thine own words: then shalt thou delight thyself in the Lord" (lviii. 13, 14). When, the natural mind is made quiet on the Sabbath, and all anxieties and cares are laid aside, and spiritual things sought and loved; then will divine joy and peace flow in: we shall delight ourselves in the Lord. There is an exhortation of the Lord in the New Testament which has been sometimes misunderstood, which exemplifies the words of the Apostle, "The letter killeth, but the spirit giveth life." The passage I mean is, "If thy foot offend thee cut it off," and the newspapers have sometimes contained accounts of persons who have gone astray; laid their fault upon their feet, and absolutely determined to cut off the supposed offending part. But sin is in the mind, the legs are not to blame. Our Lord meant, that if there were something in our daily habits or our daily business, which truth shewed to be contrary to conscience and to right, we should reject it, and not have a divided mind.

This religion of daily life is the true test of religion. WE ARE what we do. If we are inconsistent in our conduct, we are inconsistent in our minds. Our faith is seen in our works. We may have splendid fancies, and think we believe them, but our real belief is shown by WHAT WE DO. Peter said he had given up all for the Lord, and would follow Him, whithersoever He went. This was, however, not faith, it was fancy. His real belief was in taking care of himself, and denying his Lord, or whatever would bring him into danger. Hence, when the trial came, he forsook the Lord and fled. "Shew me thy faith, without thy works," James said, "and I will shew thee my faith by my works" (ii. 18). This is indeed the eternal law. Whatever a man DOES, is what he really and inwardly believes. He may think he believes in loving the Lord, and being honest, because he may admire these things in an abstract way, and when he believes his interests are not against them, but if he defrauds another when he has the opportunity, and seeks his interests unjustly, he really believes in selfishness and fraud. Hence, the importance of the teaching of the Divine Word respecting works. "And shall come forth, they that have done good to the resurrection of life : and they that have done evil to the resurrection of damnation (judgment)" (John v. 29). Their faith, their love is in their works when they are good, and have done good; and, when they have done evil, their wickedness is the embodiment of their iniquity and falsity.

Hence, too, that impressive lesson given by the Lord on the night of His last meeting with His disciples, before the supper, from which Judas went out to betray Him. He took a bason of water, and girded Himself with a towel, and then proceeded to wash His disciples' feet : but when He came to Peter, the forward disciple objected, not understanding the inward meaning of which this was the outward symbol, nor yet prepared to understand it. Lord, he said, "dost Thou wash my feet?" " Jesus answered and said unto him, What I do thou knowest not now; but thou shalt know hereafter." Peter had no loving trust in the Lord yet, but was full of his own conceit, and so he became positive, "Thou shalt never wash my feet." Jesus then spoke the memorable words which should be deeply impressed upon every heart, " If I wash thee not, thou hast no part in me." O, that every disciple of the Lord felt this. If the Lord does not wash us from our faults by the water of truth, we have no part in Him. We may be able to talk about Him, sing and pray to Him; argue for Him, write for Him, preach for Him, fight for Him, die for Him; but has He washed us? that is the question. Has He washed greed from the covetous man, bad temper from the violent? Has He washed fretfulness from the discontented, and impurity from the unclean? Has He washed us? Has He washed pride from the haughty, ostentation from the vain? and trickery from the dishonest? If that has not been done, they have no part in Him.

"Simon Peter saith unto Him, Lord, not my feet only, but also my hands and my head." Jesus rejoined, " He that is washed needeth not save TO WASH HIS FEET, but is clean every whit." Mysterious and all-important words. What the life is, that is all the rest. Let a man sincerely purify his conduct, by power from the Lord, and his faith becomes purer, his love purer. If he neglect HIS FEET, though his head may be full of sentiment, and his hands busy with benevolent objects, every work is defiled, he is still impure. He needeth but to wash his feet, the Lord will take care of the rest, BUT HE MUST WASH THEM. "Thine eyes, O Lord of Hosts, the great, the mighty God, are open upon all the ways of the sons of men; to give every one according to his ways and according to the fruit of his doings" (Jer. xxxii. 19). How many there are who, although they profess reverence for the Lord, take the outward uniform of religion, and as to modes of faith, or rather doctrine, are of the straitest sect of the modern Pharisees, but whose feet are soiled by many a fault, and many a folly. They cannot be known from other people except on Sunday. They have not washed their feet, or at best very slightly washed them, and they have no part in the Lord.

The man of genuine religion, however, carries out the exclamation of the Psalmist, "My feet shall stand within thy gates, O Jerusalem" (Ps. cxxii. 2). Not our thoughts only, or our intentions only, but our works and all our ways shall be Thine. By Thy spirit shall all our doings be wrought in us.

When we clearly perceive the correspondence of feet, we shall readily see the Divine lessons in passages of the Sacred Word which speak of walking, leaping, and running. To walk in the truth is to live an upright and heavenly life. How often in the Word, especially in the book of Psalms, this use of walking to represent living occurs, every diligent reader will know. The very first sentence is, "Blessed is the man that walketh not in the counsel of the ungodly." When we are in temptation, we are said to "walk through the valley of the shadow of death" (Psa. xxiii. 4). "The steps of a good man are ordered of the Lord, and he delighteth in His way" (xxxvii. 23.) "Teach me thy way, O Lord: I will walk in thy truth, unite my heart to fear thy name" (Psa. lxxxvi. 11).

When we reflect upon the vital importance of a truly virtuous life, both for time and eternity, it is sad to know that a large portion of the preaching, in many branches of the Christian Church, consists in persistent efforts to persuade men that they cannot keep the commandments of their Heavenly Father. Walking, purely and perfectly, is pretended to be impossible, and often in other ways shewn to be of little value. The result, combined with the tendencies of human lust and passion; is the very imperfect world we see.

Yet, why should it be thought easier to act contrary to the laws of the Creator than to walk according to them? Every humanly-constructed machine works more easily in the direction its maker intended its springs and wheels to move than if it is turned in an opposite course. How can it be supposed that the human being, that wondrous construction of infinite love and infinite skill, will work more easily when moving contrary to the laws of his construction. O let us dread this pernicious error, and walk in the way of God's commandments. The way of transgressors is hard. "This is the love of God, that ye keep His commandments:" and His commandments are not grievous (1 John v. 3). It is breaking God's blessed commands which makes almost all the grief in the world. It is grievous to hurt the kind feelings of those around us. It is grievous to be ignorant, stupid, and irrational. It is grievous to offend the divine laws, and, instead of being angel-men, to be those poor degraded beings who are insane with pride or brutalized and deformed almost to fiendishness on earth, by vile passions and degrading habits. Oh it is grievous to see one who might have been an angel degraded to "a thing that smokes and drinks." But, on the contrary, the path of the just man is increasingly easy. He has his troubles now and then, which are blessings in disguise, but his ordinary condition is one of light, joy, and peace. In the light of the Lord Jesus he can not only walk, but run. "I am the Light of the world," the Saviour said, "he that followeth me shall not walk in darkness, but shall have the light of life." The Lord Jesus is not only the light of heaven but the light of the world. If the world would but walk in His truth, as the angels do, the world would become like heaven, and rejoice in the brightness and gladness of love. They that wait upon the Lord shall renew their strength: they shall mount up with wings as eagles; they shall RUN and not be weary: and they shall walk and not faint.

We shall now have no difficulty in understanding the sort of person brought before our contemplation in the young prince the son of Jonathan, who was lame of both his feet. Jonathan, the son of Saul, represented, in the spiritual sense, those who are born again, but only to the level of the literal sense of the Word. They are obedient and orderly, but have no deep yearnings after spiritual wisdom. They rejoice in the milk for babes, but the strong meat for men they have not yet tasted. But there are those who gather their religion, such as it is, not directly from the Word at all, but from the example of good men, and what they can pick up in a general way from the good they follow. These are represented by Jonathan's son. Having comparatively little knowledge of the Word of God and Divine things, they have but little strength. They are well disposed, but they have many imperfections—they are lame of both their feet. The right foot corresponds to deeds of goodness, the left foot to words of truth. To be lame is to have many weaknesses and faults in both these respects. He was said to dwell in the house of Machir, the son of Ammiel, from Lo-debar, and this, no doubt, was literally correct. But it is equally true of those who are represented. They who are weakly religious at second hand, all dwell in the house of MACHIR, or of ONE WHO KNOWS, which that name expresses. They trust in men rather than go to the Word of the Lord, the TRUTH ITSELF. They lean upon creeds, forms, rituals, but have no clear light in their own minds. They are Christians by tradition; and the stream of truth, like other streams, gathers defilement as it goes. We should rise to the Fountain Head.

Ammiel signifies the people of God, and Machir, son of Ammiel, expresses one who has derived his information from the people of God, but who uses it to obtain spiritual influence over others. Lo-debar means the Word to him. They make themselves TO BE AS THE WORD to weak minds, and often lead men blindly in religious servility, instead of training a host of enlightened Christians. How large a portion of society, even at this day, are mere followers of men, not really disciples of the Lord. Some church or some distinguished preacher is THE WORD TO THEM, and the leaders are content to have it so. The thought with multitudes is not what the Lord says, or what is right in the sight of the Lord, but what our church says, or what the minister allows or blames. How lame is society in both its feet.

How much is there in daily life, in personal habits, and in the usages of society which weakens health and destroys usefulness? How much is there in business which is unprincipled, but which is passed over and done, because it has been passed over and done before. Men hurry themselves on in life, both in mind and body, because society does it, but it is spiritual lameness, and oftentimes they fall and can with difficulty rise again. How many words are used in daily intercourse which are not true? How many professions are made, and promises and threats used in our intercourse with children which are far from being right. Society is lame of both feet. Like the feet of Nebuchadnezzar's famous image, society rests upon some things true, but much that is spurious, corrupt, and wrong: the feet are partly iron and partly miry clay. From the Legislature downwards how many habits prevail which are contraventions of God's laws, and destructive of morality and health. Night is turned into day: the lust of making great fortunes, and making them suddenly, gives a savage energy to many, and fills the mind with anxiety and care, destructive to happiness and health. The boasting bills which cover the walls with declarations, scarcely half-true, announce how much fraud has vitiated the left foot.

When people become sensible of their weakness and imperfections, real Mephibosheths, they will be on the way to gain strength. The word Mephibosheth signifies a *confession of shame.* And a sincere confession is the way to repentance. When men can be induced to rise out of the rut of old ways, and ask not what men have taught, but what does the Lord, the living Lord our Saviour, teach now, teach to us, teach to me, we shall find the lame man will not only be comforted, but be filled with strength and joy. "Then shall the lame man leap as a hart, and the tongue of the dumb shall sing" (Isa. xxxv.). The day has come when the lame can be healed. Divine truth is given in abundance to strengthen the weak hands and confirm the feeble knees. The lame can take the strength the Lord has provided, and none need say I am sick. The great Saviour has promised, and He is now fulfilling it. " I will assemble her that halteth, and I will gather her that is driven out, and her that I have afflicted. And I will make her that halteth a remnant, and her that was cast afar off a strong nation: and the Lord shall reign over them in Mount Zion from henceforth even for ever."

David's kind feeling towards the lame son of Jonathan represents the tenderness of the spiritually-minded Christian to the weaknesses of the erring. Stern uncharitable men are harsh, hard, and forbidding, but the real Christian is tender and very pitiful. He desires to help the weak, and not to discourage them. He knows his own struggles, and his own shortcomings, and he sympathizes and desires to console and to cheer. His heart, inspired by the infinite love of the Lord Jesus, is ever asking if there be any weak one whom he can aid, and, when he finds a Mephibosheth, he is ever ready in loving kindness to encourage the weak to become strong. He never forgets the charity that hopeth all things and believeth all things, and with his kindly cheer the prodigal will sometimes come home to his father, the crooked will become straight, and the rough places plain.

SERMON XXII.

NATHAN'S PARABLE.

"And the Lord sent Nathan unto David: and he came unto him, and said unto him, There were two men in one city; the one rich, and the other poor.

"The rich man had exceeding many flocks and herds; but the poor man had nothing, save one little ewe-lamb, which he had bought, and nourished up; and it grew up together with him, and with his children: it did eat of his own meat, and drank of his own cup, and lay in his bosom, and was unto him as a daughter.

"And there came a traveller unto the rich man; and he spared to take of his own flock and of his own herd, to dress for the way-faring man that was come unto him; but took the poor man's lamb, and dressed it for the man that was come to him.

"And David's anger was greatly kindled against the man; and he said to Nathan, As the Lord liveth, the man that hath done this thing shall surely die: and he shall restore the lamb four-fold, because he did this thing, and because he had no pity.

"And Nathan said to David, THOU ART THE MAN."—2 SAM. xii. 1-7.

THE exquisite wisdom, faithfulness, and tenderness of this parable have been the admiration of every age from the time it was given. How delicately, yet clearly, the prophet showed the erring king his sin, and led him to condemn himself. With what force did the faithful words come home to the powerful offender, Thou art the man. Such is the office of Divine Truth always, and it never fully accomplishes its saving purpose until it produces in the consciences of weak and offending men the healthy and penitent conviction that leads to godly sorrow and a true amendment: "Thou art the man."

David had much altered from the days of his innocent youth. He was ingenuous, modest, frank, brave, and devoted to piety in his early years. He was called a man after God's own heart. But, he became far from a man after God's own heart when prosperity and power put self-indulgence within his reach. It avails nothing to say he wrote psalms in his mature and later days. People can write poetry, and religious poetry too, who are very bad men. And evil is evil when committed by a poet, as well as when it is done by less gifted men. Indeed, the more a person is gifted, the more blameable is he when he debases himself in his conduct to the level of the sensual, the brutish, and the ignorant. David became a polygamist, which is utterly contrary to the pure laws of heaven, and was only permitted to the Jews, when, for the hardness of their hearts, they were allowed laws which were not good, and judgments by which their souls should not live (Ezek. xx. 25). David also became extremely revengeful and cruel, and treated the people he conquered with excesses quite impossible to a good man (2 Sam. xii. 31). And nothing could be worse than his treachery to Uriah, a noble servant, subject, and soldier, who was bravely hazarding his life in the dangers of war for him, while the king was gratifying his lust, and covering himself with the infamy of adultery and murder.

The scenes of his dying bed were such as to take away all pretence of supposing David in any sense to be a saint: they exhibited revenge and uncleanness, and, while righteousness is eternal, and not a thing of change by time or place, we must confess it to be impossible to account David after his youthful virtues had passed, as anything but an exceedingly bad man. It redounds to the wonders of mercy displayed in the Divine providence that David could be made use of as a type of the spiritual man and of the Lord Jesus, and as the medium through whom those Divine Psalms could be given, which have served the Jewish and the Christian Churches as the daily food of piety, the songs of the regenerate life, and the expression of the joys and sorrows of the struggling soul, wherever the Word of God is known. David was the poet by whose heaven-inspired imagination these glorious gifts to the Church of all ages have been embodied and presented; but we must ever bear in mind they are God's Psalms, not David's. David was but the instrument, the Author was Divine.

Regarding the king in the parable before us, we must have no palliation of his grievous faults under the idea of his being a sacred personage. He was simply and atrociously bad. He was the rich man. Uriah was the poor man. His beloved and only wife was the ewe lamb, who ate of his meat, drank of his cup, lay on his bosom, and was everything to him. The traveller who came to the rich man, meant the wandering lust which had actuated the king, and led to his guilty behaviour. And here we may remark the tendency there is in Scripture, and indeed in the human mind, to personify principles as personages, which has led sometimes to serious errors. The Holy Spirit of the Lord is spoken of as he, the Divine Wisdom as she, and some have imagined that therefore they must be treated as distinct persons. Just as well might we designate

David's unclean passion a person, because it is called a traveller who came to him.

The prophet stands nobly out, confronting the king who condemns his crime severely when he judged it as the wickedness of another, and who quailed before his faithful corrector when it was brought with all its force upon his own conscience. We could wish that mighty sinners had always faithful Nathans to stand before them, to tell them of judgment to come. We should never forget all hearts in due time will be revealed, all books opened, and we shall all be judged even more faithfully than Nathan condemned his guilty master. The prophet unfolded in his parable the exceeding guilt of the rich and powerful, when they oppress the poor. The wealthy have many enjoyments, many distractions, many varieties of good. The rich man had exceeding many flocks and herds. The poor man had nothing save one little ewe-lamb. The lowly of the earth have few things upon which to pour out their wealth of affection, but those are very dear. They love intensely, and he who touches the beloved object, touches the apple of their eye. They have but few joys, but to the good poor man those few are all in all. His wife, his children, his business, his religion, and his God form the circle of his life, and he who injures these is guilty of no common crime, and will surely be found out by his sin. "Woe to the wicked, it will be ill with him; the reward of his hands will be given him" (Isa. iii. 11). David had to expiate his crime in dust and ashes, to lose the child of his crime, to be driven from his capital by his favourite son, and to learn by bitter experience that the Judge of all the earth will do right to the powerful as well as to the weak. The Most High ruleth among the children of men, and giveth to each, surely, sooner or later, the reward of his doings.

Let us turn now to the inner lesson contained in this interesting parable, and in the circumstances to which it alludes. Viewed in this respect it will remind us of the rich man and the poor man in the Gospel. The members of the Church are rich, because they have an abundance of heavenly wealth. The Gentiles are poor, because they lack all mental treasure respecting eternal things. Yet, what little good they have, they love tenderly, and love intensely. It is the want of consideration and charity displayed sometimes by the members of the Church towards those who are poor in divine things, that is here unfolded to us in the Spirit of the Word. Uriah and his wife were Hittites, or as they are often called, children of Heth.

They were a gentle and good people that inhabited the middle and south of Judah. They are brought before us in the history of Abraham, who obtained from them the cave of Machpelah where Sarah was buried, and which became the place of burial for Isaac, Jacob, and their wives: a sacred spot pointed out and jealously guarded to this day.

The Hittites are represented as friendly with the Israelites, and aiding them on various occasions. Uriah was a Hittite, Abimelech was a Hittite, and both were evidently leading men with David; Bathsheba, the mother of Solomon, was probably of the same nation. They were amiable, courteous, friendly, and good; though they were not Israelites. They represent such as are moral, and cultivate goodness in their lives, although they have little relish for spiritual attainments, or spiritual knowledge.

There are people who are kind, gentle, orderly, and upright in their conduct, who yet do not advance to the conviction of spiritual truths, with any degree of firmness or clearness. They are good neighbours, kind friends and just people, and yet confine themselves to doing their duties in this world socially and politically, as the whole duty of man, at present. These are often people of great talent, very estimable, very virtuous, and very serviceable to mankind. They are not unfriendly to religion, not opposers of spiritual truth, but they are obscure and doubtful about it. They are mentally dim-sighted probably, generally from hereditary causes, and sometimes from having been repelled by the faults and shortcomings of religious people. Judged by the Lord's standard, "those who are not against us, are on our part," the considerate spiritually-minded man will deal very kindly with this class of persons. Moral good is all they have, but they cherish that tenderly. It eats of their bread, and drinks of their cup, and lies in their bosom. They would not do a wrong thing or descend to any false or dishonourable proceeding for the world.

It is their meat and drink to do right in external things, and they are often tender, considerate and benevolent. The feelings of kindness and rectitude are to them a species of religion. "It is unto them as a daughter." They do no harm to any one, but are ready to join in virtuous and useful works. They are convinced that morality is a good thing of itself. Justice, truth, honesty, chastity, brotherly-kindness, diligence, intelligence, faithfulness, truthfulness, and sobriety are virtues they know to be above all price for this world, if there were not another. This world they confess to be full of beauty, and full of good, and their households are often abodes of greater comfort, courtesy, and satisfaction, than the homes of some of the bitterly good, or the sourly religious.

These are the spiritual Hittites, they serve in the armies of David, and are faithful and true to the side of goodness. The Lord is with them, though obscurely. Then comes a time of deeper awakening if all goes well. Some earthly sorrow, or perhaps some book adapted to their state, brings the truth home to them in a suitable way, and they rise as to a new heaven and earth. They exclaim with Jacob, "Surely the Lord was in this place, and I knew it not. This is none other than the house of God: this is the gate of heaven."

When Abraham addressed the children of Heth, he said, " I am a stranger and sojourner with you" (Gen. xxiii. 4), which in the spiritual sense means that the Lord is with them, though they do not fully know, and fully acknowledge Him. Blessed be His Holy name, how wonderful is His mercy; how vast, how unspeakably tender His loving-kindness! A mother may forget her child; but He never forgets a soul that He has made. They may not know Him, but He is with them, and in due course will reveal Himself and say, as He said to Philip, "Have I been so long time with you, and yet hast thou not known Me, Philip. He that hath seen Me, hath seen the Father. How sayest thou then, Shew us the Father? Believe me that I am in the Father, and the Father in Me" (John xiv. 9).

> "O blest be His name: who in sorrow's stern hour,
> Hears the prayer of affliction and sends forth His power,
> Like the morn o'er the valley, night-shadowed and dim,
> O'er the heart shines the Spirit of Mercy from Him.
> Bless, bless His name."

The children of Heth said to Abraham, "Thou art a mighty prince among us," which signifies that the well-disposed moral people represented by the children of Heth, acknowledge religion to be a great power in the world, and have a respectful feeling towards it. They will in due season receive it.

In the meantime, none should hurt the Hittites. They are fighting on David's side against the Ammonites, and it is a grievous evil to leave Uriah to be killed, or in other words to be anathematized and their feelings outraged in the name of a false religion. The Ammonites, against whom the armies of Israel were warring at this time, were the offspring of deplorable impurity on the part of Lot. Ammon and Moab, the twin brothers, were born in a cave.

Spiritually, they represent an adulterated religion, born in obscurity of mind.

A religion of ceremonies, rituals, and worship, without any regard to purity of heart, to heavenly wisdom, or to regeneration, is Moabite. Hence the prophet said, "Moab hath been at ease from his youth, and he hath settled on his lees, and hath not been emptied from vessel to vessel, neither hath he gone into captivity; therefore his taste remaineth in him, and his scent is not changed" (Jer. xlviii. 11). Ammon was his brother, and the Ammonites represented those in the Christian Church who support and sustain a religion of mere rituals. The Ammonites are great for creeds, ceremonies, apostolic successions, dogmas, although charity, that soul of religion, is never thought of, and a whole people are sweltering in ignorance, superstition, vice, and misery.

Such men want nothing to be changed. They are dumb dogs that never bark. They may, like swine disturbed in their mud, make now and then an unpleasant noise, but leave them to batten on their gains, and they soon go to sleep again.

Such are the Ammonites of the present day. The armies of David, or all the spiritually-minded, fight against a hollow, meaningless, impure and unjust religion, and Uriah the Hittite is amongst them. The morally good assist in all the progressive changes, that remove from the earth superstitions that cumber the ground, and do evil, in the name of the Prince of Peace.

David's crime of looking upon Bathsheba, and taking her to himself, and contriving Uriah's death while he was fighting in the field, represents the wrong done often by those who are spiritually-minded in persecuting such as are in moral good, and joining the bitterly religious in condemning them. It was evening-time when David did this, representing an obscure state of mind. There will sometimes come into the thoughts of Christians, otherwise truly earnest and good, a spirit of intolerance, a subtle lust of dominion. They become for the time readier to condemn than to help. They become filled with the persuasion that outside of a profession of religion there cannot possibly be any moral good, and they regard such as avoid Christian profession, however amiable and excellent they may appear to be, as utterly dead and worthless.

They admire morality, they see she is a beautiful woman: but they desire to appropriate her for themselves. In good time, this will come to pass, for all true morality will eventually unite itself to true religion. But such a happy realization comes with time and maturity, and cannot be forced by despotism and persecution.

A persecuting spirit is always wrong. A tree cannot be hurried in its growth, nor can the soul. We ought ever to have patience and wait, until Divine Providence brings His purposes to pass in an orderly manner, when all will be well. Bathsheba was to be the wife of David, for she was to be the mother of Solomon, the future king of Israel in its most glorious state; but not by the murder of Uriah.

When we desire things to be done, before they can be accomplished in an orderly manner, we are actuated by lust, not by principle. The spirit of lust is represented by the traveller who came to the rich man mentioned in the parable. Lust is a wandering vague desire, yearning after what is lawless and wrong. It hastes to be rich, and ruins the heart that yields to it. It pants like a bear for its prey, and can never have enough. Lust must have a thing just now, and must have it right or wrong. It is sad when it is allowed to seduce the rational faculty, for thus it carries out its schemes, but it ruins the soul, and entails the most grievous misery. We should always beware of these greedy spiritual travellers, who are thieves and murderers, and seek only to make us their accomplices, that like David we may sin, and like him only be recovered by severest sorrow and repentance.

We have said the rich man represents the spiritually-minded members of the Church, and surely they are divinely rich, and can always afford to be gentle and merciful. They are like the king who had exceeding many flocks and herds. They are possessors of the Word, which is a vast treasury of heavenly wealth—of gold, silver, and precious stones in never ceasing abundance. They possess the wealth of all the kind sentiments of innocence, charity, devotion, and heavenly affection that have placed them in relation with heaven itself.

How strange that having these riches at their command, they should forget themselves, and instead of cultivating their own heavenly-mindedness, they should descend to straining at gnats and swallowing camels.

Yet so it often is. The Lord is constantly giving us the divine advice—" I counsel thee to buy of me gold, tried in the fire, that thou mayest be rich, and white raiment that thou mayest be clothed" (Rev. iii. 18).

> "In every age the Lord was kind,
> And to His Church revealed His mind;
> But we enjoy a wondrous store,
> Of blessings never known before.
> The gold and silver,—truth and love,
> And all the wealth of heaven above,
> Are Thine, blest Lord! Thou wilt bestow
> This treasure on Thy Saints below."

And yet, instead of enjoying these heavenly treasures, which the Lord imparts in such abundance, we often allow ourselves to be drawn aside by vague feelings of an unkind character, by desires to find fault and blame others, and in various ways we increase anxiety, care, and sorrow, both for ourselves and others. Instead of having a heaven upon earth, we dwell in the wilderness, and often the divine rebuke is true of us, "Thou sayest thou art rich, and hast need of nothing, and knowest not that thou art poor and miserable, and blind and naked." How true was this of David, when he was confronted by the prophet. How small, how poor, how blind, how abject he seemed when the tremendous words fell upon him, "Thou art the man." Will it be less true with us?

Do we carefully guard against all the instigations of the lust of domineering over, and condemning others. Let us live up to the sacred gifts which divine mercy has given us in such abundance, and so shall we never hear in judgment the startling announcement of divine truth, "Thou art the man."

The sin of David in relation to Bathsheba had relation no doubt to his typical character in reference to the Lord Jesus; for David in the Word throughout represented the Lord; but we must remember that the transaction of David only represented states in the Lord, and the evil acts of David represent the evils suggested by the iniquities of our hereditary nature which the Lord deigned to take upon Him, for He was made in all points like unto His brethren, "yet without sin." No actual guilt of any kind took place with the Lord, although He was tempted that He might be able to succour them that are tempted.

To His holy spotless inner nature the shade of temptation would be immeasurably more painful and vivid than it can ever be to us. This should add to our dread of everything that is contrary to His divine purity, and our care against every sin, that we may escape the denunciation "Thou art the man," and trust hopefully to receive instead, "Well done, good and faithful servant; enter thou into the joy of thy Lord."

SERMON XXIII.

THE DEATH OF DAVID'S CHILD.

"And he said, While the child was alive, I fasted and wept: for I said, Who can tell whether God will be gracious unto me, that the child may live? But now he is dead, wherefore should I fast? Can I bring him back again? I shall go to him, but he shall not return to me."—2 SAM. xii. 22, 23.

OUR CHILDREN WHO HAVE PASSED FROM EARTH CERTAINLY GO TO HEAVEN. This great truth throws a gleam of hope and comfort over the bleeding heart, when a little darling which had been the light and the joy of home is removed.

Children bring so much of heaven with them, are so endearing, so interesting, and entwine themselves so completely with our best affections and our liveliest sympathies, that it is indeed a dreary blank when the place is empty, where so much love has been.

The little garments are laid tenderly aside. Every endearing recollection is cherished with loving care. There is a yearning towards the future better world, that raises the soul almost unvaryingly towards heaven, even if there has been but little of heavenly thought before. The death of a child seldom occurs without to some extent spiritualizing those with whom its short life has been passed, and inducing somewhat of the feeling expressed in the beautiful lines—

> "Do you moan when another star
> Shines out from the glittering sky?
> Do you weep when the raging voice of war
> And the storms of conflict die?
> Then, why should your tears run down,
> And your hearts be sorely riven,
> For another gem in the Saviour's crown—
> For another soul in heaven?"

The sadness of having the gem of our fireside removed, is often greatly lessened by our having a clear view of what Scripture teaches respecting the nearness of the spiritual world, and the ministry of angels. The sorrow which is felt when the future is quite unknown is very deep. It is as if our darlings were dropped into a hollow bottomless pit, or had floated away on a dark ever-wandering stream. But, if on the contrary, we are assured that the inner spiritual world is, as Scripture represents it, "a heavenly country,"—a real world more full of objects, more perfect in the beauty of all its scenes and arrangements than this: near at hand, though unseen; then the void we feel is much less painful.

This sense of comfort is still greater when we remember the great love of our Heavenly Father, the Lord Jesus Christ, for every child, as it is written, "It is not the will of your Father who is in heaven that one of these little ones should perish" (Matt. xviii. 14).

How tender were the incidents in which children were concerned when our Lord was upon earth. The loving mothers who were touched by His Divine words, brought unto Him their little children, that He should put His hands upon them and pray. The disciples rebuked them, but the Saviour soon shewed how much the tenderness of the mothers was in harmony with His own, and He said, Suffer little children, and forbid them not to come unto me, for of SUCH IS THE KINGDOM OF HEAVEN. Touching and divine expressions which will carry balm to bereaved hearts, through all time. OF SUCH IS THE KINGDOM OF HEAVEN.

It is a further source of comfort to remember that our children were the objects of tenderest angelic care while they lived here. Their Divine Creator had provided for their welfare of body and soul, by ministers of love appointed to take care of them both in the outer world and the inner world: parents for their outer life, and angels for their inner life. How wonderful is true parental love! How mindful, how tender, how deep, how engrossing it is! Though but a drop from the ocean of the love of God, how rich, how heavenly a thing it is. What miracles it often works! What care for all the child's little wants! what self-sacrifice! what devotion will the true mother manifest for her child! How often will the light-hearted and giddy become sedate and matronly, when such a gift from heaven has completed the marriage union. How often under the gentle caresses of baby has the dashing young father settled down to the gentle endearments of home, steady and in "his right mind."

Oh, yes a baby is a magnet that radiates love, and is surrounded by love even here on earth. But their angels, our Lord said, "do always behold the face of my Father who is in heaven." Their angels; what a beautiful arrangement for the aid of parents is announced in these gracious words. Their angels, angels especially for them, to assist in directing their young souls to thoughts of love, of gentleness, and of heaven. "Heaven lies around us in our infancy," is not a poetic fancy, but a serious truth, a law of Divine mercy and providence, that each young immortal may have its golden age. There is a holy ground implanted in each young heart, a germ of angel life, ready to receive the seed of the Word in due time, and cherish it. Their angels stimulate the desire for heavenly things. How many of those questions which children ask, and foolish parents avoid, are suggested by their angels we can never know; but if we were wise we should be delighted to store up in the young soul instruction, which would be as corn in Egypt, ready in days of sorrow and of want.

Their angels! what value must be set upon each soul by the great Parent of all, since He appoints at least two heavenly guardians and two earthly guardians to each one.

Their angels influence them happily before their parents obtain any conscious notice. A child in the earliest days of life will smile with closed eyes, and dimple its little cheek with heavenly sweetness, before it responds to any earthly prompting, even of its mother. The Irish regard the radiance of joy which beams from baby's face on such occasions as the result of "angels' whispers." And probably they are right. "The Lord has given His angels charge over them, to keep them in all their ways" (Psa. xci. 11). And the whole work of regeneration is to bring our entire spirits into harmony with the holy substance of heaven implanted in them at first. The heavenly childlike innocence implanted in our nature during our formation remains;—the child within the man, during the rude bustling of actual life, always exhibits a fellowship with children's ways and children's joys, until happily we are converted, and once more as little children become humble, guileless, unselfishly good, and ready for the kingdom of heaven: lambs of a larger growth, by the nature and the power of the Lamb of God, who is King of kings and Lord of lords (Rev. xix. 16).

Such are the considerations that group around children. In David's case there was the greatest anxiety about this child. He appears to have had for it the tenderest regard. He prayed and fasted, and took every means as a Jew to obtain from the

Lord the grace of the child's restoration ; and when this was seen to be not deemed good by the Divine Providence, the king bowed in resignation to his lot, intimating his obedience by the touching words, "I shall go to him, but he shall not return to me."

There is not much reference to the future life in the early books of the Word, and the Jewish Law was given expressly requiring obedience from the Israelites, on the ground of temporal rewards and punishments, but there is nevertheless such recognition of the future as to shew that the eternal world though dim had never quite vanished from their view.

They called dying "going to their fathers;" "sleeping with their fathers;" and when we couple with these phrases the intimation of our Lord that God is not God of the dead, but of the living, for all live to Him, it appears that the Jews never altogether lost sight of the eternal world, although their chief hopes and fears were in close relation to this.

When we remember too that angels are from the human race, and how frequently they appear in the events recorded in the Old Testament, we shall be convinced that the men of old had a firm belief that they would be men after death, in a real and everlasting world.

When, however, we remember the arrangements of Divine Providence for the good of children, we may feel certain they will not be less perfect in that more perfect world. If the Lord provided angels and parents to assist in training the beloved ones on earth in developing their minds, and implanting within them sacred principles of truth and goodness, we may rest assured that He will give His angels charge over them there. Angels suited to their tender states will lead them gently and instruct them wisely in the paradises of heaven. They will not be subjected, as children are too often subjected on earth, to see debasing examples, to hear degrading words. Children in heaven will only come into contact with what is pure, loving, gentle, and wise. They will be taught by the best of teachers. They will see only what is elevating, instructive, and beautiful. They will be taught the meaning of all they see in the deeper wisdom of eternity. They will behold goodness personified in all the angels, and from them learn to adore and love the Lord, their great Father, and behold Him in the sun of heaven and His perfections reflected in all the glories of heaven. When we consider all these things, and feel that all children, who pass from earth are safe, for ever safe, against making shipwreck of their souls, we must surely be so resigned that we would not wish them back. Though our loss is bitter, their gain is unspeakably great.

In the departure of children into the eternal world, there is also an important providential law that should not be overlooked.

As all children go to heaven, the inflowing of heaven into the world becomes stronger, because of their greater number. And, when we are aware that half of the human race die in childhood and youth, we cannot but observe the wisdom of Divine Providence in overruling the seeming evil of the death of children to advantages so vast as the extension of heaven, the multiplication of the angels, and the equilibrium of the influences which bear upon, and sustain the freedom of the human race.

The more evil the world is, the more children die; the more children die, the more angels there are, and their influence serves to restore a better state in the world. And so out of our very evils, our good Lord provides for restoration and blessing. "O give thanks unto the Lord, for He is good, for His Mercy endureth for ever."

In proportion as sin and folly are overcome in the world, children will cease to die. It is not of the Divine Will that any children die now, but only of His permission, because of the circumstances of the human race, and the prevalence of evil. When we consider the want of wisdom in parents, the heedlessness of the requirements of health displayed by too many, over-indulgence by some, harshness by others, inattention to their sleep, their habits, their appropriate food, to say nothing of the hereditary disorders of mind and body transmitted unthinkingly by parents, the wonder is that so many continue to live. It is indeed of the Lord's mercy we are preserved so long and preserved so well; but surely there is the dawn of better times. A new heaven and a new earth are opening upon us, in which true virtue, true wisdom, and true order will bring about the happy state described by prophecy. "The Lord is our judge, the Lord is our lawgiver, the Lord is our king: He will save us. And the inhabitant shall not say I am sick: the people that dwell therein shall be forgiven their iniquity" (Isa. xxii. 24).

David's child was doubtless tainted with the faults of its parents, and children similarly born, in far greater proportion than children born under purer circumstances, fail to live to become men and women. Their tender systems are corrupted from the beginning, and if they had lived, life would have been too hard a battle for them. They are taken from the evil to come. Instead of being weighed down by sins and sorrows, they become angels, and add to the glorious company of those who form the shining ranks of the blessed.

When the world has become what it will one day be, a new heaven and earth regarding in all things the principles of the Lord Jesus Christ, so that He will be the centre, and all laws and institutions will breathe His Spirit and be inspired by His Love; then will marriage, parentage, and education be regarded as things most sacred, to be entered upon with feelings of the purest kind, and carried forward with prayer, and reverential regard for the teachings of truth. Then will deformities, disease, weakness and early death disappear. In the meantime, the text describes the course to be pursued in the sufferings of our children. We must strive to obtain divine assistance; we must employ the best natural means we have for their recovery : but if that is not seen by the All-wise to be for the best, we must patiently and lovingly acquiesce. Why should we murmur when the Good Shepherd places His lambs in greater safety? He sees the end from the beginning, and He ordains all things for the best. We should strive then without a murmur to resign our dear ones to His care, and be satisfied that all is well. The more perfect circles of heaven will accomplish His blessed purposes with our children, better than the imperfect homes of earth. Let us say, "Thy will be done." They will not return to us : we will strive to go to them.

The premature death of David's child has however a permanent, abiding, and spiritual lesson for us, as well as that in relation to our children. We have mental children as well as external ones. A person's character is his child more closely perhaps than any other. Our states, our plans, our schemes of life are a species of births ; and the new Christian character we attain in our strivings after heavenly mindedness is correctly called in Scripture "the new man." In this respect we must all be "born again," and put on the new man, which is renewed in knowledge in the image of Him that created him (Col. xxxi. 10). Looked at more closely, each new principle in us is a new birth, and each new state is as a new man. The twelve sons of Jacob represented the births and developments of the leading principles in the regenerate life, and the way in which they expand within us so as to form in us the Israel of God. In spiritual things as in natural things a common failing of us all is that we would fain get to the end too fast. We too often forget, what a vast work has to be done in us, and how long it is to last, and we want to get to the end of our labour far sooner than the divine mercy and wisdom of the Lord can permit it to be done. Hence we have in our spiritual progress many failures. We have premature births and deaths before the time. Our children are not born strong enough; we have been in too great a hurry.

We hasten to be rich in spiritual things as we do in natural affairs. We do not work and wait as all great artists do for perfection, but we labour for quantity. Hence we often do what Scripture calls to conceive chaff (Isa. xxxiii. 11). Our goodness is as the morning cloud, and as the early dew it goeth away (Hosea v. 4).

This mistake of our nature is often referred to in the Word, and often represented. Jacob's wish to have Rachel before Leah was an instance of this latter kind. David's taking Bathsheba before the time, and the unhealthy result of this feeble dying child, are representative of the same unsound result. It represents sentimentality and morbid piety, not steady growth by obedience to the truth.

A sickly spirit of religion, piety without justice, and a true regard to right is sure sooner or later to die. Bathsheba was to be the mother of Solomon, but all in order and due time. Celestial states cannot be forced, any more than good earthly fruit can. In earthly things we know a child should be a child, a boy should be a boy: a boy that is a premature old man lacks the good qualities of both. It is so in religion: if a person affects states and feelings that are not the genuine growth of real knowledge, real learning, real virtuous struggles in the trials of life, real piety and real love to the Lord, affecting to be more pious and celestial that they really are, his religion is sentimentality, and ere long it will sicken and die.

We should not seek to be high-flown in our feelings, and celestial before the time, but very sensible of our deficiencies and humbly good. Peter was very demonstrative. He was ever ready to declare for His Master, to follow Him and die for Him he said. But, we know how miserably he failed when he was really tried. His faith was then an imaginative dream, it had not yet grown into principle. So David's taking the beautiful Bathsheba, whose name signifies the seventh daughter, before the time, represents the endeavour to become celestial before the state has really been attained. The result will be a sickly child, and it will die.

How often such premature states of imaginative piety are let down in the realities of life abundant experience shews. The mercy of the Lord is so good to us, that we often suppose the states of peace which we enjoy are the fruits of our advanced states in regeneration. Often, however, a change comes. We are let into ourselves. Clouds gather round, feelings we had supposed to be entirely subdued rise up again, and we are astonished at ourselves. Our bright thoughts, our states of innocence and joy, have all passed away, and we doubt whether we really have advanced at all in the heavenly life.

Such self-revealings are often most distressing. We weep, we fast, we humble ourselves, but all that is not based in steady truth must die. Much of the early bloom on many a fruit-tree is inherently weak, and must fall off when the bitter winds of spring come. So is it with the bloom of the soul. It is mixed up with weaknesses and impurities which destroy its strength and taint its beauty. Troubles will come. Our sky will be covered with gloom. We shall see our sins, and feel condemned. Our hopes and comforts for a season at least will all die, and we shall take up the pathetic sentiments of the poet—

> "Where is the blessedness I knew
> When first I saw the Lord?
> Where is the soul-refreshing view,
> Of Jesus and His Word.
>
> O for a closer walk with God,
> A calm and heavenly frame,
> A light to shine upon the road,
> That leads me to the Lamb."

Such is the spiritual state that is represented by David's sorrow over his dying child. It will not however avert the calamity. The cup of sorrow must be drunk after sin. If our religion has failed in sober earnestness, and been imaginative and sentimental, its hollowness will appear in due season, and like an untimely birth it will pass away.

But, when we see its weak and frail nature, and humble ourselves before the Lord, when we examine ourselves, and confess our faults and follies, we may rest assured of a happier season soon. This state will die, but it will not perish; it will only go before. It will be preserved in our interiors, our inner heaven. And in due season, if we are faithful and true to the Lord Jesus, our souls will become celestial. We shall go to Him; but He will not return to us.

SERMON XXIV.

DAVID DRIVEN OUT OF JERUSALEM, BY THE REBELLION OF ABSALOM.

"And the king, and all the people that were with him, came weary, and refreshed themselves. And Absalom, and all the people, the men of Israel, came to Jerusalem, and Ahithophel with him."—2 SAM. xvi. 14, 15.

To those who do not think much and deeply on divine things, it is not easy to conceive that lessons of heavenly wisdom, equally varied in their character and applying to the human mind, arise from the numerous particulars that are given in the sacred narratives. They could readily apprehend the spiritual meaning of a battle. They know good and evil, truth and falsehood are antagonistic, and strive against each other. But, when they go beyond the general idea, for want of deep reflection and steady observation they fail to perceive clearly the diversities of mind and life which nevertheless are in full play around them. The varieties of character and principle are innumerable.

Were the condition of human life so that on one side you saw the purely good, and on the other side the altogether bad, there would not be much difficulty in understanding the state of things, or in taking a side. But human life, and human souls are things far too varied, multiform, and complex for such easy observation and decision.

And how varied is human society! In what curious and ever changing proportions do you find human feelings, principles, and sentiments blended together. Some persons are truly conscientious and upright; but with notions so narrowed by prejudice, that in their demeanour they are exclusive and unamiable. Others are very good, but very weak. Others again are very good, but very stern. Some are rigid in precept, but in practice loose, others in doctrine less precise, but in conduct unimpeachable. Some are very imperfect indeed in their views, but their lives are resplendent with every virtue, others most correct in their sentiments, but with weaknesses over which the angels weep. Innumerable shades and grades of thought, principle, and practice meet us everywhere. Life is an immense kaleidescope presenting change perpetually. There are not only great virtues and small faults; and great faults redeemed by some excellencies; great mental powers allied to strange follies; but there are curious inconsistencies on all sides. There are happy inconsistencies, where persons are far more liberal than their professed sentiments; and unhappy inconsistencies, where justice, charity, order, piety are constantly in the mouth and the dogma, but very little of them to be seen in the daily actions. To represent these wonderful and countless varieties of character and life, then, we need not be astonished that the Word contains narratives and incidents very numerous, and very interesting in the letter of the sacred page, and exhibiting to man, for the instruction of all ages the mirrored reflections of himself. As the persons move in the history, so the principles they represent move in him.

"The proper study of mankind is man."

We have David in the divine narrative before us, opposed and for the time driven from his capital and his throne by his own, his eldest son.

That spiritual things may be thus represented we may be convinced by the instances the apostle Paul gives of Abraham and Sarah, Hagar, Isaac and Ishmael, which things he said are an allegory (Gal. iv. 24). Abraham, in that case, he shews, represented the Lord. Hagar the bond-woman and her son represented the Jewish Church and her members,—her children which were in the bondage of a merely external and burdensome religion. The free-woman Sarah and her son represented the Christian religion with its freedom, because of its illumination by higher, broader, more spiritual principles, which would purify the heart and mind, and thus rectify the life, and make the practice of virtue a constant joy: the glorious liberty of the children of light.

The counterpart of this is given in this history of David and Absalom, and the latter's rebellion against his father. Again, we may say, "These things are an allegory."

David represented the Lord, Absalom, his eldest son by a Syrian woman, the Jewish church with all its rituals, ceremonies, and ordinances, heaven directed and ordained in beautiful order; like Absalom's beautiful person and hair, but rebelling against Him, and driving Him out of His own Church, by making His commandments of love of none effect by their traditions. " I have nourished and brought up children, and they have rebelled against me. The ox knoweth his owner, and the ass his master's crib; but Israel doth not know, my people doth not consider" (Isa. iv. 2, 3).

David had several wives and concubines, and several sons. And just as Abraham's two wives represented churches, and his sons their members: so David's wives, concubines and children were also in like manner representative of the Lord's connections and conjunctions with His people, and the different characters thus formed.

The mother of Absalom was Maacha, the daughter of Talmai king of Geshur. The small kingdom of Geshur was in Syria (2 Sam. xv. 8). And Syria, when the Jewish Church was founded, from having been the former seat of the church, as was manifest from the names of its cities and prominent parts, had sunk down so as to be the depository only of more knowledge of heavenly things than others had. Balaam was a son of the East,—a Syrian. The wise men of the East who came to worship the infant Saviour, and brought gold and frankincense and myrrh, were also Syrians, and their journey and their offerings prove that much heavenly knowledge still existed among that people.

All these circumstances manifest the sort of character represented by Absalom. Maacha, the name of his mother, means CONSTRAINT. She was the daughter of Talmai, whose name means an OBSTRUCTOR OF WATERS. Geshur, the kingdom he ruled over, signifies THE SIGHT OF THE VALLEY.

Absalom then represents such as are born of the Lord the divine David, but in the minds of those who are very external look too much to the valley, and whose religion is one of constraint, not of affection. In such minds there is a distaste for truth: there is the influence of an obstructor of the waters there. Purifying and refreshing truths are not wanted there.

The young man was very beautiful, and his hair was very abundant, and very fine. " In all Israel there was none to be so much praised as Absalom for his beauty: from the sole of his foot to the crown of his head there was no blemish in him. And when he polled his head, for it was at every year's end that he polled it; because the hair was heavy on him, therefore he polled it: he weighed the hair of his head at two hundred shekels, after the king's weight" (2 Sam. xiv. 25, 26).

All these characteristics manifestly indicate those who are exact in external things, faultlessly beautiful there, but who care nothing for purifying truth, and nothing for goodness within. Absalom was a traitor to his father, and sought to supplant him on his throne.

It is possible to be quite beautiful in externals; in worship, in music, in knowledge, and in order; but at the same time, for want of an inward soul of use, our knowledge, our worship, and our loveliness may be as sounding brass and a tinkling cymbal.

We must derive nothing from an obstructor of the water. The father of our affection must not be Talmai. Rather must we say, "As the hart panteth after the water-brooks, so panteth my soul after thee, O God" (Ps. xlii. 1). "Ho, every one that thirsteth come ye to the waters, come buy wine and milk, without money and without price" (Isa. lv. 1). "With joy shall ye draw water from the wells of salvation" (Isa. xii. 3). "Whosoever shall drink of the water that I shall give him, shall never thirst again, but it shall be in him a well of water springing up to everlasting life" (John iv. 14). Where there is no love for spiritual water, purifying truth, in a man, he has an abundance of evil in him, though he may as yet know but little of his own real character, or why he has no concern for everlasting things. Goodness loves truth, and seeks for it, hails it when found, and rejoices over it, like the woman mentioned in the Gospel, who found her lost piece of silver (Luke xv. 9).

Not to seek the truth, to have no concern for it, no enthusiasm for it, implies that there is much evil within, and sooner or later it will break out. "Wash you, make you clean; put away the evil of your doings from before mine eyes: cease to do evil; learn to do well." This is the eternal, indispensable law. No substitute will do. No external worship or ritual, however beautiful. No music, no prayers, no creed, no amount of observances will suffice. The Kingdom of God must be formed within us. The heart must be renewed by the divine Love, until love to the Lord and to man reign therein. The spirit must be changed to yearn after and delight in the truth: to lave in it, to drink it, and to rejoice in it. Only these things will save the soul. "The Spirit and the bride say, Come. And whosoever will, let him come, and take of the WATER OF LIFE freely." "What is a man profited, if he gain the whole world, and lose his own soul?"

Absalom sought by specious pretences to withdraw the hearts

of the men of Israel from the king his father. He insinuated that the king took no notice of their affairs, and deputed no one to judge at the gate among them. "And it was so, that when any man came nigh to him to do him obeisance, he put forth his hand, and took him, and kissed him. And in this manner did Absalom to all Israel that came to the king for judgment: so Absalom stole the hearts of the men of Israel" (2 Sam. xv. 5, 6).

The absorbing character of external things, even of external worship, if there be no seeking after the kingdom of God and His righteousness, is shown by this insidious conduct of Absalom. He misrepresented and betrayed his father. He smiled upon and kissed and made traitors of the Israelites.

David as king represented the Lord as to Divine Truth ruling and regenerating the heart, restraining and then overcoming everything wrong. Without Divine Truth nothing of this kind can be done. Truth grounded in good forms our faith; truth grounded in good leads to the love of the Lord, to the love of our neighbour,—truth fortifies the soul in temptation, truth leads to order, to progress, truth consoles under trouble, and truth beautifies the spiritual man and forms him into an angel. Such truth is represented by David. To draw the soul away from such truth is a deadly error.

In times of temptation it appears to a man that the Lord does not regard him or his matters. And some absorbing passion or pursuit, like Absalom, may strongly urge that the Lord Jesus, our King David, is taking no notice of us. It is altogether false. He that watcheth Israel neither slumbers nor sleeps. He may seem to sleep in the hinder part of the ship, but let us go and earnestly seek His salvation, and He will rise and still the storm. Absalom is altogether false and wrong. He should have supported his father's government, instead of betraying it. Yet so it is, external things that are good in themselves need watching diligently, lest they seduce us from the higher principles which it should be their glory to serve.

> "How vain are all things here below!
> How false, and yet how fair!
> Each pleasure has its poison too,
> And every sweet a snare.
>
> Our friends, with whom in social love
> The path of life we've trod,
> May steal our hearts from things above,
> And turn us back from God."

As with friends, so with habits. We may be so engrossed by some external pursuit, as to increase its power over us until it weans us from the grand aim of life, and becomes our all in all, our idol.

Business becomes such an absorbing pursuit with some, art with others, knowledge with others, pleasure with others. All these and a thousand other things are good in their places, it is only when they engross us unduly, and prevent us from seeking the kingdom of God and His righteousness as our first, our pre-eminent aim, that they become traitorous Absaloms, or evils.

Absalom, David's eldest son, like Ishmael, Abraham's eldest son, represents religion, such as it is in the early portion of our regenerate life, excellent but external. It is strange, but it is true, that persons may make an idol of the externals of religion itself, until, beautiful and orderly and useful as they are in their due exercise and proper place, they may take the place of Him they profess to adore, and become an Absalom which will drive David from Jerusalem.

In our worship we must always look to the end. We must be pious that we may become humble, fearing the Lord, and having no other fear. We must be humble that we may exalt the Word above our own conceits, so that it may become our wisdom, our strength, and our glory. The Word in us must become the Lord in us, the Living Word. The Lord in us must be a man of war, until our giants are slain and every foe is overcome. The Lord God shall give unto Him the throne of His father David, and He shall reign over the house of Jacob for ever, and of His kingdom there shall be no end (Luke i. 32, 33). The Lord in us must be a Man of War. He comes not to send peace, but a sword. Envy must be struggled with until it gnaws no more. Quarrelsomeness must be assailed until it no more distresses or annoys. Ambition must be reduced until it has altogether taken up its cross, and follows the Lord, to minister and to serve, content to take the lowest place, if only good may be done and the glory of the Lord promoted. Whatever raises its head to prevent this sacred work of self-conquest, this work of salvation and redemption, from being accomplished in us, is our greatest foe. And when the outer life of religion and of worship engrosses and draws us away from really being born again, and growing up to the stature of a man, an angel-man, it is a veritable Absalom.

We may pray, or at least say prayers, and we may join daily in praise, and really be no better for it. Under these solemn sounds may burrow vanity, bitterness, hatred, malice, and all uncharitableness. The long drawn aisle is not always the place where angels walk. Anthems are not always the music of holy hearts. Some of the stupidest people in the world are those who repeat the droning round of prayers again and again, until they have as little pleasure and perceive as little sense in them as praying parrots would.

Worship is a means, not an end. Its object is to make noble men, full of charity, wisdom, knowledge, and virtue. If this be not done, it is an Absalom to us, and will betray the Lord, and drive Him out of our Jerusalem, as David was driven out of his.

The fascination of beautiful worship, when it engrosses the whole mind, and draws the mind from internal virtues, from the truth of the Word and from the Lord, is represented by Absalom's winning manners and engaging person. His lovely and abundant hair is another symbol of the overweening attention of external things, hair being the most external portion of the body.

In the statement that Absalom did this for forty years (ver. 7) we have a remarkable instance of the letter of the Word being made to bend to the necessity of the spiritual meaning. Forty signifies a full state of temptation. The rain of the deluge is said to have fallen forty days and forty nights: the Israelites were forty years in the wilderness, and our Lord was tempted forty days in the desert. Absalom, a young man, could not have been engaged in his traitorous conduct forty years literally, yet as an extreme case of temptation is meant, in which the externals of worship are suffered to continue and to prevail for a season over the real regeneration of the soul, it is said he did it forty years.

King David and his men retired on the east of Jerusalem over the brook Kedron to the Mount of Olives, grieving (xv. 23-30) and weary, and there in the words of our text refreshed themselves.

The Lord Jesus often withdrew from the turmoils and contradictions of the city of Jerusalem to the quiet and elevation of the Mount of Olives.

In both these instances it was representative of the retirement of the Lord in the soul into the inner man. The external of the mind is in disorder and insurrection. This has continued long, and there is a feeling that the Lord is weary and tired with us, and He is pleased so to represent Himself, because of the appearance to us.

When Jesus met the woman of Samaria at the well, He is said to have been wearied by His journey, and here David was weary. The expression is indicative of the Lord's patience and long-suffering. He has sympathized with us, and continued with us, and suffered our vexations and persistence in wrong, until we have the sense of His endurance being quite exhausted, as He says, "Thou hast made Me to serve with thy sins, and wearied Me with thine iniquities."

But David's retirement and refreshment on the Mount of Olives signifies that in His Divine Love, which the Mount of Olives represented, notwithstanding human follies and hindrances, there is an infinitude of affection, unwavering compassion, and persevering pity. He refreshed Himself there. In His own great and gracious tenderness, He prepares the means by which our evils can be overcome, and though disorder may prevail for a time, in His Love and in His pity He will redeem us. When He sees the right time He will come forth as one refreshed, and restore the soul to order.

"Absalom and all the people, the men of Israel, came to Jerusalem, and Ahithophel with him."

The coming of Absalom and all the people to Jerusalem signifies the prevalence in the Church for a time, of the externals of worship and religion merely, over the government and regeneration of the soul within. For a while the rule of David was suspended. Absalom became the consort of his father's concubines. These things represent that in such a state the real work of religion is suspended, and a man becomes more and more external and sensual. Low views, appearances of truth, prevail with him, and self-derived intelligence is with him. Ahithophel, the hoary counsellor, whose name signifies the BROTHER OF RUIN, was with him.

Divine Truth is a safe friend and counsellor, but self-conceit, our own wisdom, when it is set against the Lord, and against His kingdom, is a veritable Ahithophel, and while it puffs us up with foolish dreams leads down to darkness, defeat, and despair.

Let us learn from this divine lesson, not to elevate the external, even of religion itself, above its internal principle, the Son above His father, the servant above his lord. But ever seek to remember in all the means we use that the aim of all religion is to make wise, good, and happy here, and so add to the number of the blessed in heaven.

SERMON XXV.

THE DEATH OF ABSALOM.

"Then said Joab, I may not tarry thus with thee. And he took three darts in his hand, and thrust them through the heart of Absalom, while he was yet alive in the midst of the oak, and ten young men that bare Joab's armour compassed about and smote Absalom, and slew him."—2 SAM. xviii. 14, 15.

THE moment we have accepted the grand principle that David was the type of the Lord Jesus in his combats with, and victories over the powers of darkness, first in the universe in general as our Redeemer, and then in each soul as its Redeemer, we have received a principle fertile in the power of opening the Word of God. It may well be called the Key of David. The eldest son, Absalom, we then may see represents piety in the external man, the way in which religion first appears in a man, very beautiful, very attractive, and obedient for a time, but sometimes when religion stops at that, made into an idol, and turning the hearts of the people from the Lord, His Word, and His government, as Absalom turned many of the Israelites against his king and father.

Worship is a beautiful thing. It springs from the veneration which is the offspring of love. It is universal. Men always have worshipped, and always will worship. The atheist is a self-worshipper, and he worships himself as devoutly and as constantly as the Christian worships Him in whom we live and move and have our being. To worship is the deference which a sense of weakness inspires for the Omnipotent who can help. Worship is adoration which gratitude for past mercies awakens, and the utterance of loving trust for the future.

But worship always requires truth to guide it. Without truth, worship will attach itself to superstition and strange habits, which lead from heaven as much as they are supposed to lead to heaven.

To be without truth is to pass life in a dense fog. It is to make no progress; for nothing grows in the dark. Who can doubt that many nations continue in their darkness and their evils, because their consciences are benumbed by an imposing formulary, which they conceive to be satisfactory to God. They have a name that they live, and so they are satisfied. The bandit goes to church, and believes he has appeased God. The murderer makes up for his crimes by many prayers, and some gifts. Religiousness is an enemy to religion when it consists of reverence without enlightenment. They think they do God service by injuring His children. Persecutors are generally very religious in their way, but they are without truth and without charity. The stronghold of error and unspeakable mischiefs is the bigotry which is engendered by worship with no desire for enlightenment. No obstinacy is so difficult to break through as that which arises from fanaticism, in which all old abuses are sustained under the notion of doing God service, as if God could possibly be pleased, by the rejection of that truth which is the brightness of His own nature; that truth which in its essence is Himself.

Worship combined with evil is thus designated in the Divine Word: "When ye come to appear before me, who hath required this at your hand, to tread my courts? Bring no more vain oblations; incense is an abomination unto me: the new moons and sabbaths, the calling of assemblies, I cannot away with: IT IS INIQUITY THE SOLEMN MEETING." It is strange that the worship of God can be made unpleasing to God, yet so it is. Never have atrocities been so awful as those which have been done in the name of God, and been sanctified by Te Deums. Many a carnival of villainy has been hallowed by religious ceremonies, as if anything could make a whited sepulchre other than abhorred in the sight of the All-Pure and All-Merciful One, who sees it full of dead men's bones and all uncleanness.

The Lord desires us to have mercy and truth, goodness and truth, integrity and truth, light and truth, worship and truth. Worship without these inner virtues is an opiate, which benumbs the conscience, the gilding of rotten wood, a Dead Sea apple, fair to look upon, but putrid at the core.

Such a state of formal religion, worshipping without light and love, is that represented by Absalom in his war against his father David, and in the chapter before us its character, condemnation, and overthrow are depicted.

The whole Jewish Church had become such an Absalom

before the Lord's coming into the world, and often it is addressed in language very similar to the tender expressions of David respecting Absalom. Thus we read, "Is Ephraim my dear son? is he a pleasant child? for since I spake against him, I do earnestly remember him still: therefore my bowels are troubled for him: I will surely have mercy upon him, saith the Lord" (Jer. xxxi. 20). "When Israel was a child, then I loved him, and called my son out of Egypt." (Hos. xi. 1).

Absalom with his host represents perverted worship as we have described, with all the ideas, sentiments, and arguments which support such a frame of mind. David represents the Lord in the soul, with supporting truths in abundance, especially such as relate to charity, faith, and good works. The army of David was divided into three parts, each under its appropriate leader.

The wood of Ephraim, where the conflict took place, was a few miles from the Jordan, in the district of Gad.

The battle which took place there represents the struggle in the mind between goodness and truth, on the one side; and evil and falsity on the other. The two hosts marshalled against each other, represent the opposing principles in full antagonism in the soul: mere barren ceremonials on the one side, and Divine Truth, sustaining charity, righteousness, and wisdom on the other. David having retired into the tribe of Gad, outside the Jordan represents Divine Truth resting upon the necessity of a good and virtuous life, both for earth and for heaven.

Gad being strictly out of the land of Canaan represents good work, or the life of love in the world. David's being in the tribe of Gad represents to the mind the Divine Truth, saying, "All religion has relation to life, and the life of religion is to do good." The wood of Ephraim represents all the perceptions of the natural mind in perfect harmony with the teachings of the Word, and all shewing the importance of religion to life, and of life to religion. Trees grow up from seeds, and they signify the perceptions of the mind which grow up from knowledge, by meditation and reflection. The interior perceptions respecting the grander principles of innocence, love, faith, and the inner states of the soul, are represented by the more valuable trees, the olive, the vine, the palm, and others. The plainer and commoner views of rational, moral, social, and civil life are represented by the timber trees, the cedar, the oak, and others. Respecting these, we read, "I will set in the desert

of the richest ritual, the magnificence of the proudest decorations of a church, if the Word of God is not there, and its grand principles of charity, justice, integrity, usefulness, and real daily purity and virtue unfolded and enforced, are only the meretricious adornments of spiritual witchery, by which the lust of power in priests soothes its dupes and gains its ends. Bandits can listen to the soft strains of holy music, and go again to murder. The sensual can flock in crowds to grand displays of sacred show, and bow and kneel, and return to their vile debasements well satisfied that they have patronized the Deity and done the right thing.

But where, in such scenes of mere ceremonial worship, is the enlightened mind, the purified heart, the life improved, the self-denial which would not pain the affections of another by a harsh word, or the property of another by the slightest injustice? The greatest persecutors in the world, the men who have laid provinces waste by fire and sword, and destroyed the salt of the earth by thousands, have been the most punctilious in religious services, which, being the ceremonials of superstition, have soothed their consciences and fanned their pride.

The religion which opposes progress, which does not perpetually promote regeneration, which does not enlighten the mind, soften and widen the sympathies of the heart, and lead to integrity of life, is useless to man and dishonouring to God; not a blessing but a curse. This is what is meant by Absalom being suspended by the branches of the oak, between earth and heaven—useless to both.

The Christ-like man, who seeks to exalt and spread the Word of God, who leads the erring to his Saviour, who urges all men to think, to act on principle, to use their judgments to find the truth in all things, and when they have found it to love and practise it; but, above all, who remembers to put on charity as the bond of perfectness (Col. iii. 14), as the very end of the commandment, out of a pure heart, a good conscience, and a faith unfeigned (1 Tim. i. 5), such a one, whether minister or layman, is a city set upon a hill that cannot be hid; he is a ministering angel among men, a helper of the helpless, and a hope and a blessing to all around him. But the man or the system which, without Christian virtues, usurps the Christian name, is worldly with the worldly; as selfish and as vile as they; satisfied if with holy mutterings there can be the husk of religion where all is dead and unholy within; this is indeed an Absalom suspended between earth and heaven.

A religion of mere ceremony, without a living earnest use of the Word of God, an outside religion which does not insist upon love and wisdom, the spirit and life of religion, the kingdom of God within—an Absalom which opposes David—is the upholder of every abuse, the sanctifier of every stupid notion, the source of unending bickerings, the infuser of jealous divisions between men and men, the impeder of education, the drag upon the chariot wheels of progress, a dark, dull, stupefying cloud that shuts out the bright beams of the Sun of Righteousness.

And what relation does it hold to heaven? It hinders where it should help; it revolts where it should attract. The tree with an abundance of leaves but no fruit was the symbol of Judaism when it had become such a system, and evoked the withering condemnation of our Lord, "Let no fruit grow upon thee henceforward for ever." When the Supreme Owner of the vineyard, the church, sees that religion has become such a tree, and has come to it for the mystical three years without finding anything but barrenness and corruption, He says, "cut it down, why cumbereth it the ground."

Piety is not promoted, virtue is not strengthened, God is not honoured, by such a system. It puts itself in the place of God, and therefore the Lord says of it, "Thine heart was lifted up, because of thy beauty, thou hast corrupted thy wisdom by reason of thy brightness: I will cast thee to the ground, I will lay thee before kings, that they may behold thee." (Ezek. xxviii. 17). Such is the state of things symbolized by Absalom, seized and suspended in the branches of the oak between heaven and earth.

By word being brought to Joab of Absalom being thus caught and thus helpless, is represented the convictions of the mind by many evidences of the worthlessness of such worship, combined with fearfulness and hesitation in weak minds lest harm should be done by its abolition.

The Lord desires worship, that He may bless us again and again. But, when, instead of this, we are only gratifying selfishness in a more subtle form, and turning the externals of worship to be instruments of the lust of power, pelf, and hypocrisy, then He suffers Joab to marshal the army and go out against it.

Joab represents the rational faculty on the side of true religion opposing, condemning, and destroying superstition. Joab had no hesitation. He took three arrows, which signifies a three-fold condemnation. Of the Lord, it is said, "Thine arrows shall be sharp in the heart of the King's enemies" (Psa. xlv. 5). True religion is a message of glory to God in the highest, and on earth, peace, good-will towards men, but superstitious worship inaugurates war to mankind; it hates and despises them: therefore a rational view of Divine Truth condemns it. This is the first arrow. The arrows of the evil are bitter words against the good. They shoot their arrows, even bitter words (Psa. lxiv.). But the Divine condemnation of them are bitter too, and are felt by them as arrows. "God shall shoot at them, with an arrow, suddenly shall they be wounded. And all men shall fear, and shall declare the work of God: for they shall wisely consider of His doing" (Psa. lxiv. 7-9).

True religion instructs, enlightens, and elevates the mind. It is light in our dwellings. Superstitious worship shuts out the light as an owl flies from brightness. The dark places of the earth are full of cruelty, therefore a rational view of religion condemns it. This is Joab's second arrow.

True religion leads to virtuous works. It lets its light so shine before men that they may see its good works, and glorify its Father who is in heaven. Worship without truth winks at evil. Its devotees love darkness rather than light, because their deeds are evil. The corrupt tree brings forth corrupt fruit. Tear it up by the roots. Lay the axe to the root. Cast it from the garden of the Lord. This is Joab's third arrow: the third condemnation. The piercing of the heart signifies that the very essence of superstition is altogether opposed to Divine Truth.

The ten young men who bare Joab's armour, and compassed about and smote Absalom, and slew him, represent all the truths of the letter of the Word, which condemn and reject a system which, under pretence of serving God, destroys the very pith of all religion, for love to God and love to man are the very soul of all Divine precepts. "On these two commandments hang all the law and the prophets." Let us avoid the fate of Absalom; let us ever shun the form of worship filled with the spirit of evil, as the deadliest rebellion against our Heavenly King and Father the Lord Jesus Christ." Let us never forget His divine words, "Why call ye me Lord, Lord, and do not the things which I say?"

SERMON XXVI.

THE SIN OF DAVID IN NUMBERING THE PEOPLE.

"And David's heart smote him after that he had numbered the people. And David said unto the Lord, I have sinned greatly, in that I have done: and now I beseech thee, O Lord, take away the iniquity of thy servant; for I have done very foolishly."—2 SAM. xxiv. 10.

WE must never forget in reading the history of Israel in the Holy Word, that Israel was the divinely appointed type of the Church of God. They were chosen to be a nation not for themselves, and their comparatively small interests, but as a symbol of the Lord's spiritual kingdom in the world, and a lesson for mankind in all ages. They were an earthly Israel representing accurately the Israel of God.

Unless we bear this important fact in mind there will be much in the history from time to time that will be difficult of explanation, as in the subject before us. There does not appear to be any sin or impropriety in numbering a people, or in accurately examining and statistically defining a nation's resources. A tradesman who did not take stock would hardly be considered to be exercising that prudent care which would avoid serious error and lead to prosperity. To take stock of a people, to become acquainted with the facts of their national life, seems to be absolutely needful to those who desire to diminish whatever is injurious, and to promote all that would be advantageous to its well-being. If the Israelitish people had simply been as other people, it would appear very difficult to understand in what the sin of David in taking the census of the nation consisted; and yet it is clear that he had done a sinful thing; both from its being resisted by his counsellors before it was carried into effect, and from his own conscience, which smote him afterwards, and caused him to utter the words of our text.

The first verse of the chapter indicates that the Israelites had come into a very evil state. They had been triumphant under

David, and the vigour of his government, and the protection he had afforded, had brought prosperity and wealth. Forty years of valiant rule and able government had produced their usual blessings, peace and abundance; but they had brought also their usual dangers, self-elation and pride of heart. Weak, erring man is prone to forget that all he has is from God, and not from his own merit or ability; and the more he abounds in the gifts of heaven, the more he is in danger of attributing to his own skill and power what ought to induce him to be more humble daily; for the more he has, the more he owes.

Israel was constantly forgetting this, and Israel's fault has been too often repeated in all ages. It is equally the error of to-day. We ought to tremble when we are prosperous, and pray to be kept thankful, but lowly in heart. When we are straitened, we mourn and complain: when we are rich we too often glorify ourselves, are thankless and proud, forgetful of God, and greatly overlooking the slender tenure of health and of all temporal possessions. "Jeshurun waxed fat, and kicked: thou art waxen fat, thou art grown thick, thou art covered with fatness: then he forsook God which made him, and lightly esteemed the Rock of his salvation." Alas! that it should be so: but it is the old and oft-repeated story. Prosperity has more dangers, and needs more wisdom than adversity.

Outward success often induces inward poverty. "Thou sayest thou art rich, and full of goods, and hast need of nothing, and knowest not that thou art poor and miserable, and blind and naked."

This had obviously become the state of Israel; for it is said the anger of the Lord was kindled against Israel. These words are only another mode of saying Israel was in a very wicked condition. The Lord is never really angry, but He appears angry when man is wicked, as the sun appears lowring when the clouds are thick. When men are drawn away of their evil lusts and enticed, as the apostle James expresses it, they hesitate, they ponder, they debate with themselves more or less, the attraction of vice grows stronger, the allurements redouble, their self-deception becomes more persuasive, until they become defiant against the divine laws; they know they are opposed to Him, and they feel thoroughly that He must be opposed to them, and all the sorrows that flow from their sins, they thenceforward attribute to God's anger. They drive themselves against the divine laws, which cannot be altered; they suffer pain, and they cry out God is punishing them. A person who has pursued a course which has induced severe inflammation of the eyes, goes into the full sunlight, and screams with pain. He cannot bear the sun. Another has severe inflammation of the ear; he cannot bear the joyous notes of the lark: a whisper even is a pain to him. One who has an inflamed soul feels God as angry, yet it is not God; it is an evil heart which makes an evil eye. An evil eye sees everything in a perverted manner. To sombre, jealous, melancholy hearts the world in brightness and its Almighty Maker seem deriding, condemning and scorning them. To obstinate and vigorously evil men, the Lord seems angry, for they feel an opposition from Providence to their efforts constantly. The evil man's schemes fail, nothing goes well with him, and he imagines Providence to be against him. He cannot conceive that the evil is in himself: that he is his own worst enemy, and that for Providence to gratify him with success would be to do him deadly wrong. He won't humble himself, and put himself right. He becomes angry, and the more his objects are defeated, the more angry he is, and the more he supposes God is angry with him, when in reality the whole of the anger is in his own wicked heart. When God is said to be angry then, the meaning is that man is evil.

Anger has absolutely no existence in the Lord, no more than darkness exists in the sphere of the sun. Yet, in the changes of life, and in many of the declarations of Scripture, anger is attributed to the Lord, the All-merciful. In the interpretation of these we must remember that men attribute to God, as they do to their fellow-men, the states which they cherish in themselves. Jealous men attribute jealousy to others. Angry men regard others as acting from anger. And the opposition and pain they feel they charge to the anger of God.

But how wild and audacious must man be when he believes that God is angry with him. God, the centre of every blessing, the source of all the benefits and glories of earth and heaven, without whose aid no pulse would beat, no breath could be drawn, no food could be grown, no flowers would bloom, no trees would wave, no birds would sing, no sun would shine, how can He be angry with us, when He is sustaining us every moment? O how evil we must be when we fancy there is anger in Him!

When the railway train is rushing on, the steady banks seem moving in an opposite direction. When a sinner is rushing on in sin, he soon comes to sorrow, and He says God has punished him. HE HAS PUNISHED HIMSELF. And the more he persists, the longer he continues in a wrong course, the more he destroys himself soul and body; the more he feels and says that the wrath of God is heavy upon him. So with a nation, when it is puffed up with its prosperity, and insolence and pride induce in it a life of luxury, of lust, and the greed of conquest, already it is digging the grave of its happiness. When it has despised gentle warnings and remonstrances, and brought itself into calamities of various kinds, the result of licentiousness and wrong, it is said the anger of the Lord is kindled against it. The real explanation is that the nation is so utterly depraved that its blessings are turned into curses.

What a nation is so is its government. The king becomes the instrument of the spirit that reigns among the people. The king is rarely anything but the index of the general mass. What the body is that also is the head. Cruel and persecuting kings have usually had a fierce body of the nation whose prejudices against those who differed from them, and whose hate urged them on, so that like people like prince is an ancient and veritable adage. When, therefore, it is said the Lord was angry with Israel, and moved David to number the people, it means that the people and their king were inflated and depraved. The anger kindled again, signifies a deeper degree of wickedness. They wished to take stock of their numbers, their wealth and their power, that they might glorify themselves, and exult in their merit and their might.

The business being intrusted to Joab and the captains of the host, and account being only given of the men capable of wielding the sword, would seem to indicate that the end in view was to make war on the surrounding nations. The lust of conquest was the impelling motive for this numbering of the people. Hence, there is no return made of any but the eight hundred thousand men of Israel who drew the sword, and the five hundred thousand men of Judah (ver. 9).

David had become a military monarch, a warrior king. He was swelled with the pride of conquest and thought only of his warlike men, by whom he could go forth and subjugate others. The numbering itself, the pride of greatness apparent in it, and the motive involved, are all opposed to the Divine Law, and represent evils destructive of the Church.

The numbering of the people had not been forbidden by the Lord to the Israelites, but it was to be done according to prescribed rules. These rules may be found in the 30th of Exodus: "When thou takest the sum of the children of Israel, after their number, than shall they give every man a ransom for his soul unto the Lord when thou numberest them, that there be no plague among them when thou numberest them. This they shall give, every one that passeth among them that are numbered, half a shekel after the shekel of the sanctuary, a half shekel shall be the offering unto the Lord. And thou shall take the atonement-money of the children of Israel, and shall appoint it for the service of the tabernacle of the congregation, that it may be a memorial unto the children of Israel before the Lord; to make an atonement for your souls" (12, 13-16). We learn, then, that the people might be numbered, but according to the three conditions: first, they were all to be numbered who were above twenty years of age; secondly, they were each one to give a half skekel, a piece of silver of the value of one and threepence, on the occasion; and, thirdly, this was to be used for the service of the tabernacle, to make an atonement for their souls. The taking account, then, of the children of Israel was not forbidden, but, when it was done, there was to be an acknowledgment that each one was the Lord's, and that they were to perform His service.

To number spiritually is to take account of ourselves: to notice what we have received from the Lord, our faculties, powers and possessions. But in doing this, we must offer to the Lord our piece of silver, or in other words our interior acknowledgment that whatever may be our powers or attainments they are all from the Lord, they are His, not self-derived. And they ought to be used in His church, and for His service.

This was what was signified by the commands respecting the numbering. Unless, we thus acknowledge all things of the church to be the Lord's, indeed all we have, whether natural or spiritual gifts, we are actuated by the serious error of attributing merit to ourselves, of exulting in self-righteousness, of trusting in our own strength, and claiming as our own the bounties and graces which are the Lord's mercies, and should only be used in dependence upon Him.

Our strength is in dependence upon the Lord. Our weakness is in dependence upon ourselves. It is written, "O Israel, thou hast destroyed thyself; but in Me is thine help" (Hos. xiii. 9.) "Without Me ye can do nothing" (John xv. 5.) To reckon up, then, our gifts and possessions, and to inflate ourselves with the idea of our power and excellency, is to swell up with self, and to expose ourselves to certain downfall and condemnation. WHAT HAVE WE THAT WE HAVE NOT RECEIVED? The very breath we draw is the momentary gift of the Most High. Our health is imparted by His Merciful care, and if forfeited and lost, our condition is pitiful indeed. The feeblest bark might as well hope to ride safely in the wildest tempest, as a man of himself to resist the assaults of the powers of hell. As the fiercest hurricane smites the blade of grass to the earth so would the awful influence of infernal might destroy the strongest man, undefended by a strength greater than his own.

Hence the danger of self-complacency. The man who boastfully imagines he is wise or good, or strong or amiable of himself, will ere long feel the blast of a mental simoom which will leave him withered, bare and weak. Instead of having the ability to maintain God's cause, to overthrow evil and falsehood in the world, or to advance the progress of mankind in virtue and truth, he will be broken down and incapable, self-condemned and visibly paralyzed for all good. Humility is the only ground in which heavenly virtues can grow. Blessed are the poor in spirit, for theirs is the kingdom of heaven. In religion he who would save himself must lose himself. He who fancies himself rich, is poor. He only who is poor in his own estimation is rich. He who will lose himself will save himself.

The three punishments which were placed before David by the prophet Gad, represent the three ways in which the presumption of self-merit in religion produces its sad results.

In some it produces famine of soul. Seven years of famine come upon them in the land; or in other words, they become altogether unable to receive goodness and truth into their soul. The Lord "satisfieth the thirsty soul, and filleth the hungry soul with goodness" (Ps. cvii. 9), when these blessings are desired in a true spirit of lowliness and self-denial. But when the soul is puffed up with a sense of its many excellencies; when it conceives it is rich and has need of nothing; when it is vain of its virtues, and thanks God for its gifts and graces, and that it is not as other men, the leprosy taints the whole, and no heavenly goodness enters. There is a famine of the Word of God, and there is a famine of true love, the BREAD OF LIFE; the bread of God which comes down from heaven, and gives love to the world. No heavenly grace can animate our hearts while we are full of a sense of our own self-sufficiency, and imagine we are good and strong and have need of nothing.

It may be we have plenty of men of war to draw the sword. We can be victorious in argument, both on spiritual and celestial grounds, but our hearts will be cold, our interior states poor and feeble. Our food will have failed, and we shall be lean, hard, and the holy flesh will have gone off us (Jer. ii. 15). The heart will lack food, and become hollow and unsatisfied, ever yearning for, but never receiving, the rich supply of angelic life. No real good can enter, while self desires to make heaven and divine things subservient to Pharisaic pride. There will be seven years of famine, or in other words a complete deficiency of THE BREAD OF HEAVEN.

In other cases self-sufficiency in religion leads to bitter harassings and mental persecutions in matters of faith. Doubt and darkness fill the soul. Months having relation to the moon, and the moon being the symbol of faith, which illuminates our spiritual nights, to fly three months before thine enemies, as expressed by the prophet Gad to David, represents a state in which on all the subjects of faith the most painful uncertainties and misgivings shall be felt. Defeat and distress fill the soul with consternation when through interior pride it has puffed itself up with the idea of a strength of its own.

The third sad result of self-sufficiency is pestilence, or inward destruction of the good formerly received, signified by the perishing of seventy thousand men (ver. 15).

This destruction is said to have been inflicted by the angel of the Lord, who sent a pestilence which destroyed the people. There are evil angels as well as good ones, and because the Divine Providence is over all events, and rules by what He permits among the evil, down to the lowest hell, as well as by what He ordains even to the highest heaven; in this general sense evil angels that delight in smiting are said to be angels of the Lord. Of the plagues of Egypt it is written, He cast upon them the fierceness of His anger, wrath and indignation and trouble, by sending EVIL ANGELS among them (Psa. lxxviii. 49.)

This permission was for great and ultimate good, hence it is said, "When He slew them, then, they sought Him: and they returned and enquired early after God" (ver. 34). So in the case of the slaughter of the seventy thousand in this pestilence in David's old age, it induced sorrow, humiliation, and repentance. It stayed any presumptuous war, and prepared for the peaceful reign of Solomon.

Yet how sad it is that only by blows so severe can men and nations learn righteousness. What merciful reproaches are breathed in the Divine words, "O Jerusalem, Jerusalem, thou that killest the prophets and stonest them that are sent unto thee, how often would I have gathered thy children as a hen gathereth her chickens under her wings, but ye would not" (Luke xiii. 33). The death of the seventy thousand men from pestilence represented the destruction in the Jewish Church of all the holy principles of interior religion from the desire of merit and spiritual pride.

The pestilence was the blast of presumptuous eagerness to rule over all in the pride of self glory stimulated by evil spirits. This scorches up all innocence, all true virtue, and begins a spiritual death that may be palliated and stayed for a time, but goes on like a fatal disease until all is ruined.

David's giving way to this represented the tainting of conscience, so that the Divine Itself in them was clouded, and in their corruption the idea of God was perverted, and they imagined that the Lord Himself favoured their presumption and designed to lift them above all other nations, and gratify their lust of glory. The misery this induced led to repentance for a time, and the plague was stayed, but only to resume its ravages after a while, until the ruin of the nation was consummated. So is it with individuals who give way to the same spirit of presumption.

The number seventy, like seven, is used when the idea of sacredness and fulness are intended to be conveyed. The seventy elders who went up Mount Horeb with Moses and Aaron, and the seventy who were sent out by the Lord to heal the sick and to preach the gospel, are instances of the use of this number to denote the Lord's operations in His Church and in the human mind by the sacred affections of interior good, by innocence, by the love of peace and the love of wisdom. On the other hand, the destruction of these principles by the lust of merit and the profanity of self-righteousness was indicated by the seventy years' captivity of Israel in Babylon, the seventy weeks mentioned in Daniel, when it is said the Messiah should be cut off, and here the destruction of the seventy thousand from Dan to Beersheba.

As the Lord is Wisdom itself and Order itself, He cannot interpose and stay the plague until the impression of the solemn warning which will lead to repentance and reformation has been made. Then Mercy interferes and the plague is stayed. The Divine Love is full of pity and tenderness while the suffering is going on, and removes it at the earliest possible moment.

Let us learn then to avoid sins, especially the sins of self-conceit, self-merit, and the lust of power, for thus only can we avoid the destruction of the interior virtues within us, and ultimately the entire loss of our souls.

SERMON XXVII.

DAVID'S DEATH AND SOLOMON'S REIGN.

"And the days that David reigned over Israel were forty years: seven years reigned he in Hebron, and thirty and three years reigned he in Jerusalem.
"Then sat Solomon upon the throne of David his father; and his kingdom was established greatly."—1 KINGS i. 11, 12.

"CHRIST in you, the hope of glory" (Col. i. 27), said the apostle, when speaking of the governing and saving power of the Lord in the soul. And again, "God hath said, I will dwell in them, and walk in them; and I will be their God, and they shall be my people" (2 Cor. vi. 16).

The kingdom of earthly Israel was the sketch and portraiture of Israel in the soul and in the Church. Only when the Lord Jesus becomes King of kings and Lord of lords in us, can the kingdom of the soul, the little universe within, be brought into true order, real harmony, and interior peace.

This government of the Lord, however, is different at different stages of the regenerate life. It is at first the discipline of the outer man, the government of obedience, directed almost entirely to our words and actions. This is like the government of Saul. In due time our religion becomes deeper, and enters into more interior states. It is much engaged in the search for intelligence and truth. It has many conflicts, and it struggles hard for self-conquest. There are hard struggles within for purity of thought and feeling, of which the world takes no note, but which are inexpressibly real and terrible to one who desires to realize the kingdom of God. This is like the government of David. The spirit is striving against the flesh. The love of mind is increasing, and the love of the world decreasing. It is the spiritual state of man. The celestial state follows. The clashings of thought are over. The aim is only to be good, to seek peace and pursue it. In this state there is but little relish for argument; but a great concern for love, for charity, for justice, for duty, and for rest in God. A yearning for content, for quiet, and for perfection, distinguishes this stage of the Christian life. This is represented by the government of Solomon, the peaceful king, whose name signifies peace. David's reign was a very warlike one, yet it was a very necessary one. It prepared the way for that of Solomon.

The human mind, when deep thought has been awakened, and somewhat of Divine light has penetrated, discovers a host of views, sentiments, and prejudices in itself, which need to be corrected. This entails trial, sometimes severe distress of soul. "Think not that I am come to send peace upon earth: I came not to send peace, but a sword" (Matt. x. 34), the Lord Jesus said; and so He ever says to the regenerating man. He who makes no change, makes no improvement.

The period of spiritual conflict was represented by the reign of David, which it is said in the text continued forty years. Forty is used in the Word when a full state of temptation is intended to be represented. The rain that caused the flood is said to have descended forty days and forty nights. The Israelites were in the wilderness forty years. Our Lord was in the desert tempted of the devil forty days. So David's reign lasted forty years, to represent the many and varied conflicts of mind and heart, before the kingdom within is thoroughly brought under the steady government of Divine Truth. David's reign was divided into two epochs. He reigned seven years in Hebron, and thirty and three years in Jerusalem.

The seven years' reign in Hebron, the name of which signifies Friendship, represented the spiritual man as to *Love to the brethren*, without which we have no real inner spiritual life. It is charity within, and in act, which really gives heavenly life to the Christian. "Above all things, put on charity, which is the bond of perfectness" (Col. iii. 14). "By this we know that we have passed from death to life, BECAUSE WE LOVE THE BRETHREN" (1 John iii. 14). "By this shall all men know that ye are my disciples, if ye have love one to another" (John xiii. 35). To come into a state of charity, of real love for the good of others, is spiritually to reign in Hebron; and to do this for seven years means to have this state of heart completed, perfected, and made thoroughly our own. The number seven indicates the sacredness and completeness of charity. The thirty and three years' reign in Jerusalem represented the advance and completion of heavenly truth in the mind. The name Jerusalem means *the sight of peace:* the number three representing completeness as to truth; and eleven times three, or thirty-three, indicates completeness, nearly to the celestial state; twelve representing that which is full and complete in all respects.

That David's warlike reign would represent that part of the Christian life which is a warfare, will be easily admitted. He knows as yet but little of himself or of true religion, who does not know that, besides the conversion of a person at first by repentance to the side of religion, which takes place when he ceases to live a thoughtless, an indifferent, or an openly sinful life, there must be a conversion in thought, sentiments, and principle in the mind itself, before the soul is fitted for heaven. With a profession of religion, so far as to avoid sins which are not respectable, to observe the requirements of public worship, to read good books, and to contribute to the cause of spreading the doctrines of religion, we may often be pained to observe pride, vanity, self-seeking, covetousness, haughtiness, or impatience of temper, an unwillingness to make any effort for the good of others, a determination to do as far as possible what is just to our own honour, a concentration of the whole mind upon self, as if it was not a divine declaration which asserts, "Ye must be born again."

Yet, to fight against these inner evils, to struggle for victory over spiritual wickednesses, is what is represented to us by the whole life of David in its spiritual sense, and in its application to the individual Christian. In its grandest application, David's life and character represented the Lord Jesus as our Redeemer from the powers of darkness. For although His outward life had little appearance of violent strife until its close, yet the Gospels contain sufficient indications of terrible struggles in the spiritual world against the powers of darkness, during His whole career, to warrant the strong language of the Psalms and the Prophets, and to show how the earthly David in his wars could be the type of the Divine David in His awful combats with, and victories over, the world's spiritual foes:—

> "Temptation's thorny path He trod,
> In form a man, in soul a God;
> And trod the path alone.
> In vain the direst fiends assailed:
> His mighty arm of power prevailed,
> And hell was overthrown."

The redemption of the world, and the necessity of Jehovah

Himself coming into the world to be our Redeemer, are little understood, unless we are aware how closely the spiritual world is connected with ours, and how the two worlds act and react upon one another.

When the Church is corrupt, and a dispensation has become dark with falsity and ignorance, souls flock by death into the inner world, and cannot enter heaven. As the evening state of mankind becomes darker, the number of dark souls in the world of spirits increases greatly, and a stupefying atmosphere presses upon human minds receiving influences from the spirit-world, indisposing them to search for truth, to examine, to discuss, to think, to progress. "Darkness covers the earth, and gross darkness the people." Century after century passes on, and mankind live in a fog ever denser: they grope for the wall like the blind, the night of thought deepens, the captivity of soul becomes more rigid; and although there are never wanting a few pious and noble souls who cry out against the wickedness of the age, and the blindness and the supineness of the teachers, yet one after another the lights go out, and darkness and error are over all.

"Then error reigns, and earth complains."

There is, however, no help in man. At the fulness of time, the Lord Himself descends into the world of spirits as the Redeemer, and judges and clears that world. He pours from Himself an influx of glowing love and wisdom, which like a stream of fire opens all minds, called in Scripture opening the books. The simple good welcome and hail it as glorious truth, for which they have been waiting. The evil hate it, and resist it, but in vain. They are compelled to fly before it. The masses of those who love darkness rather than light oppose it, but are overthrown as David overthrew the Philistines, the Moabites, the Ammonites, and all the foes of Israel. Redemption is effected, and a new Church and a new era are begun. Daniel describes the operation of a judgment in the world of spirits when he says, "I beheld till the thrones were placed, and the Ancient of Days did sit, whose garments were white as snow, and the hair of His head like the pure wool. His throne was like the fiery flame, and His wheels as burning fire. A fiery stream issued, and came forth from before Him: thousand thousands ministered unto him; the judgment was set, and the books were opened" (Dan. vii. 9, 10).

The real nature of REDEMPTION may now again be clearly understood, and it may be thoroughly seen why Jehovah alone could be our Redeemer. No power but that of the Omnipotent could subdue the banded hosts of the evil in the world of mind, set free the myriad souls which superstition had bound as blind followers of the blind, and pour new beams of light and love into the world. The Lord as a *man of war*, as Jehovah mighty in battle, is the Divine David.

Very numerous indeed are the declarations of the prophets which speak of the Lord the Redeemer waging a tremendous warfare. Thus the prophet Isaiah, in the words which immediately precede the announcement of the Lord's coming, in the well-known declaration, " Unto us a Child is born, unto us a Son is given," foretells the struggle that would take place in the following terms : " For every battle of the warrior is with confused noise, and garments rolled in blood : BUT THIS SHALL BE WITH BURNING AND FUEL OF FIRE " (Isa. ix. 5). No such awful combat took place in the outer world : it must therefore have had its fulfilment in the inner world, the world of spirits.

Again we read, "Shall the prey be taken from the mighty, or the lawful captive delivered ? But thus saith the Lord, Even the captives of the mighty shall be taken away, and the prey of the terrible shall be delivered : for I will contend with him that contendeth with thee, and I will save thy children. . . . And all flesh shall know that I, Jehovah, am thy Saviour and thy Redeemer, the Mighty One of Jacob" (Isa. xlix. 24–26). Here it is evident that multitudes are represented in such bondage, that their freedom could not be won for them by any one but the Eternal Himself.

Similar passages are so numerous, that we must leave many unmentioned ; but two more will give us very marked testimony on the important subject of the Great Redeemer and His work. "And He saw that there was no man, and wondered that there was no intercessor : therefore His arm brought salvation ; and His righteousness, it sustained Him " (Isa. lix. 16). Again, " I have trodden the winepress alone, and of the people there was none with me : for I will tread them in mine anger, and trample them in my fury ; and their blood shall be sprinkled upon my garments, and I will stain all my raiment : for the day of vengeance is in mine heart, and the year of my redeemed is come " (Isa. lxiii. 3, 4).

That the Lord Jesus accomplished the clearance of the

world of spirits, by the warfare and judgment so strikingly foretold, is certainly taught in the Gospels. "He that cometh after me," declared John the Baptist, "is mightier than I, whose shoes I am not worthy to bear. He shall baptize with the Holy Spirit, and with fire: whose fan is in His hand, and He will thoroughly purge His floor, and gather His wheat into the garner; but He will burn up the chaff with unquenchable fire" (Matt. iii. 11, 12). Again, "I beheld Satan as lightning fall from heaven. Behold, I give unto you power to tread on serpents and scorpions, and over all the power of the enemy: and nothing shall by any means hurt you" (Luke x. 18, 19). Again, "Now is the judgment of this world: now shall the prince of this world be cast out" (John xii. 31). All these intimations show most convincingly, that while the Lord's life before men was quiet as a gentle, peaceful teacher, a loving friend, a patient sufferer, in the world of spirits He was overthrowing myriads of evil ones; and when He finished the work of redemption by His cross, "having spoiled principalities and powers, He made a show of them openly, triumphing over them" (Col. ii. 15). "By death He destroyed him that had the power of death, even the devil" (Heb. ii. 14).

Redemption, then, was the overthrow of the powers of darkness in the spirit-world, and the deliverance of good spirits and men from their infernal bondage; and David was the type of the Redeemer when engaged in this spiritual warfare. His carrying out this great work to its full accomplishment—enduring every temptation, and overcoming all foes—was represented by David's reigning forty years. His deliverance and preservation of all who were in goodness was represented by the reigning in Hebron seven years; and His delivering such from error, and giving them abundance of Divine Truths, is meant by His taking Jerusalem and reigning there thirty and three years. David's dying and being succeeded by Solomon was a type of the Lord's suffering humanity, when His redeeming work was completed, being succeeded by His Glorified Humanity, the Divine Solomon.

David being old, and getting no heat from being covered with clothes, represents the Lord rising in the mind and in the Church; His warrior character dying away, and His Glorified Humanity becoming the object of adoration. Clothes represent doctrines, and these without love impart no heat.

The remarkable circumstance of Abishag the Shunammite,

a fair young virgin, being brought to keep warmth in the king, represents the interesting law of Divine Mercy, which provides that, before a new order of things is established, an intermediate between the old and the new is permitted for a time. After the redemption of mankind was completed, and before the Christian Church was established, with the glorified Saviour as the Divine Solomon, the Prince of Peace reigning over it, there was an intermediate band consisting of the pious and pure-minded amongst the Jews, who kept up the warmth of the Lord, that is, kept the sense of the Divine Love alive in the earth. The remnant of the truly pious in one Church is the nucleus of another. They are not properly the Lord's bride, and never will be. They are not the Lamb's wife, but they serve until the Lamb's wife has grown and is ready.

They are beautiful in character and affection, they cherish and minister to the king; but in a short time their office is over, and the true Church appears. The Christian Jews were good and pious, but their mission was soon completed. They gave place to more perfect Christians, and passed away. We have taken thus a view of the passage as it represents the Lord, His victorious redemption of mankind, and the finishing of His conquests and character as the Redeemer, the warlike King. Let us resume the consideration of the subject as it applies to the work of regeneration in us. The Lord must be a David in us, and do the work of David, before He can become a Solomon.

Has David done his work in us? Has the power of Divine Truth in us smitten the Philistines? Have we overcome the persuasion, that when we know and believe the true faith it is enough? Do we think, because we are in the Church, as the Philistines were in Canaan, that we have done all that is needful, though we are bitter and quarrelsome as the Philistines were?

We must destroy this destructive error, as David slew Goliath. We must become loving and good, gentle as well as true. We must overcome envy and pride, ostentation and vanity, be pure in word, and just in deed. The only way to heaven is to become heavenly. The Lord forgives every soul which comes in sincerity to Him. But if the penitent do not proceed to root out resolutely the evil within, "the last state of that man will be worse than the first."

It is dishonour to our Lord, to think He cannot overcome

in us our evil principles and evil tempers. But the way He overcomes, is by giving us power to overcome. We must have faith in Him. Our Goliath is strong, so long as we fear and are unbelieving. When we are faithful and firm, our foe falls. To him that overcometh, the Lord gives light, love, and peace in ever-increasing fulness.

We should be encouraged by the thought that our conflict with sin is the one grand struggle in which we are certain to conquer, if we are faithful; we cannot fail if we are true. The first thing, the indispensable thing, is, that we enter into a spirit of charity, of good-will to all. Love is life. We must pray, and press, and importune the Lord, until we receive from Him the life of heavenly love, and make it our own,—dwell in it, reign in it, until it becomes our abiding nature, our new heart. This is to reign in Hebron seven years. Divine Truth will then open to us the perception that our intellectual part is not yet in thorough harmony with heaven. We imagine that in many things we must think as the world thinks, and carry out the world's maxims. And many a blind fancy, and many a lame proceeding, are tolerated in our Jebus; for these we can conquer if we try. Our thoughts are views of all the relations of life: the whole man ought to belong to the Lord Jesus, and to carry out His laws. "The kingdoms of this world shall become the kingdoms of our Lord and of His Christ, and He shall reign for ever and ever." When we set ourselves to achieve this victory, we shall be successful. Jebus will be turned into Jerusalem. The hollow maxims of worldliness, blind and lame as they are in a thousand ways, will be exchanged for the principles of true religion and of solid peace. The mind as well as the heart will fully accord with the Divine Wisdom.

Then Solomon will begin to sit on the throne of David his father, and his kingdom will be established greatly. In other words, the rule of the Lord Jesus will not now be the struggle against opposing evils and errors, but the development and establishment of goodness and truth. The new heart will abound in heavenly feelings, states, and impulses. We shall often glow with desires to do something more for the Lord, something better. We shall find grand openings of heavenly wisdom expanding themselves before us. "Our righteousness will become like a river, and our peace like the waves of the sea." The Prince of Peace will rule over us; and of His government and peace there shall be no end.

SERMON XXVIII.

SOLOMON'S PRAYER.

"And now, O Lord my God, thou hast made thy servant king instead of David my father; and I am but a little child: I know not how to go out or to come in.
"And thy servant is in the midst of thy people whom thou hast chosen, a great people, that cannot be numbered nor counted for multitude.
"Give, therefore, thy servant an understanding heart to judge thy people, that I may discern between good and bad: for who is able to judge this thy so great a people?"—
1 KINGS iii. 7-9.

HUMILITY is the true basis of every blessing. We are as nothing before the grandeur and perfection of the Lord, and ought ever to feel as expressed by Solomon, that we are but as little children, and of ourselves know neither how to go out nor to come in. Hence the importance of praying to the Lord to give us His wisdom to guide us, that we may be able to discern between good and evil. Who of himself can judge wisely in all the devious ways of practical and intellectual life? Yet it is of the utmost importance that we exercise judgment. Liberty and rationality are the truly human attributes which distinguish men from inferior beings, and from the image of God in us. By exercising these wisely, we become truly human. By exercising these wisely, we perform faithfully the part assigned to us in the household of our Heavenly Father; and our part, however small, if done well, will affect the whole for good. Considerations like these opened themselves manifestly to the mind of Solomon, when he succeeded to the kingdom of Israel and the throne of his father. He felt his important position in the midst of a people formed into a nation, with interests varied, complicated, and numerous; weighty for good if rightly directed, powerful for mischief if deficient in true wisdom. He prayed, therefore, for this all-important guidance. "Give, therefore, Thy servant an understanding heart to judge Thy people, that I may discern between good and bad." We are not all placed by Divine Providence in positions so illustrious as that of Solomon, but the essential relations of life are nearly alike for all. We have all needs which in their broad features have many similarities; and we all require similar mercies and virtues from the Most High, rightly to perform the duties of our life and station. If we are not in the midst of a great people, whose welfare largely depends upon us, we are in the midst of relations and connections far-reaching in their consequences and results; and for every one of us the prayer of Solomon is the right petition: Give me an understanding, or, as it might be more closely rendered, a listening or hearkening heart.

It may be properly remarked, that the intellect rather than the heart is the seat of understanding; and we have observed that a listening or hearkening heart would be a more correct rendering of the original words; yet the heart has a great deal to do even with our intellectual views. The eyes will never see very clearly, if the heart will not permit them to look.

A hearkening heart means an obedient will: the heart corresponds everywhere in the Divine Word to the will. What the heart is to the body, that the will is to the soul. The heart is the centre of the circulation, which sends life and force throughout the body, and really builds up the ten thousand organs and tissues of the human frame. The heart is the inner man of the body—the central palace where the blood is wondrously elaborated and prepared. The heart uses the lungs to purify the vital stream, and remove what has become worn out and injurious; and when the blood returns refreshed and invigorated, it sends it forth with all its flood of forces to give energy to the brain, sight to the eye, power to the hand, and vitality everywhere. What the heart is, that the body is. If the heart be feeble, irregular in its action, or stiff and bonelike, the lungs soon suffer, the blood becomes impure, the body by many sufferings indicates disorder at the centre, and decay and death ensue. If the heart be vigorous, firm, and healthy, the whole wondrous structure feels its grand pulsations, and thrills with energy and health.

The will is the heart of the soul. When the WILL is vigorous, the whole soul is warm. The loves, friendships, aims, hopes, ends, and affections of the will give tone and character to the whole mind. Where there is a will, there's a way. Convince a man against his will, he's of the same opinion still. These proverbs, and many others which utter the experience of mankind, teach the great truth that the will is the man; and such as is the real character of the will, such is the real character of the intellect, of the works, and of the whole man.

The will, then, is to the soul what the heart is to the body—the centre of its energies, and that which gives a character to every other faculty and every other principle, indeed to the whole man. Hence the will is called the heart, because it corresponds to it in all respects; and we have throughout the Divine Word such declarations as, "Thou shalt love the Lord thy God with all thy heart;" "I will praise the Lord with all my heart" (Ps. lxxxvi. 12); "I will walk within my house with a perfect heart" (Ps. ci. 2); "I will give them one heart, and I will take the stony heart out of their flesh, and will give them a heart of flesh" (Ezek. xi. 19); "Bessed are the pure in heart, for they shall see God" (Matt. v. 8): "Those things which proceed out of the mouth come forth from the heart" (Matt. xv. 18); "Out of the heart proceed evil thoughts" (Mark vii. 21). And in the Book of Proverbs there is a passage whose weight and importance have been often dwelt upon: "Keep thy heart with all diligence, for out of it are the issues of life" (Prov. iv. 23). And the apostle said, "With the heart a man believeth unto righteousness" (Rom. x. 10).

All these passages prove and illustrate these two facts: that the heart in Scripture corresponds to the will; that the will is the grand faculty in the soul, and that its functions to man's spiritual nature are equal in importance to those which the heart exercises in his natural body. These facts are perceived by the common sense of mankind, as is evident from the phrases of ordinary speech. When a person intends to say he will perform some work with his whole will, he says he will do it with all his heart. Of something which is not in harmony with a man's will, he is said to have no heart in it. A bad will is called a bad heart; a good disposition is designated a good heart.

So, in the prayer before us, the petition of Solomon is, "Give me a hearing heart;" that is, manifestly, "Give me a will to attend to and obey that which Divine Wisdom may utter. When God speaks, give me the grace to listen."

There is a wide-spread idea, which has been inculcated in the name of philosophy, that belief is the simple result of evidence. Faith is said to be the inevitable consequence of proof sufficient. So that if a man believes, it is simply because good evidence has induced conviction, and he could not withhold his assent; and if another man is not convinced, it is simply that proofs enough have not been supplied; and there is in neither case any room for praise or blame, merit or demerit: there is no exercise of will in obtaining faith.

The will is said to follow conviction necessarily. So that if you give a man proper evidences, he must be convinced; if convinced, he must will in harmony with his convictions: and so man is a creature of circumstances.

But experience and the Divine Word both teach a very different lesson. It is not enough to have great truths and good evidence brought before a person. He must will to believe what is true, or no impression will be made upon his mind. If a man does not desire the truth, he can listen or not listen: he can pervert what he hears, he can give prominence to some portions of what he hears, and depress and place in the background portions not in agreement with his wishes; and the result will be darkness to one who loves darkness, and light only to one who loves light. "Unto the upright there arises a light in the darkness" (Ps. cxii. 4). And with the wicked, "They love darkness rather than light, because their deeds are evil" (John iii. 19). Hence the unspeakable value of a heart that yearns for truth, that seeks for it, that listens for it.

Truth and love flowed from the Lord in one grand stream, and continue to do so; but when they arrive at human minds they separate—the soul is now in disorder, and will not receive them both at once—but, like brother and sister, they long for each other's company again. Good loves truth, and listens for it. Truth loves good, and points to it. Love, when it enters the heart in the form of goodness, makes it a listening heart, listening for the truth. This attracts the truth, as the magnet attracts iron. It embraces and embosoms truth, as the good ground receives the seed. Mercy and truth are met together, righteousness and peace have kissed each other. Truth shall spring out of the earth, and righteousness shall look down from heaven.

Thus we may see why, when the truth is addressed to a general audience, one person will receive it gladly, another will reject, a third will be indifferent.

The love of truth must be active in the soul, or there will be no reception of truth, no hearkening heart, no inward assent, no real faith. Without the love of truth, faith cannot enter the soul, salvation cannot enter. Unless truth is believed, there is no power against evil and false principles, no victory in temptation, no growth in love to the Lord or in charity to our neighbour; no attainment of spiritual beauty, of order, or of heaven within.

"Give me then a hearkening heart" should be the universal

prayer, the prayer of every one, as it was the prayer of Solomon. Solomon was prepared for this petition by the perception previously of his need and his littleness. He said, "I am but a little child: I know not how to go out or to come in."

The spirit of humility is always the true preparation for the reception of heavenly graces. "Blessed are the poor in spirit, for theirs is the kingdom of heaven."

If we think we are very wise already, we shall not seek with great earnestness for other wisdom. If we esteem ourselves very correct and good already, we shall not hunger after the righteousness of the Lord. If we deem our own lives to be faultless, we shall not seek very assiduously to become better. The very essence of heaven is that lowly spirit which feels that there is neither merit, goodness, nor wisdom in ourselves. Of ourselves, we know not how to go out or to come in. We are poor and needy, but "The Lord thinketh upon us" is the true feeling of the Christian. Humility leads to peace and to progress. "Learn of me," the Lord said; "for I am meek and lowly in heart: and ye shall find rest unto your souls." Those angels whose graces are the highest bend the lowest before the throne of the Eternal. The living ones who are in the midst of the heavenly throne are ever saying, "Holy, holy, holy, Lord God Almighty, who is, and who was, and who art to come."

The lark, high as it soars and sings, has a lowly nest. The violet, whose fragrance perfumes a hedgerow, is often hidden from sight. The heart will not be haughty, nor the eyes lofty, when self is abhorred and rejected to the depths of the sea of the soul. They who are averse to all that is evil and false because it is from themselves, and are in the affection of all that is good and true because it is from the Lord, are in humiliation, and in a state to receive goodness and truth from the Lord. Unless a man humbles himself by acknowledging that he is nothing but evil, he is in merit and self-righteousness; and as good cannot flow in, he cannot be withheld from the evils of his selfhood.

> "The saint that wears heaven's brightest crown
>   In deepest adoration bends:
> The weight of glory bows him down
>   Then most, when most the soul ascends:
> Nearest the throne itself must be
> The footstool of humility."

Humiliation bends the knee, and, when it is fullest, prostrates the whole body, before the Majesty Divine, the unutterable perfection of Infinite Mercy, Purity, and Love. It feels the truth ever to be as expressed by Solomon: "I am but a little child: I know not how to go out or to come in." Solomon was, moreover, not only the type of the Christian, but of the Lord Jesus in His glorified humanity. He was pre-eminently the Prince of Peace—the Divine Solomon. He was conscious, in His humanity, that all its powers and capabilities were from the Father. The Son was formed from the Father, lived from the Father, thought from the Father, felt and loved from the Father, yet AS OF Himself. He had a consciousness in Himself, as being a Divine Man; yet He ever felt that the Father, the Divine Love within Him, was the Fountain whence every power of the Humanity was derived. Just as the body of a man lives from the soul, speaks and acts from the soul, yet feels distinct and has a consciousness as if life were its own and in itself; so, in the Lord's human nature, He felt His thoughts, perceptions, and powers as if they were self-existent: yet He knew constantly, and constantly taught, that the Son could do nothing of Himself. He said: "The Son can do nothing of Himself, but what He seeth the Father do; for what things soever He doeth, these also doeth the Son likewise" (John v. 19). To us the Son is everything, yet everything from the Father within. "For as the Father hath life in Himself, so hath He given the Son to have life in Himself" (ver. 26). The Son was to reveal the Father, to raise a dead world to life, to give light, to impart salvation, to convey power to men that they might conquer their evils and follies, and rise to become images and likenesses of the Lord Himself. Power over all flesh was given unto Him—all power in heaven and on earth; yet all was from the Father. To us He is Wonderful, Counsellor, the government upon His shoulder; He is all and in all, the Mighty God, the Everlasting Father, and the Prince of Peace. Yet He was infinitely meek; and in comparison with the Divine Love within, He could say: My Father is greater than I. "All things are delivered to me," He declared, "of my Father; and no man knoweth the Son, but the Father." How wonderful, how mysterious, how glorious this revelation of the Father in the Son—of the Divine in the Human! The Human is a Divine Human, and to us the Mercy-seat, the Temple of the Godhead, the Sun of Righteousness; yet all from the invisible Father, the otherwise unapproachable. The Son must reveal the Father to us. "No man knoweth the Father save the Son, and he to whom THE SON WILL REVEAL HIM." Just as the body reveals the soul—in its looks, in its gestures, in its touch, in every movement—so the Son reveals the Father, not as another, but as His own inner nature. Though all the grandeurs of Deity are revealed in the Saviour, and he is King of kings and Lord of lords; yet there is this constant humility in Him, which says, in relation to the boundless infinitude of the Father within: I am but a little child; I know not of myself how to go out or to come in; but all things that the Father hath are mine. All Thine are mine, and mine are Thine; and I am glorified in them (John xvii. 10). Yet am I a little child, nothing of myself; all is from Thee. O Father, Thou only art underivedly Holy, Wise, Omnipotent, and I from Thee. I in them, and Thou in me, that they may be made perfect in one.

This perfect subserviency and response of the Humanity in the Lord Jesus, His having a hearing heart to the Divine Love in the most absolute perfection, gives a grandeur to the words of Solomon in their application to Him of the most wonderful kind. "Thy servant is in the midst of Thy people, whom Thou hast chosen, a great people, that cannot be numbered nor counted for multitude. Give, therefore, Thy servant a hearing heart to judge Thy people, that I may discern between good and bad: for who is able to judge this Thy so great a people?" Let us raise our view from Solomon and his nation—so great to him, though otherwise comparatively small—to the Saviour, ascended high above all heavens, that He might fill all things (Eph. iv. 10), ruling and blessing the heavenly in all worlds and through all ages; and we shall then obtain a glimpse of the inner glory of the Word, and perceive how far the spirit and life exceed the outward form. To the Lord Jesus the words are applicable as they are to no other. "Lo, I have given thee a wise and a hearing heart; so that there was none like thee before thee, neither after thee shall any arise like unto thee. And I have also given thee that which thou hast not asked, both riches and honour; so that there shall not be any among the kings like unto thee all thy days." Let us, however, turn from this wondrous and attractive theme, to the humbler lesson which the Divine Word contains in the blessing pronounced upon Solomon, because in his prayer he had asked only for spiritual graces, leaving all outward things contentedly to the Divine Providence. He had asked for a hearing heart, to give him perception to discern between the good and the bad. This perception is higher than knowledge, higher than reason: it is an inner sight, which comes from the union of love and truth in the interiors of the heart, making a good and supremely tender conscience.

This is indeed an invaluable gift from our Heavenly Father, an inmost blessing. Outer gifts—long life, riches, power, victories over others—may be blessings, or they may be curses. They are blessings to those who use them conscientiously; they are to others snares and curses. We do not know whether they will do good or evil to ourselves or to others; and therefore they are not proper subjects for prayer. But to pray for humility, obedience, wisdom, love, patience, and all heavenly graces, this will secure all that is needful. "Seek ye first the kingdom of God and His righteousness, and all these things shall be added unto you" (Matt. vi. 33).

What we shall eat, what we shall drink, what we shall wear, riches, power, prosperity,—these are not the subjects for prayer, but for Providence. The Lord will provide in these respects what is good for us; and while we diligently cultivate our powers, and do our duty, we should pray for content, gratitude, and peace. The one thing needful is to become heavenly, and live the life of heavenly usefulness on earth.

No wealth, no possessions, no gifts, no talents, no adornments, however rare or costly, no opportunities for distinction, no applause, no fame, can impart what the yearning heart wants, unless the Lord and His kingdom are there. Let us then pray, with Solomon, for the hearing heart, that ever listens to the voice of the Saviour in the conscience, and follows Him. Then from day to day the Lord will lead us: to trial, when trial is good; to inward peace during the struggle, and full content and prosperity when the trial is over. Weeping may endure for a night, but joy cometh in the morning. And, both night and morning, though the Lord give us the bread of adversity and the water of affliction, yet shall not our teachers be removed into a corner any more; but our eyes shall see our teachers, and our ears shall hear a word behind us, saying, This is the way, walk ye in it.

Because we ask for a hearing heart and a wise understanding, the Lord will give them. And He will give those things for which we have not asked, but which would conduce to our comfort and usefulness in this life also, when He sees they would be real blessings; not temporal only, but extending our progress and happiness through ages which will never end.

SERMON XXIX.

THE JUDGMENT OF SOLOMON CONCERNING THE DEAD AND THE LIVING CHILD.

"Then spake the woman whose the living child was, unto the king, for her bowels yearned upon her son, and she said, O my lord give her the living child, and in no wise slay it. But the other said, Let it be neither mine or thine, but divide it.
"Then the king answered and said, Give her the living child, and in no wise slay it: she is the mother thereof."—1 KINGS iii. 26, 27.

THE discernment for which Solomon prayed, and which in his dream the Lord promised should be granted to him, was soon manifest to Israel. The sagacity he displayed in finding out the real mother in the curious case submitted to his judgment produced reverence for him through the land, and a conviction that the wisdom of God was in him to do judgment.

It seemed indeed to be a matter not easy to determine. Here were two unknown women, who in one house and on the day after the other, had children. They were alone, and the second mother overlaid her child, and awoke to find it dead. The circumstances imply that she was a careless woman, with none of the mother's intensely tender feeling, but still for some reason she would rather have a living child than a dead one. She saw the other woman peacefully sleeping; her child, three days old, peacefully sleeping also. She crept stealthily with her dead babe, and took the living one from its sleeping mother, leaving her own lifeless infant with the unconscious woman, who probably in her dreams was picturing the happy future of her child.

The bereaved mother awoke, and in her love for her child, her first thought was to supply its want. She placed it to her breast but found no effort. It was still and breathless, and the conviction came that her child was dead. But, still fondling about and mourning over it, the morning came, and with the light she saw this little lifeless one was not her son. Though only three days old her love had marked the lineaments of

P

her babe upon her heart. She could not be mistaken. She had photographed with loving gaze each little feature on her warm affections, had touched with exquisite tenderness its little fingers, each little limb, and though the other shameless creature unfeelingly persisted in her wrong, yet the mother cried for justice and would not be appeased. So the case was brought before the youthful monarch. The young Solomon heard their story, listened to their assertions and denials. It was a perplexing case as there were no witnesses, and both women belonged to a class not always credited with possessing a reverence for truth.

It occurred to the king that the true mother would have far more love for the infant than the pretended one, and therefore if the child seemed to be in danger, the real mother would do anything to save it. The pretended mother who had readily parted with her own dead babe would most likely be indifferent to the well-being of that which was not hers. The king feigned perplexity, and seeming to be puzzled ordered the child to be divided and half to be given to one woman, and half to the other.

The plan succeeded. The woman who had been so cool over her own smothered child, showed very little agitation about the other. The real mother would suffer anything in her own feelings to save her child. They might give it even to her rival, but they must not hurt it. The king saw where the genuine mother's love was, and decreed accordingly. All who heard of it applauded the judicious decision, and were grateful to God who had given them, as successor to the warlike David, a prince at once sagacious and just: a monarch who would be a father in the land.

In its literal sense, this narrative is extremely interesting. It illustrates the simplicity at that time of Eastern manners. The king appears accessible to all. It was usual for the monarch to dispense justice at the gate of his palace, or the gate of the city, to all requiring it, and probably some such place was the scene of the transaction recorded. There were no pleaders, no cross-examiners, no law's delay, or long uncertainty, often so cruel in modern times, but the case was heard in the simplest manner, the matter at once decided upon, judgment declared, and justice done.

But, let us turn now to consider the deeper wisdom of the divine narrative before us; for although the incident occurred as related in the early part of the reign of Solomon, it forms part of the Word of God to afford us, in addition to the moral lessons of the letter, wider and deeper lessons for the Church and for the soul.

Solomon in his glorious and peaceful reign was the type of the Lord Jesus reigning in His kingdom, and judging in His Church.

The womanly character is represented to us in Scripture as the type of the Lord's Church, which is called His bride and wife.

The church is intended to be as warm, as true, as confiding and truthful in her affections towards the Lord as a loving, true, and faithful wife is to her husband. Hence we read such passages as the following. Thy Maker is thine husband; the Lord of Hosts is His name: and thy Redeemer is the Holy One of Israel; the God of the whole earth shall He be called. (Isa. liv. 5). Turn, O backsliding children, saith the Lord, for I am married unto you; and I will take you one of a city and two of a family; and I will bring you to Zion. (Jer. iii. 14). In the New Testament the Lord Jesus, because He was the manifested God, is represented as the Bridegroom. John the Baptist said of Him, in this respect I am not the Christ but am sent before Him. He that hath the bride is the Bridegroom: but the friend of the Bridegroom, which standeth and heareth him, rejoiceth greatly because of the Bridegroom's voice: this my joy therefore is fulfilled. He must increase but I must decrease. He that cometh from above is above all. (John iii. 29, 31). The apostle said I have espoused you to one husband, that I may present you as a chaste virgin to Christ. (2 Cor. xi. 2.)

The Church is continually represented in Scripture as a virgin, a bride, and a wife. Hence, we read such passages as the following: Hearken, O daughter, and consider and incline thine ear: forget also thine own people, and thy father's house, so shall the King greatly desire thy beauty: for He is thy Lord, and worship thou Him (Psa. xlv. 10, 11). Turn again, O virgin of Israel, turn again to these thy cities. How long wilt thou go about, O thou backsliding daughter? For the Lord hath created a new thing in the earth, a woman shall encompass a man (Jer. xxxi. 21, 22). The Church, as in future it would be an interior one among the Gentiles, is described when it is said, 'Sing, O barren, thou that didst not bear: break forth into singing thou that didst not travail with child; for more are the children of the desolate than the children of the married wife;' saith the Lord (Isa. liv. 1). Again the prophet says, "For as a young man marrieth a virgin, so shall thy sons marry thee: and as the bridegroom rejoiceth over the bride, so shall thy God rejoice over thee" (Isa. lxii. 5).

These and similar allusions and declarations evince most clearly that the Church is represented in Scripture by a virgin, a woman, and a wife, and it is not difficult to perceive the reason. The leading characteristic of the womanly nature is affection, and it is affection to the Lord and our neighbour which is the chief essential of the Church. Not cold knowledge or hard faith, but warm love unites a man to the Lord, and makes him a portion of the Lord's Church. The whole Church should cleave to the Lord Jesus as a wife clings to her husband. The Church should fix her heart upon the Lord Jesus alone, as a pure wife has one husband only. The Church should confide in the protection of the Lord Jesus as a trusting wife rests confidently in the care and strength of her husband.

The women before us were not wives, although they were mothers. They represent, therefore, a Church which has not been faithful to the Lord. When a Church has turned from the truth, and sunk into error and traditions, instead of abiding by the Divine Word and obeying it, then from a wife it becomes a harlot, or rather two harlots in one house, as represented in the narrative before us. The most awful picture of this state of things is portrayed in the Book of Revelations, where the perverted Christian Church is described as a great harlot, a woman arrayed in purple and scarlet colour, and decked with gold and precious stones and pearls, having a golden cup in her hand, full of abominations, and filthiness of her fornications, and upon her forehead having a name written, "Mystery, Babylon the Great, the mother of harlots, and abominations of the earth" (Rev. xvii. 4, 5). It is a sad and solemn symbol for reflection this perverted Church; a harlot, and a mother of harlots, with mystery for a God, instead of the God of Love.

The two harlots in one house represent a Church no longer in close communion with the Lord, but having adopted false views, and being governed by pernicious principles, making the commandments of God of none effect by their traditions. In such a Church, however, all are not alike. There are those who cherish false doctrines from ignorance, from circumstances, and an erroneous education. These would accept the truth if it were suitably introduced to them. They do conscientiously what good they know. They are often pious, humble, and tender: they live a good life so far as they understand it. These are represented by the woman with the first child. The new birth with them is solid, sincere, and good, and they cherish the new character they attain, supplying to themselves the sincere milk of the Word. These continue in an earnest and sincere state, doing good as they best can. They fear God, and work righteousness, and their child lives.

In the same house, however, or the same Church, there are those who love darkness rather than light, because their deeds are evil. On the third day, or at the end of the Church, this woman has a child, or puts on a religious character; but this child dies in the night, or in other words, when trial and dimness come, their zeal dies away, and what little profession of goodness there was perishes. The one party, the inwardly good, are better than their doctrine by far. Although they are taught to say that a good life has nothing to do with heaven, that a man is saved by faith only, if exercised at last, and however vile a life he may have led, yet they are as careful to regulate both heart and life, that both may be well-pleasing in the sight of the Lord, as if all depended on themselves.

The others, represented by the other woman, do really not care about a heavenly life. They are self-seeking and evil, governed only by a regard for appearances, when they seem to be moral and religious.

There are times, however, when the truth is brought home to them. Thou hast a name that thou livest and art dead. Their pretended good life, they then see has no life in it. Their faith alone is seen to be a dead faith. But some excuse must be made, some defence must be put forth, and they seize their neighbour's child, or, in other words, they attribute to their Church, their doctrines, their faith, and themselves, what love has brought forth in the humble minded doers of good.

It is very common for persons of this class to declare that although their only faith that Christ died for them is saving, yet that this faith is so full of godliness, that it necessarily produces good works.

They know that myriads hold this faith, and do not produce good works; nay, the vast bulk of people in Christian countries believe that Christ died for them, but they do not heartily believe that they ought to live for Him. They are ready enough to believe that Christ has suffered and done every thing for them, and the more they smell out this side of what they declare the blessed one has done for them, the less room is there for self-denial and subduing of evils which they love. But they know that the Word everywhere enjoins a good life, and commands incessantly good works to be done. They have invented therefore this theory of the necessary results of their faith, and to confirm it they point to those loving humble souls who love the Lord and love to do His will. See what good works they do, they say, what hospitals they support, what Sunday schools they carry on, what works of mercy they perform. All this is the result of our faith.

But this is only stealing their neighbour's living child and passing it off as their own.

It is true that thousands of excellent Christians do good works, and live really Christian lives, although in the doctrinal declarations they have been taught to say, faith only is saving. These persons are better than their creed. They do in their hearts believe that they must shun sin and do good, or they cannot be saved. They do indeed believe that the Lord Jesus died for them, and did and does all that the Divine Love prompts to be done for their salvation, but they believe also that He gives His Word to tell them what they have to do, and they love to obey it.

They hear him saying, if ye will enter into life keep the commandments. Blessed are they that do His commandments. While they from His Love, His Life and His death for them, are filled with love to Him, from His precepts they regulate their daily lives. They cease to do evil, and learn to do well. They work out their salvation with fear and trembling, and when they feel a difficulty in doing His Will, they look up and remember all He has done for them.

These are they who, whatever their doctrines are, become truly born again. They become as to their characters, new-born babes, and the babes are truly alive. They are "babes in Christ," for every one that useth milk is unskilful in the Word of righteousness: for he is a babe (Heb. v. 13). "Yet as new-born babes, they desire the sincere milk of the Word, that they may grow thereby" (1 Pet. ii. 2).

These babes are full of new life, and will live. They yearn to do good, and to be good, not from a sense of merit, but from love. They love the Lord, they love His Word, they love His kingdom. They live from heavenly motives, and they live for heaven.

The Word is their delight and their joy, and as they read, it is as if a voice ever accompanied them saying, If ye know these things, happy are ye if ye do them. They hear their doctrinal expounders often declare that good works have nothing to do with their salvation, and evil works will not condemn one whose faith at the last hour is right, but they pay little attention to them. They pray that they may please the Lord. They do what they believe will be well-pleasing in His sight. They obey His Word, and when evils present themselves in their hearts, tempers, or lives, they carefully struggle against them. Thus they live Christian lives, and the Lord blesses them. Their faith is seen in their works. Their lives adorn the doctrine of God their Saviour. These are they, who have the child for three days, and who rise to give it suck in the morning. The discovery that the child placed in the bosom of the mother of the living one is dead, represents that those in an erroneous church who really love virtue and heavenly-mindedness, when truth discovers to them that the religion they profess has no relation to life are shocked, and protest against it. They believe in their private way, but very really that all they do should spring from religion. There should be, they believe in their hearts, religion in trade, religion in temper, religion in everything. They will not have the dead child, they want their own living child, and however often they may be told that religion is a thing of belief and worship only, and has nothing to do with works or life in the world, they will not believe it. They treat as a delusion the pretence that a person should strive to get faith that he may be saved; but not strive to overcome selfishness, pride, peevishness, over-reaching and every known evil on peril of continuing in his sins, and being incapable of entering heaven.

They bring the matter before Solomon. They appeal to the Lord Jesus Christ. The sword which Solomon commanded to be brought is the symbol of the Word. The sword of the Spirit is the Word of God. For the Word of God is quick and powerful, and sharper than any two-edged sword . . . . and is a discerner of the thoughts and intents of the heart. (Heb. iv. 12.)

The Lord Jesus tests the real love of any one for a good life by pressing upon them the possibility of a religion in life being altogether destroyed. Those who are inwardly evil are not shocked at that. Their life in the world is a thing, they suppose, which they can conduct on selfish principles; it has nothing to do with religion. Let it be neither mine nor thine but divide it. They would be quite content to fight the fierce battle of life, while life is a scramble for wealth and distinction, if religion will only provide for their getting to heaven at last. Let living virtue be neither mine nor thine, but divide it. Let

those who care for worship have worship; it is very decent and
proper, but let them not suppose it is essential to any spiritual
growth or regeneration which is to fit them for heaven; Christ
kept the law for us, and it is not really necessary for us to keep
it, and we cannot. Let those who feel inclined to lead a
moral life do so, it is quite right; but there is no spiritual life in
that, as it is only the other half of a dead child, it has nothing to
do with salvation. If you think it has, you are quite in the
wrong way, you are taking from the glory of Christ. Such is
the way of thinking expressed in a great variety of ways by
those who have divided faith from love and life, but yet are
anxious to add to all the gains they desire to amass on earth,
all the bliss of heaven, without the labour of real self-denial.

But what says the real mother of the child, that is, those who
really desire the life of heaven upon earth. These long to see
a better world: they long to become good. If, as they are
told, the prevalence of the doctrine of salvation by faith alone
more widely, will induce a truly good life from gratitude, they
are willing it should in this, but a heavenly life, a heavenly
world, they are convinced, there ought to be. Give her the
child, they say, but don't destroy it. O for a better world. O
for a closer walk with God. O for a state in which every feeling, every thought, every act, and every word might be per-
vaded by the spirit of heaven. Let it be by this doctrine or by
that, by circumcision or uncircumcision, by ritual or anti-ritual,
but let us see faith working by love, a religion of glory to God
in the highest, and on earth peace, good-will towards men.

Now, Solomon speaks, the Lord Jesus gives His decision.
The woman who desires a living child, is the mother thereof.
Give her the child. The Lord in His judgment judges the
works of men, and the faith of any one, only so far as it is seen
in work. The Lord sees the heart, and tries the works of every
one, by the motive there was in it. Only those who love
what is good, and seek by truth to make their good purer and
purer, only these can be the mother of the living child. Except
your righteousness exceed the righteousness of the Scribes and
Pharisees, ye shall in NO CASE enter into the kingdom of heaven.
Why call ye me Lord, Lord, and do not the things that I say.
Walk worthy of the vocation, wherewith ye are called, with all
lowliness and meekness, with long-suffering; forbearing one
another, in love endeavouring to keep the unity of the spirit in
the bond of peace.

SERMON XXX.

THE BUILDING OF THE TEMPLE BY SOLOMON, WITHOUT HAMMER, AXE, OR ANY TOOL OF IRON.

"And the house when it was in building, was built of stone made ready before it was brought thither; so that there was neither hammer, nor axe, nor any tool of iron heard in the house, while it was in building."—1 KINGS vi. 7.

THE whole universe is the Temple of the Lord; the sublime outbirth and the dwelling-place of His infinite Love and Wisdom. His wisdom made the heavens: their movements are from the pulsations of His Love. The Lord hath prepared His throne in the heavens: and His kingdom ruleth over all. Bless the Lord, all His works in all places of His dominion: bless the Lord, O my soul. (Ps. ciii. 19, 22.)

Were men in true harmony with the Divine Being they would see and feel His majesty, truth, and tenderness all around them, for "in Him we live and move and have our being." But only as men become like God do they see God in all things, and perceive His Love encircling them in every object great and small, for "whatsoever the Lord pleases, that does He in heaven, and in earth, in the seas, and all deep places." Yet only when men themselves have become regenerated, and dwell in love, do they really know by experience that divine love is expressing itself in every object, and in each event. They then taste and see that the Lord is good, and are certain that the man is blessed that trusteth in Him. Each discovery one makes that the earth is full of the goodness of the Lord, comes like a voice from our Saviour repeating the tender remonstrance He uttered to Philip, "Have I been so long time with you, and yet hast thou not known me;" I was with thee when thou wast fearfully and wonderfully made in thy creation. I was with thee in thy mother's love, and thy father's care. I was with thee in all thy joys and thy sorrows, thy waywardness, thy pains, and thy penitence. Surely goodness and mercy have followed thee all the days of thy life; and thou shalt dwell in the house of the Lord for ever.

To reveal what man must become to be attuned to the harmony and bliss of the universe, and thus by Divine aid build himself up for heaven, the pattern of heavenly things was shewn to Moses in the Mount, and it was enjoined upon him that he should make a tabernacle, and all instruments suitable for worship exactly according to the pattern there exhibited. "Look that thou make them after their pattern, which was shewed thee in the Mount." (Ex. xxv. 40.)

The temple was a still more complete and full pattern of the constitution of heaven; and because it was a likeness of heaven, it was also a pattern for the church, which is the Lord's heaven among men, and likewise a pattern for a heavenly human mind, for this is a heaven in its least form. For all, then, who desire to become heavenly, the study of the Temple as the model of order amongst heavenly things, both amongst angels and men, may well become an object of meditation and earnest thought.

The divine direction was not only given to Solomon to build the Temple, for which David had stored up many of the materials, but it was expressly said, "concerning this house which thou art in building, if thou wilt walk in my statutes, and execute my judgments and keep all my commandments to walk in them; then will I perform my word with thee, which I spake unto David thy father: and I will dwell among the children of Israel, and will not forsake my people Israel." During the days of the typical church it would be the Lord's peculiar dwelling-place among them,—the centre of protection and blessing. There they should adore the Lord, and ask from Him direction and guidance in the things belonging to their peace, and there He would fulfil His gracious promise, "I will meet with thee, and I will commune with thee from above the mercy-seat, from between the two cherubim which are upon the ark of the testimony, of all things which I will give thee in commandment." (Ex. xxv. 22.)

The temple at Jerusalem was the visible sign and symbol of that still more glorious and celestial building THE CHURCH, which in due time would be formed among men, and of which the apostle speaks when He says, "Now, therefore, ye are no more strangers and foreigners, but fellow-citizens with the saints and with the household of God; and are built upon the foundation of the apostles and prophets, Jesus Christ Himself being the chief corner stone: in whom all the building fitly framed together groweth unto a holy temple in the Lord: in whom also ye are builded together for an habitation of God through the Spirit." (Eph. ii. 19, 22). And, again, "Know ye not that ye are the Temple of God, and that the Spirit of God dwelleth in you. If any man defile the Temple of God, him will God destroy: for the Temple of God is holy, which Temple, ye are." (1 Cor. iii. 16, 17).

The Temple was very moderate in dimension. A building thirty yards long, ten broad, and fifteen high can only be considered modest in relation to the wonderful structures of ancient and great numbers of those of modern times; but it was magnificent in the richness of its materials, and above all in the divine order and arrangement of all its parts, to represent perfectly the order of heaven and the church. Every part was full of significance, and spoke of heaven. This will equally appear if we consider the general configuration of the temple, and also the materials of which it was constructed.

The temple was threefold in all its proportions. There were the Holy of holies, the Holy-place, and the Porch. Inside the temple there were three galleries on three sides, one rising above the other, each gallery being wider than the one below it, the higher jutting over the lower, being supported by three rows of pillars, each row increasing in height towards the outside, and the lowest gallery front within the temple resting on cedar pilasters or half pillars. The galleries were filled with small chambers. The chambers of each upper gallery being larger than those of the gallery beneath. The lower gallery was five cubits in width, the middle six, and the highest seven.

The temple was surrounded on all sides but the front with three rows of pillars, forming three passages between them, all round, for exercise and meditation.

This general description can hardly fail to exhibit to the thoughtful Christian that the heavenly world represented by this temple with its three galleries has three grand degrees in it, the lowest heaven, the middle, and the highest, called elsewhere the heaven of heavens. The little chambers in each gallery will represent the specific societies in each heaven, for "in our Father's house there are many mansions." Variety in harmony is the order of divine works in all things, in the heavens, as well as on the earth, and may we not say on all the earths of the universe. "Each star differeth from each other star in glory." The number FIVE is used in Scripture when things of small value are treated of, and was the measure of the width of the lowest gallery : the number SIX, derived from the six days of labour, represents the attainments of the spiritual man, which are of great value, but have something of labour associated with them; while the number SEVEN, the width in cubits of the highest gallery, reminds us of the day of rest, and is expressive of the celestial state, the state of the perfect angel; the state of full peace enjoyed by those who are more than conquerors through Him that loved them. The number seven is also the Hebrew word for perfect. The uppermost gallery was ordained to be seven cubits in width, because it represented the highest heaven, and the perfection in love of the angels who are there.

The temple was wider as it became higher. (1 Kings vi. 6. Ezek. xli. 7). And, this was to denote doubtless the greater power and the influence of the angels, as they belong to higher states in the regenerate life, and so possess the higher homes of the blessed. The angels of obedience who inhabit the lower courts of our Heavenly Father are happy to the utmost of their power of reception, and their ministering influence is employed by the Lord to sustain the virtue of novitiates who have been won from darkness to light, for there is joy in heaven over one sinner that repenteth. But the angels of light have a wider vocation and a vaster power. They awaken the intellect, and extend the view. They scatter doubts and allay fears, as ministers of the blessed Saviour. They aid the "children of the light," to see the Word in its inner beauty, and from them flashes many a gleam of brightness into the hours of gloom and sorrow. They enable the soul to realize the gracious words, "Unto the upright there ariseth a light in the darkness."

But, above all are the ANGELS OF LOVE. These have passed through much tribulation and the deepest states of self-denial, and received from the Lord Jesus the holiest likeness of Himself. They are meek and lowly, from Him, the meekest and the lowliest. They have sought to be lambs from the innocence of the Lamb of God, and their gentle spheres enter more deeply, and affect more widely than any other order of angelic being, and to represent this the upper gallery of the temple was the widest of all.

A similar order exists in the church on earth. The discerning eye can easily discriminate and delineate three great classes of Christians. There are nicer shades innumerable, for there are no two souls alike. But, just as we distinguish between the three kingdoms of nature markedly enough, although on their confines they shade off one into the other, by almost imperceptible lines, so can we perceive three definite stages of the regenerate life, and three well-defined groups of Christians. There are men of the letter of the Word, men of the Spirit of the Word, and men of deep humility and holy love. These latter who have passed through the former grades of the Christian life, and been tried and found faithful again and again, acquire a maturity and gentleness, which affects sometimes a whole generation, and many a generation for good. Like the scented violet, their fragrance fills the air, though they themselves are little seen. They are celestial babes and sucklings, whose youth is renewed like the eagles (Psa. ciii. 3). They be like John, near to the Redeemer's breast, and like him, they dwell in love, and are beloved.

The three materials of which the temple was chiefly constructed were, stones for the foundations and the walls, cedar wood for wainscotting and covering the stone within (v. 14–18), and gold plates with which the whole interior of the house was covered,—floor, walls, and ceiling alike (v. 22).

The appearance of the temple within must have been indeed magnificent, and its costliness when erected, was truly a mark of the devotion of both king and people. This also was representative. Gold, the best of metals, the purest, most ductile, and most valuable, was the inmost everywhere, because the celestial state of the church is strictly represented, in which love to the Lord is the chief and all pervading principle.

We have treated hitherto of the temple as representing the heavens in general, and the church in general; and indeed the same divine order which prevails in general, prevails in each particular and in every part. But, we must now notice that specifically the temple of Solomon represented the celestial church, and the church as its principles exist in a celestially minded man. In such a one the golden spirit of love to the Lord Jesus, derived from Him, is everywhere within. He adores from love, he thinks from love, he acts from love. He heeds continually the gracious words, "I counsel thee to buy of me gold tried in the fire that thou mayest be rich." (Rev. iii. 19.)

The cedar-wood which was laid between the gold and the stone represented rational good. The grand old cedar-trees with their outstretched branches and boughs are the symbol in Scripture of the protective power of the rational mind. The Assyrian was a cedar in Lebanon, it is written, with fair branches, and a shadowing shroud and of a high stature. (Ezek. xxxi. 3.)

That keen and reasoning people were thus represented by the cedar, and they became magnificent like those noble trees.

The cedar wood was everywhere placed underneath the gold to teach us that what love dictates is always truly rational. There is often a great difference between reasoning, and being rational. When a person loves rightly and does rightly, he is truly rational, whether he can give a reason to others or not. He has got the cedar-wood under his gold. He reasons best, who does best, though he may never be able to wrangle. To teach this it was that Solomon sent his hewers, thirty thousand men into Lebanon, with the assent of Hiram the king of Tyre, and obtained abundance of cedar and overlaid the whole of the stone with its wood.

The stones themselves got from the neighbouring mountains by fourscore thousand hewers, are called great stones, costly stones, and hewed stones. They were prepared by exact rule in the mountain quarries probably near at hand, and they fitted so exactly, that in the words of our text, neither hammer, nor axe, nor any tool of iron was heard in the house, while it was in building.

The mountains represent the Divine Love of the Lord in all its manifestations as Creator, Provider, Redeemer, Saviour and Regenerator. Thy righteousness is like the great mountains. (Ps. xxxvi. 6.) I will look to the mountains from whence cometh my help. My help cometh from the Lord who made heaven and earth. (Ps. cxxi. 1.) The stones represent the truths of religion, and their being hewed out of the mountains and prepared there for the building, was to be a lesson for ever, that when Christians have arrived at the celestial state they perceive all the truths of religion to be derived from the Love of God. They see the Lord as their Father, their Saviour, their all in all.

Men of celestial love perceive that the truths of religion must be as they are represented. They understand what the Lord Jesus meant when He said, "Let your communication be yea, yea, and nay, nay, Whatsoever is more than this cometh of evil." The law is written on their hearts, and in building up their Temples, there is no noise heard. They love, they meditate, they build up, and make themselves into living Temples of the Lord. Love thinketh no evil, but thinketh all good, rejoices in the truth. Love knows what Divine Love will do, because the likeness of Divine Love is in itself.

The hammer, axe, and tool of iron are symbols of the Word, which when compared to the spiritual sense is as iron compared to silver. The hammer represents the letter of the Word employed to overcome errors of the will. Hence it is said, Is not my Word like a hammer that breaks the rock in pieces? (Jer. xxiii. 29.) The axe represents the letter of the Word when employed to remove intellectual difficulties, as the woodcutter fells the trees of the forest. The tool of iron represents the sharpened intellect when employed upon smaller faults, and particular errors, and the work of these things has been done long before in the regenerate life. Hence they have nothing to do in the celestial state. In former days there was work for hammer to break down evils in abundance, the axe had often to be brought into play, and of many a corrupt tree it needed to be said, "cut it down why cumbereth it the ground." The chisel had often been required to make the crooked straight and the rough places plain. But now there is no need of that. The soul is at peace. It seeks to be all love, and loving adoration. Nothing of self mingles in its desire to be wholly the Lord's. As the stones are made ready in the mountains, as the truths of heaven descend from the Divine Love, it desires no alteration from self-conceit, prejudice, or vain imagination, but with peaceful, quiet, holy readiness it accepts them and builds them up in the soul into a Temple of the Lord. Nothing of mere science in divine things, nothing of the mere letter of the Word need be consulted; the perception that has been attained is enough to bring the headstone of the inner Temple forth with the exulting, the adoring outpouring of the heart. Bless the Lord, O my soul, and all that is within me, bless His Holy Name.

The Oracle or Most Holy place, the central and most sacred object, containing the ark enclosing the tables of the law, and Aaron's rod that budded, and surmounted by the Mercy-Seat, and the Cherubim, all of cedar-wood covered with gold, represented the Lord's inward dwelling-place in man. From this divine abode in the soul the Lord is ever a God at hand, a gracious presence in our hours of joy, and a very present help in trouble. In Him is the Fountain of Life, and in His light we see light. How excellent is thy loving kindness, O God! Therefore the children of men put their trust under the shadow of thy wings.

We have considered generally the wonderful structure Solomon was inspired and directed to build; and the heavenly lessons it was intended constantly to represent among men; but there are two additional portions which were striking objects while the Temple stood, and respecting which very minute and copious descriptions are given. These are the two great pillars which supported the vestibule of the Temple, and were called Jachin and Boaz. Jachin, which was the pillar on the right-hand side, signifying in Hebrew, *He that make stedfast;* and Boaz, *He who is in strength.* The right referring to the strength of good in act, the left to the strength of truth.

They were formed of molten copper, and like everything else in three portions. They were hollow, the metal being of the thickness of a handbreadth. The shaft or main portion of each pillar was eighteen cubits high; this was surmounted by another portion five cubits high, surrounded and ornamented with SEVEN strands of network decorated with one hundred figures of pomegranates: over this again was the capital of the column crowning the whole in the shape of a lily, four cubits high. They were in all, twenty seven cubits in height, and four cubits or six feet in diameter.

Being the prominent objects which would meet the view of every one about to enter the Temple, they would represent religion as it should present itself in the world. The pillars represent integrity in work and word.

Copper represents the GOOD of a virtuous life. It is the symbol of the external of that religion, in which gold is the symbol of the essence. Where brass occurs in the Old Testament it would be more correctly rendered copper, for the mixture called brass was not at that time known. When the Lord, by the prophet Isaiah, declared that for mere moral virtue, he would bring in among men goodness flowing from love to Him, He said, "For copper I will bring gold, and for iron silver."

The constituents of this religion in daily life, this integrity in deed and word, and we should remember that words are also deeds, and deeds of weighty responsibility, the chief elements are represented by the lily at the top of the column, which our Lord desires us to regard and thus dismiss anxious care. Consider the lilies how they grow: they toil not, neither do they spin, yet I say unto you, that even Solomon in all his glory was not arrayed like one of these. The network beneath represented the adaptation of means to ends, the busy lacings and weavings of the intellect, while the solid shaft represented the solid integrity of the result. "What doth the Lord require of thee, but to do justly." Let this be always the entire embodiment of thy religion; and thou wilt be like these two pillars in the Temple of thy God,—Jachin and Boaz.

SERMON XXXI.

THE QUEEN OF SHEBA'S VISIT TO SOLOMON.

"And when the queen of Sheba had seen all Solomon's wisdom, and the house that he had built, and the meat of his table, and the sitting of his servants, and the attendance of his ministers, and their apparel, and his cup-bearers, and his ascent by which he went up into the house of the Lord; there was no more spirit in her. And she said, It was a true report that I heard in mine own land of thy acts, and of thy wisdom. Howbeit I believed not the words, until I came, and mine eyes had seen it; and, behold, the half was not told me: thy wisdom and prosperity exceedeth the fame which I heard. Happy are thy men, happy are these thy servants, which stand continually before thee, and that hear thy wisdom."—1 KINGS x. 4-8.

THE prosperity of the peaceful reign, and the magnificence of the temple, of the king's house, and the house for his queen, the daughter of Pharaoh, spread the fame of Solomon through the surrounding kingdoms. The queen of Sheba, or Abyssinia, excited by what she had heard of his great wisdom, and pressed by many anxious questions which she thought he might possibly solve, made the long journey from her country to his. Her labour was not in vain. She was astonished and delighted with all she saw, and all she heard. She contrasted the grandeurs she beheld with the very modest structures of her native land, poor then as now in noble buildings, and the splendours of art, and she felt no comparison could be made. The interesting and beautiful language of our text informs us of her increasing admiration until she could no longer contain her ardent and astonished feelings, and exclaimed, "It was a true report I heard in mine own land of thy acts and of thy wisdom. Howbeit I believed not the words, until I came, and mine eyes had seen it: and, behold, the half was not told me."

We may view this divine history in many ways. It may be regarded as a manifestation of the will of the All-wise, that beauty and goodness should exist together among men, as they do in His glorious works, and in heaven.

We sometimes meet with good people who suppose that the surroundings of religion cannot be too plain. They shrink from anything but the veriest simplicity in places of worship, and fear that anything but the most modest appearance there is unbecoming, and tends to draw the soul away from devotion. Yet, if we consider that all beauty and all true art are from God, who is Himself the Infinitely Beautiful as well as the Infinitely Good and True, we may see that real beauty like real blessing should raise the soul to Him. "Honour and majesty are before Him: strength and beauty are in His sanctuary. O worship the Lord, in the beauty (the beautiful things) of holiness: fear before Him, all the earth."

The splendid tabernacle, and the still more magnificent temple, constructed by the directions of inspiration, will certainly be testimonies and illustrations of the truth, that if the inner beauties of the heart and mind are kept supreme within us, in our devotions, it is becoming also to adorn our piety with such forms as may suggest that true beauty and true goodness are from the same source, and should, as far as circumstances permit, go hand in hand together. The Christian in a cottage should make it as neat and pretty as he can. The Christian of ampler means should not neglect to surround himself with graceful forms of art, which are the blending of loveliness in mind and matter from the source of grace and grandeur. And the Christian should not be slow to make his church beautiful, to manifest that he deems nothing too good for the worship of Him, in whose hand his breath is, and who by His beautiful flowers, and beautiful sights and sounds, as well as by His lessons of holiness and wisdom, prepares the soul for the land of living loveliness and everlasting peace.

The King of the spiritual Israel is the Lord Jesus, the King of kings and the Lord of lords. This Divine Prince of peace was represented by Solomon, the peaceful king. And, the three houses which Solomon built, the house of the Lord, the house of the king, and the house of Pharaoh's daughter, were types of the Church, as it exists amongst the celestially-minded, where heavenly gold or love is the chief feature, as it exists among the spiritually-minded, in which truth is the leading characteristic, as cedar was in the house of the king; and the condition of the Church amongst those whose delight is mainly engaged in the art and science of religion, which was portrayed by the house of the daughter of Pharaoh. The Lord Jesus, when He had redeemed man by conquering the powers of darkness, and was fully glorified, was represented by Solomon.

When, therefore, we read of Solomon's great wisdom, of the

peace of his kingdom, and the abundance of gold in his time, we must remember that in the supreme sense "a greater than Solomon is here." He is meant who is high, above all, who imparts in abundance the blessed gold of celestial love, and who diffuses over the soul interior peace. Hence, in the 72d Psalm, which is said to be for Solomon, it is evident that the language can only be fitly and fully applied to the glorified Saviour. Of this Solomon it can alone be true that " He shall come down like rain upon the mown grass; as showers that water the earth. In His days shall the righteous flourish; and abundance of peace, so long as the moon endureth (ver. 6, 7). For, He shall deliver the needy when he crieth: the poor also, and him that hath no helper. He shall spare the poor and needy, and shall save the souls of the needy (ver. 12, 13). His name shall endure for ever: His name shall be continued as long as the sun: and men shall be blessed in Him: all nations shall call Him blessed" (ver. 17). These words can only be true of the Lord Jesus, the Divine Solomon. Of Him only can it be said, He shall save the souls of the needy, and men shall be blessed in Him. When, therefore, the psalm is said to be for Solomon, it is to Solomon as the type of Him, in whom is all wisdom, and from whom alone we can derive true peace.

The queen of Sheba, who had heard of the fame of Solomon concerning the name of the Lord, and who came to prove him with hard questions, represented those who yearn for the Lord Jesus, who seek for communion with Him, and desire to lay their perplexities before Him. The soul, when it turns to its Saviour, has many hard questions. Can the selfish become truly humble, the sinful become really pure? What shall I do to be saved? Is the Lord indeed a friend above all others, or is He only an avenging God? How is it so many good people are tried and straitened in the world, and so many wicked flourish? How is it after death? How is it in heaven? Will the Lord speak to me and whisper peace? These and a thousand other hard questions move the minds of those who are represented by the queen of Sheba, and who commune with the Saviour, the Divine Solomon.

These are represented by a female, because in the Word of the Lord, they who can be received into the Church, because they are in the affection for truth, are represented usually by a virgin, a bride, and a wife. Hence we read of the virgin daughter of Zion, the virgin daughter of Jerusalem, the bride, the Lamb's wife, and other expressions involving the idea that those are meant who love the truth, as a maiden loves the object of her choice, and who will be faithful to the truth, as a genuine wife is faithful to her husband. This real and earnest affection for truth constitutes the central point, the fulcrum on which all spiritual progress turns. If the affection cherished for truth be deep, then the good seed of the Word will sink deeper and grow, and bring forth fruit. If there be no affection for the truth, there is nothing to lay hold of the means of salvation. The Lord calls, but there is no response. The Divine Love invites, but the heartless object of His affection throws the priceless boon of His love away.

Not so with those meant by the queen of Sheba. They come and open their hearts to the Chief among ten thousand. The Lord displays to them His Church. They see the house that He has built. They behold its proportions, and its adornments. Its glorious truths of every kind are like gems, shining on every side. It is the house of which it is written, "I will lay thy stones of fair colours, and lay thy foundations with sapphires. And I will make thy windows of agates, and thy gates of carbuncles, and all thy borders of precious stones." Of the same house the apostle says, "These things I write unto thee . . . that thou mayest know how thou oughtest to behave thyself in the house of God, which is the Church of the living God; the pillar and the ground of the truth." The Lord's Church is a home for all who desire to live for heaven: it is indeed a heaven below, a vestibule to that above.

When one who has been troubled with hard questions, cast down, dismayed sometimes, with doubts and difficulties, comes to see how complete a provision the Lord has made in His Church for all the soul's wants, even beyond all its hopes and wishes, like the queen of Sheba he is lost in wonder and delight, and exclaims—

> " Here will I take my joyful rest,
> Nor ere from Salem roam;
> For ever, and for ever blest,
> In this my happy home."

What next excited the admiration of the queen of Sheba was the "meat of his table." The soul has appetites as well as the body. Blessed are they that hunger and thirst after righteousness; for they shall be filled. The varied assortments of Divine Wisdom which afford food for meditation, for comfort, and for joy, are so many dishes of heavenly meat on which the spiritual appetite may feed, and indeed enjoy a sacred banquet. "When I found thy words," the prophet exclaimed, " I did eat them, and they were the joy and rejoicing of my heart." The Word is a divine table on which there is prepared an unlimited supply of all that the soul can want. The Book of Psalms may be truly called the Christian's Daily Bread. He who will devoutly in the morning extract heavenly nourishment from one psalm will find himself strengthened for the day. There is that heavenly good which is the bread of life, the holy wisdom which is the wine that cheers both God and man. There is every supply which can strengthen hope, impart consolation, and fortify the Christian for virtuous duty. It is the dinner of the King in the Gospel; the supper in which our Divine Friend will sup with us, and we with Him. He spreads a table before us in the presence of our enemies, and enables man to eat angels' food. The meat of His table is sweeter than honey, or the droppings of the honeycomb. It is meat that endures to eternal life. Those, then, who are like the queen of Sheba, when they have seen and partaken of this bread of heaven, join with the disciple in saying, " Lord, evermore give us this bread."

Another delightful feature of the arrangements of this palace, as we learn in the text, is, the " sitting of the servants." Sitting, in the spiritual sense, implies settlement and satisfaction. They who are at rest sit down in the kingdom of God. They are neither hesitating nor disquieted, but in repose. They have been pilgrims, but are now at home. They sit, as belonging to the household. Each has his place, his dignity, and his enjoyment. They sit as the guests of the king, each in order, and each satisfied, as forming part of the company of their Heavenly Father, the highest and the best of beings. Some too were lower ministers, delighting to serve, but glorious in their apparel.

When doctrinal truth has been made the Christian's own, and fitted to his soul, it is called, " a garment of salvation," " a robe of righteousness." The spirit walks in Heavenly purity. Its dress is white, with a golden tinge. Thou hast a few names in Sardis, who have not defiled their garments: they shall walk with me in white, for they are worthy." Heavenly thoughts are heavenly clothing; for thoughts clothe affections, and words clothe thoughts, just as raiment clothes the body.

Some people have noble impulses, but cannot clothe them in suitable dress so as to bespeak for them attention and acceptance: others as wolves in sheep's clothing. But when we behold angelic innocence and earnestness clothed with purity and wisdom, we see immortal excellences holily attired, and we understand those gracious words in the parable of the prodigal son, respecting the penitent returned: "Bring forth the best robe and put it on him, the ring upon his finger, and the shoes upon his feet." There are immortal thoughts for the whole immortal being. Thoughts of hallowed reverence which are constantly suggesting supreme gratitude to the Lord, who is the infinitely tender and All-Good, form the mitre for the spirit's head-dress, on which is written " Holiness to the Lord."

Thoughts of charity and good-will are the clothing of the breast, or vest encircled with a golden girdle. Thoughts of conjugial love and ever-increasing union are the clothing of the loins, and thoughts directing our daily life make the lower portion of our raiment down to the feet. "Let your feet be shod," said the apostle, "with the preparation of the Gospel of peace" (Eph. v. 16).

The queen of Sheba admired the apparel of the ministers, and was struck also with the cup-bearers. When we remember that there is heavenly wine we shall understand there must be heavenly cup-bearers. The Psalmist exultingly exclaimed, "My cup runneth over." There are seasons when out of the abundance of the heart the mouth must speak. There are occasions likewise in which the wearied and tried spirit becomes faint and languid: strength and hope are flagging, and at a very low ebb, and we greatly need counsel and support. In such states, when comforting friends come gently to us and administer in sympathizing kindness themes of consolation and peace, we then, like the queen of Sheba, make note of the cup-bearers. Our Lord desires that we should have ever ready the blessed cordial that strengthens the weak and cheers the weary, and should thus all be cup-bearers. "They put new wine (He said) into new bottles, and both are preserved" (Matt. ix. 17).

The angels in their office of ministering spirits doubtless often exercise the office of cup-bearers. They infuse the balm of comfort into the bitterness and vexation which have tried us deeply, and well nigh multiplied our sorrows beyond what we can bear. A strange and wonderful peace will sometimes be imparted in our darkest hours, like a beautiful light in the gloom, and we feel our hearts cheered and our souls refreshed. No doubt, it is wine new from our Heavenly Father's kingdom, gushing fresh from the Fountain of Peace, which had thus suffused its blessed balm throughout our being: and the angels are the cup-bearers. While we acknowledge that the Lord's mercy has held us up, and His comforts have delighted our souls, yet let us not forget to bless Him that He has made His ministers to be our cup-bearers. Lastly, the queen observed with admiration and delight the ascent by which He went up into the House of the Lord. All creation is connected together by degrees above and below. Stage above stage, we rise at every point from Nature up to Nature's God. The natural is surmounted by the spiritual, the spiritual by the celestial, the celestial by the divine. The universe of God, like the Word of God, is a ladder whose foot is on earth, whose top reacheth to heaven, and above which is Jehovah Himself. In each degree there are numerous subdivisions, having relations above and below and ramifications on all sides.

"All are but parts of one stupendous whole."

We live on the skin of the vast body of universal being; and when we see the correspondences, analogies, and relations of one grade of existence with another, of one stratum of life with the next above it, like the queen of Sheba, our spirits sink within us, and we are lost in wonder, love, and praise.

All orderly and beautiful things on earth are images of things in heaven, and steps of ascent to them.

From the humblest forms, from mosses to fruit trees, from creeping things to the animals in immediate attendance upon man, there is a continual ascent of being. All have relation to man, a certain resemblance to him, even to his body. His body corresponds to his mind, which is a higher—a spiritual body. And this is in the image and likeness of the Lord, the Divine Man, the Almighty. Man's will is intended to be the receptacle of the Divine Will, which is Infinite Goodness; man's understanding of the Divine Understanding, which is Infinite Wisdom. Thus from the Supreme there are degrees downwards, all things in the universe having relation to His goodness and truth. From the atom upwards, there is a constant ascent towards the Lord, and all things are seen to be derived from Him, and to return through man's acknowledgment and worship to Him.

It is just so in the Word of the Lord when understood in the Church. In it and by it, there is an ascent from the letter to the spiritual sense, from the spirit to the celestial sense, and from this to the Divine, for in its origin and highest essence the Word is God (John i. 1). Thus, everywhere in the Church, those represented by the queen of Sheba are shewn the ascent by which they can go up into the House of the Lord, by which they can touch all around them, and see and feel this chain of being everywhere, while they, filled with awe and adoration, exclaim with the patriarch of old, " Surely God is in this place, and I knew it not. This is none other but the house of God: and this is the gate of heaven."

There is said to be no more spirit in her: that is, self was entirely humbled and abashed, and could no more be seen. Yet these words are more fully and divinely true when uttered by the humblest Christian, than they were in the case of the queen of Sheba.

By unregenerate nature we are, like the Abyssinian queen, inhabitants of a far country, rough and poor. We have felt how dark we are, and how much there is we would like to know. We have heard of the fame of Solomon, and of the glory and peace of his kingdom. The Divine Saviour is known to be condescending, powerful, glorious, and full of wisdom. We are troubled with hard questions. Why are we tossed about on a sea of uncertainties? Whence are we? What are we to become? Can we really be made into angels? What are the monstrous propensities and lusts which press themselves upon us? Can our passions be subdued, and our life in this world be made even in a feeble way to resemble the life of the blessed? Can we indeed find peace? What is death? What is there beyond the grave?

These are hard questions which have made us ponder, as they have perplexed those who have gone before us. Let us go to the great Prince of Peace in our day, and commune with Him of what is in our hearts. In prayer and meditation, He will speak to us, and give us replies; not only to what we have asked, but tell us much more than we have sought to know.

It is astonishing that an immortal being, placed for a season between two seas as it were, THE PAST, of which he is a product, THE FUTURE, in which he is everlastingly to live, can remain in apathy, nor ask whether he is on the assured road, which will lead to eternal peace. A night of darkness may be around us, but let us not rest, let us not sit down in the valley of the shadow of death. Let us at least unceasingly inquire, Watchman, what of the night? Watchman, what of the night? Let us rest assured that if we thus inquire earnestly and perseveringly the gracious Saviour, who intends to turn our darkness into day, will reply, The morning cometh.

SERMON XXXII.

THE ABUNDANCE OF GOLD IN THE REIGN OF SOLOMON.

"And all king Solomon's drinking vessels were of gold, and all the vessels of the house of the forest of Lebanon were of pure gold; none were of silver; it was nothing accounted of in the days of Solomon."—1 KINGS x. 21.

IF the world were full of the love of the Lord Jesus, our Creator, our Saviour, our Father, and our King, and of our fellow human beings as His children, what a glorious world it would be! a world of wisdom, peace, and blessing. Even the conception of such a state of things seems but the faint imagining of a condition, beyond all hope of possible realization, which can only be regarded as

"The faint exquisite music of a dream."

Yet why have we day-dreams at all, except to foreshadow what may be. The world has had a golden age, why may it not return?

It is true that cruel phantasies at present possess mankind. Men are like inhabitants of a low dark valley, spending their time in gathering its dust into heaps, and contending to the death for the privilege of owning the largest hillock. But everyone feels impulses higher and nobler than this. Each immortal being has yearnings for unselfishness, for innocence, for virtue, for wisdom, and for peace. Why cannot we seek first the kingdom of God and His righteousness, and depend that all other things will be added unto us?

The Scriptures undoubtedly in multiplied and varied phrase proclaim that a period will be arrived at on earth when "The Lord shall be King over all the earth," when "The knowledge of the Lord shall cover the earth, as the waters cover the sea; and none shall hurt nor destroy in all the Lord's holy mountain" (Isa. xi. 9). Far, very far off it may be before this and many a splendid divine declaration of Scripture concerning the future glory of the world shall be realized, but the Word of God will be fulfilled for all that. The Lord's kingdom will assuredly come, and the Lord's will shall undoubtedly be done on earth, as it is done in heaven.

In the typical dispensation of the Jews, this celestial condition of the Church and the world was represented by the wealth, the glory, and the peace of the reign of Solomon. It was literally true in the reign of that son of David, that peace, and all the arts of peace, brought prosperity, wealth, and abundance to the extent described in the text. Trade and commerce connecting Israel with distant lands in ties of mutual benefit, poured riches around, so that not only was plenty enjoyed, but sumptuousness and magnificence were attained; and gold to an unparalleled extent was seen, and silver was accounted of but little.

Yet this is written in the Word of God, not to make us proficient in history, or to excite our admiration for this abundance of earthly splendour, but to represent to us the glorious state that shall be: the golden age again; when men shall beat their swords into plough-shares, and their spears into pruning-hooks; when nation shall not lift up itself against nation, neither shall they learn war any more (Isa. ii. 5; Micah v. 3). Gold is regarded in divine things as the symbol, among metals, of the highest good, that is, love to the Lord. The qualities of gold perfectly correspond to those of the golden principle of love to the Lord supremely, and for this it is used in Scripture. Hence, we may readily perceive that the abundance of gold in Solomon's reign typified the abundance of love, and all heavenly treasure, which will exist when the Church has accomplished its victories over naturalism and selfishness, and the Lord Jesus reigns over a regenerated world as the Divine Prince of Peace. As to the world in general, having regard to its present condition, it might indeed be thought that such views of the future, if not Utopian, can have no practical value, but it is well to remember that the Word of the Lord reveals such truths for our comfort, and it can never be wrong to learn what Divine Wisdom teaches. And, besides that, the order of progress for the world and the order for one individual are the same, and though we may not hope to behold any great advance of the general state of mankind in our time, yet individuals may realize golden things for themselves. They may receive from the Lord the gold of heaven, and be solitary pioneers of exalted states and of blessed achievements, in which perfect humility and heavenly wisdom shall give perfect peace.

That gold is recognised in Scripture as corresponding to heavenly goodness of the highest kind, may be gathered not only from the direct words of our Lord, "I counsel thee to buy of Me gold tried in the fire that thou mayest be rich" (Rev. iii. 18), but from its use in every part of the Divine Word. In the first land mentioned as being watered by the first river flowing out of Eden, now known to be an allegorical representation of the highest state of happiness, it is said "in that land there was gold, and the gold of that land was good" (Gen. ii. 11, 12). When the ark, the mercy-seat, the altar, and the vessels of the tabernacle were commanded to be made of pure gold, we cannot fail to feel there must have been a divine propriety in the choice that these patterns of heavenly things, as the apostle calls them, should be made of that valuable metal. And that reason can hardly be any other than that gold, the best of the metals, is the appropriate symbol of love, the best of heavenly principles.

When the Lord through His prophets foretold the wonderful change which His coming into the world would make in religion, by the substitution of the spirit of religion for the mere symbolic form of it which existed among the Jews, He said "For brass I will bring gold, and for iron I will bring silver, for wood brass, and for stones iron: I will also make thy officers peace, and thine exactors righteousness" (Isa. lx. 17). The explanation virtually follows in the succeeding verse, "Violence shall no more be heard in thy land, wasting nor destruction within thy borders: but thou shalt call thy walls salvation, and thy gates praise." For what can take away all violence, wasting and destruction, but that Christian love which is the essence of good-will, and, as the apostle says, "fulfils the law" and "worketh no ill to the neighbour." The prophet Jeremiah speaks of gold manifestly in the same way. He says, "How is the gold become dim? how is the most fine gold changed?" The stones of the sanctuary are poured out in the top of every street. The precious sons of Zion, comparable to fine gold, how are they esteemed as earthen pitchers, the work of the hands of the potter (Lam. iv. 1, 2).

The seven golden candlesticks mentioned in Rev. i. are called the Seven Churches (ver. 20), and although it is indeed a chief duty of a church to hold up the light of truth amidst surrounding darkness, yet love is the golden substance from which alone she can do it effectively. The Lord Himself was seen by St. John as girded around with a golden girdle, because this symbolized the divine affection, from which descends the sphere of love which is derived from Him, which encircles His children, uniting them to each other and to Himself. Lastly, the holy city, New Jerusalem, the Church now diffusing itself among men, AND THE GRAND CHURCH OF THE FUTURE, is said to be a golden city. "The city was PURE GOLD, like unto clear glass;" "and the street of the city was PURE GOLD" (Rev. xxi. 18-21). What can that pure gold be, but the spirit of pure love?

> "For love within itself includes
> The source of all beatitudes."

Love is the golden principle. Love enriches, embellishes, and blesses mankind. Without love nothing can impart true and lasting felicity. With love the humblest gifts are valuable and valued, and the humblest position of life contains the real essentials of happiness. The gift of loving is heaven's greatest boon to man. And he who cannot love may have splendid talents, may win position, wealth, applause, and fame, but will never succeed in possessing that without which all other possessions are cold, hollow, and valueless, the gift of being happy, in making others happy. This is divine gold. Gold abounded so much in the reign of the earthly Solomon, to represent that in the celestial condition of the Church, when the Lord Jesus in His glorified humanity would be truly and supremely loved as Lord of all, there would be an abundance of this spirit of holy Christian love. The whole interior of the Temple was covered with gold, the altar, and all the consecrated vessels were of gold: there were ten great lamp-holders of gold: the throne of the king was covered with gold. There were "two hundred targets" (or large shields), and "three hundred (other) shields of gold:" and "all king Solomon's drinking vessels were of gold, and all the vessels of the house of the forest of Lebanon were of pure gold; none were of silver: it was nothing accounted of in the days of Solomon."

If we notice the leading qualities of gold, we shall discern how perfectly they correspond to the leading qualities of heavenly love.

There is its wonderful malleability and ductility. Though

very heavy it can be beaten out until it is lighter than air. It is so ductile that it is said a comparatively small portion could be drawn out as wire to compass the whole world. It will enter into and cover, embellish, and improve objects of all shapes and sinuosities. All patterns can be gilded, and brightened, and however old, or however often used, the gold retains its intrinsic value. Gold never corrupts or grows old.

All this can be truly said of genuine Christian love. It is the most solid and the most sacred substance the human soul can have, but how wonderfully it can be stretched out. Its sympathies flow forth in all directions. There is no sorrow to which it will not bend, there is no grandeur which it will not adorn. Love will clothe the house of prayer with devotion, and it will wipe away the orphan's tear. Colour and distance of country make no difference to love; it will gild and glorify them all. It will penetrate the prison and the forest, to liberate the captive and to elevate the savage. Love will circumnavigate the globe to carry out its mission of raising the down-trodden, and replacing the manacles of misery by the golden links of mutual affection. Love is the grand miracle-worker. It turns a barren waste into stores of blessing. It transforms the wilderness into an Eden, and the desert into a garden of God. Love never dies. Like the soul, in its inmost being it is blest with perpetual youth. Talents become feeble, and knowledge grows dim, but love, the true vestal and perpetual fire, burns on with undiminished flame even among the mists of this lower world, until it is transplanted to the warm mountains of the better land, where it will glow and bless for ever.*

Gold is superior to the action of acids. Inferior metals are fretted and agitated by the bitter action of acrid fluids, but gold remains uninjured. Let the acid be keen and biting as it may, true pure gold remains with its substance unhurt, and its lustre undimmed. It is exactly the same with true heavenly gold. The acids of bitter temper, the provocations of satire, and the jeers of malice, make disturbance enough in the affairs of the world, but where genuine Christian love exist they assail in vain. Love never faileth. " Love suffereth long and is kind. Love is not easily provoked, thinketh no evil: rejoiceth not in iniquity, but rejoiceth in the truth: beareth up all things; believeth all things; hopeth all things; endureth all things."

One of the amazing things in the world is the enormous production there is of mental acid. Every little thing that is unusual will excite some people. Charity suffereth long, but they will suffer nothing. A word, a look, will be enough for a sulk, or enough for an open quarrel. They don't believe they ought to bear anything; and if the whole world does not give way to their humour, the gall of bitterness comes from them in streams of malicious words. Many of these are professing Christians, pretended servants of Him who is the Divine Lamb. Instead of forgiving their brother seventy times seven, their spite and venom are often more withering and enduring than will be found among many who make no profession of following Him who said, " Love one another, as I have loved you."

These often excuse themselves, and lay the fault upon their temper, as if temper were something distinct from themselves. Self-love is always bad tempered to those who thwart it. If our religion does not soften and sweeten our tempers, we may be assured that it has very little heavenly gold in it. If we are ready to say sharp words at every little excitement, if we retaliate bitter word for bitter word, scorn for scorn, fretfulness, impatience, and vexation for every little inconvenience, mishap and disadvantage, we may depend upon it, there is much alloy mixed up with our gold, or what we take to be gold is only some baser metal. If true heavenly love be in us, we shall have heavenly patience. The more heavenly love we have, the more gentleness we shall have, the more self-conquest, and the more true gold.

It is said all the drinking vessels of king Solomon were of pure gold. The streams of intelligence and wisdom are represented in Scripture by things which can be drunk. For these, the soul can be thirsty. Hence we read, " Ho, every one that thirsteth come ye to the waters. Come, buy wine and milk, without money and without price" (Isa. lv. 1). There is wine from our Father's kingdom, the sincere milk of the Word, and living water, to which every one is invited to come.

These can feed, cheer, purify, and satisfy us at every stage of our spiritual pilgrimage. But, when we have arrived at the celestial state, we shall always get our supply with golden drinking vessels, or in other words we shall seek by every draught of wisdom we take to become more loving, more innocent, more pure, and more kind. We shall desire the truth from love, as well as speak the truth from love. From love we shall read, from love we shall study, from love we shall learn, from love we shall meditate, from love we shall act, or from love refrain from acting. This glorious principle will be the ground of all our activities, and of all our peace. On the two commandments of love, our Lord said, all the law and the prophets hang, and from the spirit of love to the Lord, and to our neighbour, all the efforts and the acts of the Christian who has become more than conqueror through Him that loved Him will be derived. All the drinking cups, and all the vessels of the house of the king, the house of the forest of Lebanon will be of pure gold.

The phrase house of the forest of Lebanon was given to the house of the king, because of the abundance of cedar-wood used in its construction. That grand tree the cedar of Lebanon is the symbol in nature and in the Word of God of the rational faculty, especially in its expansive and protective power. The rational faculty, with its great lines of thoughtful reasoning, is like the cedar with its branches, which are so many arms and hands covering and defending all who shelter under it from danger. The cedar-wood represents the results of reasoning, or reasons, when the reasoning has ceased. The cedar-wood was present under the gold, but was not seen. The cedar of the house within was carved with knops and open flowers, all was cedar: there was no stone seen. The knops were egg-shaped fruit, opening and disclosing somewhat its interior, the flowers were unfolding their graces to the observer.

When the regenerated Christian acts from the high and pure principle which animates him, it includes the truest reason, but without reasoning. He does what is right from love. His communication is yea, yea, or nay, nay. The law is written on his heart. He feels rather than reasons, but if the most perfect reasoning be applied to it, it will confirm all that has been done.

These carved ornaments would indicate that in every rational conception of the regenerate mind there is a tendency to goodness and truth. There is no barren reason—all flows forth into genuine piety and genuine righteous works. There are opening flowers. Sweet conceptions of heavenly things delight and edify the mind. All things tend heavenward. In the whole frame of thought there is the divine stamp upon it. It fructifies and it adorns. There are knops and opening flowers.

The gold of the New Jerusalem is said to be transparent gold. " The street of the city was pure gold, as it were transparent glass." On earth, certainly, we have no transparent gold. But, in the spiritual world, into which John's spirit was enabled to see, there are many forms of substances unknown in this outer material sphere of things, and we doubt not among these will be transparent gold. It would seem to imply that the objects were full of love, and at the same time clearly wise—golden and transparent. The lesson is very nearly the same as that taught by all Solomon's drinking cups, and all the vessels of the house of the forest of Lebanon being of gold.

Oh, what a grand state of man is that, when all he receives, as well as all he does, is from the golden spirit of love. Now, alas! too many spend their whole lives in empty nothings—in grovelling in the dust. It is said there is a nation of dirt-eaters in central America, who eat voraciously, but are gaunt, unsatisfied, and ever-hungry, because they are aiming to extract nourishment from that which is not bread. A sad picture it is, but a true illustration of the aims of those who are seeking angelic nourishment from sordid pleasure and earthly gain.

O, let us live for the golden age again! Let us seek from our Saviour the gold He invites us to receive—the love from Him, to Him and to all that are His. Let us seek His purity, though we may be tried in the fire of many a temptation and many a trouble. He will preside over the process by which we are rendered loving and good; and when the fires shall have done their work, we shall enjoy truly Christian love, and a calm and blessed peace. All our drinking vessels will be of gold: all the vessels of the king's house of pure gold.

Silver, it is said, was nothing accounted of in the days of Solomon. Silver represents the spirit of the Holy Word, as distinguished from the letter, which is represented in Scripture by iron. The spiritual sense of the Word glitters before the eyes of the understanding more than the letter, as silver shines with a richer radiance than iron. Silver is of great value in purifying gold, but after that work is done, would be little accounted of where gold was vastly abundant. So, likewise, when a soul has gone through its spiritual states in which the intelligence of inward truth, spiritual silver, leads it, and has entered into the celestial state in which love is all in all, then it will be truly said, silver is nothing accounted of. All our vessels, all our faculties will be formed of purified gold. The spirit of love, of holy celestial charity, has transfused itself from the Lord into our entire being. The Lord has been to such celestial Christians as a refiner and purifier of silver first, and He has purified them as the sons of Levi (Mal. iii. 3), He has then purged them as gold, that they may render to Him offerings of righteousness, and live in His golden city for ever and ever.

SERMON XXXIII.

SOLOMON'S WIVES AND CONCUBINES.

"But king Solomon loved many strange women, together with the daughter of Pharaoh, women of the Moabites, Ammonites, Edomites, Zidonians, and Hittites: of the nations concerning which the Lord said unto the children of Israel, Ye shall not go in to them: for surely they will turn away your heart after their gods: Solomon clave unto them in love. And he had seven hundred wives, princesses, and three hundred concubines: and his wives turned away his heart."—1 KINGS xi. 1-3.

AFTER the glorious things which made Solomon's reign for a considerable time so illustrious, it is sad to record its strange decline and miserable termination. It was a magnificent morning and noon, followed by a dark evening and a stormy night. The subject of polygamy, or the marriage of several wives by one man, has been excused by some and approved by others, because it was not distinctly condemned and forbidden to the Israelites. It was practised by Abraham, Jacob, Saul, David, and here declared to have existed to an enormous extent with Solomon.

Had the Jewish Church been a real church, and its distinguished men examples for us, the difficulty of revering them as being patterns for us, and yet repudiating this very important part of their conduct, would have been great indeed. But such is not the case. They were none of them examples for Christians. They were not a church, but only a type of a church which was to exist in the world's dark midnight, until its darkest hour had come, and a new morning could be introduced by the Lord Jesus, the Divine Sun, who would arise with healing in His wings.

Polygamy was a permission to men whose nature had become so depraved that it was needful, in order to keep them in any association with religion, that their habits in this respect should be, as the Apostle terms it, winked at. "And the times of this ignorance God winked at, but now He commandeth men everywhere to repent" (Acts xvii. 30). True marriage is the holiest institution among men, and can only exist between two who, in love to God and the righteous, are accordant in aims, hopes, wishes, and virtues, and feel a soul-fitness and inward preference for each other. The Lord Jesus said, "Have ye not read, that He who made them at the beginning, made them male and female; and said, FOR THIS CAUSE shall a man leave father and mother, and shall cleave to his wife, and they twain shall be one flesh? Wherefore they are no more twain, but one flesh. What therefore God hath joined together, let no man put asunder" (Matt. xix. 5).

Marriage is therefore the blending of two souls into one harmony of sentiments, desires, and purposes, so that they act as counterparts of each other, the one viewing every circumstance and event from the intellectual side of our nature chiefly; the other from the love side, but both working together: she perceiving God's wisdom in him, he perceiving God's love in her, and both striving daily to become one more and more. This union is a type of the union of the Lord and His Church (Eph. v. 32). It is a type of heaven. It is the centre of those homes in which angels are intended to be born and trained for a heavenly life and heaven itself. True marriage is the bond of society, the soul of progress, the essential life of business, and of usefulness, the spring of education, and the blessing of the world. Blissful married homes are little heavens upon earth, and the truest resemblances of the grand home, the everlasting home of men in heaven, which is called married land (Isa. lxii. 4), and where they are invited to partake of the marriage supper of the Lamb (Rev. xix. 9). Every departure from this truest and highest order of life is a departure from right, and though God permitted it to the nations of the East, and to the Israelites as a portion of those people; yet evidently, like the sacrifices of animals, instead of the offerings of the heart in worship, it must be regarded as of that class of laws of which the prophet Ezekiel speaks, "He gave them statutes which were not good, and judgments whereby they should not live" (xxi. 25). The prophet Jeremiah speaks of the same rebellious and depraved disposition of heart among the Israelites, modifying the providential relations of the Most High in regard to them. "Put your burnt-offerings to your sacrifices, and eat flesh. For I spake not unto your fathers, nor commanded them in the day that I brought them out of the land of Egypt, concerning burnt-offerings or sacrifices; but this thing commanded I them, saying, Obey my voice, and I will be your God, and ye shall be my people; and walk ye in all the ways

that I have commanded you, that it may be well with you"
(vii. 21-23).

The worship consisting of the sacrifices of slain beasts, and the burnt-offerings of their carcases, was never the intention of the Most High, but the old nations, and the Israelites amongst the rest, could not be brought up to the pure offerings of righteousness (Mal. i. 11), the adoration of the heart, the dedication of holy and innocent intentions; of thoughts and sentiments of judgment and justice; and the consecration of the whole man to be a living sacrifice to holiness, wisdom and love (Rom. xii. 1). In the meantime they must worship, and therefore they were suffered to worship in their own rude way, and the worship was regulated and commanded to be a shadow of good things to come, until the Lord Jesus came and brought a better dispensation, a real, a universal, and a spiritual church which could and would worship God in spirit and in truth (John iv.).

We must always keep brightly before us the truth, that the grand aim of the Word of God is to give us spiritual truth, to impart to us the thoughts of God. Its histories are true histories, with the exception of the allegories of the purely allegorical times of the oldest ages of the world. But the histories also are allegories, as the apostle Paul observes, of the history of Abraham and his two wives, "Which things are an allegory: for these are the two covenants; the one from mount Sinai, which gendereth to bondage, which is Agar. But Jerusalem which is above is free, which is the mother of us all" (Gal. iv. 24-26). We know from Luke xvi. 22, that Abraham, the husband, represented the Lord our Maker, who is the husband of His church (Isa. liv. 6).

Thus we rise from regarding these ancient personages as to their own individual characters. Of these they would give an account in their judgment in the eternal world, where the hearts and reins and all things are tried and laid open in their own characters, and every one is judged according to his works, but they are mentioned in the Divine Word in their allegorical aspect only, and as, the apostle says, the Lord and His church.

The church is portrayed as a woman and wife, because the leading feature in the womanly character is affection, and Christian love, not belief, is the central virtue of Christianity and of all true religion. "By this shall all men know that ye are my disciples, that ye love one another" (John xiii. 35). By this we know that we have passed from death to life; because we love the brethren" (John iii. 14). The church then is a woman. When she yearns for the truth sincerely, then she is a virgin, the king's daughter all glorious within, the virgin daughter of Zion, the virgin daughter of Jerusalem. When she has fully received the truth and seeks supreme communion with the Lord, and is full of the desire to do His will, she is a wife; and when she abounds in members, and trains, comforts, educates and strengthens them, she is a nursing mother, with children abounding on every side.

The desire of the Lord to unite the Church to Him as a virgin is represented in the sweet language of the prophet Hosea: "And I will betroth thee unto me for ever; yea, I will betroth thee unto me in righteousness, and in judgment, and in loving-kindness, and in mercies. I will even betroth thee unto me in faithfulness: and thou shalt know the Lord" (ii. 19, 20). The internal church, once flourishing in early times, barren among the Jews, but restored again in Christianity, is described in Isaiah, when it is written concerning the Lord's wife, "Sing, O barren, thou that didst not bear: break forth into singing, thou that didst not travail with child: for more are the children of the desolate than the children of the married wife, saith the Lord. For the Lord hath called as a woman forsaken, and grieved in spirit, and a wife of youth, when thou wast refused, saith thy God" (liv. 1, 6).

Here are two wives of the Lord described, one which had had many children, the married wife, the Jewish representative of a church, and the other, which had been a wife of youth, long unable to travail with child, but about to break forth on the right hand and on the left, her seed inheriting the Gentiles and making the desolate cities to be inhabited (ver. 3).

The Church is one wife, when in her perfect state, all her parts loving the Lord supremely, loving and learning His Word fervently and intelligently, loving one another, but when the fervid days of supreme love are over, and opinions begin to have more weight with men than charity, there then ceases to be a strict unity, and there comes to be many wives. There may still be unanimity—difference with concord—many Churches with one Lord—harmony with variety—many creeds with many forms, but equal love: this is represented by the seven hundred wives of Solomon.

Seven hundred represents the sacredness, and the perfect conjunction there may be with the Lord in all the diversity which may exist in inferior matters. Each member may say of another in any of these diversified forms, this is my brother, for he is a good man, he loves the Lord and strives to do His will.

The Lord will manifest His love to all these, and form of these one grand heaven. "Other sheep," He said, "I have that are not of this fold: them also must I bring: and there shall be one fold, and one shepherd." Those churches who accept the Word, and receive their dogmas and directions from its hallowed pages, though they may lay some great stress upon parts which do not strike others as of so great importance, and magnify some truths at the expense of others, and so constitute differences; yet because the Word is their great teacher, they constitute wives of the Lord. They are united by the ties of greatest dignity. Such churches or communions as are not united by the direct teachings of the Divine Word, but only in a secondary way by tradition handed down from times more or less remote, are secondary wives, or concubines. Yet, they are not disdained. There are three hundred concubines. The number three has more relation to truth, while seven is used where good is more the leading object concerned.

There is some truth involved in every sort of religion, in every sort of superstition even. By the truth it continues, and serves in some distant way to keep men in connection with their God—

"The poor Indian whose untutored mind,
Sees God in clouds or hears Him in the wind,"

is better for seeing and hearing in some form that which is higher and nobler than himself. So there are wives and concubines. All men all over the world are conjoined with their God by ties direct or indirect. The Apostle Peter said, when the world was covered with idolatry, and Christianity was confined to the city of Jerusalem, "Of a truth, I perceive that God is no respecter of persons: but in every nation, he that feareth Him and worketh righteousness is accepted of Him" (Acts x. 34, 35).

Then, the Hindoos had their numerous deities, the Thibetans and Chinese their Boodha, the Greeks Zeus and other Olympian deities, the Romans Jupiter and his subordinates, while the Northern nations had Woden, Thor, Balder, and the Walhalla, but still the Apostle said, "in every nation he that feareth God and worketh righteousness is accepted of Him." The leading features of all these are so much alike as to suggest that they are all parts of a grand system which once prevailed over the world, an ancient Church. Glorious truth! Outbirth of the God of Love! It must be so. How horrible and unworthy of that Glorious One, Whose tender mercies are over all His works, is the notion that the Divine Father has created and is creating hundreds of millions of human beings who never heard of the Bible or of Jesus, and yet would be passed over by God until death ushered them to everlasting torments, for not having believed that of which they had never heard. The higher truth of mercy and love is meant by the spiritual sense of the fact, that Solomon had his seven hundred wives and three hundred concubines. Solomon, as the husband of these wives and concubines, represented the Lord Jesus, no longer as the one grand embodiment of infinite love; as a glorious Divine Man, keeping ever open the means of communication between the human race and heaven; but the Lord as He appears to different churches and communities. He is worshipped under many forms. But so far as God is really and sincerely worshipped from the heart, it is a Divine Person who is sought, worshipped and loved, and there is no other Divine Person but the Lord Jesus Christ. "He is the Alpha and the Omega, the beginning and the end, the first and the last, who is, who was, and who is to come" (Rev. i. 8, 17).

In some of the beautiful myths of the Middle Ages we are told of a little child imploring a boatman to row him over a river for charity, for he has nothing to pay, and he will perish if he cannot get across; the boatman ferries the child across, and then discovers that the distressed child was the Saviour Himself: or a poor pilgrim solicits a morsel of bread or a lodging for the night, and on some compassionate person supplying his needs, the pilgrim is transformed into the Lord Himself, and gives the merciful donor His blessing. The lesson taught is that the Lord is present in every form of good, and accepts as done for Him whatever the heart sincerely intends for the love of Him.

In thousands of cases the Lord Jesus is worshipped as a crucified one, still bleeding on the Cross, although He now reigns in unspeakable majesty in the Sun of heaven, the glorified King of kings, and Lord of lords. In other cases, almost beyond number, He is adored as a little baby, as if He had never got beyond that condition in His mother's arms. In Spain and her dependencies the worship of the Virgin has quite eclipsed that of the Saviour, the churches being so filled with pictures and symbols referring to her that very little room indeed is left for her Lord.

Yet, under all these forms the Lord is worshipped by the sincerely good, they mean it for Him, the Highest and Best, and when their mistakes are corrected in the eternal world, they will all be found to have been gravitating towards the one grand Centre who said, "And I, if I be lifted up, will draw all men unto Me" (John xii. 32): "I in them, and thou in Me, that they may be made perfect in one." And if these incorrect forms of the Saviour among Christians may be regarded as errors which will be removed in the world where those servants who knew not their Lord will be beaten with few stripes, why not the incorrect forms of Gentile lands? That which they lovingly do for worship, is done to God as they understand Him. Will it not be accepted by Him, who looks not on the outward appearance, but who looks upon the heart.

Go on, then, Christian men, if you find your money and your labour are not needed in the heathen parts of your own countries, in the slums and the cellars where vice and poverty and misery degrade and destroy all that is noble in the soul, but do not imagine that three-quarters of the world had no taste of God's mercy before you got there. The eternally Good is eternally active, He neither slumbers nor sleeps, and where the African has sighed for God, and the Asiatic in far distant lands has groped after every ray of light from far-off hoary centuries, the true light that enlighteneth every man that cometh into the world has not failed them, and He will remember them in the day when He makes up His jewels. Solomon in his degenerating state, we have said, represents the Lord, when the state of the Church degenerated, and they came to have less faithful and pure views of Him. It is interesting to notice the order in which the strange women who began to affect Solomon are mentioned.

First, we have women of the Moabites, then of the Ammonites, next of the Edomites, followed by the Zidonians and the Hittites. The Moabites, spiritually, are those who are much taken up with ceremonies in religion, who are much concerned with the beautiful in service, but neglect the inward struggles against self and sin, which alone produce the new heart and the right spirit in us. "Moab hath been at ease from his youth, and he hath settled upon his lees, and hath not been emptied out from vessel to vessel, neither hath he gone into captivity: therefore his taste remained in him, and his scent is not changed. All ye that are about him, being on him; and all ye that know his name, say, How is the strong staff broken, and the beautiful rod!" (Jer. xlviii. 11-17). With all the strength of seeming grandeur, and the most perfect finish of the most beautiful ritual, if there be no change of heart, all will be vanity and vexation of spirit. Moab is exceeding proud. We have heard the pride of Moab, his loftiness, his arrogancy and his pride, and the haughtiness of his heart (v. 29).

Next, there are mentioned the Ammonites. Ammon was the brother of Moab. They were both born in disorder, in a dim cave. The Ammonites represent, spiritually, those who are as eager after mere creeds and modes of faith as the Moabites were after ceremonies." "If we have the gift of prophecy and understand all mysteries, and all knowledge, and though we have all faith, so that we could remove mountains, and have not charity, we are nothing" (1 Cor. xiii. 3). Then come the Edomites, who represent merely natural men; the Zidonians, the inhabitants of Tyre and Sidon, who, in their avidity for trade, are the emblems of those who are eager for knowledge, who were the good-natured moralists of old times.

All these form their God, somewhat after the fashion of their own predominant predilection, but they are not on that account forsaken by their Heavenly Father. "If thou, Lord, should mark iniquity, who shall stand? But there is forgiveness with Thee that Thou mayest be feared." When Jeremiah went by divine command to the house of the potter, he saw there was a work on the wheels. "And the vessel was marred in the hand of the potter: so he made it again another vessel, as seemed good to the potter to make it. Behold, as the clay is in the potter's hand, so are ye in mine hand, O house of Israel" (Jer. xviii. 4, 6). So is it with all divine operations. The Lord desires to make the very best vessel, whether it be of church or man. If these, however, fail, and the vessel is marred in the hands of the potter, he makes the second best, and so on the best possible of every one of us.

In the glorious part of Solomon's reign, the Church in its highest state was represented; all was magnificent, beautiful, and happy: the Lord Jesus, the Prince of Peace reigning over, and blessing His pure and united Church. This, however, after a time changed, and divided and subdivided, but nevertheless the divine goodness imparted some blessing to all, for He had seven hundred wives and three hundred concubines.

SERMON XXXIV.

SOLOMON'S OLD AGE, DECLENSION FROM GOD, AND DEATH.

" For it came to pass, when Solomon was old, that his wives turned away his heart after other gods; and his heart was not perfect with the Lord his God, as was the heart of David his father. And Solomon slept with his fathers, and was buried in the city of David his father, and Rehoboam his son reigned in his stead."—1 KINGS xi. 4, 43.

THE reign of Solomon during his early glorious years was the type of the early and most sacred time of the Christian Church. The reign of Solomon, spiritually, is the reign of the glorified Jesus, the reign of love, the reign of peace. When we read of the earthly Solomon, of his early soundness of judgment, of his devotion, his costly and splendid temple, and of his magnificent works, and then turn to contemplate his latter years, we cannot but sadly think how great a fall was there. Prosperity is a more dangerous tempter than adversity, more destructive because more insidious. Our strength is sapped by luxury, and we often suffer the grand promise of our youth, by the enervating influence of self-indulgence, to fade away into weakness and sensuality. So was it in Solomon's case. So has it been with many a ruler, with many a successful merchant and tradesman whose sun of early promise shone brilliantly, but went down while it was yet noon, surrounded it may be with earthly splendour, but with wearied and famished souls: in the Lord's sight miserable and poor, and blind and naked.

How sadly the reflection comes home to us, when we contemplate the excellence and the brightness of the early years of Solomon's kingly life, Why could it not continue! How strange that he who ran so well for a time should become weak, and stumble and fall so strangely. Yet so it is, unless we keep constant watch, and guard against self-indulgence continually, the old, old story will repeat itself again, and the fair young spring of immortal life with us will dissolve into a blighted autumn and a dreary winter; when all that could have warmed and blessed the heart has expired under the baleful activities of egotism and lust.

But if such reflections press sadly upon us when meditating on the glory and declension of Solomon's life and government, still more seriously do they affect us when we contemplate the early centuries of Christianity of which they were the symbol and the foreshadowing. Not less glorious spiritually than the magnificence of Solomon was the pure and beautiful condition of the Christian religion when love was its grand and central law.

The Lord Jesus was to them supremely the God of Love and the Prince of Peace. To be a Christian was to be humble, wise, and good. To be a Christian was to love the Lord Jesus above all things, to love the brethren, and to do God's commandments in relation to all men under all circumstances. When brought before persecuting governors, Christians called themselves sometimes God-bearers, sometimes Christ-bearers; for they said they bore Christ in their hearts. The apostles preached love, and those who were genuine and acknowledged Christians lived in love.

See how these Christians love one another, said the observers of their lives and characters, and when John, the last of the apostolic twelve, could no longer walk to the little company of brethren at Ephesus, and was carried still to be present with them in their worship, he is said, when entering and retiring, to have repeated the words, "Little children, love one another." Love to the Lord Jesus, and the keeping His commandments, were at that time considered the all in all of Christianity.

"And above all things have fervent charity (or love) among yourselves." "And, besides this, giving all diligence, add to your faith virtue, and to virtue, knowledge: and to knowledge, temperance: and to temperance, patience: and to patience, godliness: and to godliness, brotherly kindness: and to brotherly kindness, charity (or love)." "Whoso keepeth His Word, in him verily is the LOVE OF GOD PERFECTED. Hereby, know we that we are in Him." "We know that we have passed from death to life, because WE LOVE THE BRETHREN." "He that loveth not, knoweth not God, for GOD IS LOVE." "God is love, and HE THAT DWELLETH IN LOVE, DWELLETH IN GOD, AND GOD IN HIM." "There is no fear in love, but PERFECT LOVE CASTETH OUT FEAR." "By this we know that we love the children of God, WHEN WE LOVE GOD, AND KEEP HIS COMMANDMENTS. For this is the love of God, that we keep His commandments: AND HIS COMMANDMENTS ARE NOT GRIEVOUS."

Such was the universal teaching of Christianity in its warm and best days. Such were its grand principles when its real and genuine triumphs were obtained. Its progress then was that represented (Rev. vi. 1) by the rider on the white horse, with the bow in his hand, who went forth conquering and to conquer. These were its golden days. It was then a real temple of the Most High, not made with hands, but formed of devoted hearts, and minds radiant with the wisdom of heaven. The Christian assemblies there were held in very humble places, but they were glorified by faithful adherence to grand principles which were to form "a new heaven and a new earth," principles before which Jupiter and his pantheon, and a thousand deities beside, became what they really were, mere things of nought.

These, then, were the days represented by the glorious years of the reign of Solomon. The Lord Jesus was their King, their Judge, their law-giver. The life of His religion was to do good. For nearly three hundred years this pure and blessed state of Christianity existed and spread, but some time before, Constantine blended it with the pagan world and gave it political power and patronage. It had been losing its faithful and spiritual character, and exchanging the spirit that giveth life for the letter that killeth. In gaining external influence and dominion, the disciples of the Saviour lost in purity and love. The Lord Jesus, in their minds, was no longer the pure God-Man, the actual God manifest in the flesh, who had lived a real life on earth, who loved us, died for us, and redeemed us from the powers of darkness, that He might regenerate us, and make us as His angels on the earth, but strange delusions of the wildest kind were entertained.

Some declared that He was not the same Divine Being as Jehovah, but that He came to put Him down. Some declared He had had no proper body, but that His appearance was only a shadowy phantom life. Others maintained He had no real proper Divinity or Divine Humanity, but that a distinct spirit at His baptism entered into Him for a time, and then left Him before His crucifixion.

These phantasies, and many others, adjoined to the doctrine of the Lord, like the strange women of Solomon, quite altered the Church's view of her Saviour; they began to make Him in imagination what their false philosophers dreamed over, long before the real incarnation of the Lord.

They were the strange wives spiritually, and to professed Christians, that turned away Solomon's heart, and made Him to the Church no longer what He had been, the God of love, the God of peace, regeneration, and progress; but the God of wrangling, of dispute, and of battles, and since that time the wars waged by Christians and in the name of Christ have been as murderous, as cruel, as vindictive, and as revengeful, as ever were those of ancient Babylon, Nineveh, Greece, or Rome.

The very vision of the cross by which Constantine, as it was pretended, was converted, was a vision which he understood to mean, that by the power of the Lord Jesus he would overcome the other tyrant Maxentius, against whom he was at war, and would thenceforward be sole ruler of the Roman Empire.

Shortly afterwards the doctrine of three divine persons was set up, and the real divine power in the Church passed away from the Saviour, and was awarded to the first Person of the Trinity separate from Him, and a God as terrible as ever the Jews had thought Him, or clothed with attributes still more transcendently dreadful. Thus was the time changed from being a reign of peace, wisdom, purity, and the glory of being good, to a condition little better than heathenism once more, but heathenism clothed with Christian names. It was in all respects like the early happiness of the government of Solomon, transformed into the disturbed condition of his later years.

Why should we ever lose the truly Christian state, or turn it to anything of a contrary character? Why should Solomon be degraded and die, and give place to the fierce Rehoboam? Jesus, our Divine Creator and Saviour, has made us to be orderly and blessed, and formed the world to be our happy training place, preparatory to our blissful everlasting home. He has given His Word to guide and delight us, and all things around contribute to our comfort and delight if we conform to the just and kind requirements of heavenly order. While industry, virtue, and kindness reign, all things go well. Life is golden; and hope gilds the future with hues still more lovely. Life's ways are ways of pleasantness, and all its paths are peace. Why should it not always be so? We are not suffering privation unendurable by being good. We are but living rationally. It is life in its truest sense. Could it but continue, our graceful and noble youth would be perfected to a more noble and maturely graceful middle age, and our after years but ripen us for heaven. Then could it be said of each of us, and "all that Solomon did, and his wisdom, are they not written in the book of the acts of Solomon." Our whole life would be a life of wisdom, and the book of our lives written by ourselves on the pages of our affections and thoughts, would be a book whose opening in the eternal world would not make us ashamed, but grateful to Him who had made us images and likenesses of His own eternal wisdom and love. When Solomon had declined from God, the state of peace no longer fully existed. He was harassed by Hadad the king of the Edomites (ver. 14), by Rezon king of the Syrians, who reigned at Damascus (ver. 25), and by Jeroboam, who afterwards, in the days of Solomon's son Rehoboam, became king of the separated kingdom of Israel (ver. 40).

True devotion to our Lord Jesus, the Divine Saviour, the meek and blessed one, who is also the Everlasting Father, keeps everything in its place. A peace unspeakable possesses the soul that is at peace with Him.

When, however, we no longer are right with God, we find ourselves wrong in many other ways. We are out of harmony with creation. Troubles of various kinds arise, and we are at peace with nothing. We are divided from the Lord Himself, and we are out of joint with His world, which is His servant, and will not freely serve His rebels. A world of trouble comes when we quit the orderly sphere of the Prince of Peace.

The enmity of Hadad arose from the former severity of Joab, who abode in Edom six months, and slew every male who had not fled. Hadad and certain others took refuge with the Egyptians, and in time, when they found Solomon's power waning, they returned to assert the rights of their country, and to do mischief to the subjects of Solomon.

The Edomites, who were the descendants of Esau, represent the affections of the natural man. The attempt to slay all the male inhabitants of Edom represents the endeavour of those who are in narrow conceptions of the letter rather than in the spirit of religion, to do away with the natural man altogether. They would have no husbands and wives, they would not eat if they could help it, they are under the mistaken persuasion that nature is not equally with spirit a child of the Divine Being, but is His enemy: hence they strive to destroy every male in Edom. Happily, however it cannot be done. Enormous mischief arises from the attempt, and both Solomon and the Edomites suffer, religion is made sour and bitter, and the world defiant, repulsive, and contemptuous. The truth however is, that nature has her claims and her rights, as proper to be granted in their own sphere as those of religion in the higher duties of life. The impulses, instincts, and pleasures of our lower affections are not to be stifled or destroyed, but to be purified, directed and kept healthy. The pleasures of the world are to be kept in subordination to the Lord's divine laws, and that secures their orderly life and enjoyment, and prevents their declining into pain. And thus is fulfilled the blessing pronounced upon Esau, "Behold, thy dwelling shall be the fatness of the earth, and of the dew of heaven from above" (Gen. xxvii. 39). The Saviour shall come upon Mount Zion, to judge the mount of Esau: and the kingdom shall be the Lord's.

When Christianity had ceased to a considerable extent to be the loving, wise, and peaceful kingdom of the Lord Jesus, the religion of simple goodness and truth, a strange fanaticism began to trouble the Church, rude extravagant minds determined if possible to banish all natural delight, under the delusion that they would thus become more spiritual. For this object, they went into deserts to live apart from human kind. They eschewed the sweet relation of society, and lived in strange uncouth ways, until they became like animals. Thinking they could become more, they became less than men. They became brutish, irrational, covered with hair, and fearfully ferocious. Some lived in dens, and on pillars for years, filthy saints, fed by the charity and ignorant superstition of the honest and industrious but mistaken people of the neighbourhood. They were continually degenerating into wild and inhuman excesses, and gave terrible illustrations of the truth, "It is not good for man to be alone." Orders of monks and nuns were formed which were constantly degenerating into hotbeds of luxury and vice. Industry and social life are the divine safeguards of virtue. This state of things was what in the spiritual sense was represented by Joab's attempt to destroy every male in Edom, and subsequently of Hadad the Edomite and his subjects harassing the latter days of Solomon.

There will be no persistent enmity if the world, on the one hand, has its claims allowed and blest; and religion, on the other, is exercised as a benign and holy influence uniting earth and heaven, time and eternity, in sacred links of order and well-being.

The Syrians equally waged war against the Israelites in the latter years of Solomon. "Rezon (the lean) gathered men unto him, and became captain over a band, when David slew them of Zobah: and they went to Damascus, and dwelt therein, and reigned in Damascus. And he was an adversary to Israel all the days of Solomon, beside the mischief that Hadad did: and he abhorred Israel, and reigned over Syria." Syria was an ancient kingdom, having Damascus for its capital, one of the oldest cities of the East, renowned for its refinement, its skill in the fine arts, and the elegancies of life, as well as for its literary treasures, as Egypt was for its science. Syria was the land of trade and knowledge. Tyre and Sidon were its great ports, and through these Spain and Britain, and all the great and busy states which clustered round the Mediterranean, ministered to the Syrians, frequently called "the children of the East." Balaam was a Syrian, and evidently had a knowledge of correspondences, of the true God, and of divine things, which shewed that ancient wisdom still existed there. The wise men of the East that followed the star which guided to the new-born Saviour exhibited again the possession in Syria of knowledge lost in many other lands. Syria then is the type of the region of literature, of the knowledge of religious, social, and moral life.

When religion has lost its true character of love to God and man, and has become superstition, literary men become scoffers. Syria is an adversary to Israel all the (degenerate) days of Solomon. Let religion, the daughter of heaven, be pure, humble, holy, and true, and there is no antagonism between knowledge and religion. Literature rejoices in illustrating and enforcing, in her own domain, whatever tends to make homes elegant and amiable, to embellish, purify and dignify society, and elevate the characters of men. To have antagonism between religion and philosophy is disastrous to both. But it is inevitable, when religion has become impure and superstitious. The very keystone of the social arch then crumbled into corruption, and everything becomes disjointed.

Philosophy disdains a religion of fear, or a religion of folly. It sneers and laughs at the God of crouching terror and wild fanaticism. And this war between the two will continue until religion is restored to that sacred condition which the apostle James so well describes, as the "wisdom which is from above, which is first pure, then peaceable, gentle, and easy to be entreated, full of mercy and good fruits, without partiality, and without hypocrisy. And the fruit of righteousness is sown of peace of them that make peace."

Jeroboam, the son of Nebat, was the third great opponent which troubled the declining years of Solomon, and ultimately established Israel as a separate kingdom, formed of ten tribes; leaving only two to form the kingdom of Judah.

The reason of this division was that Solomon's strange wives had led him and his kingdom to forsake the Lord, and follow

Ashtaroth, the goddess of the Zidonians; Chemosh, the god of the Moabites; and Milcom, or Moloch, the god of the children of Ammon (ver. 33).

Ashtaroth, the moon-goddess, or queen of heaven, as she was called (Jer. vii. 18), was woman-worship, which extended over many countries, as far as Spain, where it was especially prevalent, and where it was introduced into the Christian religion. It continues to the present day, only the queen of heaven, anciently called Ashtaroth, is now called the Virgin Mary. The outward worship of this female phantasy is symbolic of the Church worshipping herself and forsaking her Saviour.

Chemosh, the god of the Moabites, was a Baal, or sun-god; and the Moabites in the Church are those who make religion a ceremonial ritualism, to the neglect of love, justice, and wisdom.

Moloch, or Milcom, of the Ammonites, the burning god, to whom children were destroyed, represented the infernal lusts and passions which exist, and strengthen, in a perverted church, to the destruction of pure and innocent feelings, and sentiments.

When the Church of the Lord Jesus was thus bereft of its pure order and character, and a semi-heathenism defiled and weakened it, destroying its genuine and heaven-derived authority, then division came, and unity was destroyed. "To your tents, O Israel!" was cried by leaders and people, and a separate nation was formed by Jeroboam and his successors.

In the corrupt Christian Church "To your tents, O Israel!" has again been cried, and continues to be cried, by those who have protested against the corruptions which have been introduced into the once pure, spotless, and peaceful Church of the Saviour. And now, another city is placed before those who wish to be saved, both from the corruptions of corrupt Judah and of rebellious Israel, a city of gold, a new Jerusalem. Again the laws of divine order are given, again the Word is unfolded, and a greater than Solomon is here. Let us enter this glorious city, and walk in its light. Let us avoid for ever all strange and curious superstitions of every kind, remembering only what divine truth reveals to us, and that its sure, its grand, its ever-recurring lesson, both for earth and heaven, is this: "What doth the Lord thy God require of thee, but to do justly, love mercy, and to walk humbly with thy God?" Let our only struggles be the fight against self, against bad tempers, passions, and lusts. O Jesus, Saviour, Divine Solomon, restore Thy government of golden peace within us, and let Thy throne be established for ever and ever!

SERMON XXXV.

REHOBOAM'S BAD REIGN.

"And Rehoboam the son of Solomon reigned in Judah. Rehoboam was forty and one years old when he began to reign; and he reigned seventeen years in Jerusalem, the city which the Lord did choose out of all the tribes of Israel, to put his name there; and his mother's name was Naamah, an Ammonitess."—1 KINGS xiv. 21.

THE history of Rehoboam's rash conduct at the commencement of his reign yields a lesson of deep significance; it is a history of the result of ruling without affection. He had succeeded to a glorious heritage. His father and grandfather had consolidated the kingdom and extended the influence of Israel far and wide. The incident of the Queen of Sheba coming to learn the wisdom of Solomon shews that distant Abyssinia had heard of the fame and glory of the realm which owned the line of David for its monarchs.

Though the extent of Israel forbids a comparison with many ancient empires, or with the stupendous monarchies or republics of modern times, yet it had become a great and splendid kingdom for its epoch, and it had one glory peculiarly its own—one surpassing every other—the glory of being the depository of the Word of God. A thoughtful, wise, and prudent king had a wide career for good before him, yet Rehoboam threw his opportunity away, and dwarfed his kingdom to a comparatively small sovereignty, entailing also many generations of quarrel and conflict in which Judah vexed Ephraim and Ephraim weakened Judah. The adage "Divide and rule" was exemplified in many an invasion and disaster which Israel suffered, including captivity and exile, and the numberless sorrows of contention and animosity, where all ought to have been union and peace.

The circumstances suggest that there was a species of election in the succession of the kings. "Jeroboam and the congregation of the people came and spake to Rehoboam," and proposed their terms, which were very reasonable. His father's government had degenerated, and become burdensome to the subjects. With a new reign they desired new and easier regulations. Certainly this was a natural expectation, and with a new monarch, unfettered by old ties and associations, not a difficult achievement. The experienced counsellors of his father were strongly in favour of meeting the just wishes of the people, and the king took three days to consider the matter fully. At the end of that time, when the assembly of the people again demanded his answer, the monarch preferred the folly of reckless insolence to the wise courtesy of experienced age, and gave the bitter reply, "My father made your yoke heavy, and I will add to your yoke: my father also chastised you with whips, but I will chastise you with scorpions." Ten of the tribes, disgusted and outraged by so wild and rash a reply, refused their allegiance to a person so full of harshness and bitterness, and commenced under Jeroboam a separate national existence, adding another illustration to the many which the history of other lands affords, that pride is the highway to destruction, and that the spirit which would usefully rule others must ever commence by ruling itself. "He that humbleth himself shall be exalted, and he that exalteth himself shall be humbled."

When all Israel saw that the king hearkened not unto them the people answered the king, saying, "What portion have we in David? neither have we inheritance in the son of Jesse: to your tents, O Israel! now see to thine house, David."

Of course kings rule, and the great have their privileges for the good of the universal people. When they forget this, and rule not for the public good, but for the gratification of self and selfish lusts, they destroy the reason and the basis of their exalted position, and justly forfeit the advantages they abuse. Monarchs, like the Sabbath, were made for man, and they ought in all their relations and activities, public and private, to remember that they are clothed with especial advantages that they may promote the general good. When they forget this they forget the very law of their being, and may most righteously be set aside.

So Rehoboam lost the greater part of his dominion, and so will selfish domination ever lead to its own curtailment and ruin. Oh, that men would learn that the true law of greatness and happiness is to minister to the happiness of others. The Lord Himself ministers to all. He serves the meanest insect and the feeblest worm; His angels are ministers serving each other, and ministering to man. The reward an angel seeks who has bestowed some good on another, is to be permitted to do the like again. The ministries of loving usefulness one to the other are the very balsam and blessedness of society: they yield a sense of security, satisfaction, and peace, while they secure progress and fill the world with beauty and with good.

No one is wise, rich, or great for himself alone, but for the use which he can perform and the good he can communicate to others. The delight of the love of uses is a heavenly delight. "Love and wisdom exist and subsist in usefulness, and true use consists in a faithful, sincere, and diligent discharge of the duties of our calling." What great and numerous delights therefore wait upon the office of a king, if in all his acts he is guided by the law, and animated by justice and judgment. What beneficence will abound in his kingdom, where freedom reigns protected by the power, and stimulated by the example of the just magistrate. How will the arts of peace flourish when all can feel that safety is ensured by the vigilant suppression of crime, and the constant smile of power on virtuous labour? A true king is a blessing to all his subjects, high and low: a selfish king is a universal blight. The one is like Solomon in all his glory, the other like the rash and miserable Rehoboam, a bane to his kingdom, an adept only at the baleful art of reducing a great state into small, jealous and opposing sections. On a wider sphere, however, must we now contemplate the sad state of things when love waxes cold, and hard vindictiveness takes the place of heaven-born charity. Israel was the type of the Christian Church. It was the type of that Church in its rise, in its mid-day glory and in its decay.

In the Christian Church there was a Divine David, a Divine Solomon: that is, Jesus was the Redeemer and the glorified Prince of Peace, and regarded by the Apostles and the majority of the Christians of the first three centuries as their All in all (Acts x. 36; Col. iii. 11), as the Father in the Son, THE DIVINE LOVE INCARNATE. He was succeeded by a harsh spirit in the Church, a bitter Rehoboam. Then first arose in the Christian Church harshness, the spirit of pride and the love of pre-eminence. This was for a time associated with the worship of Jesus, but associated with disputes and bitterness concerning creeds, which did much to banish loving-kindness from the Christian assemblies, and instead of sympathy, gentleness, and devout spiritual-mindedness prevailing, there arose among Christians themselves the old strifes with new names.

Peace was again banished from the earth. Different modes of worshipping the Lord Jesus arose, some with more of ritual, some with less, some with semi-pagan rites, images, forms, and customs, but with Christian designations.

As there had been gods of different places, and presiding over different occupations and departments of life, so now there were introduced saints to be patrons of countries, cities, battles, trades, and occupations. St. James was supposed to fight desperately for Spain. St. George, who had been a soldier of very bad character in Cappadocia, was credited with being the champion of England. The old heathen worship of a queen of heaven, Ashtaroth, was continued, only devoted to the Virgin Mary. This state of things was symbolized and foreshadowed by the idolatry to which Solomon attached himself in his later years. But a time came when the proper Deity of the Lord Jesus was called in question altogether. Arius arose, and although he was combated and defeated in his attempt to set aside the worship of the Lord as Very God, yet, owing to the low, natural state of the Church, the worship of the Lord the Saviour, God manifested, was subordinated to the invisible and unknown God again. Jesus remained on the lips, but in the heart and in the conduct the God of the Church was the great and terrible God, whom men should fear and dread, and make other men fear and dread. This was the state of the Church represented by the reign of Rehoboam. Then came the idea of converting men by the persuasion of the sword. Then came crusades and persecutions, wars for religions, far more bitter than heathendom had ever waged, until it has been said with too much truth, that war is the normal state of Christianity. Truly of this degenerate condition of the Church may it be said as Rehoboam said, "My little finger shall be thicker than my father's loins. And, now, whereas my father did lade you with a heavy yoke, I will add to your yoke: my father hath chastised you with whips: but I will chastise you with scorpions."

Let any one read the terrible annals of France, Spain, the Netherlands, Germany, Italy, or our own country even, and learn what cruelties Christians have inflicted upon Christians, and he will turn with horror and loathing from the cruel records and ask if this indeed be the religion of the merciful Saviour. Certainly it is not, it is the reign of Rehoboam. He was chastising the Church with scorpions.

This terrible condition of the Church, heathenism and cruelty gilded with Christian names, is clearly foreshadowed and foretold in the Word in many places, as well as here, by Rehoboam's reign following Solomon's in typical Israel. Our Lord said, "Because iniquity shall abound, the love of many shall wax cold" (Matt. xxiv. 12). Again, "When ye therefore shall see the abomination of desolation, spoken of by Daniel the prophet, stand in the holy place: whoso readeth, let him understand." The abomination of desolation stands in the holy place when self-love stands in the centre of the Church, where the LOVE OF THE LORD JESUS alone should be.

The same impressive lesson was taught when the Lord said, "Immediately after the tribulation of those days shall the sun be darkened, and the moon shall not give her light, and the stars shall fall from heaven, and the powers of the heavens shall be shaken." For, what can be more manifest than that the SUN OF DIVINE LOVE, the Sun of Righteousness (Mal. iv. 2), had become darkened in the firmament of the Church, when the struggles for pre-eminence, with all its hates and animosities, its desolations and slaughters, had wasted the Church and so-called Christian nations. Love was quenched in hate, revenge and massacre. The Church had become a pandemonium. Not the religion of Jesus, but the revenge of ferocity was there. In like manner, the moon of divine faith did not give her light. When love becomes cold, light becomes dim. Hear what a famous bishop, St. Hilary so-called, said of the Church when it had become political and merely natural: "It is a thing equally deplorable and dangerous, that there are at present as many creeds as there are opinions among men, as many doctrines as inclinations, and as many sources of blasphemy as there are faults among us; because we make creeds arbitrarily, and explain them as arbitrarily. As there is but one faith, so there is but one only God, one Lord, and one baptism. We renounce this one faith when we make so many different creeds, and that diversity is the reason why we have no true faith amongst us. We cannot be ignorant that since the Council of Nice we have done nothing but make creeds. And while we fight against words, litigate about new questions, dispute about equivocal terms, complain about authors, that every one may make his own party triumph; while we cannot agree, while we anathematize one another, there is hardly one that adheres to Jesus Christ." "We make creeds every year, nay, every moon we repent of what we have done. We defend those that repent, we anathematize those we defended. So we condemn either the doctrine of others in ourselves, or our own in that of others; and reciprocally tearing one another to pieces, we have been the cause of each other's ruin." No friendly moon was shining then to light the spiritual traveller on his way. The darkness of folly had taken the place of the beautiful and blessed perceptions of true wisdom. The stars fell from heaven, and the powers of the heavens were shaken, that is, the blessed lights of Scripture, each verse shining like a star when truly regarded, became extinguished, or used only for selfish and earthly ends, the powers of heavenly virtue were all shaken and ready to perish. Then came the dark night of superstition and the terrible reign of ferocity. The dark places were full of cruelty. It was the time of Rehoboam and his successors. The reign of the Prince of Peace was over.

"Rehoboam was forty and one years old when he began to reign, and he reigned seventeen years in Jerusalem." These figures intimate no doubt the literal times in relation to Rehoboam, and express them correctly; but they have also a spiritual and prophetic signification. Forty in Scripture is used to indicate a full state and period of tribulation. The rain causing the flood fell forty days and forty nights: the children of Israel wandered forty years in the wilderness: the Lord fasted forty days. It was of Divine Providence that Rehoboam should be forty and one years old when he began to reign, to indicate that when the Rehoboam state would come in the Church it would have endured a full wasting by tribulation; its spirituality would have departed, and a new condition had set in, a condition of the letter that killeth, of the letter perverted, materalized and misunderstood. Only when spiritual things had become desolated, and a state of superstition had set in—was it possible to inaugurate the reign of cruelty in the Church. How terrible the change! The religion of meekness, of charity, of doing unto others as we would they should do unto us, of returning good for evil, of humility, of meekness and peace, was made into a reign of terror, of fires to burn heretics, of fiendish inquisitions, of massacre and death. Rehoboam was forty and one years old when he began to reign. Only when love to the Lord, true charity, and real faith had been fully wasted by persistent quarrels, and persevering bigotry, could hate and cruelty in the Church begin its rule.

The seventeen years he reigned in Jerusalem reminds us also of the seventeenth day of the month when all the fountains of the great deep were broken up in the days of Noah, and of the age of seventeen years attained by Joseph, when his great trials began. This number, made up of ten and seven, in its spiritual sense implies the period of temptation and trouble for the good, who have however been mercifully prepared to endure it. His mother's name was Naamah, an Ammonitess.

The Ammonites in the Church represent those who make creeds of trifles, and are bitter for beliefs. Ammon originated in a dim cave, and though near to the Israelites, the Ammonites were ever quarrelsome and opposed. No Ammonite was to come into the congregration of the Lord to the tenth generation (Deut. xxiii. 3). The Ammonites in the Church are the hairsplitters, the wranglers, those who neglect the sweet graces of charity, of deference, gentleness and peace, and are indifferent to integrity and genuine faithfulness to the duties of life. They are diligent to foment discord, ready to join in with the first dog that barks. Like the wasp which instantly perceives the slightest crack in the grape, and destroys the fruit, so the Ammonite, fierce for his crotchet, however trifling it may be, destroys genuine religion in the bitter war of words. He strains at gnats, but swallows camels. He is ready to fight for what he calls his religion, but never attains the religion of humble love and genuine virtue. Concerning the Ammonites, thus saith the Lord, "Hath Israel no sons? hath he no heir? why then doth their king inherit Gad, and his people dwell in the cities?"

Rehoboam's mother was an Ammonitess, to teach us that cruelty in the Church is born of the grim spirit of bigotry. The name Naamah means, *vehemently moving:* and thus it denotes the eager energy of those who are fierce for their opinions, who disturb the world about their notions, but have little, very little to do with humility, wisdom, regeneration, and the thousand blessings of peace within and peace around.

And now let us gather the whole lesson to a close. The sum of it is: this, woe comes to the Church when we depart from the sweet government of our blessed Saviour Himself, the Divine Prince of Peace, and let the spirit of despotism and domination take His place.

Of Solomon it is said, as the type of our blessed Lord, "He shall judge the poor of the people, He shall save the children of the needy, and shall break in pieces the oppressor. They shall fear Thee as long as the sun and the moon endure, THROUGHOUT ALL GENERATIONS. His name shall endure for ever: His name shall be continued as long as the sun: and men shall be blessed in Him: all nations shall call Him blessed" (Psa. lxxii. 4, 5, 17). When the blessed Jesus is king in the Church, His Holy Spirit descends "like rain upon the mown grass, as showers that water the earth: in His days do the righteous flourish, and there is abundance of peace" (ver. 6, 7). Why should we not all say "Reign for ever, Prince of Peace." In Him is light, comfort, strength, and every blessing. What is there that the soul cannot find by abiding in the Saviour alone? When He was on earth, the sick went to Him and were healed, the penitent went and had their sins forgiven, the lepers were cleansed, the lame were made to walk, and the dead were raised. He never directed the sorrowful soul to any one else, for in Him was the Father of Mercy, from Him is His Holy Spirit.

To the early disciples the Lord Jesus was all in all. He was their theme. He was their Guide, their Consoler, and their Helper. Let us now go back to Him. It was a sad thing for the Church that the easy yoke of the Redeemer was changed for the grim rod of Rehoboam. Let us go back to Him who is the Way, the Truth, and the Life, and thus resume the long broken connection, the centre of unity, love and peace.

How constantly He calls mankind to Himself. "Come unto ME all ye that are weary and heavy laden, and I will give you rest. No man cometh unto the Father but by ME. Whosoever cometh unto ME I will in no wise cast him out. He that seeth ME, seeth HIM that sent ME. I am come a light into the world, that whosoever believeth on ME should not abide in darkness. These things I have spoken unto you, that in ME ye might have peace."

Even so, blessed Saviour, Father, Son, and Holy Spirit, may Thy reign be perpetual! Govern and regenerate our hearts, diffuse thy love throughout our works and ways, raise us far above harshness and animosity, and let Thy Spirit of peace diffuse concord in our hearts, our homes, and throughout the world, that there may indeed be "one King over all the earth," one blessed Lord, thy own reign, O Lord Jesus, and "His name One."

SERMON XXXVI.

THE KINGDOM OF ISRAEL DIVIDED INTO TWO, JUDAH AND ISRAEL.

"But the Word of God came unto Shemaiah the man of God, saying, Speak unto Rehoboam, the son of Solomon, king of Judah, and unto all the house of Judah and Benjamin, and to the remnant of the people, saying, Thus saith the Lord, Ye shall not go up, nor fight against your brethren the children of Israel: return every man to h' house; for this thing is from me. They hearkened therefore to the word of the Lord, and returned to depart, according to the word of the Lord."—1 KINGS xii. 22-24.

THUS was the separation of the hitherto united band of Israel into the two kingdoms of Judah and Israel completed. Happily it was done without bloodshed. Rehoboam would have added to his previous folly that of attempting to compel the tribes whose hearts he had alienated to return to their allegiance by force, but he was forbidden by Divine command, and the two kingdoms were suffered to consolidate themselves in peace.

A quiet separation when their hearts were united no longer was evidently the wisest course, and thenceforward the two peoples had a separate nationality and a diverse history. But they are still interesting to us, because they still describe the Church, which has also had its division into two, the one in which affection prevails over intellect, signified by Judah, and the other in which the intellect prevails over affection, represented by Israel.

The kingdom of Judah continued to exist with a very chequered history until the time of Nebuchadnezzar the king of Babylon, who destroyed the temple, burnt Jerusalem, and carried the remaining Jews away into captivity in Babylon. The kingdom of Israel continued with Samaria for its capital, until it became extremely corrupt, and at length was destroyed, and the inhabitants were carried away into Assyria.

Religion in its rising state is like Israel up to the time of Solomon, constantly more and more united and powerful.

When religion is declining it separates and divides. Strong minds take some single characteristic, or some few characteristics, and make a distinct church of these, and so distinct communities or separate sections or divisional churches arise.

Although when love is warm, and charity reigns in a communion, all will tend to harmony and unity in the church, when love grows cold and charity decays there is a tendency to division, and separate communions have their use. They mutually keep guard over each other and connect each other. They detect faults and chastise follies, and though a decaying church will deteriorate to its end, called in Scripture the end of the world, yet its downward course is arrested, and made much more gradual, and its corruption at last is probably not of so deep a dye as it would have been but for its division into separate parts, and these protesting against each other.

Had Israel not separated from Judah in Rehoboam's time with so self-willed, furious, and corrupt a king, and the entire kingdom, with undivided wealth and power, remained at his command, his capacity for evil would have been far greater, and the mischief he had done in the world much more. As it was, "Judah," we are told, "did evil" in his time "in the sight of the Lord, and they provoked Him to jealousy with their sins which they had committed, above all that their fathers had done." "They did according to all the abominations of the nations which the Lord cast out before the children of Israel" (1 Kings xiv. 22-24).

This division then was of Divine Providence for good, and the divisions in the Christian Church into Protestant, Roman Catholic, and other sub-communities have in like manner been for good under the circumstances, the Church being a declining one. They have checked each other, and they have checked the tendency of the great body to become so material, superstitious, and stupid, as they would otherwise have become. The two sides of the Church are affectional and intellectual, or celestial and spiritual.

The affectional or celestial in tendency of character is represented in Scripture by Judah. The members of it are more earnest in worship and praise than in exercises of the intellect. The name Judah signifies praise to Jehovah. The Christians represented by Judah, are in general amiable and earnest, but they are often rather averse to the exercise of much intellectual vigour. They willingly do as their fathers have done, and even increase their exercises and energy in that direction; but they dislike change and are shy of inquiry. They are willing to worship and to praise and to love, but are not much given to thought and reflection.

The virtues they practise when in the earnestness of warm young affection look beautiful and are interesting, but in their ground partake much of natural feeling; and self-love in some form will attach itself to them. A sense of merit intrudes and induces self-righteousness, or they will multiply forms, and thus become a great source of superstituous observances, bigotry and exclusiveness. Goodness, without truth to purify the motives and direct the aims of a man, often does mischief from its blindness, and no man is so obstinate as he who is well-intentioned but is destitute of good sense, and will not seek to learn by patient inquiry. He is constantly confounding his own conceptions with the will of God, and he struggles as a martyr for heaven, when he is only an obstinate adherent of folly. Hence, this description of Christian character is the dupe and the prey of designing priests. Such simple minds confide implicitly in those on whom they have bestowed their esteem, and sustain by their countenance and their blind adhesion, abuses and follies of the most injurious character. The kingdom of Judah sunk at last entirely under the power of Babylon, and the people became captives in that land.

Spiritually, those who give themselves too exclusively to good, without the effort to learn truth, fall under the yoke of that lust of dominion exercised by lordly priests who are meant in the Word of the Lord by Babylon. They become ritualists, Romanists, blind adherents to some poor creature not a whit wiser than themselves, and probably not so good; who is audacious enough, or stupid enough, to set himself between them and that God who sends out His mercy to all, but who also sends out His truth for every soul.

It is a sad thing to abjure the mental eyes which the Lord has given us to enable us to behold the wonders of His works and the glories of His Word.

Should we see in the world of nature some human being with closed eyes, content to shut out all the beauties of the universe, the magnificence of the firmament, the loveliness of flower and shrub, and all the soul-inspiring changes of the human countenance, and be told that this strange abnegation was the result of an amiable weakness, which had been persuaded by some authoritative guide thus to submit, and take in exchange for the God-giving faculty of sight just so much of a report of the splendours of nature as the guide thought fit to impart, how deeply should we be moved with pity at so cruel an abuse of misplaced confidence. But the eyes of the understanding are infinitely more valuable than the eyes of the body. The world of mind, of knowledge, of intellect, is vaster, grander and immeasurably more important to our true interests than the world of outward vision, and yet there are those who can be induced to conceive that mystery and darkness, at least on religious subjects and on science, if science interfere with some old cherished fallacy of theirs, are to be preferred to the Divine light of the grand universe or to some new disclosure of wisdom and of truth.

Such are Judah separated from Israel. Sooner or later, those who are careless of truth become careless of goodness, and descend from bad to worse like Judah, of whom we not only read that they committed serious evils in the days of Rehoboam, but frequently, as we learn from their history, king after king walked in the sins of his fathers or became worse than those who went before him; until the last king, Zedekiah, had his eyes put out, and was bound in fetters at Babylon. They were the sad symbols of those who may begin with a profession of good, but who despise the truth which alone makes man free, and defends, purifies, and exalts him to become a child of the light and an angel of love.

The kingdom of Israel separate from Judah represents those in the Church who give predominance to intellect, who think more of truth than of good.

These are often to be met with, and are greedy of knowledge. They cultivate the intellectual side of religion. They desire to give a reason for the hope that is in them, but sometimes when they have got reasons, and give reasons, they consider their whole duty to be done. They cultivate the intellect, ever the intellect. They do not consider religion as the means of making us humble under a sense that our graces are all gifts of unpurchased and undeserved mercy. Love to the Lord, filling us with the graces of the heart, making our lives and tempers pure; faith gentle, true and good: but they regard doctrines chiefly, and esteem them as things to be discussed and proved, and discussed and proved, and discussed and proved again. They are eager disputants, always going over evidences.

"E'en though vanquished they can argue still."

Such are Israel without Judah, and in this state of mind

pride of intellect often creeps in, and a vain, conceited, and unpleasant character is formed. Persons in this state make sometimes an idol of the intellect, and vain fantasies flit over the mind, like bubbles of the brain. Reasoning is mistaken for reason. The delusive fancy will sometimes creep into the intellectually clever that nothing is true but what they make true, that they can make anything true or anything false, and ultimately that their self-will, their caprice, ought to be law.

Israel in this separated character is often described in the prophetical Word, especially in the prophecy of Hosea: "Israel is an empty vine, he bringeth forth fruit unto himself." "And the pride of Israel testifieth to his face: and they do not return to the Lord their God, nor seek Him for all this. Ephraim also is like a silly dove, without heart; they call to Egypt, they go to Assyria."

"For from Israel was it also, the workman made it, therefore it is not God; but the calf of Samaria shall be broken in pieces. For they have sown the wind, and shall reap the whirlwind."

Sometimes Israel is described by her chief tribe Ephraim, and it is said, "Ephraim feedeth on wind and followeth after the east wind: he daily increaseth lies and desolation: and they do make a covenant with the Assyrian, and oil is carried into Egypt." The emptiness of a religion of the intellect, which never rises to pure love to the Lord, or goes down to genuine integrity of conduct, is described and condemned as a mere following after wind. Alas, the mere play of the intellect after every wind of doctrine is but following after bubbles as vain and empty, as superficial and evanescent as the filmy playthings of the giddy child.

Israel at length became the captive of Assyria, whose help she had often courted, as Judah became the slave of Babylon, because Assyria in the Word of God is the symbol of the rational power of the mind, sound when subservient to religion, but a bitter tyrant when exalted above religion, and the tool of an infidel spirit.

The mere reasoner becomes a slave of reasoning, and goes on his ceaselesss round of wrangling, like the gin-horse that still plods in the same circle and makes no progress. He reasons, and reasons and reasons, and dies, sure of nothing.

Would we make advancement in heavenly things we should carefully inquire into divine truth, and earnestly strive to understand it. As we do this from the affection for the truth perception comes in and we perceive it clearly. When we thus see the truth in light we should in faithfulness reduce it to practice, and it will be confirmed by its fruits. "What doth the Lord thy God require of thee, but to do justly, love mercy and walk humbly with thy God?"

We have seen the result of separating the two grand departments of religion, as represented by the separation of Judah and Israel into two kingdoms, and ending in the one becoming captive to Babylon, and the other to Assyria, let us now consider the effect of their reunion, for this also is copiously described in the Divine Word.

We must not suppose however that all was continued calamity with the two kingdoms of Judah and Israel after their separations. Both had times of comparative prosperity. Both had intervals of comfort, peace, and well-being. Such is the plenitude of Divine Mercy that the Lord blesses the sincere according to their lights always, and gives to those who do not live in the most perfect state as much of benediction as their conditions of mind and life will enable them to receive.

So, in the separated communities of the Christian Church, there have been multitudes of Christians not only true to what they consider their duty to uphold in contradistinction to others, but bright with every virtue of heart and life. Men of humility, men of benevolence and self-sacrifice, men of active virtue, and diligent in works of worth, in learning, and every excellence which dignifies our humanity as the image of the Divine Humanity of love, wisdom, justice and beneficence. Christians with these rich graces have illustrated and adorned every section of the Christian Church, even in its divided condition, and so will all be found united in the eternal home provided for the good of every name. The Lord has said, and it may be applied to each, "Other sheep have I that are not of this fold, them also must I bring, that there may be one fold, and one shepherd."

Israel re-united forms the theme of many a glorious declaration of the prophets. Isaiah, Jeremiah, and Ezekiel are especially rich in these; but their predictions were but faintly fulfilled in the return of the scattered people from Babylon, Assyria, and other lands, after the seventy years' captivity. Thus we read in Isaiah: "And in that day there shall be a root of Jesse, which shall stand for an ensign of the people; to it shall the Gentiles seek: and His rest shall be glorious. And it shall come to pass in that day, that the Lord shall set His hand again the second time to recover the remnant of His people which shall be left, from Assyria, and from Egypt, and from Pathros, and from Cush, and from Elam, and from Shinar, and from Hamath, and from the isles of the sea, and He shall set up an ensign for the nations, and shall assemble the outcasts of Israel, and gather together the dispersed of Judah from the four corners of the earth" (xi. 10-12). This passage was given by divine inspiration, with many others of similar import, long before the seventy years' captivity in Babylon; and was literally fulfilled by the return of Judah and Israel to their own land in the time of Ezra, where they formed one nation with a temple again at Jerusalem, and once more all Israel dwelt in their cities" (Neh. vii. 73); "for God had made them rejoice with great joy: the wives also, and the children rejoiced; so that the joy of Jerusalem was heard even afar of" (xii. 43).

In their spiritual import, however, these magnificent prophecies of the reunion of Israel and Judah point to the united church of the New Jerusalem. In that church, the grandest unfoldings of knowledge and faith will be united to the deepest humility and the holiest love. The diffusion of light will be abundant with a plenteousness beyond all former days, but a light leading ever to heavenly-mindedness and genuine affection. Goodness and truth will again be hand in hand. The church will be one, because all the portions of it gather round the Saviour who is one. "In His days Judah shall be saved, and Israel shall dwell safely: and this is His name whereby He shall be called THE LORD (Jehovah) OUR RIGHTEOUSNESS" (Jer. xxiii. 6). No church could ever be truly one, and therefore universal, unless it provided for the cultivation and consecration of all human faculties. A church that could act upon the maxim that ignorance is the mother of devotion, would be certain to be degraded to stupid mummeries by its followers, and be condemned and protested against by those who seek for and reverence the truth. Blind superstition excites pity, and in some contempt. On the other hand, a church full of intellectual glory, but defective in humility, charity, piety, and virtue, is like the noon of a wintry day, bright but cold.

True religion is a broad and comprehensive thing. It aims at making man a full man, the image of all the perfections of his Maker. The true disciple of the Lord must abound in knowledge, for wisdom and knowledge are the strength of his salvation. He must be painstaking, studious, and thoughtful. He must be bold for truth, and strictly and rationally follow where truth leads, for only thus can he attain safe paths in which to walk; but he must also be full of adoring reverence for the Lord, the ALL-GOOD, and for gentleness, loving-kindness, and tender mercy. He must be faithful to every iota of duty. "He that is faithful in that which is least is faithful also in much." The least of real good is superior to a thousand truths without goodness, but nothing excellent is attained without the union of both.

These are the lessons we are taught by all those declarations of the Word, which proclaim for the grand future a Church in all respects united. "Behold, I will take the children of Israel from among the nations, whither they be gone, and will gather them on every side and bring them into their own land: and I will make them one nation in the land upon the mountains of Israel: and one king shall be king to them all: and they shall be no more two nations, neither shall they be divided into two kingdoms any more at all. And David, my servant, shall be king over them, and they shall all have one shepherd: they shall also walk in my judgments and observe my statutes and do them" (Ezek. xxxvii. 21, 22, 24). The restoration and elevation of all Israel upon the mountains of Israel represents the union of all those who know the truth of every name with each other by the exalted affections of love to the Lord Jesus and mutual kindness to each other. They become one grand Church, one holy nation under one king, the Divine Saviour who is King of kings and Lord of lords. He is called my servant David, because David was the type of Him, and because David means the Beloved One. The Divine David then, the Divine Shepherd, the Beloved One, the God-Man, the centre of every excellency, will reign over His united and regenerated Church. It will be, as declared of the New Jerusalem, a golden city, and clear as crystal, golden with celestial love, and clear with the brightness of wisdom, and the members will walk in the light of the Holy City (Rev. xxi. 24).

They shall fight against nothing but evil. "I will save them out of all their dwelling-places wherein they have sinned, and will cleanse them: so shall they be my people, and I will be their God." Their worship, then, shall be full of feeling, full of adoration, and of blessing. "My tabernacle also shall be with them; yea, I will be their God, and they shall be my people."

SERMON XXXVII.

THE SUN GOING BACK ON THE DIAL OF AHAZ.

"And Hezekiah answered, It is a light thing for the shadow to go down ten degrees: nay, but let the shadow return backward ten degrees. And Isaiah the prophet cried unto the Lord: and he brought the shadow ten degrees backward, by which it had gone down in the dial of Ahaz."—2 KINGS xx. 10, 11.

THE very remarkable circumstance related to have taken place as a sign that the King would be restored by the mercy of the Lord, was no doubt calculated to impress him and his people with a sense of the goodness and providence of the Most High.

Though the son and successor of Ahaz, one of the most wicked sovereigns who ever desecrated the throne of David, he was a devout and faithful ruler. He had put away the idols, which his father had multiplied, and led back his kingdom to repentance and to order. "He did that which was right in the eyes of the Lord, according to all that David his father did." He removed the high places, and brake the images, and cut down the groves, and brake in pieces the brazen serpent that Moses had made: for unto those days the Children of Israel did burn incense to it, and he called it Nehushtan (that is, derisively, a piece of brass)—chap. xviii. 3, 4.

Hezekiah's faithfulness arrested the sinking condition of the nation, and brought again for the almost ruined land a period of truth, righteousness, and peace, very superior to the condition in which the kingdom had been in the wicked times of his father's reign. In this respect, the declining sun of the nation's prosperity went back ten degrees. And no doubt the miracle had an application to the career of the kingdom, as well as the condition of the king. Decay had written its marks of misery over all the land: now penitence and reformation brought prosperity once more, and men were able to sit under their own vine and their own fig-tree, none making them afraid.

The Divine narrative is interesting, as containing the first known account of any instrument for the measurement of time.

The dial must have been a vertical one, probably fastened to a wall or pillar. Ancient writers say dials were invented in Chaldea, and from the intercourse between Babylon and Israel, it is most likely this dial was obtained by Ahaz from the former country, and from its novelty was called the dial of Ahaz. The dials of Babylonia were made of stone, semi-circular, marked with divisions, parts of a circle, making probably 180 degrees, and were built into walls. In that case, ten degrees would mean two-thirds of an hour, and although such a going back could not be done at an appointed time by any other than Divine power, yet we shall easily see that a return of the shadow ten degrees on the dial, could be effected without any further alteration than a slight change in the density of the atmosphere.

The sun every day at his rising and setting appears by refraction in a different place, by eighteen degrees, from that in which he really is. Sometimes, seen through a thick atmosphere, both sun and moon appear two or three times larger than their usual size, and occasionally extra suns and moons are seen, yet in reality there is no disturbance, except in the refraction of the light. So in this merciful sign to Hezekiah, we must not suppose that the sun really was arrested in his course, or the earth stopped in its daily revolution, but simply that such a refraction was produced in the air as to cause the backward motion of the shadow, and thus strengthen the faith of the king, by the conviction that the Ruler of nature was about to restore him to health, and prolong his life.

In the dispensation of outward religion during the Jewish age, by which the Most High kept earth united to heaven, and preserved mankind until the better dispensation of the Gospel should be opened, many signs and wonders and extraordinary events took place in the representative Church of Judea, which were types needed for them, and full of meaning for us; but we may rest assured that they were all kept within the bounds of Divine Order. Nature was not really turned back, or confounded in her operations. A grand lesson was given to king and people, by this apparent arrestation and turning back of the shadow on the dial. This lesson meant, that by genuine repentance and turning to God, the descending sun of their prosperity would return to its splendour, and all would be well with them. But no further change was necessary to give this lesson than takes place in the mirage of the desert, in which sometimes a wide lake stretches out before the traveller, which vanishes, however, on his nearer approach. A ship, or an army, is seen in the air, which excites wonder, but speedily vanishes away.

The people of Jerusalem would understand the sign, for they were accustomed to regard the progress of the sun as a symbol of their well-being or otherwise. When all was dark and gloomy in their affairs, they said the sun had gone down over the prophets, and it is dark with them (Micah iii. 6). When great calamity was to come suddenly upon them, it was said,—" And it shall come to pass in that day, saith the Lord God, that I will cause the sun to go down at noon, and I will darken the earth in the clear day" (Amos viii. 9). This was language not to be understood of movements in nature, but as symbolic of their condition as a nation. When they were doing well, the sun was shining brightly over them: when they were disobedient and ruined, their sun had gone down.

In the same character and application of language, the end of their dispensation altogether was described by the prophet Joel as a complete darkening of the heavenly bodies. It is written, "I will shew wonders in the heavens and in the earth, blood, fire, and pillars of smoke. The sun shall be turned into darkness, and the moon into blood, before the great and terrible day of the Lord come" (Joel ii. 30, 31). Yet these words were fulfilled; the Apostle Peter said on the day of Pentecost, "This is that which was spoken by the prophet Joel: I will shew wonders in heaven above, and signs in the earth beneath; blood and fire and vapour of smoke. The sun shall be turned into darkness, and the moon into blood, before that great and terrible day come" (Acts ii. 19, 20). Evidently the desolation and end of the Jewish dispensation are described figuratively by the decay and extinction of the great lights of nature; but they were only symbolic forms of speech, not to be understood as literal facts.

The destruction and end of Babylon are described by very similar language: "For the stars of heaven and the constellations thereof shall not give their light, the sun shall be darkened in his going forth, and the moon shall not cause her light to shine. And I will punish the world for their evil, and the wicked for their iniquity; and I will cause the arrogancy of the proud to cease, and I will lay low the haughtiness of the terrible. And Babylon, the glory of kingdoms, the beauty of the Chaldees' excellency, shall be as when God overthrew Sodom and Gomorrah" (Isa. xiii. 10, 11, 12).

In like manner the punishment and destruction of the kingdom of Edom are depicted: "And all the host of heaven shall be dissolved, and the heavens shall be rolled together as a scroll; and all their host shall fall down as the leaf falleth off from the vine, and as a falling fig from the fig-tree, for my sword shall be bathed in heaven: behold, it shall come down upon Idumea, and upon the people of my curse to judgment" (Isa. xxxiv. 4, 5).

Evidently, a catastrophe of nature is used as an emblem of the ruin of a kingdom, and such language is not to be construed as a literal prophecy, but as a figure of moral desolation. In like manner, when similar language is used concerning the end of the Church by the prophets of the Old Testament, or by the Apostle Peter in the New, it should be understood only of the decay and darkening of the Church, not of any wild crash of suns and worlds. The great universe is a Divine work, and will be sustained for ever by the same eternal Love and Wisdom which originated it, and constantly renews, strengthens, and extends it. It is the illimitable field of His adorable goodness, in which ever-increasing numbers of immortal beings can be trained for heaven.

The sun of nature is a symbol of the Lord, and especially of His Divine Love. As the planets have originated from the sun, and are still maintained in their courses by his attractive force, so have we all originated from the Lord, and so are we sustained in our life and movements by His almighty power. The sun pours forth his heat and light, and all the myriad forms of beauty and good with which the earth blooms and is enriched owe their existence to his beams: so is it with the human mind. The Lord, as the Divine Sun, is the true light which enlighteneth every man that cometh into the world. As the Divine Sun, He blesses the angels, and warms the soul. As the Divine Sun, He draws us to Himself. As the Divine Sun, all inferior being is sustained by Him, because it is derived from Him. As the Divine Sun, He shines for ever. "The Lord is a sun and a shield. He giveth grace and glory: no good thing will He withhold from them that walk uprightly" (Ps. lxxxiv. 11). "Thy sun shall no more go down, neither thy moon withdraw itself, for the Lord shall be thine everlasting light, and the days of thy mourning shall be ended" (Isa. lx. 20).

Of this Divine Sun, the earthly sun is necessarily the representative, for it is its out-birth. Hence, in the earliest and best ages of mankind, men everywhere knew and adored this Divine Sun, as the Apostle Paul knew and adored Him, as the blessed and only Potentate, the King of kings and Lord of lords, who only hath immortality, dwelling in the light which no man can approach unto, and whom no man (*by material eyes*) hath seen or can see (1 Tim. vi. 15, 16). As men became, however, of the earth earthy, carnal, and sensual, they lost sight of the Eternal Sun, and of the inner light and inner love which from Him radiated into their souls, and transferred their adoration of the Divine Sun to the sun of nature—from the cause to the effect, from the reality to the image. Hence arose Sun-worship in all its various forms. Afterwards, images of the sun were made, and ultimately these images were worshipped, and endowed with divine powers. So senseless does man become, when he looks downwards to earth in the indulgence of his lusts and carnal appetites, instead of looking upward, and striving continually to become spiritually-minded.

For us, the path of wisdom is to turn upward to the light which shines from the Lord Jesus. The Divine Sun is incarnated in Him, and in His face beams the glory of God. God is manifest in Him, and His countenance is as the sun shineth in his strength (Rev. i. 16). This Sun of the soul is the grand CENTRAL SUN of all the spiritual being. He is the Light; He is the Love; He is the Power, which draws all men unto Himself, and in whom they will find their true Centre, their Father, their Saviour, their Regenerator, their Friend; the King of kings and Lord of lords; the Prophet, Priest, and King. It was to represent the movements of this Divine Sun in the penitent soul, sin-sick, that the miracle was wrought for Hezekiah, and recorded in the Divine Word. The sick king represents the soul conscious of discomfort, weakness, and wrong, and convinced that without Divine help it must die utterly immersed in evil: there is no salvation in itself. The sun-dial was a reflector of the light, and an indicator of its progress. The rational mind is a mental sun-dial. When it is dark, there is no light of truth in the soul. When the spirit is in deep sorrow, and surrounded by dark clouds of doubt, difficulty, and despair, the sun-dial's use is only negative. That it gives no indication, should lead to humility, to prayer and research. Try yourselves, and search the Scriptures, are admonitions which we should never forget in trials of the soul. When we break through the clouds, and light comes in—the light which shews us our state—some advancement has been made. If the light we have tells us the day is already far spent, the summer is nearly ended, and we are not saved, then does it in reality urge to fly for help and refuge to Him who is mighty to save.

Isaiah the prophet was to Hezekiah what the doctrine of the Word is to us. He assured the king that in three days he would be healed, his life should be lengthened fifteen years, and his country should be delivered from the Assyrians. The suffering king was very fearful, and asked for a sign that these blessings would certainly be given. The prophet, willing to comfort him, assures the king that a sign would be granted, but it must be in accordance with his own free will. Would he have the shadow go further forward and down, or would he wish it to return and to rise up ten degrees? Evidently it is past noon, the sun is going down. The sun of Judah's prosperity had been going down since the time of Solomon. To go down further was easy; to return back, that would be the hard thing. Hezekiah had the wisdom to ask for the shadow to go back, and rise up ten degrees. This was well, and Judah's decay was arrested during his time. The sign that this would be was that the shadow went back on the sun-dial ten degrees.

It is an important spiritual truth, that whatever state of good we can understand to be desirable and yearn after, we can certainly attain. It is in fact, in embryo, already attained. We long for peace, and grieve that we do not possess it. We do interiorly possess it, and it will certainly increase, and become in due time altogether ours. "Blessed are they that hunger and thirst after righteousness, for they shall be filled."

To give us a view of Divine things without the power of attainment, would be a tantalization impossible to be attributed to Infinite Love. Hence, animals have no capacity of noticing or conceiving spiritual and eternal things, because they have no power of enjoying them.

What we conceive and wish, then, we can have, nay, already have in embryo. Let as never be hopeless, but know that our hope is a true prophet, and only anticipates what we shall certainly enjoy. This foretoken of a better state is represented by the shadow rising on the sun-dial. To see the truth clearly, is given us for the end, that we may love and do it. When we love the light, we easily see the light: we have a ground of good from which we see, and we pass in time from shade to brightness. Hence the infinite importance of getting light on our mental sun-dial. The reason why truth is covered in the world with some degree of difficulty—with shade, parable, and cloud—is that our love may be tested. If we have no desire to labour for the truth, we shall not make good use of it when we obtain it. Better is it that we should remain without it. "Unto you our Lord said, it is given to know the mysteries of the Kingdom of God, but not to them which are without."

But if we are sad at our spiritual sickness and feebleness, and pray as Hezekiah did for deliverance, light will come into the mind. "Unto the upright there ariseth a light in the darkness." And in that light we see where we are and where we ought to be. We discover we have been losing time, living heedlessly, and suffering decay and degeneracy. We turn heartily to the Lord, and the light rises on our sun-dial. Hope and faith come to our help, and we are animated by the conviction that we can live a new life, that we can be conjoined to the Lord and attain a present heaven. Hezekiah was restored to health. We too can attain to new strength, and realize a new possession of heavenly life and vigour. The ten degrees up which the indicator of the sun-dial rose, would probably, in the spiritual sense, refer to the sacredness of the Divine Commandments. They are called the ten words, the ten pieces of silver. We have known the Divine law, but we have neglected it. We now perceive that it is all holy, pure, and good. It shall henceforth be our glory to love and do the Divine will. We see the Commandments are the utterances of Divine Love, "for our good always." "Great peace have they that love thy law, and nothing shall offend them."

The light has risen ten degrees. The soul now perceives the Divine truth in fulness, and is invigorated and blessed. It is assured, comforted, and cheered. It can work out its salvation, though with fear and trembling, and filled with gratitude it exclaims, I cried with my whole heart; hear me, O Lord: I will keep thy statutes.

> "O blest be His name, who in sorrow's stern hour
> Hears the prayer of affliction, and sends forth His power."

The sun-dial is designated the sun-dial of Ahaz, and Ahaz was an unfaithful and wicked king. He probably obtained this sun-dial from Babylon, as we are told he had an altar, which he saw and admired, brought from Damascus. The sun-dial, however, we may gather was a true one, although it had belonged to a wicked king, and may have been derived from Babylon.

All religions include much truth, although that truth may be associated with many things not true. Pious and sincere souls have an instinct for the truth, however it may be wrapped in error, and by that truth they strengthen their spiritual life. They scarcely see the errors of their system, and never dwell upon them. Hezekiah's being comforted and helped by the light rising on the sun-dial of Ahaz was probably intended to teach us that in each religion, however imperfect, there is a sun-dial; and if we devoutly pray to the Lord, and look believingly to Him, He will illumine our minds by that which is Divine in every form of faith, and we shall be spiritually healed. He saves in various ways; He has ten thousand methods of diffusing His love into the weak and the weary. But if the suffering heart really seeks Him, He will be found; if we knock, it will be opened; if we ask in earnest humility, unto us shall be given.

Hezekiah's life was lengthened fifteen years. Fifteen consists of two sevens and one, and corresponds to a new spiritual state, but one rather feeble. It was the fifteenth day of the second month when the Israelites commenced their journey into the wilderness. Hezekiah's condition was one struggling to be faithful, surrounded by general decay. A soul in such circumstances secures some heavenly good—what he feels to be a great blessing; but is conscious of lacking power to arrest the general downward tendency. Such a soul saves itself, but sighs that it cannot do much more, and its comparative feebleness is expressed by this number fifteen.

Yet, to be rescued from disease, to come into light and love, to enjoy a sense of spiritual life and peace,—these are great mercies, and may well inspire the soul to say, as Hezekiah did, "The living, the living, he shall praise Thee, as I do this day: the father to the children shall make known Thy truth. The Lord was ready to save me; therefore will we sing my songs to the stringed instruments all the days of our life in the house of the Lord" (Isa. xxxviii. 19, 20).

SERMON XXXVIII.

HEZEKIAH'S SICKNESS AND RECOVERY.

"And Isaiah said, Take a lump of figs. And they took and laid it on the boil, and he recovered."—2 KINGS xx. 8.

THE character of King Hezekiah, as presented in the Holy Word, is that of a good man and a good king struggling with great difficulties. He had inherited the throne of his father Ahaz, who had been an extremely bad monarch. Ahaz had suffered idolatry to spread over the land. He copied some of the worst practices of the worst of the neighbouring nations, and under the king's example the people increased in their unhallowed habits, and the land became corrupt and degraded, very little different from the nations around.

Under these circumstances, King Ahaz no longer felt the protection of the Most High about him and his people, as it had been about David and Solomon; but he courted the alliance, and trusted in the power of the kings around, especially of the potent monarchs of Assyria. Having despised and neglected the protection of heaven, he sought the defence of the most powerful rulers of the time, and lived in fear of them, instead of relying on the arm of that God whose worship and whose law his nation had been marvellously raised up to preserve amongst men.

To the unhappy state which his father had thus impiously and unwisely governed and degraded, the good Hezekiah succeeded. He laboured to undo the mischief iniquity and folly had produced in the land. "He did that which was right in the sight of the Lord, according to all which David his father did." In one respect he gave an admirable example: he found that the brazen serpent which Moses had made had become an object of idolatry, by the superstition of the ignorant people, and he broke it to pieces. The harmless memorial of one time may become a snare to weak minds at another; and when that is the case, we learn from this example of Hezekiah, and from many other examples furnished by history, the prudent legislator will remove it out of the way.

There is a tendency in many minds to cling to forms, and not to penetrate to the substance and essence of things; and these rest in and deify objects and modes which have lost their use and meaning. Hence come the preservation of relics and customs, which are not only useless, but injurious. Thus the brazen serpent, which when set up as an emblem by Moses of the Lord's glorified humanity, had saved those who looked upon it with faith in the Divine protection from the fiery flying serpents; but when it was regarded, not as a symbol, but itself as a God, and foolish people burnt incense to it, Hezekiah caused it to be broken to pieces, and used the expression Nehushtan, *a bit of brass,* to intimate its true character.

The Cross, which among the Egyptians, thousands of years before Christianity, was the symbol of spiritual life; and after Christianity became blended with love for the Saviour, who died to redeem us to spiritual life, became in the dark ages an instrument not only of superstition, but often of the vilest knavery. To bear our mental crosses with patience, and even to be thankful for them as means of chastening and purification, is truly Christian. Only those who thus humbly bear the cross, can ever wear the crown of righteousness. But to imagine there is anything Christian in adorning ourselves with a cross as an ornament, is rather to feed vanity with a not very elegant form than to promote religion. It is the new heart and the right spirit; the love of God and goodness; the promotion of wisdom; the affection for all that is noble and pure; the shrinking from all that is mean, false, and dishonourable; the inward seeking for the kingdom of God and His righteousness, supremely, which form the Christian character and make us fit for heaven. If crosses are substituted, in however small a degree, for these interior graces, then we should do well to remember with Hezekiah they are but bits of metal, wood, ivory, or stone. They are Nehushtan.

Many a lying cross in England, where wicked monks deceived the ignorant populace by voices and machinery, the treacherous contrivances of bad men, were righteously exposed at the Reformation, and cast into fires with a noble zeal like Hezekiah's. God can only be served by purity, truth, and righteousness.

The object of our sojourn on earth is that we should become thoughtful, intelligent, pure, wise, and good. Everything which conduces to this training is valuable. Those things which have contributed in former times and other circumstances to good government and well-being, but have lost their significance or their utility, should be served as Hezekiah served the serpent of brass, and removed out of the way. Other times, other manners. Laws and customs, once valuable and laudable, may become an offence; and the course of the wise man is decently to inter that which was good in its day, but has ceased to have any real life. But, faithful as Hezekiah was, he inherited many troubles. He could not escape the results of the bad courses of his father and his country. He was threatened by the power his father had courted. The unwise alliance with Assyria was a continual annoyance. And when he declined to become an abject slave to that giant monarchy, the king Sennacherib brought a vast host around Jerusalem, and with the most contemptuous language summoned Hezekiah to submit. Encouraged by the prophet Isaiah and his own trust in God, the king courageously resisted, and awaited deliverance. The enemy actively threatened; but the king relied upon the Lord, and was saved.

It was in this time of peril, and probably from continued anxiety, that Hezekiah's health failed. He is described as afflicted with a boil or abscess. His pain and distress, as we learn from his prayer, and reflections given in Isaiah, chapter xxxviii., were extremely severe; but he was consoled by the prophet, and directed to use a poultice of figs, and the ulcer was healed. Thus was the suffering monarch restored, and soon after relieved also in an astonishing manner from the besieging army of Assyria. He lived in grateful recognition of the Divine goodness to him for fifteen years, and his excellent reign greatly retarded the fall of his kingdom, by the restoration of virtue and true religion. It does not appear that Hezekiah's troubles were owing to any misconduct of his own; they were hereditary. We are informed that "He clave to the Lord, and departed not from following Him, but kept His commandments which the Lord commanded Moses, and the Lord was with him;" and even in his illness he pleaded without rebuke that "He had walked before the Lord with a perfect heart, and had done that which was good in His sight." But yet he was greatly troubled.

There are many anomalies in life. We see but the outsides of things, and we see but a little way. A more interior view, and our sight of truth in our eternal life will no doubt explain them all. Divine mercy does not give outward prosperity to some, BECAUSE He is giving them something better, truer, and more lasting. Hezekiah had walked well; but he was capable of being led to walk better, and hence, through sorrow, he had to be purified and elevated. His troubles arose from his hereditary difficulties, and they were severe, but they were salutary. By their means he was enabled to say, " O Lord, by these things men live, and in all these things is the life of my spirit: so wilt thou recover me, and make me to live. Behold, for peace I had great bitterness; but thou hast in love to my soul delivered it from the pit of corruption, for thou hast cast all my sins behind thy back." We are also often spiritually sick for similar reasons, and from similar causes. We have walked, for anything we know, uprightly. Yet afflictions come, adversity sets in; perhaps sickness and misfortune come together. A sorrow of soul comes over us. We are chagrined and unhappy. Coldness is within us, and darkness around us. We have no pleasure in what we do; we are fretful, easily annoyed, and dissatisfied. A miserable change has come. We examine our conduct, and cannot trace to anything wrong in our ways this strange unhappiness, and our continued sapless life. A great gloom is around us, and continues for a time distressingly long. We cry sometimes very long, and apparently in vain. But light comes at length.

The soul has its diseases, as well as the body, and corresponding in all respects to those of the body. There are spiritual heats and spiritual chills—spiritual fevers and violent spiritual inflammations. There are spiritual palsies and spiritual lamenesses. There is spiritual jaundice which discolours the whole mind, and induces us to distort and disfigure everything which prejudice has led us to dislike. There is spiritual consumption—a wearing and wasting down of our strength, until our life is all gone. We have been living in bad air, and our lungs have got out of order. Our spiritual blood is not purified, and the whole tissues of our souls become weak. We become spiritually lean and feeble, expectorating the very substance of our lungs. Our flesh wastes away, our skin is scrofulous, and a settled low fever wastes us, and we become almost sleepless, until we pine and fade away. In other words, from heedless indifference to the evil customs and impious maxims of bad society, the atmosphere of our souls is poisoned, and all our thoughts are corrupted and vile; we gradually lose all pure, tender, holy, virtuous, and manly feeling, we reject all rational remonstrance, until we lose the very faculty of noble or heavenly thought, and die to all that is good. Or, it may be, a spiritual abscess has formed, a large boil increasing from time to time,—some settled envy or constant fretfulness, or rooted malice, or lasting discontent.

Our self-love has taken some offence against God or against man, and we dwell upon it, feed it, recur to it again and again; words, looks, every act of the offending individual, or the abhorred condition, all are construed by the unhappy one bad feeling we have cherished; and the swollen sinfulness attracts our spiritual life, turns it into grim dislike, ever growing, and incapacitates us for loving work and holy states. We grieve, we hate, we gather malice, we sink in moody misery, and after years of self-inflicted anguish die. Such is the unhappy state, without its fatal termination, that Hezekiah's boil would represent.

These soul sicknesses are often alluded to or described in the Word. All spiritual evil is a disease of the soul. The world is a great hospital. None are quite without disease. If we could but realise the truth, it would help us often, both in our own cases, and in those of others. We should seek help from the Great Physician, and we should often pity others, as weak sufferers, whom now we harshly condemn. The Word affords abundant recognition of these spiritual ailments. How frequently do we read in the Psalms plaintive prayers for the soul to be healed of its sorrows. "Have mercy upon me, O Lord, for I am weak: O Lord heal me, for my bones are vexed" (Ps. vi. 2). "I said, Lord be merciful unto me: heal my soul, for I have sinned against Thee" (Ps. xli. 4). How soothing is the beautiful language of the 103rd Psalm: "Bless the Lord, O my soul: and all that is within me, bless His holy name. Bless the Lord, O my soul, and forget not all His benefits: Who forgiveth all thine iniquities, who healeth all thy diseases (1-3). The name of Saviour, one of the dearest names of our Lord, means Healer, Giver of spiritual health. Salvation means health. Health of the body is the type taken to be an image of a true, heavenly, and happy state of the soul. "Thou shalt call His name Jesus, for He shall save His people from their sins" (Matt. 1, 21).

We may as easily recognise spiritual disease, if we consider it as the disease of the body. A person knows he is physically unwell when he suffers pain, or when he is weak, too weak to perform the duties or enjoy the pleasures of life. We are spiritually unwell when we feel unhappy, are careworn, anxious, harassed, weary, and unable to perform with pleasure the duties and enjoy the blessings of spiritual life. How few there are who in this aspect can be regarded as entirely well. The universe of our Heavenly Father is indeed streaming with delights. How innumerable are the charms of earth and heaven, in the midst of which we live! But how few are content! How few are happy! How few are grateful with the present lot, and feel sure that it is the place for them which Infinite Love and Wisdom deems the very best. How few there are who are not wrestling to quit their present position, who have tried but little to realize the heaven of doing their duty in their present position.

"Blessed are they that do His commandments." "Great peace have they that love Thy law." "The Kingdom of God is within you." These are the Divine maxims for happiness, and if we are not happy, under ordinary circumstances, we should seek the causes in ourselves. Of course, we are not speaking of unusual cases, of bitter persecution, or extraordinary trial, but of the conditions of ordinary life. Yet how many are far from happiness. How many are the mentally sick.

Some have many small boils that harass them, petty vexations, which, however, prevent them from enjoying rest. Now and then, there is a great misery, a rooted sorrow, such as Shakespeare alludes to:

> "Canst thou not minister to a mind diseased;
> Pluck from the memory a rooted sorrow;
> Raze out the written troubles of the brain;
> And with some sweet oblivious antidote,
> Cleanse the stuffed bosom of that perilous stuff,
> Which weighs upon the heart?"

To a great wearing misery like this, malicious humours make their way, and constantly increase. The heartache is deep and lasting. It sleeps with its victim, and wakes with its victim. The face may smile, but the sorrow is rankling there. There may be interruptions, chequered changes, but the bitter misery returns again, and makes content and peace impossible. Like the woman in the Gospel, the soul tries many physicians, but there is no healing; the soul gets worse, and will still become worse, until we go to the true Physician. The Great Saviour can heal, and none but He can thoroughly heal the soul. "Is there no balm in Gilead? Is there no physician there? Why then is not the health of the daughter of My people recovered?" are the questions of the Lord Himself. "Come unto Me all ye that are weary and heavy laden, and I will give you rest."

The method by which Hezekiah was healed, as recorded in our text, is the Divine means of restoration in a case of spiritual abscess. The prophet Isaiah came to him. The prophets of those times were to Israel what the Word of God is now to us. When we search the Bible, the prophets are speaking, and indeed the Great Prophet is delivering His counsel to us, and he says, " Take a bunch of figs." Figs are the emblems in the Word of God, and in nature, of the virtues of everyday life. They were the common fruit of Palestine. They were planted on the way-sides, and as they stood with their noble leaves and their nutritious and pleasant productions, inviting, useful, and delicious everywhere, they represented the good man whose fruits of integrity and kindness are the true products in their season of his religion in the path of duty, genuinely right and cheerfully rendered.

The fig-tree in this respect is frequently referred to in the Divine pages. In the book of Judges, it was one of the trees invited to become the king, and it is represented as refusing, and saying, "Should I forsake my sweetness and my good fruits, and go to be king over the trees?" (ix. 11). Far better is it to be useful ministers in the walks of daily life, and desire to bless others in the genuine performance of our duty, than to seek pre-eminence over our fellow-men in the vain desire to rule. Good figs are represented as corresponding to good people, in the prophecy of Jeremiah : " Like these good figs, so will I acknowledge them that are carried away captive of Judah, whom I have sent out of this place into the land of the Chaldeans for their good ; for I will set mine eyes upon them for good, and I will bring them again to this land" (xxiv. 5, 6.) The fig-tree which the Lord Jesus went to examine, as He passed along the way from Jerusalem, desiring to find fruit, but only realizing leaves, was the symbol of the Jewish Church of the time, plenteous in profession—abundance of leaves, but totally wanting in good fruit. The good fruit of the fig-tree corresponding to the lowest virtues—external acts—the lesson afforded is that the Jewish Church at that time was not only not productive in the higher excellencies of exalted love or wisdom, but even the homely virtues were wanting. They had made the commandments of God of none effect by their traditions.

Take a lump of figs, then, would mean, determine to do good, to perform kind and just acts to the person against whom you have strong dislike. The great law of loving our neighbour as ourselves, is often felt to be difficult of exercise towards persons who are disagreeable to us. The exclamation will sometimes be heard,—" How can I like people whom I don't like ?" I wish I could alter my disposition towards such or such persons, but indeed they are very disagreeable. I cannot pretend to be pleased with them when I am not pleased. It would be hypocrisy. Religion cannot require that. The Divine method in our text tells us what to do. We cannot directly or immediately alter our interior disposition, but we can determine our acts. We can embrace every opportunity of doing good, that is, of doing right to every one, and when we compel ourselves to do kind acts towards those to whom we have felt bitterly, the Lord will alter the disposition. You get the lump of figs, the Lord will heal the boil.

Oh, it is a sad thing to have a rankling spirit of enmity where love, joy, and peace should prevail. Yet sometimes jealousy, pique, prejudice, a readiness to take offence, will embitter the soul towards those with whom there should only be loving intercourse. We fasten upon every little word, look, and act, and gather matter of offence; and the boil which gives us excruciating pain continues and increases. Take the Divine counsel. Look up to the Lord, and determine to do them good. Look out for an opportunity of serving them. It does not imply that we should fawn and flatter those for whom we have no respect, but we should desire really to serve them, and rejoice in the opportunity of performing towards them acts of real justice, real kindness, and real good. Do this, and the mental boil will disappear in three days, or when your kindness is fully carried out, and you, like Hezekiah, will recover.

A kiss for a blow. "Love your enemies, do good to them that hate you, bless them that curse you, and pray for them that despitefully use you." These constitute the Divine method, and they are infallible in their power of healing. But often the irritating boil is not even the bitter feeling induced by an enemy, but the misconception, the misconstruction, the misunderstanding of the spirit and language of our friends—of those who really mean well, and who, when they see by our kind actions that we desire their good, will at once reciprocate, and change the gloomy frown into a cheerful smile. What we most need in the world is sympathetic love, is open-hearted kindness. Vast numbers of persons mean well, but want helping out. They may be weak, and they may sometimes fall; but a kindly word and a kindly act will often strengthen them, and allure them back to good. The Lord helps all; we should help each other. If we would strive to do this, and actually apply this spirit of kindness to our souls, we should find our own boils to disappear, and in blessing others we should ourselves be blessed. "Do good and lend, hoping for nothing again, and your reward shall be great, and ye shall be the children of the Highest; for He is kind to the unthankful and the evil. Be ye therefore merciful, as your Father also is merciful."

SERMON XXXIX.

THE DESTRUCTION OF SENNACHERIB'S ARMY.

"Therefore thus saith the Lord concerning the King of Assyria, He shall not come into this city, nor shoot an arrow there, nor come before it with shield, nor cast a bank against it. By the way that he came, by the same shall he return, and shall not come into this city, saith the Lord."—2 KINGS xix. 32, 33.

THE second great empire of the world's early history was Assyria. That of Babylon was the first. In the vast and fertile plains watered by the Euphrates and the Tigris, arose those mighty nations; and burning with the lust of power, they extended their conquering efforts far and wide. They had an amazing career. They began in feeble communities. By constant growth and cultivation they attained to conditions of magnificence only equalled by the mightiest states of modern times; having capitals of a size and splendour which seem, as ancient history recounts their glories, almost beyond belief. After a lengthened existence they sank so low, that scarcely anything remained of them but their names, and certain vast mounds, the wonder of the wandering Arab. So passes the glory of the world.

"Ambition vast, at which the world grew pale,
Then points a moral, and adorns a tale."

Assyria, at the time of the siege of Jerusalem alluded to in our text, was at the summit of its extraordinary splendour. Nineveh was its capital, a city sixty miles in circuit, containing probably a million of inhabitants, and including in its palaces embellishments of art and magnificence only surpassed by the most splendid examples of modern times. It was an offshoot from Babel, and in time surpassed its parent state. We are informed in Genesis that "Nimrod was a mighty hunter before the Lord. And the beginning of his kingdom was Babel, and Erech, and Accad, and Calneh, in the land of Shinar. Out of that land went Ashur, and builded Nineveh" (x. 9-11).

Babylon and Assyria had a most interesting existence and history, as presented to us in Holy Writ. We meet with them first in the peculiarly allegorical portion of the Word; and they would therefore represent persuasions or religions of that early time.* They next fixed themselves in towns and cities and governments, and became immense empires, dominating the then known world; and lastly, when they disappeared as nations, they were still retained in the Divine Word, on account of their spiritual signification. Hence, we find Babylon in the book of Revelation, hundreds of years after its entire destruction as a nation and a city, as a symbol of the dreadful lust of spiritual power over the souls of men; that unhallowed lust which in Babel in very ancient ages, and in the Rome of more recent times, has been the mother of delusion, uncharitableness, and persecution; the stimulant of separation, strife, and ill-will. Assyria was formed out of Babel: "Out of that land went Ashur, and builded Nineveh." In these simple words we have revealed to us the Catholicism and Protestantism of the very remote times. The same things under other names. The lust of power clothing itself in ceremony and superstition is Babel. The intellect protesting against delusion, striving for knowledge, intelligence, and rationality, denying the unproved to the extent sometimes of doubting all that cannot be exhibited to the senses, is Assyria.

The proselytizing spirit which craves influence not for real good, but for the sake of power, out of which both the Babel and the Assyria of ancient times arose, is what is really meant by hunting before the Lord, or Jehovah, which is ascribed to Nimrod: "Even as Nimrod, the mighty hunter before the Lord." To hunt souls before the Lord, is to seek to proselytize men that the proselytizing zealots may rule over them, or make gain by them. It is to have a creed which may easily accord with pride, vanity, and selfishness, in a thousand forms, and seek, by cajoling and vehement zeal, to obtain for it numerous adherents. The hunters of souls do not unfold the loving yet pure commandments of the Lord, and the requirements of the regenerate life, encouraging men to real virtue, and insisting upon doing right under all circumstances from the love of right; but they persuade, captivate, and ensnare men's minds, by flattering them in the pursuit of sensual objects and unworthy indulgences, tempering religion to the tastes of those they hope

---

* In fact, all ancient nations were embodied religions, their kings being the chief priests.

to gain, with a secret aim to the promotion of their own exaltation.

Of such hunters of souls the prophet Ezekiel speaks:—"Woe unto the foolish prophets, that follow their own spirit, and have seen nothing." "Will ye HUNT THE SOULS of my people, and will ye save the souls alive that come to you? And will ye pollute me among my people for handfuls of barley, and for pieces of bread, to slay the souls that should not die, and to save the souls alive that should not live, by your lying to my people that hear your lies? Wherefore thus saith the Lord God, Behold I am against your pillows" (or soft flattering persuasions), "wherewith ye there HUNT THE SOULS to make them fly, and I will tear them from your arms, and will let the souls go, even THE SOULS THAT YE HUNT to make them fly." "Because with lies ye have made the heart of the righteous sad, whom I have not made sad; and strengthened the hands of the wicked, that he should not return from his wicked way, by promising him life" (xiii. 3, 18, 19, 20, 22).

Out of such hunting, then, in hoary antiquity Babel rose, and out of Babel came at length Assyria. But how small the beginning of the power of the Assyrians was at first, and how vast it became in the course of ages, we can only briefly tell.

Nineveh was founded in a region eminently suited to be the seat of a mighty empire. Where the river Zab falls into the great and rapid river Tigris, there are the ruins which mark the spot where the great city stood for ages. Twenty miles long, and about twelve miles broad, as the mounds which cover the ruins indicate, was the enormous capital, the focus of the Assyrian power. There are now ample historical proofs that it had a king and strong government, more than two thousand years before the coming of Christ. So completely had Nineveh been ruined by its overthrow and destruction by fire, along with its last king, Sardanapalus, that up to a recent period nothing but shapeless mounds remained. So vast were they, that they were believed both by the inhabitants of the region and by travellers for many ages to be hills of natural formation. But recently, by the sagacity, skill, determination, and perseverance of several learned men, and pre-eminently of our own countryman, Mr. Layard, these mounds have been explored, and found to contain remains of sculptures, painted walls, and other objects, so numerous and so varied, as to lay open once more the whole life of the nation. The appearance of the ancient Assyrians, their dress, their modes of life, their religion, their palaces, are all portrayed on their sculptured slabs and walls. Their history, which had been inscribed in a language in arrow-headed letters, which had ceased to be used so long ago as the epoch of Alexander the Great, has been brought to light again, and all deciphered by the marvellous sagacity and industry of the learned. This extraordinary nation of antiquity may be said to have been called into existence again, to bear witness to the faithfulness and accuracy of the Bible, and to illustrate the Divine wisdom of its teaching.

One of the most astonishing disclosures which has thus been brought to light is, that the greatest mound, that of Kouyunjic, was composed of the covered ruins of the palace of Sennacherib. His name has been deciphered on almost every slab and brick of the vast building; the archives of fourteen years of his reign have been made out from records upon tiles contained in a chamber which may be regarded as the record-room of the palace, with an account of his conquests, his victories, the plunder he made, and a likeness of himself.

On one slab is the following inscription, "Sennacherib, the mighty king, king of the country of Assyria, sitting on the throne of judgment before the city of Lachish, I give permission for its slaughter."

In another record on a tablet of this king, it is stated that he obtained from Hezekiah, king of Judah, THIRTY talents of gold, exactly what is stated in the previous chapter of this book (v. 14). In another portion of the same record, it is stated,—"Hezekiah, king of Judah, who had not submitted to my authority, forty-six of his principal cities and fortresses, and villages depending upon them, of which I took no account, I captured, and carried away their spoil. I shut up himself within Jerusalem, his capital city."*

This marvellous disentombment of records made by the monarchs themselves, buried for thousands of years, yet coeval with the sacred writers, confirms to the utmost our confidence in the genuineness of Holy Writ, and thus prepares us for the higher wisdom which is enclosed in the spiritual lessons taught in the inner sense of the Word of God.

Assyria in Scripture is the type of the rational faculty of the mind, and of men prone to the supremacy of the intellect. The intellect, in harmony with religion, is a glorious power, exalted, noble, God-honouring, capable of progress, both heavenward

---

* See *Nineveh and Babylon*, pp. 144-152; also *Nineveh and its Remains*: Layard

and earthward, the protective against superstition and folly, a defence against absurdity and sensuality. "Come now, and let us reason together, saith the Lord: Though your sins be as scarlet, they shall be white as snow; though they be red like crimson, they shall be as wool" (Isa. i. 18). Religion, true religion, hails true reason, and rejoices in it; but absurdity and superstition dread it. The keen powers of the intellect discover the discrepancies in fallacious views, and the vain dreams of narrow bigots flinch from its investigations. Piercing as arrows are the glances of minds sharpened by investigation and reflection, and humdrum dogmas of a traditional belief cannot bear their searching inquiries.

The relations of the intellect to religion,—to false religion and to true religion—are what are described in the Divine Volume by the relations of Assyria to Israel and Jerusalem. The intellect may become lawless, and inflated with self-sufficiency, and then it is like Assyria, boasting and arrogant, sneering, contemptuous, and sarcastic, insolently defying God.

Such a state is represented by Assyria in our text, under Sennacherib. The ground of the correspondence of Assyria was the intellectual character of the people. As we look upon their noble countenances, the full eye seems charged with intellectual power. They were veritable lords of men.

The name Ashur signified arrow. They worshipped God, as the infinite in understanding, and represented Him by the symbol of an eagle, which the word Nisr means in their language. Sennacherib was worshipping in the house of Nisroch his god, when his sons smote him with the sword. The Assyrians often represented men with eagles' heads, and frequently portrayed an eagle-headed figure overcoming a lion, or bull, which, as Mr. Layard suggests, "may denote the superiority of intellect over the lower faculties."[*] In one of their wise sayings preserved by Eusebius, we read, "God is he that has the head of a hawk (or an eagle). He is the first, indestructible, eternal, unbegotten, indivisible, dissimilar; the dispenser of all good; incorruptible; the Best of the good; the Wisest of the wise; the father of equity and justice; self-taught, perfect and wise, and the only inventor of the sacred philosophy. They pictured almost everything with wings; their men, their lions, their bulls, were all used symbolically with wings, because they contemplated everything in its relation to the intellect. Thus in all things they soared from earth to heaven.

[*] *Nineveh and its Remains*, vol. 2, p. 458.

Their victories and wide-spread dominion were the result of their culture and intelligence. Knowledge is power; and intellect must triumph over sense, mind over matter. This was true in their days, and will be true for ever. There is a prediction of wonderful majesty and beauty in the prophecy of Isaiah, in which the orderly connection of science and intelligence, and the subordination of both to pure religion, is described under the form of the union of the three countries, Egypt, Assyria, and Israel:—" In that day shall Israel be the third with Egypt and with Assyria, even a blessing in the midst of the land : Whom the Lord of hosts shall bless, saying, Blessed be Egypt my people, and Assyria the work of my hands, and Israel mine inheritance" (xix. 24, 25).

Egypt has but little now to do with the true worship of God; Assyria has long disappeared altogether as a nation; and Israel will never more, as a people, inhabit the hills and vales of Palestine. The hour-hand of Divine Providence never goes backward; progress for the human race is the order of heaven. Nevertheless the prophecy will be fulfilled. Science, the possession of Egypt, and rationality, the possession of Assyria, will be united and subordinated to holiness, the true "Israel of God," and the Divine blessing will be upon them all.

It is a very curious circumstance, and a peculiar feature in our mental history, that while as to every other faculty it is admitted to be its office to perceive as much as it can, and enjoy as much as it can of the objects which it is fitted to embrace,—the rational faculty, with one class of minds, rejoices only in resisting; it closes its eyes, and defies you to make it see; it doubts, doubts, doubts, and keeps trying to say, No; it is ingeniously negative; it will not have a Divine Friend.

This state is represented by Assyria, the rational faculty, warring against Jerusalem. Sennacherib and his army represent negative reasoning, and all its supporting ideas, resolved to crush the Church.

The three personages, Tartan, Rabsaris, and Rabshakeh, who so insultingly addressed the Jews, as recorded in the previous chapter, are now known to have borne these names as official ones. The Tartan means the commander-in-chief; the Rabsaris is chief of the eunuchs; and the Rabshakeh chief of the butlers. They were the ministers of state of the king of Assyria. The perverse spirit of infidel doubt has such ministers of state, who deny and defy, and think they can conquer religion. The vindictive feeling of bitter opposition to the

Lord's kingdom is the Tartan. The ever-ready doubt is Rabsaris, the chief of the eunuchs; it is barren, and incapable of producing any soul-ennobling project of good. The chief of the butlers is Rabshakeh, who represents the plausible spirit of delusive reasoning, which presents its flatteries and persuasions as draughts of seductive wine, to make its victims intoxicated with folly and inflamed with a spirit of delusion.

What is religion, say these, but the dream of dotards, the scheme of priests? Away with the vain fancies of the life of angels, and be content with being a finely organised specimen of dust, a bubble of froth tossed up on the billows of time's tremendous sea, and soon to sink into its native nothingness. "Let us eat and drink, for to-morrow we die." This boastful derisive rationalism, which is as far from true reason as darkness is from light, is Assyria beleaguering Jerusalem.

The true Christian knows in whom he has trusted. He knows what heaven is, for the kingdom of God is within him. If he can really reason well, he can soon scatter the legions of false argument which are based only on the fallacies of the senses. If he cannot reason much, he will still be safe, for he has a faculty above reasoning, the perception which shines from goodness. He dwells in love, and therefore he dwells in God and knows God, for "God is love" (1 John iv.) Such a man will remain firm, and pray. This was what Hezekiah did, and the Divine promise of our text came. It amounts to this: Mere reasoners will fall of themselves; don't trouble yourselves about them. Give blasphemous reasoning a little time, and it will refute itself. "In quietness and confidence shall be your strength."

This angel of the Lord is generally and properly considered to have been that terrible blast of Eastern deserts, the simoom. In the previous chapter we read, "Behold, I will send a blast upon him" (v. 7). It is called an angel or messenger of the Lord, as all things are under the control of Divine Providence—the evil and the good—and by permission, as well as by ordination, they work out His Divine purpose, which is the greatest good possible for the human race, and the least evil for any one. Like the "evil angels" mentioned in Psalm lxxviii., as being sent among the rebellious Egyptians (v. 49), the angel of the Lord here was a power acting by permission for wise ends, and for the universal good. The Lord is Mercy itself, and only for purposes of mercy does He act. "He slew famous kings, for His mercy endureth for ever" (Ps. cxxxvi. 18).

"Evil shall slay the wicked, and they that hate the righteous shall be desolate" (Ps. xxxiv. 20).

There is always a pressure from the dark world seeking to destroy men; but the Divine Sphere of the Lord arrests it, and every moment preserves the human race. When, however, the preservation of the good, as in the case before us, can only be accomplished by the overthrow of the wicked, Divine Providence can no longer avert it, and then, either by war, pestilence, earthquake, storm, or simoom, the wicked are overthrown.

We are not told the entire number of the Assyrian host. Their armies in those days were very large; but probably the greater part of the immense mass lay suffocated by the awful minister of death. When the rest awoke in the morning, there was a plain covered with corpses. The horrid blast of the desert, stimulated by the inner blast of an opened hell, had done its fearful work.

> "Like the leaves of the forest when summer is green,
> That host with their banners at sunset were seen;
> Like the leaves of the forest when autumn hath blown,
> That host on the morrow lay scattered and strown."

The scene must have been surpassingly dreadful; and it is the symbol of what happens always, sooner or later, to the boastful scorner of religion. From the terrible hot-bed of his lusts there comes an influx which breaks him down. To assail the Church, there must be an appearance of morality; but the evil one is really burning within, as the prophet says, "as an oven heated by the baker" (Hos. vii. 4); and the day comes at last when the impure blast breaks forth and destroys all spiritual life. They become all dead men. Like the volcano which has long been sleeping, but bursts out, scattering dismay and death, so is it with inward passion and sin. Its scathing power rushes forth irresistibly at last, and the soul becomes only a living death.

Let this terrible Assyrian example teach us never to oppose the Church of the living God, the heavenly Jerusalem; but come up there to worship the King, who liveth for ever and ever.

There is a beautiful prophecy in Isaiah, the converse of our text, to which the mind can turn with delight, for it opens up a fountain of hope to those who have strayed from the truth:—
"And it shall come to pass in that day that the great trumpet shall be blown, and they shall come who were ready to perish in Assyria, and the outcasts in the land of Egypt, and shall worship the Lord in the holy mount at Jerusalem."

SERMON XL.

THE BURNING OF THE TEMPLE AND CITY OF JERUSALEM BY NEBUCHADNEZZAR, KING OF BABYLON.

"And in the fifth month, on the seventh day of the month, which is the nineteenth year of King Nebuchadnezzar, king of Babylon, came Nebuzaradan, captain of the guard, a servant of the king of Babylon, to Jerusalem; and he burnt the house of the Lord, and the king's house, and all the houses of Jerusalem, and every great man's house burnt he with fire."—2 KINGS, xxv. 8, 9.

THUS perished Jerusalem, the city of David, Solomon, and the prophets—the city of the temple of God, the divinely appointed type of the Church in every coming age—the city of Sacred Song—the beautiful capital of Judea. It had intrigued and coalesced with Babylon, and by Babylon it was destroyed. The house of the Lord, the king's house, and all the houses of Jerusalem were given to the flames, were consumed by fire.

Babylon, which comes out so terribly before us in this passage as the polluter, and then the destroyer of Jerusalem, is much treated of in the Word of God. The city of Babylon was built on the river Euphrates, which flowed through the midst of it. It was the settlement of that class of mankind who were animated by the lust of making themselves great, and ruling over others through the means of perverted religious teaching.

The instincts of our religious nature are the deepest of all those gracious affections which our Creator has fixed within us. They are universal and everlasting. Men must worship: they will worship. He who will not worship the infinite and all-good Father of all, will worship a stick, a stone, a beast, or will offer in self-flattery secret worship to his own supreme excellence. Worship thus exists everywhere, and has existed in every age. Subtle seekers after power see this, and construct a religion by means of which this feeling of adoration may be associated with mysterious doctrines, of which they claim to be the only guardians and expounders, and in the name and by the authority of which they obtain influence, dominion, and wealth. Its mysteries overawe the vulgar, its splendours flatter the great. Where ignorance reigns, and the prestige of long ages exists, such a system continues firmly rooted. The fears of mankind, combined with intellectual sloth and a cowardly dread of danger in following the inquiry after truth, give a long life to Babylon. Yet the superstition, the delusion, the separation, and the persecution the system engenders, have been, and still are, among the world's greatest errors and greatest miseries.

We first read of Babylon or Babel—for Babylon is only the Greek form of Babel—in the very early annals of mankind. The allegory of the building of the city and tower of Babel was the description of the development of the lust of spiritual domination and humanly contrived mysteries in the early world. The confusion this engendered in the place of the simplicity of clear Divine truth is indicated by the word Babel, which means confusion. Men before this time had been invited in a spirit of charity and of light. Their souls were simple, and they followed the simple truth. Nothing is more clear than truth to the soul which desires to obey it. Whoso will do His will, our Lord said, shall know of the doctrine whether it be of God. "Let thine eye be single, and thy whole body shall be full of light." True religion is itself light to the soul. Darkness is the condemnation of itself. It does not come from God, in whom there is no darkness at all.

The Babel builders, however, said, "Let us make us a city and a tower whose top shall reach to heaven, and which shall make us a name." The bricks which they made for stone mean the artificial opinions they invented instead of Divine truths, the stones of which the Church is constructed; the slime which they had for mortar is the symbol of the impure lust of self-aggrandisement, by which they sought to hold their system together; and the thorough burning of the bricks represented the burning zeal by which they contrived and sought to spread the system of mystery and falsity they had thus unhappily introduced among men. That wondrous allegory unfolds the whole subject to the devout mind, and the division which happened from the Lord's coming down, or when Divine Truth was brought home to them, intimates the disunion which ever distracts a community when each seeks selfishly and vehemently to intrude his own opinion upon others, instead of all cultivating the spirit of loving the truth and loving one another.

Such was the character of Babel as a system of pretended religion. Subsequently it embodied itself in an actual city and state, and became in power and magnificence the wonder of the ancient world. Its armies overrun the neighbouring nations. In the time of Nebuchadnezzar it attained its greatest splendour and extent. Subsequently it descended into the lap of luxury and effeminacy, and after a long downward career, it ultimately perished by the attack of the enemies whom its arrogance had provoked. It became a heap of ruins. The wandering Arab passed by the mysterious mounds, and told stories of buried treasure and buried giants; but the name of Babylon had perished from the land of its ruin, and if its name and history had not been preserved by ancient historians and in the Bible, it would have passed altogether from the records of men.

Babylon was wonderful in its origin, wonderful in its magnificence, wonderful in its fall, and wonderful in the insignificance into which it sank. The city of Babylon was placed on the great river Euphrates, and was admirably situated for commerce with the whole world. Eastward, it could easily reach India by the Persian Gulf, and through the mountains of Armenia by land; while its power, exercised on the west by Tyre and Sidon, could communicate with every nation in Europe and on the coast of Africa then known. It was on the highway of intercourse between every civilized portion of the world, and the enterprise of its inhabitants never failed to make the best use of their position. The manufactures of Babylonia attained to wonderful perfection very early. We read in Joshua of a goodly Babylonish garment being very highly prized, for Achan became a traitor to possess it. And the remains of jewellery which still exist, and the descriptions of ancient historians of the magnificent palaces and temples of Babylon, of the paintings and sculptures, confirmed by the wonderful specimens of vessels, statues of men and animals, which recent excavations have brought to view, all disclose an advanced condition of society which gives ample room for reflection, as well as it fills the mind with astonishment. The city was square; the walls were fifteen miles on each side, making sixty miles in the entire circuit. A vast ditch surrounded the whole. There were twenty-five gates in brass, very majestic, on each side of the square. The walls were eighty-seven feet thick, three hundred and fifty feet high, and surmounted by two hundred and fifty towers. Certainly, no modern city is so strong against the modern appliances of warfare as Babylon was against the ancient ones; while we read also with surprise that a tunnel under a river—that triumph of modern engineering—was formed at Babylon under the Euphrates, which is there nearly two hundred yards wide.

Babylon became the emporium of the world, and a system of navigable canals united the Tigris and the Euphrates, and every important part of Chaldea together, with a regard to principle and convenience not surpassed by any modern country. Looking at this city, so vast, so splendid, so majestic in its might, the seat of an empire of unbounded wealth, ruling probably over twenty subject nations, an empire not only of physical might, but of intellectual grandeur and ancient prestige, it seemed destined to be perpetual. But no; it was founded on wrong principles. It became great on superstition, zealotry, ambition, and unprincipled magnificence. Its decay and death were certain to come. Nothing but truth, and virtue in accordance with truth, is everlasting. Where Babylon once stood, the land had returned to its ancient solitude three hundred years before Christ. It is at this day, as the prophets Isaiah and Jeremiah prophesied, confused heaps and "pools of water." The small town of Hillah, with its mud huts and scanty population, represents NOW a portion of the site; but all around is desolation and wilderness, a land of marsh and misery, the home of the bittern and the cormorant. The words of the prophet Isaiah have been literally fulfilled: "Babylon, the glory of kingdoms, the beauty of the Chaldees' excellency, shall be as when God overthrew Sodom and Gomorrah." "Wild beasts of the desert shall dwell there; and their houses shall be full of doleful creatures; and owls shall dwell there, and satyrs shall dance there" (Isa. xiii. 19, 21).

But what really was Babylon? It was the papacy of ancient times. Dr Hinks, who, with Colonel Rawlinson and others, have successfully deciphered the ancient inscriptions of Nineveh and Babylon, informs us that the title of the king of Babylon, constantly met with, means priest-king. The king of Babylon was the pope of those early ages, the spiritual despot of remote times. He had his hierarchy. The wise men, the astrologers, the magicans, and the soothsayers, spoken of in Daniel (ii. 27), were just the various ranks which corresponded to the eminences, right reverends, and other great dignitaries with grandiose titles of modern days. Hence it is that Babylon has still its signification in Holy Writ. It was a religion of human mystery and mummery in the name of God. They cajoled and ruled over men in ancient times, and therefore, in the Word, their state became the symbol of a religion of that kind. So it is described by the prophet concerning Babylon: "Thou hast said in thine heart, I will ascend into heaven; I will exalt my throne above the stars of God: I will sit also upon the mount of the congregation, in the sides of the north : I will ascend above the heights of the clouds; I will be like the Most High " (Isa. xiv. 13, 14). " Thou saidst, I shall be a lady for ever; so thou didst not lay these things to thy heart, NEITHER DIDST REMEMBER THE LATTER END OF IT. Therefore hear now this, thou that art given to pleasures, that dwellest carelessly, that sayest in thine heart, I am, and none else beside me : I shall not sit as a widow, neither shall I see the loss of children." "Thou hast trusted in thy wickedness, thou hast said, None seeth me. Thy wisdom and thy knowledge perverted thee, and thou hast said in thine heart, I am, and none else beside me. Therefore shall evil come upon thee ; thou shalt not know from whence it ariseth : mischief shall fall upon thee; thou shalt not be able to put it off: and desolation shall come upon thee suddenly, which thou shalt not know" (Isa. xlvii. 7, 8, 10, 11).

In these astonishing descriptions and predictions we might be reading the character and fate of the modern Babylon, the papacy as developed in Christendom, and crumbling into dotage and destruction in our own days. In the book of Revelation, we have expressly delineated there a system which is called Babylon the great, the mother of harlots, and the abominations of the earth, as one that would be developed in Christendom. The form, spirit, extent, and fall of it, are exactly detailed in chapters 17 and 18. The church is represented by a majestic woman, the bride, who would become the Lamb's wife. The rival system is represented by a woman, a harlot, having upon her forehead, "Mystery, Babylon the great, the mother of harlots, and the abominations of the earth " (v. 5).

Every one knows that such a system did develop itself, and grew and increased in the dark ages which supervened on the fall of the Roman Empire, and usurped the place of the Lord Jesus, ruling by the fears, ignorance, and superstitions of princes and people, until Christianity became but baptized heathenism. As many saints were worshipped as idols had been worshipped before; a queen of heaven was adored just as the Babylonians had their queen of heaven. Particular places and buildings were visited in pilgrimage for counsel, favour, and cure, just as the famous oracles of the heathen priests were thronged for their wonderments in older times. The pure wisdom and simple holy commands of the Gospel were entirely covered, and made of none effect, by relics and observances which are but stupid substitutes for the Kingdom of God, within an enlightened mind and a loving heart.

At length the whole of Christendom became a vast field of dense ignorance, of wild ambition, passion, and ferocity; very faintly, indeed, moderated by a few good men here and a few there. A remnant remained, watched over by the Lord, under every name, but captive and depressed by the darkness which covered the church, illumined only by the flashes of terrible struggle, of wild hate and defiance, in which the cruel of one class battled fiercely against the cruel of another; or in which the fiendish despot who would murder a nation not obsequious to his senseless tyranny and his stupid priest, was met by the fierce gallantry of heroes of liberty, and a people in arms. But where was Christianity in these awful times? Jerusalem had been set on fire and destroyed by Babylon. What a marvellous view it gives us of the Word, and of the Lord's Providence, when we comprehend the great lesson, that the record of the career of Jerusalem in the Old Testament is the prophetic delineation of the Christian Church, the Jerusalem which the Lord Jesus established. Yet it is manifestly so.

"Ye are come unto Mount Zion," said the Apostle to the Christians, "and unto the city of the living God, THE HEAVENLY JERUSALEM, and to an innumerable company of angels, to the general assembly AND CHURCH OF THE FIRST-BORN" (Heb. xii. 22, 23). Again, he is not a Jew who is one outwardly, but he is a Jew who is one inwardly (Rom. ii. 28, 29). And still again, Jerusalem which is above (the earthly Jerusalem) is free, which is the mother of us all (Gal. iv. 26).

If, then, the Jerusalem of the Old Testament was a figure, a shadow going before of the Christian Church, the Jerusalem of the new, what will the degeneracy of Jerusalem, its courting communion with Babylon, and ultimately its destruction by Babylon, mean, but that the Christian Church would degenerate, would become corrupted by Babylonish intercourse, and ultimately be destroyed by Babylon? The consequence seems to be inevitable; there appears no escape from such a conclusion.

The Christian Church, as the Lord Jesus founded it, and the Apostles spread it, was a city suffused and filled by this spirit of humility, love, and the wisdom of humility and love; it was the city set upon a hill, the Jerusalem which was holy, pure, and free. How came it then to become the church of contradictory mysteries, of violent antagonisms, of fierce struggles, and burning hates? How came its great men to become monstrous for their crimes and their cruelties? Whence came the Torquemadas, the Alvas, the inquisition, the centuries of persecution, of cruelty, and bloodshed in the name of the religion of the Prince of Peace? It was from Jerusalem shewing her treasures to Babylon, as in the days of good, but weak Hezekiah.

The Church having lost her first love, and manufactured the new creed of three divine persons, began to borrow showy rites and gaudy ceremonies from heathenism. Instead of kindling the fire of love in the hearts of men, she lighted plenty of candles; instead of holy truth, she provided holy water; instead of taking up the daily cross of the Gospel—the cross of subduing evil tempers and unhallowed desires, she put crosses on her buildings and into the hands of the people—rough crosses and dainty crosses—covered her priests with crosses in grand colours, quite as grand as those of the old priests of Thibet, or the priest of Egypt, which they flaunted in processions centuries before Christianity existed; she made and blessed jewelled crosses for wicked men and women of princely position and high degree, who were a scandal not only to religion but to mankind; instead of removing sin, she pretended to forgive it and satisfy God by saying many hurried prayers with unchanged hearts, and living as wickedly as before. To preserve this masquerade of religion, she martyred the true children of Christ, and massacred nations. O Lord Jesus, Saviour, infinite in purity, wisdom, charity, and holiness, was this Thy Church, for which Thou didst bow the heavens and come down? Was it for such a system as this Thou wert God manifest in the flesh, and didst suffer and die for men? Assuredly not. Thy Jerusalem had mixed with Babylon, and at length Babylon had burnt and utterly destroyed it.

Nothing but the Word of God, loved and obeyed, can change the human heart and mind: and the Word of God was closed from the people, and mysterious looking mummeries instituted instead; and so the fires of evil lust and passion, at one time smouldering in the heart, at another raging forth in cruel violence and battle, until Jerusalem was entirely destroyed. "Wickedness burneth as a fire" (Isa. ix. 18). "Behold, all ye that kindle a fire, that compass yourselves about with sparks; walk in the light of your fire, and in the sparks ye have kindled. This shall ye have at my hand, ye shall lie down in sorrow" (Isa. l. 11). The so-called Christian nations, sunk under Babylonish principles, did surely kindle enormous fires, and did indeed lie down in sorrow.

The name Nebuchadnezzar is found so abundantly upon the broad bricks or tiles of Babylon, that not only is his extraordinary grandeur fully testified by the extensive remains of the wonderful palaces and other great structures he built, but scarcely any remains are found of the city as it was before his time. The Birs Nimroud, four miles from Hillah, which had been long supposed, without any evidence, to be the remains of the Tower of Babel, has on every inscribed brick which has been taken from it the name of Nebuchadnezzar.*

But this king, great as he was, typified a principle far more terrible and powerful than he. The name Nebuchadnezzar means *the anguish of judgment;* and the name of his general Nebuzaradan means *the fruits of judgment,* also *the winnowing of judgment.*

When a church has lost its soul and life, and instead of its own nature and strength has borrowed from Babylon its influence and right to be, a time comes when even the appearance of it, the remains of it, will not be tolerated. All regard for gentleness, wisdom, justice, truth, and everything of the angelic character, will be thrown off, and it will stand out only what Nebuchadnezzar has made it, a ruin, a misery, and a desolation. His general, the winnower, will scatter everything inconsistent with Babylonish rule, and the Church will be judged by its own manifestation, a home for falsity, destitute of true goodness, true life, true wisdom, and true peace.

But, blessed be Infinite Mercy, Jerusalem was to be built again, and it was built again. The second temple was more glorious than the first. The Prince of Peace came and inhabited it in person; and in that house, as the prophets predicted, He gave peace (Haggai ii. 9).

Jerusalem was to be inhabited as "towns without walls, for the multitude of men and cattle therein." The Lord declared He would be a wall of fire round about, and a glory in the midst of her (Zech. ii. 4, 5). And so it is once again. The New Jerusalem, THE SECOND SPIRITUAL JERUSALEM, the Church of great principles, revealing truths infinite in number and grandeur, and love extensive as heaven and earth, and embracing peoples, nations, languages, and tongues in all-encircling charities, now appears. The Lord is in her. His love surrounds her as a wall of fire. Come and see the bride, the Lamb's wife, the city of the great King. Let us hail the glorious dwelling, and say, "This is my rest for ever; here will I dwell, for I have desired it."

* *Nineveh and Babylon,* p. 496.

SERMON XLI.

EZEKIEL'S VISION OF THE WHEELS.

"When those went, these went; and when those stood, these stood; and when those were lifted up from the earth, the wheels were lifted up over against them; for the spirit of the living creature was in the wheels."—EZEK. i. 21.

IN meditating upon the Word of the Lord, we may observe that one of its features of perfection is, that its letter partakes of the genius of the age and place in which it was given. It not only embosoms Divine wisdom in every page, but it so enters into the spirit of the literature and circumstances of the period in which it was imparted, that it contains confirmations of its truth, which commend it more and more to the studious mind, the more it is examined. This characteristic illustrates and confirms to the thoughtful inquirer, the genuineness and the naturalness, so to speak, of each portion of the Bible. It is strikingly exhibited in the book before us, in several leading particulars.

Ezekiel prophesied in the land of the Chaldeans, near Babylon, at the time when the Jews were suffering the seventy years' captivity. He was commissioned to console the captives, who were now bowed down in penitence, to raise their hopes by consolation. He was to impart the promise of a return once more to their beloved country. They should build once more the temple, the centre of their best aspirations, and restore Jerusalem, their sacred city.

Now, at Nineveh and Babylon, the mythical genius of the people displayed itself in marvellous allegorical forms of sculpture and painting. If we look at their recovered monuments, now displayed so largely at the British Museum, and in many other national collections, we see winged men, winged animals, extraordinary compounds of men and animals, no doubt representing their conceptions of the intellectual and animal nature in the human mind, and their views of these, both in order and in struggle. In such representations they abounded.

Manifestly in this opening of the magnificent prophecy of Ezekiel, we have disclosed to us the very same thing. There are the winged cherubim with their marvellous forms, compounded of man and animal. There are the wings and the mysterious wheels. We have evidently the Word clothed with the Chaldean genius. It is the Divine Truth, as it were, incarnated in the wondrous representations of that age and country. The same peculiarity is observable in the fourth chapter. It was the custom of the Chaldeans to write and paint upon tiles of baked clay. When the prophet was commanded to represent the siege of Jerusalem, it is said, "Take a tile, and portray upon it the city, even Jerusalem." It is not take a scroll, or take a book, as we find in other parts of Scripture, but take a tile. The same characteristic is manifest in the thirty-seventh chapter, in the resurrection, which is represented as taking place in a valley of dry bones.

The Babylonish people in very ancient times were remarkable for their spiritual character. They had, however, at length sunk into an exceedingly carnal state; and from worshipping the Lord, the Sun of heaven, the worship of the sun of the world became prevalent: from regarding the fire of love as the worthiest possession of spiritual life, they began to deem earthly fire as something sacred, and keep it perpetually burning. They had believed with the rest of the world in the resurrection of the spiritual body; they sank into the idea of the resurrection of the *material* body. The Jews had never held the latter doctrine before the captivity, and no traces of it appear in the books of Scripture revealed before that seventy years' residence in Babylon. But now, Ezekiel uses the resurrection believed by the Babylonians as a symbol of the resurrection of the Jews as a nation, and their return to their own land. He gives us the meaning in verses 11 and 12, but he uses the figure. Of course, in the spiritual signification, it means what the apostle calls the resurrection from the death of sin to the life of righteousness; the regeneration of the soul and of the church. There is a similar figure used by Daniel in chapter xii. verse 2, evidently with the same signification, that is, the resurrection of the Jews from the dust of captivity, to national honourable existence again. Anywhere else, as in Greece, Rome, or India, where the people only thought of the resurrection of man, not of the scattered dust, such a figure would have been strange and outrageous; but in Babylon, where the resurrection of the flesh and bones had already obtained credence as a doctrine, the prophets who prophesied there could use it as a metaphor. Thus does the Word of God, enclosing in its bosom the infinite wisdom of the Most High, yet clothe itself with the language and ideas of those to whom it is given, that it may dwell among us.

Let us now turn to consider the vision which the prophet says he beheld. It was a vision full of hope and comfort. The heavens, he said, were opened to him, and he saw visions of God (verse 1). The poet says, "Heaven lies around us in our infancy," and it is true. "Their angels," the Saviour declared, "do always behold the face of our Father in the heavens." But it is also true, that heaven, though invisible, is not very far from every one of us: "He has given his angels charge over us, to keep us in all our ways." Ezekiel had not to go far to see the heavens opened. It needed only his own spiritual eyes to be opened, and he beheld the heavens, which were present like an inner atmosphere around him, though unseen. It is well for us, when we realize the truth which Jacob discovered in the wilderness—"Surely God is in this place, and I knew it not. This is none other than the House of God, and this is the gate of heaven."

The prophet saw first, he informs us, a fire, with a glorious brightness, a fire ENFOLDING ITSELF. Out of this came the likeness of four living creatures, and wheels of a marvellous and magnificent construction. The living creatures had the general appearance of a man, but with the additional faces of an ox, a lion, and an eagle. Their substance was as if of fire, and the soles of their feet were like the sole of a calf's foot: that is, the hoof was divided. The wheels were wonderful in their grandeur. They seemed full of eyes (verse 18); and they were as "a wheel in the middle of a wheel" (verse 16). The vision was a representation of the array of means arranged by Divine Providence for the regeneration and progress of the human race. The fire expresses the ardour of the Divine Love. The enfolding, or catching itself, means that the burning glow of the Divine Love often withholds the fervour of its affection from man, when required by a consideration for his eternal good. Divine Love has always eternal ends in view; and when these ends would best be accomplished by hiding its holy ardours, and leaving a man to be chastened, yet purified and hallowed, by trouble, the fire restrains itself, but mercy earnestly remembers us still.

A good parent does frequently the same thing. Love often

the ages move, and by which each single soul advances; for truth lights the way, and gives the power to advance—truth, that is to say, impelled by love. The majesty of the Word is portrayed by the wheels being so high as to be dreadful (verse 18).

The four wheels, like the four gospels, represent the Divine Truth as applied to the internal man, and the external man, and the will and understanding in each. The "wheel in the middle of a wheel" expresses the inner meaning of the Word—the spirit —within the letter. The spiritual sense treating of heavenly things, and then of still higher—of the Divine—is always to the thoughtful mind "as a wheel in the middle of a wheel." So, in nature, the laws of Divine Providence are higher and lower, and wonderfully through one end attaining another; through chastenings, troubles, and afflictions, evolving eternal good. Through earthly changes, unions, and separations, through afflictions and health, joy and sorrow, sunshine and shade, by things seen to things unseen, man proposing and God disposing, it is ever "as a wheel in the middle of a wheel."

The wheels were said to be full of eyes; for truths impart to us the power to see. Each truth, when clearly understood, is as an eye placed in the mind, which perceives the good and the evil, to which otherwise we should be blind. The eyes of the Lord, in this sense, are said to run to and fro in the earth. What a Divine gift the Word is shewn to be, when we regard it as imparting to us powers to perceive on all subjects and on all sides, as full of eyes.

We shall now be prepared to apply the somewhat mysterious language of our text, When those—that is, the living creatures —went, these—the wheels—went; and when those stood, these stood; and when the living creatures were lifted up from the earth, the wheels were lifted up over against them; for the spirit or life of the living creature was in the wheels. We have seen that the living creatures represent the affections of love, which are given to warm the heart. The wheels are the truths of the Word by which the soul makes progress. When the heart is warm, the mind advances: when the heart is cold, the mind is slow—the progress stops. All advancement is by intervals of lively action and repose; indeed, we move by cycles. We commence a career in spiritual things with great vigour, and we are astonished and delighted as one bright state after another is realized, one bright lesson after another learned. We seem to be passing rapidly through a beautiful country, and our attainments and our enjoyments fill us with gratitude. We look round, and we look up, and bless the holy name of the All-Good for the heavenly career thus hopefully and joyously made. A change, however, comes over us. We more or less lose our first love. The spiritual spring and summer fade away into autumn and winter. We begin to feel cold. No longer do the gushing sentiments of a warm affection flow on, and give to all things the feeling of beauty and life. We are languid. We don't read as we did. We don't feel the same joy in worship which once filled us with interior delight. We are more conscious of faults than we were, and sometimes we have an unpleasant tendency to look more at the faults of others than at their excellencies. We often imagine that the persons and scenes around us are less excellent than they used to be. The impression has not entered our minds that the change is in ourselves. Yet so it really is. When the living creatures stood, the wheels stood. The affections are the motives,—the springs of progress. If we prayed to the Lord to warm us when we are cold, to impart more love, more charity, a holier glow of tenderness for others, and of affection for His Word and its truths, the fires would again flame out cheerfully, the wheels go merrily, and the chariot of progress would become for us, like the chariot of Elijah, a chariot of fire with horses of fire.

When those stood, these stood, and when those went, these went.

> Did we the sighs we vainly spend,
> To heaven in supplications send;
> Our cheerful song would oftener be,
> Hear what the Lord hath done for me.

We read further: "And when those were lifted up from the earth, the wheels were lifted up over against them." The lifting up of the living creatures represented the exaltation of the affections. The affections are exalted, when we yearn to become heavenly-minded. The heavenly mind makes heaven. The spiritual affections express themselves in utterances like those of the Psalmist—" O send out Thy light and Thy truth; let them lead me, let them bring me to the mountain of Thy holiness, and to Thy tabernacles." "As the hart panteth after the waterbrooks, so panteth my soul after Thee, O God. My soul thirsteth for God, for the living God; when shall I come and appear before God?" When we yearn for spiritual truths, the Word becomes to us spiritualized. We see things in it we never saw before, because we were not prepared to see them. The higher we go, the farther we see. The disciples of the Lord did not perceive their heavenly Father in Him, until they were prepared to see Him. The Jews only saw a splendid land in the hills and valleys of their country: the Christian by faith beholds a glorious heavenly Canaan. The carnal mind sees only earthly views in the Word. To the Egyptians, the protecting cloud was dark; to the Israelites, all brightness and splendour. " Blessed are the pure in heart, for they shall see God."

Oh that we could ever keep this in view, the state of our affections governs the state of the intellect. When the living creatures are lifted up, the wheels are lifted up over against them. Keep self low, and heaven high, and the confession of the soul would much oftener be that described by the prophet: " When I found Thy words, I did eat them, and they were the joy and rejoicing of my heart." A good spiritual appetite makes a splendid feast. The Lord spreads a table before us in the Word; He anoints our head with oil, and our cup runs over. Blessed be His adorable name. Let us lift up the living affections of the heart, and the wheels of intellectual perception and progress will be lifted up over against them; for there is the closest correspondence between them. Love and truth answer to one another like heart and lungs. "The spirit of the living creature is in the wheels."

We sometimes fail to perceive the love of our heavenly Father in every part of His Word; but it is there. Upon love to God and love to man, our Lord says, hang all the law and the prophets. In every atom of the world there is stored up fire; we call it latent heat. Coal is in reality embodied and embedded sunbeams, poured over the trees when growing, and fixed in their wondrous and beautiful organizations, to be called forth when required by the exigencies of human life and skill. So in every phrase of the Word, in every verse, Divine Love lies hidden, —" The life of the living creature is in the wheels."

We sometimes see no life, but rather condemnation in the Word. "It is a savour of life unto life," writes the apostle, "and a savour of death unto death." But, in themselves, the words of the Lord Jesus are always, according to His own declaration, "spirit and life." "My words, they are spirit and they are life." Do we then fail to find in the blessed pages of Revelation the counsels of consolation, the food of everlasting life, the streams of Divine Wisdom and Love unspeakable from the eternal Living Fountain? Let us never forget that it is certainly there: "The life of the living creature is in the wheels." Let us ask until it is given unto us, let us seek until we find, let us knock until it is opened.

SERMON XLII.

JONAH'S ORDER TO GO TO NINEVEH, AND HIS DISOBEDIENCE.

"Arise, go to Nineveh, that great city, and cry against it; for their wickedness is come up before me. But Jonah rose up to flee unto Tarshish from the presence of the Lord, and went down to Joppa, and he found a ship going to Tarshish: so he paid the fare thereof and went down into it, to go with them to Tarshish from the presence of the Lord."—
JONAH i. 2, 3.

IT seems a strange reluctance that the prophet Jonah had to go at the Divine command, and strive to arrest the wickedness of Nineveh. That city was then the great city of the world. Through the enterprise of its inhabitants, and the vigour and perseverance of its rulers, its power was felt far and wide, and those vast structures were built which have lately been largely explored, and which testify to the magnificence of the empire, and the splendour of the capital. With palaces so grand, and so much enriched by art, with immense bazaars, and miles upon miles of streets, vast avenues fifteen miles long, and all the varied signs of wealth and greatness which the mighty metropolis of the then most powerful nation of the world exhibited, its inhabitants must have had feelings like those which animated the old Romans when they spoke of Rome as the Eternal City. But wealth and security allured to luxury and self-indulgence; the monarchs of Assyria became distinguished for voluptuousness, and the example of a pampered court weakened virtue and integrity throughout the land. The signs of a tottering state were already multiplying, and though the end was deferred through several reigns, it surely came. The last king, whose name, Sardanapalus, became a type of soft self-indulgence and magnificent vice, lost both crown and life in the overthrow of the empire and the burning of the capital by the Medes and Babylonians.

So is it ever with a luxurious and unprincipled state, and a vicious and frivolous people. The enchanting dream of thoughtless folly and giddy pleasure extends, until integrity and virtue become empty names, the jeers of fools, despised and neglected, and a fatal though gilded rottenness extends and saps away the entire strength of the nation. When the dread hour of trial comes, such a state falls like a tree whose heart has all gone. It has stood a mere shell, deprived of all power of endurance, and it sinks a prey to its own weakness. Virtue alone gives safety to a people. Wickedness is a leprosy which taints and destroys all national vigour, as well as individual health. Sin let loose speaks punishment at hand. So has it ever been, so will it ever be. The wages of sin is death, for men and nations. So Babylon found it, and so Nineveh. Only righteousness exalteth a nation.

It was a strange circumstance, then, that, being a prophet of the Lord, and a preacher of righteousness, Jonah should have hesitated to fulfil his sacred mission He resided in Galilee, at Gath Hepher, in the days of Jeroboam, the second of Israel (2 Kings xiv. 25), and was a great comfort to his nation. But, in this he was fully their type; he supposed God entirely taken up with the Israelites, having no regard for other nations. One great error of the Israelitish people was, that Jehovah was their national God, preferring them to all others, and absorbing His Providence entirely in care for them. They knew that the Lord had done wonderful things for them, had led them from bitter bondage, and constituted them a nation endowed with privileges and benefits most bounteous and tender. They had not learned, however, that what the Lord had done for them was not for them only, but, as He had declared to Abraham, that "in him and his seed all nations should be blessed."

When the world in general was in sin and darkness, Israel was appointed to receive and preserve the Word of God. When there was scarcely any real spiritual church left among men, they were made the representative of a church, a figure, an outward shadow of a church, until a true inward church could be restored by the Lord Jesus. The oracle, the temple, the sacrifices, the prophets, the splendours of worship were theirs, but they were theirs not for their own sakes alone, but through them for all mankind. Each nation has its mission, equally with each individual. Nothing lives for itself. It is part of the great whole, and is intended to contribute to the universal well-being. The sun shines not for himself, but to warm and brighten all around him. The fountain springs not for itself only, but to send forth its rill or stream to refresh men and animals, and fertilize the land. The flowers bloom and the trees bear for the general good, not for selfish existence. So was it with Israel. They were constituted to preserve the great truths that there was one holy and good Father of all worlds, and of the vast family of man. That His Word ought to guide all, and He only should be worshipped. This was their mission, their glorious part in the ordination of Divine Providence. Doing this, they were fulfilling their charge; they were the salt of the earth, a city set upon a hill. They were set up, however, that they might diffuse light, not that they might hide it. Their national selfishness, however, led them to suppose that they were particular favourites, and they must hide their light under a bushel. They imagined that God only regarded them, and other nations were contemned, and uncared for, by Him who cares for the sparrows. There is in every human heart a spirit of egotism, which suggests phantasies like this; and instead of repudiating such monstrous notions, not Jews only, but other nations, and not nations only, but sects and parties, great and small, and sometimes very small, have set forth this narrow and unworthy folly, and made a religion of it. But God is no respecter of persons or nations. "He is good to all, and His tender mercies are over all His works." "God is love. It is not the will of our Father in the heavens, that one little one should perish." "God willeth that all men should come to the knowledge of the truth and be saved." To teach Jonah this, the exhortation was given to him which we find in our text—"Arise, go to Nineveh, that great city, and cry against it; for their wickedness is come up before me."

Here was a great city, of probably a million of people, immersed in luxury and vice, hastening to ruin. The Lord was caring for them, and providing the means of repentance and salvation. Here, too, was a prophet, the inhabitant of a small town, in a small country, but absorbed by the idea that he had no concern with these multitudes who were perishing. Jonah would not go if he could help it. He thought the Lord was only present in Israel, and he fled "from the presence of the Lord," and went down to Joppa.*

This avoidance of the work of preaching repentance, and going into a ship, was indeed what Jonah really did. He paid his fare, and entered upon his voyage to Tarshish, probably a

---

* Joppa was the seaport of Palestine. Thence voyages were taken and commerce fostered. Going to Joppa, spiritually means to addict one's self to acquire knowledge,—quite a good thing in itself, but not when we should be DOING the work of repentance.

part of Spain now called Tartesus. This was then near the pillars of Hercules, then regarded as synonymous with the end of the world. In all this Jonah was a type, a type of his nation, and of a large portion of mankind at all times and in all nations. They avoid applying themselves to repentance; they prefer to betake themselves entirely to some doctrinal system, and thus go sailing in a ship when they ought to be subduing wickedness. To go to Tarshish is to sink into the lowest trifles of life, and to spend one's time in frivolity. "From the end of the earth I will cry unto Thee when my heart is overwhelmed; lead me to the Rock that is higher than I" (Ps. lxi. 2).

A ship corresponds to a system of doctrine, because by its means we can sail over the sea of human knowledge safely. Noah was saved in a species of ship; our Lord frequently taught from a ship; and as we all have to make the voyage of life, it is essential that we should have a good stout ship. "They that go down to the sea in ships, that do business in great waters, these see the works of the Lord, and His wonders in the deep." The word nave, for the body of a church, derived from the Latin word *navis*, a ship, was no doubt used from some perception of doctrine, being as valuable to enable us to pursue our spiritual journeys over the sea of thought, as a ship to navigate the wide world of waters.

But a person may engross himself too much in doctrine. He may be attending to doctrine, when he should be engaged in the struggles of life, in the work of religion. This was what Jonah was doing. He ought to have been preaching to ignorant and perishing multitudes, repentance and salvation from sin; but he went on board a ship, out of the way, and there he went to sleep. The sea is a symbol in the world and in the Word of the vast element of external thought, in which men live as fishes in a sea. In all its aspects the sea resembles the phases of the general mind, and in an individual case the sea means the thoughts of the natural man. Sometimes the general state in which we live is like a placid sea; all is calm, quiet, and silvery, like a vast mirror. We sail smoothly along, the waters below reflecting the bright grand heavens above, and we enjoy the tranquil pleasure. A condition like this is represented by the sea of glass mingled with fire, on which John saw those standing in heaven, who had gotten the victory over the beast, and had the harps of God (Rev. xv. 2). At other times the sea is restless, unquiet, and with much that is unpleasant about it. The wicked are like the troubled sea, when it cannot rest, whose waters cast up mire and dirt. "There is no peace, saith my God, to the wicked" (Isa. lvii. 20, 21).

There are occasions more terrible than this, when the sea is wild and furious, and ships, ill-made or with rotten timbers, fail and founder, and even the best vessels are tossed and buffetted, and have a hard struggle for existence. These are spoken of in Scripture constantly as mental storms. David says, "Let not the waterflood overflow me, neither let the deep swallow me up, and let not the pit shut her mouth upon me" (Ps. lxix. 15). "Deep calleth unto deep, at the noise of thy waterspouts; all thy waves and thy billows are gone over me" (Ps. xlii. 7). These mental tempests will come, and they require a good spiritual ship.

Jonah, however, evidently wished to have a smooth life, and thought he could get out of the difficulty of reproving and overcoming wickedness, by getting into a ship, and closing his eyes. The Jewish nation strove to do the same, even to the last. They were far busier about their traditions, their washing of hands and pots, as matters of religion, their tithings of mint, anise, and cummin, than about the weightier matters of justice, mercy, and faith. This was mentally getting into their ship, rather than do the work assigned them by the Lord, to preach repentance and obedience to Him.

They are not alone in this. Myriads at the present day do the same. They enter a church, that is to say they confess a doctrine, and enrol themselves amongst its adherents. They pay their fare, they give their warm assent, and undertake the support of their particular form of religion, and attend to its external requirements, and then, like Jonah, they go into the sides of the ship and fall fast asleep. They have cleansed the outside of the cup and the platter, but the inside, the thoughts of the mind, and the affections of the heart, are taken up with self and selfish fancies, just as much as the worldliest of the worldly. External pleasures and greatness charm them as much as others; the demands of fashion are as imperious for them, and similar vices, if not the more deadly secret lusts of the soul, are as little combatted against in them, as in those who make no profession against whatever the Divine commands forbid. Cease to do evil, and learn to do well, in reference to fashionable evils, and sins not shocking to the ordinary usages of society, is a Divine law which gives their inward consciences no concern. Jonah is fast asleep. They have paid their fare; they meet all the demands made upon them; and they consider that things are all right, or ought to be. Some are so besotted as openly to say they leave religion to the ministers, whom they pay to attend to it. They are dead asleep to the awful words spoken by the Highest, "Ye must be born again." Their tempers, hasty or sulky as the case may be, are unsoftened and unrenewed by the adorable spirit of Him who said, "Take my yoke upon you, and learn of me, for I am meek and lowly of heart, and ye shall find rest unto your souls." They are vigorous at self-indulgence; but for the advancement of real religion they are fast asleep.

Going to sleep, however, has never been found to be a successful way of overcoming difficulties. The evils increase. What might have easily been removed becomes rooted and ramified. We should be up and doing. Success means going early to work, and working well. The very worst of all ways of accomplishing anything is GOING TO SLEEP. To such sleepers the Apostle Paul cried, "Awake thou that sleepest, and arise from the dead, and Christ shall give thee light" (Eph. v. 14). Too many, however, instead of walking in the holy light of Divine Truth, lie quiet, slumber on, and think all is right,—they have paid their fare, and are in the ship. Yet the storms of life will come. Prepared or unprepared, trials will arise, and occasionally become fierce tempests; and woe to him whose conscience has not been purified and renewed, only benumbed by mental opiates.

Such will find the storm rage wildly, and no remission. They will trim their sails, and cry in wild alarm, but the tempest will not be stilled. The waves and the billows will roll over them. They mount up to the heaven, they go down into the depths, their soul is melted because of trouble. They reel to and fro, and stagger like a drunken man, and are at their wits' end. They have fled from the presence of the Lord, the only stiller of tempests; and now the sea rages, and becomes tempestuous more and more. At length inquiry is made throughout the whole mind, and Jonah is wakened up. By the secret providence of the Lord, represented in the narrative before us by the casting of lots, it is seen that upon Jonah is all the blame. Jonah sees it himself. The sleepy religion is fully wakened up, and filled with terror and self-condemnation. Confession is made by the conscience that it is a Hebrew, that it has been born for heaven, and ought to have been doing the work of heaven. A great dread comes over the soul. All the intellectual powers, represented by the mariners, are filled with awe and amazement at the folly of man, and the majesty of Divine Omnipotence. Self-condemnation comes on. The soul condemns itself to utter unworthiness, as only worthy of the earth to which it has clung, or to hell itself. It is totally unfit for the church, it prays to be cast overboard, to be rejected as a worthless thing, as a mere cumberer of the ship. Before any one is saved, he must become lost. The Son of Man comes to seek and to save those who are lost. This is represented by Jonah being cast overboard.

Now, the Lord, however, had prepared a great fish to swallow up Jonah (verse 17). There has often been great difficulty felt in this announcement, that the Lord had prepared a great fish, that the prophet for three days and nights existed in a trance state buried in the animal, for the sake of the spiritual lesson to be taught. Yet, when we remember the far greater wonders which indeed formed the very life of the Israelitish Dispensation, —the deliverance from Egypt, the passage of the Red Sea, the supply of Manna in the wilderness for forty years, all for the sake of that representative Church which was for the time "SALT OF THE EARTH," the preservative of religion and the world—we need not hesitate at the statement that the Lord prepared a fish to swallow Jonah. Far more wonderful are the amazing laws which operate every day in the mighty world of waters. Who raises the tide, and moves the enormous mass of ocean with so much gentleness, that when we look upon the wondrous scene we lose the idea of omnipotent effort in the perfect ease? Who governs the myriads of living creatures which inhabit the watery world, assigning to each its food, and its particular geographical province, as perfectly as the birds of the air and the beasts of the land have their climates and regions adapted to each?. All these things are wonderful to the thoughtful mind, and not less wonderful because they are common. The Lord prepares and sustains them all for the purposes of infinite love and wisdom, and for the same gracious purpose He prepared this great fish for Jonah.

In spiritual things, fish—because they inhabit and enjoy the water—correspond to the appetites for knowledge and science which explore and enjoy the sea of information. When science is kept subordinate to the higher and grander aims of the religious life and virtue, the soul is in order, and the mind has all manner of beautiful and useful ideas, clear courses of thought flow like clear streams, swarming with graceful fish. Distinct conceptions are the fish mentioned by the prophet Ezekiel as living where the waters of the sanctuary came (xlvii. 9).

It is possible, however, for a person to be too much absorbed in science, and too little concerned about his affections, or about his conduct. He may be curious to know, busy to conceive and to argue, but heedless of loving the Lord and His kingdom, slow to recognize the higher and more generous impulses of the angelic part of our nature. Such persons are cold-blooded and flat like a fish. They are altogether enveloped by the lower intellect, and are often a painful compound of great knowledge and great vanity. The Word describes Pharaoh, king of Egypt, as such a one. It is written, "Behold, I am against thee, Pharaoh, king of Egypt, the great dragon that lieth in the midst of his rivers, who has said, My river is mine own, and I have made it for myself" (Ezek. xxiv. 3).

Vanity often says, My river is my own, and I have made it for myself; and does not know that its poetry, its painting, its eloquence, its wealth, its greatness, whatever it may be, is a talent from the Lord, a gift as surely of His as our life is, and should be used for Him. But to be absorbed in scientific life, and in the cares, anxieties, and carnal indulgences of sense, with scarcely a thought or feeling for eternal interests, is to be swallowed up in a great fish. It is a paralysis of the best side and the higher region of man. And if we learned that he had chosen this condition, and prided himself upon it, and imagined he was rather a superior kind of man, our hearts would be filled with pity. Yet this is just what the man of science is, who rejects all higher things. It is Jonah buried in the fish.

Happily, the Lord prepared the fish. The Lord does not leave us, though we flee from His presence. He over-rules our earthly affairs, and our very talents, so that, if possible, our hearts may again be turned to Him. Sometimes by failure and afflictions, sometimes by observing the afflictions of others, sometimes by family sorrows, sometimes by a dear one being taken away, sometimes by all our plans being scattered, and in a thousand ways known and over-ruled by Infinite Love, men are trained for the better life; because the Lord has prepared all things, that they may form His immortal children for their everlasting good.

Jonah was in the belly of the fish three days and three nights, because these times represent in the Divine speech a full experience, both of the full joys and the full sorrows, the full lights and the full shades, of a merely external life, until we are taught how narrow, poor, and low is the life of mere science and earthly thought; and we are all brought, like Jonah, to pray that we may be drawn from the darkness of earth into the glorious sunlight of day once more, a day to become brighter and brighter until we are settled in the perpetual glory of heaven.

JONAH'S PENITENCE IN THE FISH.

"When my soul fainted within me, I remembered the Lord: and my prayer came in unto Thee, into Thine holy temple. They that observe lying vanities forsake their own mercy."—JONAH ii. 7, 8.

IT was a strange, cramped, confined sort of life that Jonah experienced in the fish. He seems to have had an inner consciousness of what was passing around, while the external was helpless, and as if paralysed. A similar life is sometimes realised in a trance state, and in some conditions of the dying. They perceive what is passing around, but have no power to stir a muscle. The external has fainted, but the internal is fully alive. Some who have recovered from apparent death by drowning have declared that their inner perceptions and sensations were quite vivid, when their outward powers were suspended, and their whole life seemed placed before them in the strongest and clearest light. Others have heard and known what was passing around them, but with no power to speak a word or move a limb. Jonah perceived the waters about him, and that he was deep down in the sea—the heart of the sea he calls it, verse 3, in the Hebrew. He felt the weeds floating and wrapping themselves about his head, but he knew he had no help for himself; he saw the real nature of his folly, and his utter incapability to procure for himself deliverance, and he remembered the Lord. His prayer was heard from the depths of the sea. "My prayer," he says, "came in unto Thee, into thine holy temple;" and he was delivered to know and to say, "Salvation is of the Lord."

In the depth of his distress he remembered the Lord. How strange it is that he, or any of us, can ever forget the Lord. He is goodness itself, and has loaded us with tender mercies. We live every moment by His life. Our talents, our gifts, our daily support, the marvellous arrangements of our being, both

in soul and body—and these are not only wonderful, but
miraculous—are all from the Lord. Yet so short-sighted, so
heedless are we, that when we are in the full enjoyment of
these, and our bark is sailing smoothly on the sea of life, we
soon forget Him by whose mercy we exist, and transgress
those Divine laws by which alone we can be truly happy.
Then storms come—storms terrible to endure; sometimes only
mental storms, but sometimes also attended by loss of wealth,
fame, estimation of friends, domestic comfort, children, health.
Our trials multiply, for sorrows, like joys, often come in groups.

> "First a speck, and then a vulture,
> Till the air is dark with pinions.
> So disasters come not singly,
> But as if they watched and waited,
> Scanning one another's motions.
> When the first descends, the others
> Follow, follow, gathering flock-wise
> Round their victim, sick and wounded;
> First a shadow, then a sorrow,
> Till the air is dark with anguish."

So was it with the self-willed prophet. The sea raged, the
tempest howled; the mariners were at their wits' end. Inquiry
brought home the conviction to Jonah that all this storm was
the result of his disobedience, and at length the lot announced
that he was indeed the culprit through whose misconduct
everything had gone wrong. He was cast overboard, completely overwhelmed by the waters, and swallowed by the fish.
In the dim sensations of his condition, he felt the waves and
the billows were rolling over him; and in the darkness and
deeps of the bottom of the sea, there seemed no room for a
ray of hope. Then he remembered the Lord, whom he had
forsaken. Yet why had he ever forgotten Him?

Here let us pause for a moment to consider the exact state
of this case, for it is illustrative of innumerable others. Jonah
had only been required to do a very proper, a very reasonable,
and a very merciful thing. The Divine tenderness honoured
him with the commission of rescuing a vast community from
sin and impending ruin. What was there in this from which a
prophet ought to have fled? It was an errand full of mercy,
and no doubt would be full of blessing. But self-willed Jonah
would not have it. What trouble he took to escape it!
Jonah was typical of his nation. He would have no dealings
with the Gentiles. A vast city was there, crowded with inhabitants—with women and children—almost a kingdom in itself.

But Jonah was hard and unfeeling towards them, and to avoid being employed on a work of mercy towards them, he would fly even to the ends of the earth—for such Tarshish was then considered.

There are many mysteries in the world, many mysteries of things in heaven and things on earth; but one of the mysteries most inscrutable of all, is the mystery of human folly—the astonishing fatuity by which great numbers take incredible pains, and persist with pertinacious obstinacy, to inflict upon themselves palpable misery and bitter and lasting ruin. In the depth of his despair Jonah discovered this, and cried out, "They who follow lying vanities forsake their own mercy." How stupid was the "lying vanity" to which he had given himself. He would not do the work of brotherly love the Divine Father of all had laid out for him—had, indeed, given him the privilege to do. He would rather leave his home and country and tempt the dangers of the sea, than go and do that which was an honour, and should have been his happiness to do.

The Jewish nation was selected in like manner to receive the doctrine of the unity and universal Fatherhood of God, and the universal brotherhood of man, as well as by an elaborate symbolism to represent regeneration, and the spiritual kingdom of the Lord. They were chosen for the sake of the whole family of man, and not for themselves alone. But they did not regard it so. They shut themselves up from others, and considered Jehovah as their national God, rather than as the universal Father of mankind. They treated other nations as heathens, and often with contempt and hatred. The result was isolation and hatred for themselves. Their religious system became thus to them merely a sectarian scheme, a system of science rather than of brotherly love. They were absorbed in the requirements of this system, doing their round of observances, detailing and practising their traditions, rather than purifying their hearts, and living and working in the generous sympathies of mutual love.

As this state of self-seclusion grew upon them, as they shut themselves up more and more in selfish isolation, their condition became narrower, darker, stormier, more cold-blooded, until at length they were shut out from other nations, and then divided from one another. A very small proportion confined their esteem to themselves alone, and there were no dealings even between the Jews and the Samaritans (John iv. 9). They made the commandments of God, those broad, grand laws of heaven, of none effect by their traditions. They were great at tithes of mint, anise, and cummin, but very small at judgment, charity, mercy, and faith (Matt. xxiii. 23). Such a close, flat, flabby, cold, and narrow life, dark, conceited, and confined, destitute of the gushing energies which flow from a warm love of God, and a glowing charity to all mankind, is like the half-life of a man enclosed in a fish.

If we could discern with the spiritual eye the spheres of men, and groups of men, as expressed by their moral conditions, we should behold strange forms unveiling themselves before us. The dragon, out of whose mouth John says he saw three unclean spirits like frogs come forth (Rev. xvi. 13), can surely only mean a presentation to his spiritual sight of a selfish hypocritical system, which sends forth croaking assailants of the noble principles which constitute genuine Christianity. The Egyptians, as they became when they secluded themselves in their religious system, and prided themselves in their abundant and curious knowledge, were regarded by Ezekiel as a great dragon-like fish. Their religion was all allegory and ceremony, derived from previous revelation, not, as they imagined, self-originated. They exulted, however, in their system for its own sake, and prided themselves simply because they knew it, and because it was theirs, and they are therefore thus described and denounced by the prophet: "Speak, and say, Thus saith the Lord God, Behold I am against thee, Pharoah king of Egypt, the great dragon that lieth in the midst of his rivers, which hath said, ' My river is my own, and I have made it for myself.' But I will put hooks in thy jaws, and I will cause the fish of thy rivers to stick in thy scales, and I will bring thee up out of the midst of thy rivers, and all the fish of thy rivers shall stick in thy scales. And the land of Egypt shall be desolate and waste: and they shall know that I am the Lord; because he hath said 'My river is my own, and I have made it'" (Ezek. xxix. 3, 4, 9).

In the vast sea of thought and knowledge there are abundant means of amusing the fancy of a man, and inflating his pride. He can glide about from one portion of knowledge to another, and from speculation to speculation, like a fish swimming about in the waters of truth. True life is, however, something far more than thinking. Life means evils to be corrected, and virtues to be performed. Life means duties to be done, and charities to be embodied. Life is fraught with hopes that need to be realized, with efforts and energies that should go forth to heal some of the sorrows of mankind, to make the sum total of misery less, and the amount of human enjoyment more. Men ought therefore to be up and doing, so that charity may have her perfect work, and thus follow the example and act from the power of Him who is Perfect Love, embodied in unceasing activity.

Jonah remembering the Lord represents the only course open to the Christian when he has felt his forlorn condition. He is full of penitence. He sees how much he has missed his way. Troubles and darkness surround him. The waters of sorrow and despair oppress him on every side. Chilling, harassing, depressing views succeed each other and weigh him down. Falsities gather about him, and deep revelations of interior corruption are unfolded to him. He cries like Jonah, "The waters compass me about even to the soul: the depth closed me round about, the weeds were wrapped about my head."

The Psalmist describes a similar state to that represented by Jonah: "Save me, O God; for the waters are come in upon my soul. I sink in deep mire, where there is no standing: I am come into deep waters, where the floods overflow me: I am weary of my crying: my throat is dried, mine eyes fail while I wait for my God (Ps. lxix. 1–3). Could the state described by the Psalmist be rendered visible to the spirit's eye, it would have presented a graphic form of a man enclosed in a fish, and tossed about in a stormy ocean. The thoughts are troubled and confused, the bewildered soul looks and mourns, and feebly expects, but all is dark, and no change comes. He loathes himself, he loathes his state, he feels himself like being in hell, and, indeed, he is surrounded for the time with infernal spheres, and may properly, though but temporarily, be said to be in hell. "Out of the belly of hell cried I," the prophet said, "and thou heardest my voice" (verse 2). "For great is thy mercy toward me: and thou hast delivered my soul from the lowest hell" (Ps. lxxxvi. 13).

One thing, however, was ground for hope. There was still some life,—that is, some love. "Yet hast thou brought up MY LIFE from corruption, O Lord my God." In spiritual things, as in natural things, while there is life there is hope. Persons in periods of temptation, and deep and lengthened trial, may be infested with thoughts, impressions, and persuasions, strange, low, impure, corrupt, and altogether foreign to their disposition, and this for weeks and months together; yet if these are regarded with aversion, and the heart turns from them with horror and grief, deliverance will surely come. It is love that decides the character. What we really love will assuredly mould all our faculties, and our very form itself, to its own likeness. Hence Jonah said, "Thou hast brought up MY LIFE from corruption." Let the LOVE, the inner LIFE, be kept pure, let the inner affections of the heart yearn and pray for salvation, and undoubtedly it will come. No person can be in a more unlikely place to be heard than Jonah, yet he was heard and delivered. The soul fainted, yet the life was preserved. The intellect was enfeebled and oppressed, yet the love was preserved, and salvation surely arrived. We remember the Lord, and we find He has never forgotten us. We have said in our bitterness—

> "I would but cannot love,
> Though woo'd by love divine:
> No arguments have power to move,
> In such a state as mine."

Yet we may be comforted by the assurance that if the love of goodness and truth remains, the jewel, the heart of the soul, is safe, and the long winter of our misery will be transformed into a glorious summer.

> "But if indeed I would,
> Though nothing I can do,
> Yet the desire is something good,
> For which my praise is due."

The Lord is near, the angels are near us, though unseen. Our sincere prayer reaches them. Heaven is meant by the Lord's temple, for it is filled with His adoration and praise. Our prayer reaches unto His holy temple, for the blessed ones have charge over us, sympathise with us, and rejoice in our humility and penitence. Our prayers announce the states into which the Divine blessings can descend.

To come even into the temple of the Lord, in its highest application, is to be received by the Lord in His Divine humanity. The Lord God Almighty and the Lamb are the temple of it. We may be assured that every prayer of sincerity reaches the ear and the heart of Him in whom dwells all the fulness of the Godhead bodily, and who is constantly saying, "Come unto Me all ye that labour and are heavy laden, and I will give you rest."

Jonah learned a great truth besides that of the ineffable kindness and pity of the All-good to the sufferer—namely, that the highest mercy is to keep man in order, and to restore him to order if he has departed from it. Mercy is extended to all finite creatures at all times, from the highest angel to the lowest subject of the King of kings. Our holy things need to be viewed by mercy, to pardon their shortcomings. And although it is mercy which touches our failings with a tender hand, it is also even fuller mercy when the righteous are rewarded according to their works (Ps. lxii. 12). It is not to any merit of ours, or of the highest seraph, that the riches of heavenly peace and joy are imparted, but only that to heavenly-minded ones, though still imperfect, Mercy can bestow angelic bliss. He charges His angels with folly; but His angels see and shun and detest their folly, keeping self under their feet, abiding in Him, and His Divine Love and Wisdom abiding in them.

It is merciful to impart to a suffering wayfarer a little help for present needs, and to alleviate immediate sorrow; but how much greater is the mercy which takes the erring one by the hand, strengthens and guides his feeble virtue, restores him to order, and preserves him in constant well-being. The higher the angel and the greater the mercy he feels, and he adores. "Holy, holy, holy, Lord God Almighty, who was and is and is to come. Just and true are Thy ways, thou King of Saints. Who shall not fear Thee O Lord, and glorify Thy name; for Thou ONLY art holy." Such are the confessions of all the blessed. The adoring seraph covers his face. The higher in grace and the deeper in humility are all the inhabitants of heaven. They follow Divine truths, and thus are preserved, elevated, and blessed by Infinite Mercy. Mercy framed the heavens, mercy redeemed and regenerated every angel of heaven, and mercy imparts to each one, according to his capacity, eternal peace and joy. The things which induce men to forsake THEIR OWN MERCY, are, indeed, LYING VANITIES, as Jonah came to see by bitter experience.

What a lying vanity is pride! It fills the heart of its possessor with vain phantasies of his self-sufficiency—of self-sufficiency when he knows his heart would not beat once, nor one breath remain a moment, if a power higher than his own, were for one moment withdrawn. Yet this lying vanity makes its possessor insolent, ambitious, envious, anxious, suspicious, defiant against God, and rebellious in opposition to the blessed commandments which mercy has imparted as the means of wisdom, health, happiness, and heaven. For this "lying vanity" thousands forsake their own mercy. What a "lying vanity" is inordinate worldly love. The preference of glitter and show for a moment, over the solid worth of spiritual graces and heavenly gifts, which endure for ever; of a fleeting earth to an everlasting heaven, is a folly so great that did we not know it as a common fact, we might well be incredulous of its possibility. Yet, for this lying vanity, myriads forsake their own mercy. What a "lying vanity" is impure pleasure! It promises bliss, and it leads to pain. It spreads before its dupes dreams of passionate enjoyment, it allures by phantoms of gorgeous felicity, of degraded but voluptuous and extatic bliss, and the reality is broken character, broken fortune, broken health, decay, imbecility, ruin, death, fiendishness. Oh may we shun these "lying vanities," and follow for ever that true wisdom which is from above, and which purifies, enriches, and ennobles both soul and body. Let us bless that unutterable mercy which has provided a shining way along which the humble tread, which leads to "Whatsoever things are true, whatsoever things are honest, whatsoever things are just, whatsoever things are pure, whatsoever things are lovely, whatsoever things are of good report," and conducts its lowly but pure-hearted traveller into the higher country of his Saviour, the realm of endless peace.

SERMON XLIV.

THE REPENTANCE OF NINEVEH.

"And God saw their works, that they turned from their evil way; and God repented of the evil that He had said that He would do unto them."—JONAH iii. 10.

THE fundamental error which the book of Jonah is designed to correct, is that God was concerned with the Jews only, and His mercies and His laws had no relation to the world at large. Nineveh, the magnificent capital of the proud empire of Assyria, then in its greatest glory and extent, represented the world outside of Judea. The world of Assyria, as seen in its metropolis, loaded with wealth and glittering with splendour, was giving itself to wild indulgence, giddy mirth, forgetful of the great aims of life; was flitting from one gay scene to another, until all serious purpose was lost in sensuous profusion and unprincipled extravagance. Let us eat and drink, dress and pamper ourselves, lead dainty lives, and disdain all useful pursuits, esteeming those who follow them as the meaner herd, whose business in life it is to minister to our pleasures and passions. Such were the thoughts of the gay crowds of Nineveh in olden times, even as of those of many a modern capital.

All this may go on for a time, for man is a wonderful being, not easily spoiled; but when principle has been dethroned, and lawless luxury is the passion of the hour, the wheels of the chariot of judgment will be heard in the distance by the ear of the wise; and if repentance—real repentance—come not, the day of chastisement will arise. "Know, O man, that for all these things God will bring thee to judgment." By Divine mercy and forbearance it may seem that judgment is long deferred, but it will surely come. For men and nations the law is precisely the same: "If thou doest well, shalt thou not be accepted? and if thou doest not well, sin lieth at the door" (Gen. iv. 7).

Because Jonah conceived that God had no concern with Ninevites, or others than Jews, he avoided the duty which the Divine command had given him to perform. To teach him and us that the law is universal, God enforced his going, and manifested that He was good to all, and His tender mercies are over all His works. Jonah, however, not only exhibited repugnance to go on the mission Divine Providence had allotted to him, but manifested his narrowness of character in the lamentation he made when the threatened overthrow of Nineveh was averted by the repentance of the people, high and low, from the king to his meanest subject.

Jonah was more concerned for his message than for the safety and wellbeing of that vast multitude of people. "And he prayed unto the Lord and said, I pray Thee, O Lord, was not this my saying when I was yet in my country? Therefore I fled before unto Tarshish: for I knew that Thou art a gracious God, and merciful, slow to anger, and of great kindness, and repentest Thee of the evil. Therefore now, O Lord, take, I beseech Thee, my life from me; for it is better for me to die than to live." What a strange complaint, and what a perverse conclusion! Surely the object of his mission was warning and repentance, not merely to announce destruction. The end was most successfully accomplished, and yet here is this poor prophet filled with a sense of his own importance, and bewailing the fact that, from the goodness of God, penitent Nineveh was not to be destroyed. That was just cause for gratitude and thanksgiving, not for lamentation.

The prophet Jonah, however, was the type of the Jewish Church in their narrowness and bigotry. He valued the means more than the end; he wanted to have his consistency and importance secured, although men, women, and children should perish in myriads. Not so, however, with Divine mercy. It is the goodness of God which leads man to repentance. The Sabbath was made for man, the Church was made for man, the Word was given for man, the ministry exists for man, the world itself and heaven exist that men may become angels, and ever-increasing multitudes become everlastingly happy. The pharisaic system, which cared more for the sect than for the people, more for the ceremony than for regeneration, more for the Church than for man, was never any part of the Divine government. Through varied means ever to operate to attain the end in view, and that end to rescue as many as possible from the dominion of sin, such has ever been the design of the Most High, who is the Most Merciful. Such will ever be the aim of those whose hearts beat in harmony with Him Who desires not the death of a sinner, but that all should turn to Him and live.

THE REPENTANCE OF NINEVEH. 347

Jonah complained that his warning, "Yet forty days, and Nineveh shall be overthrown," was not fulfilled to the letter. But as a prophet, and as an Israelite, he should have known that all warnings and all promises are conditional. Whether expressed or not, there underlay the warning that Nineveh should be overthrown, the condition, unless it repented. How plainly this is stated in the prophecy of Jeremiah: "At what instant I shall speak concerning a nation, and concerning a kingdom, to pluck up and to pull down, and to destroy it. If that nation against whom I have pronounced turn from their evil, I will repent of the evil that I thought to do unto them. And at what instant I shall speak concerning a nation and concerning a kingdom to build and to plant it: if it do evil in my sight, that it obey not my voice, then I will repent of the good wherewith I said I would benefit them." It was simply in harmony with this well-known principle that penitent Nineveh was spared, and most unreasonable as well as pitiless was it of the prophet to seek that his consistency should be maintained even if a whole repentant people perished.

At the same time we have a lesson for all time of the efficacy of repentance, and its indispensable character. Repent and live; repent not, and you will assuredly perish. This doctrine of repentance is often evaded at the present day, but in the nature of things it is the only way to happiness. Prophets, Apostles, and the Divine Saviour himself declare, "Except ye repent, ye shall all likewise perish." The universal necessity for repentance arises from the fact that all men are born with tendencies to evil, and all suffer themselves, more or less, to go into actual sin. "All we like lost sheep have gone astray." "All have sinned, and come short of the glory of God." All do wrong—one in one way, and another in another; but all feel within them capacities for still greater wrong. If the law and usages of society did not restrain men generally, we should be appalled at the infernal nature which would manifest itself where now things appear tolerably smooth and decorous. In a seditious riot, or the sack of a city after a siege, when authority is briefly suspended, the wild lusts which rush forth for insane gratification tell of the smouldering fires of horrid passion which are usually hidden under a decent exterior.

Thus it is that society presents so strange a mixture of virtue and vice, order and disorder, beauty and deformity, joy and sorrow. Minds are mixed. There is something from heaven -- the remains of man's once-glorious nature, the ground of conscience—still within, and giving to every one the capacity to receive truth, to reform, become regenerate, and eventually be an angel in heaven. But equally, it must be confessed, there is in every one a nature which is carnal, sensual, and devilish. In this part of man's compound being SELF reigns king, a very MOLOCH. The trail of the serpent is over it all. A dreadful hierarchy surround the throne of King Self: ambition, pride, envy, hate, greed, lust, anarchy, pollution, falsity, revenge, remorse, with thousands of subordinates, occupy this portion of the territory of Mansoul. From these rebellion and opposition arise from time to time; and until this lower region of the nature of man is subdued, reformed, and regenerated, there can be no true and lasting peace in the soul, no lasting order or happiness at home or in the world.

After the knowledge of God and His Divine will, as embodied in His blessed commandments, exists with us, responded to as it is by the impulses of conscience within, the first decisive step in the way to heaven is repentance. We examine ourselves, and see, by the light of the Divine law, in what we do wrong. Do we set pride where the Saviour should be, fashion for faith? Do we neglect the Word of God or the worship of God? Do we prefer the world to heaven? Do we injure others in mind, body, or estate? Are we unjust to the claims of duty and honesty? Are we careless of truth when we think lies or prevarications would better serve our purpose? Are we envious or covetous of what is possessed by others? These are the inquiries to be made honestly by one who desires genuine repentance, and he will not fail to find wherein he has done amiss. By the law is the knowledge of sin. With the knowledge of sin will come the knowledge of the consequences of sin—depravity of the soul, the wreck of peace, being shut out of heaven, everlasting ruin. The more we ponder over these, the more shall we be filled with sorrow, even to anguish and despair, while we are led to "the Saviour, the Living God, who is the Saviour of all men, and specially of those that believe."

We must not confound sorrow with repentance. Genuine sorrow leads to repentance, but it is not itself repentance. Repentance is CHANGE OF MIND, manifested by change of conduct. It is willing not to do the evil things we have done, because they are sins against God, proved by actual change. Cease to do evil, learn to do well. Genuine repentance will be attended by severe struggles in proportion as the evil has been long rooted and much practised; yet with faithfulness to truth and perseverance there is no evil, however inveterate, but can be fully subdued, and the soul be saved alive.

To acquire spiritual victories over ourselves—the most real and true victories that are achieved in the world—there must be no illusions, no substitutions, no hiding our sinful propensities from ourselves, but honest confession and honest change. We must really do as they did at Nineveh, TURN FROM OUR EVIL WAY. If we have cherished pride or vanity, we must do so no more. If we have blasphemed, we must swear no more. If we have lied, we must be true and frank ; we must prevaricate no more. If we have been peevish and violent, we must become gentle, courteous, and considerate. If we have sought dishonest advantages, we must become fair, upright, and true to every engagement, in every office, duty, and employment. Only thus will genuine repentance proceed. Everything less than this is only imposing upon ourselves. "When the wicked man turneth away from his wickedness that he hath committed, and doeth that which is lawful and right, HE SHALL SAVE HIS SOUL ALIVE. Because he considereth, and turneth away from all his transgressions that he hath committed, HE SHALL SURELY LIVE, HE SHALL NOT DIE" (Ezek. xviii. 27-28).

These lessons are so plainly and so palpably the dictates of common sense, as well as the direct teachings of Scripture, that we are amazed at objections being made to them, yet objections are widespread and frequent. The selfish, natural man will strive to change anything but himself. To avoid this he will turn, and argue, and wrangle to the last hour, and then expect to be changed by a prayer or a belief at his last gasp. His secret belief is that what is wanted is to change God and make Him favourable, and then he will be allowed to enter heaven ; and then he proceeds to devise how it can be done. Some imagine delinquencies in the week can be made up for by attendances at meetings, and what are called the means of religion, while their native greed, covered by a plan of religion, grows on during life, and they become hard gripping masses of selfishness, miserable in themselves, and close and bitter enemies of all who are not subservient to their gains. Others suppose that certain ceremonies of religion and the verbal assurance of forgivenness by a priest will make them all right; and when they have made what they call a clean breast of it, they have done what religion requires, and go and indulge their appetites and their passions again, thus staving off that inward change of heart, mind, and life which introduces heaven at home, and thus prepares for heaven hereafter.

A third class, and that a very demonstrative one at the present day, for real repentance, substitute what they call faith—a very small faith—a belief of the one fact that the Lord Jesus died to save sinners, and to save them individually, and this belief only secures the favour of God, and brings forth of necessity all manner of good works. It is perfectly true that the Lord Jesus died to save sinners, and every one may add with devout gratitude, to save every man, and to SAVE ME; but it was to enable me to repent, and to win my heart that I might be induced to repent. If, unhappily, I substitute this condescension of Infinite Mercy for my duty of repentance, I am destroying myself by the very means of help. The Lord Jesus, after His resurrection, sent forth His disciples, "That repentance and remission of sins should be preached in His name, among all nations, beginning at Jerusalem" (Luke xxiv. 47). He exalted Himself "to be a Prince and a Saviour, to give repentance to Israel, and forgiveness of sins" (Acts v. 31). The Lord is not slack concerning His promise, as some men count slackness; but is long-suffering to usward, not willing that any should perish, but that ALL SHOULD COME TO REPENTANCE (2 Peter iii. 9). "As many as I love I rebuke and chasten: be zealous therefore and repent" (Rev. iii. 19). "Repent, or else I will come unto thee quickly, and will fight against them with the sword of my mouth." "Remember therefore from whence thou art fallen, and repent and do the first works: or else I will come unto thee quickly, and will remove thy candlestick out of its place."

Indeed, the indispensable character of repentance is insisted upon by every part of the Word—Law, Prophets, and Gospel. The Lord Jesus constantly preached repentance, and exhorted men to bring forth fruits meet for REPENTANCE. It is said, however, that this particular faith will of itself produce the rejection of all evil, and perfect obedience to the Divine commandments, and yet we are often told, and the burden of half the sermons in thousands of pulpits is, that no one can keep God's commandments either with or without this faith. It is said that God's commandments are something so hard, and so extensive, and so difficult, that no one has kept them, or can keep them. But how contrary this is from the representations of the Divine Word, and from the very nature of things, a very little consideration will clearly show. God's commandments are the laws of right. Is right really so much harder than wrong? Is speaking the truth so much harder than speaking lies? Is a career of honesty harder than a career of crime? Is a life of pollution, with broken health, broken character, and a depraved mind, really easier than a course of virtue, purity, and chaste feeling? Has it ceased to be true "that the way of transgressors is hard"? Does the Almighty no longer say to the wicked man, "Thine own wickedness shall correct thee, and thy backslidings shall reprove thee: know therefore and see that it is an evil thing and bitter that thou hast forsaken the Lord thy God, and that My fear is not in thee"? Have our Lord's words really ceased to be true—"My yoke is easy, and My burden is light?" Indeed, all the talk of many preachers, who are very zealous but very unwise, is really a libel upon the Divine Majesty they desire to serve, as if He had made a universe that will not work by the laws upon which he constructed it, that evil beats Him in His own field of operations, and He can only get men into heaven on another plan.

But it is not true that the way of righteousness is hard, or that repentance is difficult to the person who is genuine and sincere. Let a person pray before the Lord Jesus for help against his sins, and avoid the temptation to commit it, and help will be given. He must not let his mind hanker after it, though his feet may be turned in another direction. He must turn his mind away, and shun his old associates, and the scenes of former indulgences, praying the Lord to give a new heart and a right spirit, and after a little perseverance he will find he loathes what he once loved, and loves what he once loathed. The Divine aid will be given him, and the Divine benediction will make him happy. The slain lion of his sin will soon be found full of honey. His wilderness will smile like Eden, and his desert like the garden of the Lord. Joy and gladness shall be found therein, thanksgiving, and the voice of melody. The heart of the true penitent will soon be filled with love, his mind with light, and his life with virtue. He must not, however, suppose that these things will come of themselves. Faith will not produce good works of itself. Faith alone will produce nothing; it is itself dead. Faith, warmed with love, will show the Lord the fountain of goodness, will teach what to shun, and what to do, and throw light over every motive to virtue, and then we must work out our salvation with fear and trembling. We must work, because it is right to work. We must work until we delight to work in the service of Him who is always working for us. We must work until it is our very heaven to do our Heavenly Father's will. And this will come, for in doing His commandments there is great reward. "Let your light so shine before men, that they may see your good works, and glorify your Father, Who is in heaven."

If in the early days of your repentance you slip and fall, try again. The child seldom learns to walk without a fall or two. Try again. Look in hope and confidence to the Saviour God, and keep as far as possible from temptation, praying earnestly for Divine assistance, and you will conquer again and again, until you can not only walk in the path to heaven, but run. "They that wait upon the Lord shall renew their strength; they shall mount up with wings as eagles, they shall run and not be weary, and they shall walk and not faint." Let the repentant sinner look to his compassionate Saviour, and his very nature will become transformed. He will eat the Saviour's flesh, and drink His blood. His Divine goodness and wisdom will be imparted to him, and he will realize His image and likeness. He will become a little heaven, and thus prepare for the greater. He will receive heaven into him, and thus learn by sure experience that heaven will receive him into it. Of the Ninevites it is said that God repented of the evil that He had said He would do unto them. This is, however, only the language of appearance. God never does evil to any. God never repents (Num. xxiii. 19; 1 Sam. xv. 29). Because God maintains the wise and righteous laws by violation of which the wicked endure punishment, He is said to punish them. The real truth is, they punish themselves. The sun is said to torture the inflamed eye. Remove the disease, and the same sun delights and cheers. So when Nineveh repented, the evils passed away, and God, whom their sins had hidden behind a lurid cloud, now came forth in brightness and in blessing. To them it seemed that God had repented. The reality was that God, who had been waiting to be gracious, could now shed abroad upon them His grace and peace. Let the sinner turn from his evil way, from faith in His Saviour, who is a Father of love, and to him the Sun of Righteousness will arise with healing in His wings.

JONAH AND THE GOURD.

"Then said the Lord, Thou hast had pity on the gourd, for the which thou hast not laboured, neither madest it grow; which came up in a night, and perished in a night: And should not I spare Nineveh, that great city, wherein are more than sixscore thousand persons that cannot discern between their right hand and their left hand; and also much cattle."—JONAH iv. 10, 11.

DIVINE Mercy had warned and preserved the great city of Nineveh, but the narrow-hearted prophet Jonah was disappointed and angry. He would rather his consistency had been maintained, although a whole people had perished. He had gone to the outside of Nineveh. He made a small booth to shield him from the hot rays of the sun, and watched and waited to see what would be the fate of the city. The day was hot, and the prophet vexed, fretful, and weary. After one day thus spent, during the night there grew up a plant of the melon or calabash kind, with green wide-spreading leaves, and this gave an agreeable shelter to the prophet for another day. Another night came, and as it passed into morning the gourd, so grateful to the heat-harassed prophet, was seen to have lost its vigour; it was blighted by a worm, and no longer lent its pleasant shade. It was dead. Fainting beneath the breath of the hot wind, the prophet wished to die. He was disappointed and forlorn; he could see no use in his life. He was despairing, and sighed to quit his post. Like many a weary soul deficient in faith, he had not yet learned submission and confidence, and pined and prayed that his toil and his life might end, as if He who gives our life, and sees our future, did not best know the time, place, and way in which to draw it to a close.

God is said to have prepared the gourd, and prepared the worm, and also the vehement east wind which the prophet felt to be so distressing, because He intended to give Jonah a lesson, and through him to give a lesson to all who would narrow Divine mercies to their own little stand-point, and to teach that all mankind are His children, for whom He cares. Each community, each dispensation, each section of mankind, has its own work and its ministration to do, but not for itself only. It is part of that grand whole, that entire humanity, which the Eternal governs with equal wisdom, and regards with equal love. Jonah was the representative of the Jewish nation in its exclusiveness and intolerance towards others. He would have nothing to do with the nations around if he could help it. Such was the feeling of the Jewish Church. How unworthily this sectarian exclusiveness was, the Lord taught the prophet, by representing the church he loved as a gourd, a mere temporary plant, which speedily lives and speedily dies, not a grand enduring thing at all. It sprang up in a night, and it perished in a night. To show the unworthiness and smallness of the bigoted sentiment, the Lord secondly led him to consider that as he loved his gourd which had interested his affections, although it had grown up without his labour, had been so temporary, and was so slight, how could he fail to see that the Universal Father must love the vast multitude WHOM HE HAD MADE, and who in their weakness and their ignorance so much needed His mercy and His care.

We have said the Jewish Church was like a gourd. Its growth was quick, it had an imposing appearance, but it was not solid; in fact, was not a real, enduring church at all. It had a shadow of good things. It was a figure of the true, but it was only a figure. It was as a gourd is to the nobler trees, the olive, the vine, the fig, or the timber trees. It was a gourd that grew up in a night. The outward circumcision was not that inward purification which a real church requires—the circumcision of the heart. The sacrifices of lambs, sheep, goats, bulls, were but coarse things for worship, though they were the necessary symbols of the affections which offer the sacrifices of thanksgiving, the offerings of self-dedication, the worship of the broken and the contrite heart. The elaborate and minute ceremonies, the numerous statutes, the hierarchial and decorated priesthood, and indeed all the arrangements of Israel in Canaan, were expedient for a time, until the Divine Saviour should bring glad tidings of great joy, which should be for all people; tidings of fatherhood for all men, brotherhood for all men, regeneration for all the obedient, and heaven for all who would live for it.

The Jewish Church, like the gourd, grew up in a night. It was a dark night indeed of idolatry, superstition, and depravity when that church was founded, and long centuries were to pass on before men could learn to worship their heavenly Father in spirit and in truth. Even a poor literal symbol of a church must be endured until the fulness of time should come, the dark midnight when men became even false to their symbols, and substituted their own miserable traditions, making the commandments of God, even as they understood them, of none effect. They would then go down in a night, and a new day from the Sun of Righteousness would dawn upon the world. How accurately the gourd, a sort of great herb, represents the Jewish Church, and its very external character will be evident if we reflect that the noble and enduring trees correspond to the interior and enduring principles of Christian love, Christian faith, Christian virtue, and Christian intelligence. Thus the two olive trees which Zechariah saw in vision, right and left of the golden candlestick which poured forth golden oil, and which are said to stand by the Lord of the whole earth (iv. 14), can be no other than the two grand affections of love to God and love to man, from which the sacred oil, the golden oil of sympathy, diffuses itself among mankind. That oil softens every asperity, heals every wound, and fills the hearts of men with joy (Isa. lxi. 3). These are the two olive trees which no man must kill, or he will spiritually kill himself, and shut up heaven against him (Rev. xi. 5, 6).

The vine, too, which produces the wine which "cheers both God and man," corresponds to the faith which imparts confidence, makes the eye gleam with victory, and inspires with hope, exhilaration, and the foretaste of peace. "I am the vine," said the Lord Jesus, "ye are the branches. He that abideth in Me, and I in him, the same bringeth forth much fruit, for without Me ye can do nothing" (John xv. 15). This faith is the tree, whose seed is at first the smallest of all seeds, the faith which is like the mustard seed, minute, but warm, and which, as we are faithful, grows up, expands its principles like branches, until they protect and bless the whole mind. The fig tree, though it produces less precious fruit, still brings forth fruit, and corresponds to that obedience in daily life which induces honesty, integrity, usefulness, without which society is unstable, like a house without solid foundations.

> "Religion's path they never trod,
> Who equity contemn;
> Nor ever are they just to God,
> Who prove unjust to men."

When Jesus found no fruit upon the fig tree, He said, "Let

no fruit grow on thee henceforward and for ever." If there were none of the lower virtues, it was quite useless to expect the higher.

Even the timber trees correspond to great principles of understanding which grow up in the intellect, and make the mind like a goodly park, diversified by pastures of instructive nutriment, unfoldings of glorious perceptions, and grand developments of thought. "I will set in the desert the fir tree, the pine and the box tree together, that they may see and know and understand together that the hand of the Lord hath done this, and the Holy One of Israel hath created it" (Isa. xli. 19, 20). The trees which are to be planted to enable us to see and know and understand together, can only be such trees as grow from the seed of the Word of God (Luke viii. 11), and tend to make the soul like a watered garden, as the Lord promised by the prophet (Isa. lviii. 11).

All the trees, however, which we have enumerated, and which correspond to grand interior principles, are firm, enduring, noble trees, which are not only valuable by their fruits, but endure for ages. The gourd is a very different production, and when the gourd was presented to Jonah as the symbol of that system or dispensation he so much loved, it was to intimate its temporary and inferior character. It grew up in a night, it would perish in a night. It was an agreeable shade while it lasted. It was an assurance of the Divine protection in the storms of life, and from the hot breath of ambition which blew from the world around them, in which proud conquerors trampled on subject and subjugated nations, but it would serve only for the little day of human life. It concerned this world only. Its rewards were temporal, its punishments temporal. If they were willing and obedient, they would eat the fruit of the land; but if they refused and rebelled, they would perish by the sword, for the mouth of the Lord had spoken it (Isa. i. 19, 20).

The Israelitish dispensation, so far as it was merely national and purely Jewish, was a gourd, a temporary expedient among people essentially external and interiorly idolatrous, whose aims, even in religion, were to be great, rather than good—who sought by worshipping God to abound in temporal wealth. Such a dispensation could only be of a transient kind. It was a figure, as the Apostle said, "for the time then present, in which were offered both gifts and sacrifices, that could not make him that did the service perfect, as pertaining to the conscience; which stood only in meats and drinks, and divers washings and carnal ordinances, imposed on them until the time of reformation" (Heb. ix. 9, 10). Such a system must in its very nature be transient. When spiritual and eternal principles were brought in by the blessed Redeemer Himself, who was our heavenly Father, manifesting Himself in Christ, the figures would give way to the true—the shadows would pass and disappear before the splendours of a new and brighter day. The gourd would die, but the olives, the vines, and the fig-trees would flourish, and bless mankind. Yet Jonah loved his gourd, and the Jews loved deeply their Jerusalem.

Men of profounder nature can only faintly realize the intensity of feeling with which a Jew regards his ancient country. Jonah loved his gourd. Other lands may be more beautiful, more fertile, and more productive. Other nations may be, and other civilizations are more powerful; but in Jerusalem his fathers worshipped, there God manifested Himself to His people, there the temple stood, and to it all his hallowed memories fondly turn. Wherever the Jew may have been, he has still had his heart attached to Jerusalem by the most surpassing literature, the most tender and magnificent poetry in the world—the literature and the poetry in which Infinite Wisdom has enshrined diviner things. The Jew in foreign lands has been taught with deepest feeling to say, If I forget thee, O Jerusalem, let my right hand forget her cunning; if I do not remember thee, let my tongue cleave to the roof of my mouth, if I prefer not Jerusalem above my chief joy. Jonah has loved his gourd, and when it perished, as all human things perish, when they enclose in their heart of hearts the worm of gnawing selfishness, he suffered bitterly, and said, "It is better for me to die than to live." Each Jew was angry with the Divine Providence, and said "I do well to be angry even unto death."

It is to this state of mind that Divine Mercy addresses the argument of the remaining portion of the text. It is as if He said, "You are very tender and affectionate to your dispensation, for which you indeed did not labour, but which was My gift; how much more should I care for the world outside of you, to which in comparison ye are only as a gourd compared to the vast city of Nineveh? That city contains more than a million of people whom I created, and whom I every moment preserve, for 'in Me they live, and move, and have their being.' Can it be, think you, that I do not care for and love them, and the thousand millions of mankind, when I care for and love you who are so few? Look, too, at the vast number of the ignorant. In

Nineveh there are one hundred and twenty thousand persons so young, and so ignorant, that they cannot discern their right hand from their left. They are in the innocence of ignorance; must they perish in whom there is no actual sin? Know you not that 'it is not the will of your Father in heaven that one of these little ones should perish?'"

With this Divine lesson before them, is it not extraordinary that there are readers of the Bible, and professors of Christianity, who imagine that none but those who believe as they do can avoid everlasting misery? The remonstrance to Jonah, brought home to him as it was by Divine Wisdom, exhibited the error into which he had fallen, so that there was no possible reply. But what was that mistake to the monstrous idea that Infinite Mercy will make the salvation of millions upon millions of the human race to depend upon a few persons who shall go and preach to them certain opinions upon which these persons lay exaggerated stress. It is true that we read in Scripture that "without faith it is impossible to please God." But faith means the trust which makes a man faithful to what he understands to be truth. Faith is faithfulness to God and God's laws, which is shown in loving the one and obeying the other. Faith is not a set of opinions or doctrines which a person or a party may dignify with the name of the true faith; but it is a firm and faithful confidence in what a person's intellect assures him is true, and therefore he believes to be right. There is a glimmer of truth handed down from past ages in every part of the earth, however little may have been heard of the Gospel, or the name of Christian. This glimmer of truth testifies that there is a God, and that He is the rewarder of those who do His will, and shun what He declares to be wrong. He who is faithful to this has faith—it may be only as a grain of mustard seed; but it is that out of which may in good time come, as more truth is disclosed after death, if not in this world, the grand tree of a fully developed religion, under whose branches every bird of soaring heavenly thought may make its nest.

Let the cruel phantasy that God has no mercy, no pity, no love, except for Roman Catholics, or except for Protestants, or except for Methodists, or Calvinists, or some little sect, be resigned for ever. Let it die like Jonah's gourd, for in truth it is a gourd with a worm in it. Self, wrapped round with religious profession, must the conceited notion be, that God deals round His favours only to those who think as we do. "Other sheep," the Lord Jesus said, "I have, who are not of this fold; them also must I bring, and they shall hear My voice, and there shall be one fold and one shepherd" (John x. 16). "Of a truth," the Apostle Peter declared, "I perceive that God is no respecter of persons; but in every nation he that feareth Him, and worketh righteousness, is accepted of Him" (Acts x. 34, 35). In every nation, when Christianity had as yet only been preached in a few cities out of Jerusalem, and when consequently systems of idolatry prevailed almost all over the earth—notwithstanding that, in every nation those who feared God under any name, and worked righteousness, were accepted of Him. "As many who have sinned without law shall also perish without law; and as many as have sinned in the law, shall be judged by the law. For not the hearers of the law are just before God, but the doers of the law shall be justified. For when the Gentiles, who have not the law, do by nature the things contained in the law, these having not the law are a law unto themselves."

They who are faithful to the law of God as given in Judaism, or in any of the hundred forms of Christianity, or the hundred forms of Mohammedanism, or the hundred forms of Brahminism or Buddhism, will be accepted by their heavenly Father in the Eternal World, as He has fed them, and caused His sun to shine upon them in this; and the mistakes of their religious teaching will be corrected in that world, where the secrets of all hearts will be made known, and every man be rewarded according as his work shall be (Rev. xxii. 12). Jesus is still the only Saviour, for He is the only God of heaven and earth. Every man who adores God under any name, has in his secret thought the idea of God, vague or clear, in a human form, and God in a human form is the Lord Jesus Christ. All power is His, in heaven and on earth: whoever therefore prays to God for power, for light, for strength, for comfort, for progress, and feels that Divine help is given, is receiving aid from the blessed Lord and Saviour, and being saved by Him. How could the ignorant all over the world, who, like those of Nineveh, cannot discern between their right hand and left, otherwise be saved at all?

Those of this description in Nineveh were no doubt very young children; but there are multitudes in every age, and all over the world, of whom it may be said, as to their spiritual condition, they cannot discern between their right hand and their left. Vast numbers make no clear mental distinctions. They do not discriminate between what they like—which is with them at the right hand,—and what their intellect teaches should be done, but which as yet is only at their left hand. Evil impulses as yet are in the first place, the teaching of better things only in the second. They have not well weighed and discerned the immense difference between them. There is a remarkable reference to the right hand and the left in their spiritual relation in Gen. xlviii. 13, 14. In blessing the sons of Joseph, Ephraim and Manasseh, the dying patriarch Israel put his hands crosswise, his right hand on the hand of Ephraim the younger, and his left hand upon Manasseh, who was nevertheless the first-born. The spiritual lesson indicated is, that the left hand side, or the intellectual side of a man's character, must for a time take the lead, until the will is regenerated; then the right hand side will again be restored to its proper place, and what we love to do when our hearts have been regenerated will also be right to do.

At the present day, however, those who do not spiritually discern between their right hand and their left are numerous indeed. There is also much cattle. Thinking, discriminating, judging, and daring to decide, those noble human activities are avoided, and often condemned by those who should know better. They treat mankind as the common herd, as dumb driven cattle, and have so stinted them, and kept education from them, that many are very little more intelligent than the cattle they tend. There is much cattle. Numbers do not rise far above the impulses of their animal nature; yet the Lord, in His mercy, cares for them all. Infinite Love—Love itself embodied in the Lord Jesus—pities them, spares them, in a thousand ways arranges circumstances to favour the highest possible good for them. Let us then in all things adore the Divine Goodness and Providence. "Bless the Lord, all His works in all places of His dominion: bless the Lord, O my soul!"

SERMON XLVI.

DANIEL AND HIS THREE COMPANIONS IN THE PALACE AT BABYLON.

"Now among these were of the children of Judah, Daniel, Hananiah, Mishael, and Azariah: Unto whom the prince of the eunuchs gave names, for he gave unto Daniel the name of Belteshazzar, and to Hananiah of Shadrach, and to Mishael of Meshach, and to Azariah of Abednego."—DANIEL i. 6, 7.

ONE of the marks of sterling worth in a man, is the courage to do rightly and to live modestly in the midst of fashionable splendour and luxurious indulgence. To choose and to follow the true path in ordinary circumstances is virtuous and commendable; for in all conditions there are temptations to hinder progress, and in all characters weaknesses to guard, which need care and fortitude, if we would walk steadily on the path that leads to life. But, in the palace of a great king, where superabundance invites to ease and self-indulgence; where wealth clothes itself with magnificence, and the vain and the ostentatious assemble, and claim the court as their own peculiar arena, to deviate from fashion is to provoke dislike. However meekly virtue may bear itself among glittering crowds, its purity is felt as a reproach, and hence it needs a high degree of courage to be simple without singularity, to be just, temperate, true, conscientious, and modest, in an atmosphere tainted with prodigality, flattery, and parade.

Daniel and his youthful friends exhibited this rare virtue. The court of Nebuchadnezzar must have been an extremely brilliant one. Babylon stood unrivalled in the days of that mighty monarch, the capital of a vast empire, upon which genius and wealth had combined to lavish all their embellishments. The grandeur which art had there exhibited, especially in the great extension effected by Nebuchadnezzar, has excited the admiration of ancient historians, as we find it inflated with pride the great king himself, when he uttered the memorable words, "Is not this great Babylon, that I have built for the house of the kingdom, by the might of my power, and for the honour of my majesty."

Daniel and his companions had been selected from the crowd of captives from Jerusalem, and treated with tenderness, and might thus have been expected to be induced by gratitude to fall into the habits of those around them, especially when those habits were such as to commend themselves to thoughtless gaiety and youthful inexperience. But Daniel and his three friends were a model to young men. They shewed how great men—true men—are made. They were abstemious amidst abundance; self-denying and thoughtful, where they were moved to be giddy and reckless; determined to preserve themselves pure and unspotted in the world. Thus, as in the case of Joseph, their great ancestor, did noble youth lead to noble manhood, and Babylon, in the proudest noontide of its glory, saw young men walking firmly amidst its blandishments, true to their God, and faithful in their obedience to His Divine Will.

Jerusalem had been overthrown, her temple ruined, and the fire no longer burned on the sacred altar; but these youths were exhibiting amidst Gentile voluptuousness their nation's truest glory, the glory of training men to serve the Living God. From such men in due time would restoration come. To avoid stimulating food, and especially stimulating drinks, is ever the path of safety for young men. The strong health, the bounding energy, the warm passions of youth, need no extra stimulation, and a sound body, the chaste but vigorous dwelling-place of a sound mind, the abode of health, and the servant of the soul, is best secured, as in the case of these noble Hebrew youths, on plain but sufficient food.

The history of Daniel and his friends, illustrates also the arrangements of Divine Providence, in preserving always a virtuous remnant, from which, as seed, when one dispensation of religion has ended, another can take its rise. Infinite Mercy and Truth are never left without a witness in the world. The Lord's flock may thus become a little flock, but the promise is nevertheless given, "Fear not, little flock, it is your Father's good pleasure to give you the kingdom." This provision of a virtuous few, the remnant or the remains of a dispensation which has in general lost its light, its strength, and its goodness, is frequently referred to in the Word. "Except the Lord had left unto us a very small remnant, we should have been as Sodom, and we should have been like unto Gomorrah" (Isa. i. 9). "And the remnant that is escaped of the house of Judah, shall again take root downward, and bear fruit upward: for out of Jerusalem shall go forth a remnant, and they that escape out of Mount Zion: the zeal of the Lord of Hosts shall do this" (Isa. xxxvii. 31, 32).

There is a beautiful account in the prophecy of Micah of the blessed influence on the world at large of a truly heavenly-minded few. They make little noise, and no ostentation. They rather do great things than talk them. They are modest and gentle, but they are the "salt of the earth." "And the remnant of Jacob shall be in the midst of many people, AS A DEW from the Lord, as the showers upon the grass, that tarrieth not for man, nor waiteth for the sons of men" (Micah v. 7). The remnant tarrieth not for men, but they wait upon the Lord and renew their strength. They ask neither councils, parliaments, nor congresses what they ought to believe, but they meditate upon the Word of the Lord day and night. They are the poor in spirit, whose is the kingdom of heaven. They are the pure in heart, who see God. They follow not a multitude to do evil. They are content to be right with two or three, rather than wrong with all the world. Daniel and his companions were the remnant still left of Israelites indeed, and the Lord honoured and blessed them, as He always will those who maintain His truth against popular error and popular guilt. They may be a poor and despised minority for a considerable time, but minorities who love and follow the truth are honoured as the creators of majorities in after days, and the Lord will remember them in the day that He makes up His jewels (Mal. iii. 17).

Let us take these lessons from the letter of the Divine Word; especially let the young keep before their minds the pure youth, the noble manhood, and the grand career of Daniel and his young friends, that they too may become strengthened in the path of purity and right, bear witness for the truth, like Joseph, Daniel, and a long line of worthy youths, be examples of all that is good in manhood, and through a saintly old age, make the last preparation for heaven.

Let us now rise to contemplate this Divine history in its higher and more spiritual point of view. For Israel's contact with Babylon is fraught with instruction, and with warning for every age. The earthly Babylon, in its greedy ambition, its wide-spread dominion, its vast extent, its unparalleled pomp and splendour, its hierarchy of priests, and its priest-king—for the King of Babylon was supreme Pontiff of Nebo, the sun-god, as appears from his history now deciphered in the arrow-headed characters disentombed from buried Chaldea—was in all respects the antitype of the mystic Babylon which St. John saw in vision, and which has displayed itself in Christianity in awful lineaments of superstition and cruelty, too palpable to be ever mistaken or forgotten.

Babylon was the type of the lust of spiritual dominion, seeking power at first by a diligent acquisition of the knowledge of holy things, and a great zeal in the ministration of the ceremonies and the externals of religion. Babylon can receive the truth, and be most vehement in the proclamation of it, can be most zealous for souls, and for the progress of religion, and yet the real source of all this zeal, be lust of power. Babylon is called the Lucifer, the light-bearer, the son of the morning, on account of this pristine zeal for religion. Yet, within, there may lurk a lust such as the prophet describes when he says further, "Thou hast said in thine heart I will descend into heaven, I will exalt my throne above the stars of God: I will sit also upon the mount of the congregation, in the sides of the north: I will ascend above the heights of the clouds; I will be like the Most High" (Isa. xiv. 13). The approaches of this lust are insinuating, subtle, and smooth; very zealous for God, and goodness, in a certain way. But, when this tremendous lust has developed itself, it becomes the most audacious, the most extravagant, and the most cruel of the insanities by which the human race has ever been infested and cursed.

The hateful ambition of the warrior would spare, where the ambitious priest would slay. Dunstan, Dominic, Torquemada, Bonner, these are names which have become appellations of horror, for they exhibited Babylon full blown; Babylon the great, with mystery on her forehead, the mother of harlots, and abominations of the earth, drunken with the blood of the saints, and with the blood of the martyrs of Jesus. The treatment of Daniel and his three friends, in the spiritual sense, is a description of the manner in which the Babylonish persuasion treats the Word, and the three great essentials of religion, charity, faith, and good works, in seeking to make them subservient to its ambitious views.

The Babylonians had destroyed Jerusalem, burning the house of the Lord and the king's house, carried away the monarch, put out his eyes, and bound him in chains, keeping him captive in prison, in Babylon, to the day of his death (Jerem. lii. 11). Part of the vessels of the house of God were carried away, and brought into the treasure-house of the Babylonish god Nebo (Dan. i. 2), whose name appears in the word Nebuchadnezzar, and many other names which occur in the Divine history. This destruction of Jerusalem by Babylon represented the entire desolation of true religion, when true religion has been weakened by unworthiness in those who profess it, and their disregard of its virtues and its aims. A time of judgment and condemnation surely comes on those who are unfaithful to the light ; at length their eyes are put out, the very faculty of understanding truth becomes lost. This terrible result is announced often in the Word, and is meant when we read in the warning to the the church of Ephesus, " Remember, therefore, from whence thou art fallen, and repent, and do the first works ; or else I will come unto thee quickly, and will remove thy candlestick out of his place, except thou repent" (Rev. ii. 5). Where Babylonish pride and pomp prevail, all true and genuine regard for that new birth which changes the human character, spiritualizing the mind and heart, and planting heaven in the soul, is kept down and imprisoned as inimical to the parade and mummery which constitute the paraphernalia of Babylon, bewitching the senses, but leaving the inner man untouched.

Some of the vessels of the house of God were carried to Babylon, and added to the treasures of their idol god. The names of Christianity, and such parts of religious knowledge as can be made serviceable to further the aims of ambition, decked out in gaudy religious forms, are taken and used. The splendour of the high priest, the incense, the washings of the Mosaic law, the names of distinguished persons, the Divine names, the Virgin, Peter and the Apostles, and certain parts of the letter of the Word, are used and paraded, but for purposes very different from those of true religion.

Very much astonished, indeed, would the lowly and modest mother of Jesus, according to the flesh, have been to find her history travestied, and herself transformed into the likeness of the queen of heaven of the Babylonians, whose worship, when it tainted Israel, was so sternly denounced by the prophet (Jerem. iv. 4). So, with other Scriptural persons and phrases, they are the vessels of the house of the Lord carried to the treasure-house of the god of Babylon, and, mixed up with contemptible rags, relics, and forms, they constitute the means of amusing and deluding the vulgar, who are kept ignorant that they may the better remain obedient to devices and influences so poor and weak, yet to minds fond of show so alluring as these.

Daniel, the young prophet, represented the Word ; the three friends, the three grand essentials of religion, like Peter, James, and John in the Gospels. They are said to be of the king's seed, children in whom there is no blemish, but well-favoured and skilful in all wisdom, because these principles are indeed derived from the King of kings, and are full of wisdom and heavenly skilfulness imparted from Him. They are said to be intended to be prepared for the Babylonish court, and to add to its splendour by being fully devoted to the king, by eating of the king's meat and drinking of the king's wine for three years (verse 5). The provision of the king's meat consists of the delights of ambition; the wine of Babylon is the inebriating persuasion that it is charming beyond all other charms to have millions submissive to your nod, to say to this man go, and he goeth, and to that one come, and he cometh. It is the flattering potion for which the conqueror thirsts and pants, and which he procures often at an appalling cost of tears and blood. This wine of Babylon is formed of a witching mixture, of a few truths, so blended with the spirit of proselytism, and so spiced with flattering deference to the splendid tastes of the great, and the weaknesses and vices of the multitude, that the desire to be greatest may be fully attained; and religion, whose very essence is humility, and whose very spirit is the love of use by ministries for the good of others and the sacrifice of self, comes out with claims for lordship, before which all other ambitions are pale and weak. The greatest of the earth are required to kiss the feet of the pretended representative of the Lowly One, who washed the feet of His disciples; and the lowliest priest claims to be higher than the proudest potentate, as if religion of any kind was not the destroyer of the lust of being greatest, by the virtue of being useful, not for self-aggrandizement, but from the truth and goodness of Him Who only is wise, Who only is good, and Whom to serve is life eternal.

It is a horrible thing when the worship of the Lord is turned into the worship of men, and when to bring this about, religion is transformed from being the light of heaven, guiding men rationally to regeneration and to wisdom, into mysteries paralysing the rational faculty, and excusing almost every sin and every folly, if only priestly rule be magnified. The cunning persuasions by which these things are accomplished are the wine of Babylon. The same wine is described in the book of Revelation: "Come hither, I will show unto thee the judgment of the great whore, that sitteth upon many waters; with whom the kings of the earth have committed fornication, and the inhabitants of the earth have been made drunk with the WINE OF HER FORNICATION" (xvii. 1, 2). Again, "And he cried mightily, with a strong voice, saying, Babylon the great is fallen, is fallen, and is become the habitation of devils, and the hold of every foul spirit, and a cage of every unclean and hateful bird. And all nations have drunk of the WINE OF THE WRATH OF HER FORNICATION."

Daniel purposed in his heart that he would not defile himself with the portion of the king's meat, nor with the wine which he drank, therefore he requested of the prince of the eunuchs that he might not defile himself (verse 8). The prince of the eunuchs had the direction of the servants and the arrangement of the court in eastern monarchies, and spiritually he will represent the directing and managing power in the system of Christian Babylon. Daniel's repugnance to the king's meat and wine, signifies the aversion of the entire spirit of the Word to the lust of dominion, and to all persuasions leading to or justifying self-aggrandizement. The two systems are as opposite as heaven and hell. The Word abases human pride, and induces innocence, purity, and the love of use. The lust of dominion inflates self-importance even to insanity, and leads weak and erring mortals to deck themselves with gaudy names and meretricious parade, in ostentatious contrast to the meek principles of the Prince of Peace. But Daniel declines for himself and his companions to receive the training, or defile themselves with the dainties and the allurements of Babylon. They are pressed but they remain firm. The prince of the eunuchs regards Daniel especially with love and favour, because the Word, which Daniel represents, is essential to furnish the few texts and the authority upon which spiritual ambition founds its claims. It loves the Word, and it does not love it. It is with them, the beast that is, and is not, and yet is. The Word with spiritual self-seekers IS,—their treasury of means and weapons, IT IS NOT,—as a means of subduing their pride and regenerating their souls, and it IS,—still to confront them at last, and be their judge (John xii. 48).

The alteration of the Word of God, and the adaptation of the great principles of religion to their own purposes, is represented by the prince of the eunuchs changing the names of Daniel, and the distinguished three who were his friends. Daniel, which signifies God's judgment, was changed into Belteshazzar, that is, HE WHO LAYS UP TREASURES IN SECRET,— an alteration implying a change from the free and open character of Divine wisdom, to the mysterious closeness which implies there are vast treasures in Divine things, but they are the secret property of priests. The change of the other three names is equally significant. Hananiah, Mishael, and Azariah, which, interpreted, are THE MERCY OF JEHOVAH SENT FROM GOD, and HEARKENING TO JEHOVAH, were altered to Shadrach, Meshach, and Abednego, that is, Shadrach, *a tender nipple ;* Meshach, *that draws with force ;* and Abednego, or the *servant of Nebo.*

When a church becomes Babylonish, love, THAT HIGHEST CHARITY, which was the evidence of Jehovah's mercy, becomes alms-giving—a tender but enslaving nipple. Truth, sent from God, becomes strong persuasion; and obedience to Jehovah, whose service is perfect freedom, is transformed into slavery to the ecclesiastical system. Azariah became Abednego. These three principles, charity, faith, and good works, may still be used, and made to support Babylon, and they will look well upon pulse and water, or supported by the letter of the Word, and give *eclat* to a system from which they are interiorly foreign, and to which they are interiorly opposed.

Daniel is said to have understanding in all visions and dreams, that is, the Divine Wisdom of the Word instructs in all things which throw light on immortality and revelation from heaven. The other three are said to be ten times better than all the magicians and astrologers in the realm of Babylon. For "charity, faith, and good works," however externally regarded, lend force and recommendation to any system into which they are incorporated, far beyond the cunning devices and magical support which it may otherwise receive. These are Divine things, and they speak to human sorrows and to human wants. They commend themselves powerfully to the instincts of the soul, and touch the secret springs of human sympathy with a tenderness far beyond all juggling cleverness. It is the good still left in a fallen church amongst humble pious souls, far better than their doctrines, which prolongs its life, and keeps it lingering on, even when obviously out of harmony with the new age, which the Lord in His Providence has given to the world. Daniel is said, at the end of the chapter, to continue even unto the first year of king Cyrus; that is, the Divine Word continues even to the coming of the Lord afresh to found a new church. Cyrus restored Jerusalem; the Lord restores His church by founding it in a new form, and giving it new prophets. Yet in the old dispensation the Word continues until the very end, and then arises into new glory, for though Nineveh may expire, and Babylon perish, the Word of the Lord abides for ever. Let us pray for the peace of Jerusalem. Let us avoid all contact with Babylon, but walk in the light of that golden city, which is clear as crystal, and glows with the glory of God.

SERMON XLVII.

NEBUCHADNEZZAR'S DREAM.

"Thou, O king, sawest, and beheld a great image. This great image, whose brightness was excellent, stood before thee; and the form thereof was terrible. This image's head was of fine gold, his breast and his arms of silver, his belly and his thighs of brass, his legs of iron, his feet part of iron and part of clay. Thou sawest till that a stone was cut out without hands, which smote the image upon his feet that were of iron and clay, and brake them to pieces. Then was the iron, the clay, the brass, the silver, and the gold broken to pieces together, and became like the chaff of the summer threshingfloors; and the wind carried them away, that no place was found for them: and the stone that smote the image became a great mountain."—DANIEL ii. 31-35.

THE dream of King Nebuchadnezzar is introduced to us in a very striking manner. It evidently impressed and alarmed him to an extraordinary degree. There are no doubt differences in dreams as in all the other occurrences of life. There are dreams and dreams. There are many people who will dismiss dreams altogether as idle impressions of no significance, mere results of certain states of the stomachs. Yet it cannot be denied that the annals of mankind shew that dreams are sometimes remarkably fulfilled, and considering how large a portion of human life is passed in dreaming, it does not seem altogether rational to suppose that they are absolutely without any meaning or import whatever. How many dreams, too, there are related in the Word containing circumstances in which Divine instructions were given to men involving the weightiest consequences. For instance, the dreams of Joseph, the dreams of Pharaoh, the dreams of Joseph the husband of Mary.

Dreams may be regarded as having a weighty lesson to teach, if we consider them as shewing our capacity for realizing a life quite independent of the body or the outward world; and if we think of them in relation to the truth that we are associated mentally with good spirits or with bad, and conceive that good dreams, like good thoughts, come from our angelic friends, and bad dreams, like evil thoughts, come from evil spirits, unpleasant dreams will then serve to put us on our guard, and intimate that danger is near. Such appears to be the teaching of the very interesting and striking passage in Job, "For God speaketh once, yea twice, yet man perceiveth it not. In a dream, in a vision of the night, when deep sleep falleth upon men, in slumberings upon the bed, then He openeth the ears of men, and sealeth their instruction, that He may draw man from his purpose, and hide pride from man" (xxxiii. 14-17).

Some dreams make an impression upon the person who is their subject that cannot be shaken off. He endeavours to turn his mind from them, and to think of them no more. But quite in vain. And many are the recorded instances of such dreams, having weighty significance, having reference to some crisis in the person's character or condition, which perhaps strengthens his conviction that the Most High ruleth in the kingdoms of men, and thus to conduce to check his self-conceit, and withdraw his soul from pride. Such a dream was this of the mighty king of Babylon. He could not remove the impression that it was a Divine message. He was deeply moved, so much so, that he felt if his hierarchy of priests could not explain it to him, it was their condemnation, their system was false, and they and it should perish. This arbitrary and awful decision spread consternation through Babylon. It was a hard thing which the king required. He insisted, first, that the wise men should tell him the dream which he had himself forgotten, and then he thought he would have a warrant that their interpretation might also be believed. To the forlorn priests of Nebo, the condition of the king was simply an impossibility. They were the blind leaders of the blind; the numerous supporters of a worn-out superstition. They could only say to this extraordinary order like the chiefs of other worn-out superstitions of our own time, *Non possumus;* we are not able.

But Daniel, who heard of this amazing occurrence, and was concerned—for he too, and his friends were to perish like the rest—and being a seer, "with understanding in visions and dreams," he knew that the dream had been given from the spiritual world, and if well-pleasing to the Lord, it could easily be repeated to him. He prayed, and asked his friends to pray, and lay the whole case before the Lord. The secret was revealed to him in a night vision; that is, his spiritual sight was opened, and he beheld the scene which had been presented to the king in a dream, and with such impressiveness that he had no doubt upon the subject, and he broke out into that glowing expression of thankfulness—"Blessed be the name of God for ever and ever: for wisdom and might are His. I thank and praise thee, O thou God of my fathers, Who hast given unto me wisdom and might, and hast made known unto me now what we desired of thee; for thou hast now made known unto us the king's matter."

Daniel desired to be led before the king; and having, with great modesty and diffidence disclaimed any peculiar art, skill, or merit in himself, he claimed to be able, by the merciful revelation which the God of heaven had vouchsafed in answer to his prayer, to relate to the king the impressive and marvellous dream which he had perceived in the night, and then forgotten. When he had drawn back to the king's recollection the dream which had made so deep an impression, and then so mysteriously vanished from memory, he would proceed to give the interpretation. All this he did so completely to the conviction and satisfaction of the monarch, that he exclaimed, " Of a truth it is, that your God is a God of gods, and a Lord of kings, and a revealer of secrets, seeing thou couldst reveal this secret." The king made Daniel a great man, and gave him many great gifts, and made him ruler over the whole province of Babylon, and chief of the governors over all the wise men of Babylon.

And now let us observe a little more closely this dream and its interpretation. It was a great image that the king saw, bright, imposing, and terrible to view. The image's head was of fine gold, the breast and arms of silver, the belly and thighs of brass, the legs of iron, the feet partly of iron and partly of miry clay. Then a stone was cut out of a mountain without hands, and smote the image, broke it to pieces, and dissipated it, and itself became a great mountain, and filled the whole earth.

The king confessed the exactitude of the recalled dream, and his full acceptance in consequence of the interpretation. That interpretation he received in its literal bearing on the political career of his empire. It commenced with himself, the head of gold. He had unrolled, as it were, before him the broad pages of the imperial career of Babylon. There would come the Persian monarchy after his own dynasty had ended, represented by the silver breast and arms; then the Greeks, under Alexander and his successors, would constitute the kingdom of brass ; then the Romans, the fourth kingdom, would come and trample down all opposition, and continue in one form or another until the kingdom should be born and grow which would break in pieces all other kingdoms—the kingdom of truth derived from love (the stone out of the mountain), which would grow until it had filled the whole church, and the whole earth, and it should last for ever.

But this literal interpretation, as given by the prophet Daniel to Nebuchadnezzar, and referring to the stages of decline through which his empire of Babylon would pass to its end, though most interesting to him, and to those who were concerned in the political changes of that remote time, have only a general, a very general interest for us. The political rise and fall of kingdoms have no very enduring impressions upon character. The movements of the church affect our nature and our everlasting condition more deeply, and hence it will be more profitable for us to make a more interior inquiry into the spirit of this wonderful vision of the king of Babylon.

It is reasonable to conclude that a vision so introduced, with such remarkable circumstances, showed plainly that a Divine hand was engaged in it, and disclosures worthy of infinite wisdom were, by its means, intended to be made. It is interesting to observe, also, that in the oldest known poem out of the Bible, that by Hesiod, who lived two centuries before Daniel, the progress of humanity is described by the succession of metals of precisely the same kind as in this vision : the age of gold, the age of silver, the age of brass—or more properly copper—and the age of iron, which he describes as the one in which men were then living. This great image, then, would represent the career of humanity; the march of the world; the succession of ages; all the race represented as one vast form, to the period when truth from Divine Love would restore to the world a state of universal loving-kindness, and none would hurt or destroy in all God's holy mountain (Isa. xi. 9). The golden age of Hesiod, like this head of gold, would represent the age of innocence and love, the same as in the early part of Genesis is meant by man in the garden of Eden. This most ancient church was the babyhood of the world. We know not how long it lasted, probably an immense period. The people were not wise in science, they probably knew as little of mechanics as babies, but they delighted in the wisdom of being good. They were ignorant of worldly ways, and of literary skill, but in the wisdom of being innocent, guileless, pure, and loving, they far surpassed all who have succeeded them.

The earliest records of the old nations—the Hindoo, the Chinese, the Persian—all speak of this age of gold; and gold in Scripture is used as the symbol of the highest love of the soul. All things in the temple were covered with gold. "I counsel thee," the Lord Jesus said, "to buy of Me gold tried in the fire, that thou mayest be rich" (Rev. iii. 18). The street of the city of New Jerusalem was to be of gold (Rev. xxi. 18). Gold is the most valuable of the metals, and therefore properly represents love to the Lord, the most valuable of all principles. Gold is unaffected by acids. Gold can be drawn out and applied to all sorts of forms. It has been used from the remote times, long before history, for the ring, the emblem of indissoluble affection, which joins human beings in the closest and most self-sacrificing of all unions. The golden age was the age of pure love, that Eden state of the world, guileless, pure in heart, in all the gushing innocence of childhood. "Of such was the kingdom of heaven." The head of humanity was then this head of gold. This was the celestial church; the most ancient church.

The second age of humanity was the age of silver. The breast and arms were of silver. These simple words unfold before us another dispensation, the ancient church, the dispensation in which men chiefly delighted in spiritual truth, for this is heavenly silver. This ancient church is meant in Scripture by Noah and his family, and that dispensation lasted also a very long period. It was the age in which allegories and beautiful personifications had their rise, representing the attributes of God, and spiritual things in lovely natural forms, the degeneration of which gave rise to idolatry. Silver in Scripture corresponds to spiritual wisdom. Hence we read, "Ye shall be as the wings of a dove covered with silver" (Ps. lxviii. 13). The words of the Lord are pure words, as silver tried in a furnace of earth, purified seven times (Ps. xii. 6). For iron I will bring silver, the Saviour said (Isa. lx. 17). And the age of silver was the age when men valued heavenly truth above all earthly good; it was the age of faith, corresponding to that time of early youth, when the young soul has not yet learned to doubt, but believes that things and persons are what they affirm themselves to be, and the eye glitters with truthful confidence. The breast and arms are said to have been of silver, for spiritual truth inspired all who lived then with charity, and what their hearts felt, they stretched out their arms to do.

The age of copper was that which the human race next realized. The good nature and genial integrity of the next succeeding age, the age of the Melchisedeks and patriarchs, when people lived simply and kindly in tents, was that which succeeded the age of silver, and was compared with the age of celestial love and innocence, as copper in relation to gold. They lived lives of virtue, but not from motives and principles so pure, so high, and so heavenly as those which actuated the age of gold.

Then came the age of iron, when men were altogether ruled by force, by force of law, or force of hand. God's Word was still given to men, and still to a large extent obeyed, but it was the Word understood only in the very letter. Men were then ruled with a rod of iron. The iron Romans compelled order. This was the Jewish age, extending through the mercy of a loving Saviour and Redeemer, under Christianity, to barbaric peoples the knowledge of the law, the prophets, and the Gospel, throwing off what was peculiarly national in Judaism. The Gospel was only the enlarging of the sphere of the age of iron, and blending with the nations far and wide. It was not ruling the Jews only with a rod of iron, but ruling all nations. And when we look over the Christian centuries, and observe the wars, the persecutions, the controversies which have been waged among Christian nations, and the immense mass of impurity which has ever clung to Christian profession, we must humbly confess that, with the iron truth which has taught us our duty, there has still been found too much miry clay.

Miry clay means moral defilement (Ps. xl. 2, lxix. 2). But, at last a stone was seen, cut out of a mountain without hands, and it became a great mountain, and filled the whole earth. Stones correspond to doctrinal truths. In large blocks they make foundations on which to build, and in detail they furnish us with the means of erecting houses and building walls. Will the Stone cut out of the mountain without hands be any other than the head-stone of the corner, which the builders rejected, the true doctrine of the Lord Jesus, as the Only God, in whom is all the Trinity. "No other foundation," said the Apostle, "can any man lay, than that is laid, even Jesus Christ" (1 Cor. iii. 2).

When this truth is given to the world again, as we are assured in the Gospel it will be in fulness, from the Divine Love of the Lord, it is indeed the stone cut out of the mountain without hands. It is the foundation-stone, and the head-stone, the All in All. This will shew us plainly of the Father. This will reveal in the Glorified Redeemer Himself, the First and the Last, the Root and the Offspring of David, the Bright and the Morning Star, and the Sun of Righteousness. The Son of Man in Him will be brought near to the Ancient of Days, so near, that it will be seen that He and the Father are one: all things that the Father hath are His. He that seeth Him seeth the Father. A dominion will then be given to Him, and glory and a kingdom, that all people, nations, and languages shall serve Him. His dominion is an everlasting dominion, which shall not pass away, and His kingdom that which shall not be destroyed (Dan. vii. 13, 14). This kingdom of the Lord Jesus, in His true character as Father, Son, and Holy Spirit, in one unutterably Glorious Person, Divine Love and Wisdom embodied, the One King who shall be over all the earth (Zech. xvi. 9), is that which is further described by Daniel when he said, " And in the days of those kings shall the God of heaven set up a kingdom, WHICH SHALL NEVER BE DESTROYED, but it shall break in pieces and consume all these kingdoms, and IT SHALL STAND FOR EVER (verse 44).

This kingdom of the Lord Jesus Christ is now being realized. It is yet small and feeble, but it has manifestly begun, and its influences are already being felt throughout the world. Bibles are issuing forth in a broad stream which has never before been equalled. There is more of loving-kindness, less of sectarian separation, than any previous age has seen. There is more care for universal education for children, more true sympathy for others, incalculably more diffusion of good of every kind, more horror of war, and ardent thirst for the true progress of humanity, than any age has seen since the time of history began. It is the age of hope. All seems young and progressive once again. There is evidently a fresh spring, the foretoken of a glorious summer, WHEN ALL SHALL KNOW THE LORD. Oh may the growth of this glorious stone from the mountain hasten and remove the rust of ages. Oh may the kingdom of God come, in which there shall be no tears, nor pain, nor death (of sin), but healthy, happy youth grow up to healthy, happy maturity, and useful, noble, spiritual, orderly, heavenly lives, announce that God's will is done on earth, as it is done in heaven.

It is written that the stone struck the image on its feet, that were of iron and miry clay, and brake them to pieces. The stone striking the feet signifies the manifestation by Divine truth of the worthlessness of the life produced by the decayed systems of the old dispensations. All interior things result in conduct, and rest upon daily life, as the body rests upon the feet. A man really is WHAT HE DOES. The deeds of the world are the result of the principles of the world. And, when it is palpable to all that national life is but little better than national selfishness, commercial life grievously tainted in all its parts with fraud, domestic life largely soiled with domestic impurity, there can be no difficulty in admitting that the doctrine of a pure and loving Saviour will strike these feet. The superstitious remains of the grand old religions of ancient times, not the good things themselves, but the dead image of them; the lingering lifeless remains of glories, holy virtues, and bright truths, now old, worn out, and meaningless, must disappear, and the newly revealed truth make a new heaven and a new earth. Hasten, O Merciful Adorable Saviour, this pure, loving, bright, and blessed age. Let the weary shadows of wrong and misery disappear, and do Thou thyself arise amongst us, and Thy glory be seen upon us.

SERMON XLVIII.

NEBUCHADNEZZAR'S GOLDEN IMAGE.

"Then an herald cried aloud, To you it is commanded, O people, nations, and languages, that at what time ye hear the sound of the cornet, flute, harp, sackbut, psaltery, dulcimer, and all kinds of music, ye fall down and worship the golden image that Nebuchadnezzar the king hath set up."—DANIEL iii. 4, 5.

IF experience had not assured us of multiplied facts of a similar kind, we could hardly have believed it possible that the same king, who had acknowledged his conviction of the Divine Sovereignty of the God of Daniel, had returned to his idolatrous inclinations, made a golden god, and commanded that all the subject peoples of his empire should fall down and worship it. Yet so it was. The Israelites furnished many instances of a similar kind. Though they had been brought out of Egypt through astonishing displays of Divine power; though they had witnessed with profound awe the sublime grandeurs of Sinai, yet forty days afterwards, when Moses did not reappear, they were worshipping and dancing about the golden calf, and exclaiming, These be thy gods, O Israel. Pharaoh, though often convinced for the moment, soon relapsed again, and finished his obstinacy in the Red Sea.

Miraculous impressions enter very slightly into the mind. They touch and pass away. Only that which enters into the soul through the understanding, by deep consideration, and then is accepted into the heart, and brought into the conduct of life, remains. Our Lord did no miracles to convince men of his truth, but only for purposes of benevolence and mercy. It is written, "He did not many mighty works there, because of their unbelief" (Matt. xiii. 58). The soul that would come into the light must not ask for miracles to be convinced, but must think, consider, weigh, and meditate, from the love of truth. "He that received seed into the good ground is he that heareth the Word, and UNDERSTANDETH it, who also beareth fruit, some a hundred fold, some sixty, some thirty" (Matt. xiii. 23). The reason of the instability of those who have been for the moment overwhelmed with some miraculous evidence, exists from the inrooted and overwhelming power of the ruling love. That love may be depressed and overawed by vivid demonstrations from without, but it will re-assert itself, and remain fixed and triumphant in the character, unless a man himself freely and earnestly desire to be enlightened and led by the truth. Divine power operating by the truth can make the soul free, and bring it into the light and the love of heaven. Nothing else can. Hence Nebuchadnezzar, convinced for a time of the Divine Wisdom and Majesty of the God of Daniel, contrived to set that conviction aside, by arguments easily conceivable; probably attributing Daniel's wonderful discovery to some unknown power in nature, or some secret disclosure he had made in his sleep, or in some self-assuring way not needful to dwell upon, but all-important to one who wishes to find excuses to do what he is anxious to do, and turn away from the truth he hates to the darkness which inflates his own importance.

In the chapter before us, Daniel is not once mentioned—an evidence that the king had resolved to have his own way, but still respected Daniel too much to defy or insult him. His image of gold was probably an image of Nebuchadnezzar himself, covered with golden plating. One of the insanities of ancient mighty potentates was to be deified in their lifetimes, and they set up statues of themselves, that they might by obsequious and flattering multitudes be thus adored. This practice is often mentioned by ancient writers. It prevailed also in the later and more currupt centuries of the Roman Empire, to the extent, that Caracalla directed the Roman people not only to adore his statue, but his horse. But whether the statue was only a larger and more costly idol in honour of Belus or Baal, the chief god of the Chaldeans, or one in honour of himself to be adored as god, is of little importance to know, for their idols were just the reflection of themselves, and were endowed with the attributes they most esteemed.

In Mars, the admirers of war idolized the desire for military glory; in Bacchus, the love of wine. Each idol was an image of what its worshippers loved, and in adoring it they were worshipping themselves. Belus, Bel, or Baal, whose worship, with slight differences, was widely spread over all the East, was especially prevalent in Babylon, and also in Canaan—as the frequent mention of places with Baal attached proves—was the Sun-God. It was an image of the sun, originally of the Sun of the Eternal World, and of the soul, " the true light, that enlighteneth every man that cometh into the world." Then, as men became carnal, sluggish, and coarse, the sun of the world became considered to be a god, and the Baal images were images of him. Then the images themselves began to be considered as gods, and the superstitious ascribed wonderful things to them. Thus men sank from one dark folly to another, until gods many and lords many, covered the earth, and gross darkness and fearful cruelty filled the gloomy places of the world.

All this declension was provided against in the Divine commandment, " Thou shalt not make to thyself any graven image, or any likeness of anything in the heavens above, or the earth beneath, or in the waters under the earth. Thou shalt not bow down thyself to them, nor worship them." The manifest reason for this prohibition was, that every man has been created to be conjoined in heart with God Himself, to love from His Love, to think from His Wisdom. God is Infinite Love and Infinite Wisdom. He has created in man two grand receptacles—the will, for the Divine Love to enter in and inspire with all holy motives and desires; and the understanding, into which the Divine Wisdom can flow, and diffuse and unfold noble thoughts and hallowed views. A man can have no real happiness but in this supreme conjunction with the Lord, in the interiors of his being. He must abide in God, and God must abide in him, or everything in him becomes loose, irregular, and unbalanced. There is something wrong at the mainspring, and the whole machine of man's soul and body works mischievously; love becomes lust, thought becomes phantasy, and the energies of the soul become wild and hurtful efforts, instead of earnest powers for good. Hence the Lord is said to be a jealous God, because His Love is indeed most tenderly and wisely jealous that no selfish intrusion, like the worm at the heart of Jonah's gourd, should destroy man's happiness at its centre.

Hence the Lord has always revealed Himself as the great and only object of man's supreme love. This has ever been the first and great commandment. It was reiterated from Mount Sinai, but it had been the centre and soul of every dispensation. "Hear, O Israel: The Lord our God is one Lord: and thou shalt love the Lord thy God with all thine heart, and with all thy soul, and with all thy might. And these words which I command thee this day, shall be in thine heart." The will, the understanding, and the operative energy, are the heart, the soul, and the might, and these comprise the whole man.

The same truth was given to Abraham in the marvellously touching and beautiful words, "Fear not, Abraham, I am thy shield, and thine exceeding grand reward" (Gen. xiv. 1). Again, "I am the Almighty God: walk before me, and be thou perfect."

To preserve to man this supreme felicity of his being, and defence against all wrong, Revelation has constantly declared that God is One, and that He is loving, wise, and all-powerful. He is our Creator, our Saviour, our Redeemer, our First and Last. "Before Me, there was no God formed, neither shall there be after Me. I, even I, am Jehovah, and beside Me there is no Saviour." "For thy Maker is thine Husband, Jehovah of Hosts is His name: the God of the whole earth shall He be called."

In the New Testament, God manifest in the flesh, and Who became thus manifest for this very purpose, to reveal Himself anew, in the deepest depths of our darkness, as constantly invites us to be conjoined with him. "Come unto Me, all ye that are weary and heavy laden, and I will give you rest. He that abideth in Me, and I in him, bringeth forth much fruit: for without Me ye can do nothing." "Behold, I stand at the door and knock; if any man will open the door I will come into him, and sup with him, and he with Me." This reciprocal conjunction of man with God and God with man, is the safeguard, the glory, the defence, and the happiness of the human race. It is man living as the servant, the friend, the child of God, his Eternal Father, in His palace, which is then His glorious home; in the world in time, in the better world in eternity.

But idolatry severs and destroys all this. The idol-maker worships, but he worships something of his own divising. Instead of his worship being a source of perfection and of peace, it is a constant source of degradation and declension. What can be more stupid than for man to put himself, his own follies and passions, in the place of the Divinely Wise and Good. Nebuchadnezzar's image, all plated with gold, represented self, all decorated with Divine attributes. That poor helpless figure, however gaudy, could neither hear nor see, speak nor walk. In the spiritual Babylon, in Christian times, when men decorate themselves with Divine attributes, they cannot really do a single Divine thing, although they claim to forgive sins, to open heaven, and to close heaven, and really to sit in the place of God. The priesthood pretending to have Divine powers is really as helpless as an image, either in changing the heart, casting out sin, or building men up for heaven.

The gold with which the image was covered represented the profession of love to God with which the lust of spiritual power covers itself. Self-seekers, in this respect, have salvation upon their lips, and piety in form and manner, but the secret purpose is the enslavement of human souls. They seek not to educate, to elevate, to make all men free and noble, and thus from principle to make earth heavenly, but to live only to spread their dominion, to extend their system. "What profiteth the graven image, that the maker thereof hath graven it; the molten image, and the teacher of lies, that the maker of his work trusteth therein, to make dumb idols? Woe unto him that saith to the wood, Awake; to the dumb stone, Arise, it shall teach. Behold, it is laid over with gold and silver, and there is no breath at all in the midst of it. But, the Lord is in His holy temple: let all the earth keep silence before Him" (Hab. ii 18-20). Again, "But they are altogether brutish and foolish: the stock is a doctrine of vanities. Silver spread into plates from Tarshish, and gold from Uphaz, the work of the workman, and of the hands of the founder: blue and purple are their clothing; they are all the work of cunning men. But the Lord is the true God, He is the living God, and an Everlasting King" (Jerem. x. 8-10).

They who made these idols of gold knew, at first, that their handiworks were lifeless, helpless stocks, and metal. But such is the amazing power of self-deception, that after a time they become oblivious of their origin, and cried aloud as if the stocks could hear, and command, as Nebuchadnezzar did, that all people should do the same. So with modern Babylon. They who have set forth the Pope and the priesthood as possessed of Divine power upon earth, and able to open and close heaven, know that they cannot explore the motives and secrets of human hearts, or, in reality, judge and know the real interior states of any one. They know that the Popes have been, as a class, not very different from other classes of people, some good men, many indifferent, and some fiends in human form. Their foolish pretensions, like Nebuchadnezzar's image, are merely vain and stupid things; a doctrine of vanities. It is vain to deck it round with gold; it is merely a stock. The makers may forget that they made it, as it is written, "A deceived heart hath turned him aside that he cannot deliver his soul, nor say, 'Is there not a lie in my right hand'" (Isa. xliv. 20).

The image was set up in the plain of Dura, probably the same district mentioned in Genesis as the plain in the land of Shinar, referred to in the account of the Babel-builders of old. Dura signifies *habitation*, and setting up this image on the plain of Dura means that this system of priestly dominion is not a speculative thing, it is to come into practical life. It will be brought into the habitations of men, to their business and their bosoms. None shall buy nor sell but those who have the mark or the name of the beast, or the number of his name (Rev. xiii. 17). The instruments of all kinds of music which were intended to usher in the worship of the golden image, represent the attractions of all kinds, the plausibilities, the sensuous charms, with which the lust of priestly ambition clothes itself in seeking to obtain its end. All sweet appliances and indulgences will subdue the soul to soft compliance, if only it will resign itself to deify men, and regard them in the place of God.

The image was sixty cubits high, and the breadth thereof six cubits. The same system of priestly ambition is described in the book of Revelation by six hundred threescore and six. Six, in a good sense, expresses all the truths which concern the states of the regenerate life, in allusion to the six days of labour. But six, when applied to an idol or a false system, will signify the falsities which result from a complete perversion of all truth; the holiness is not genuine holiness, the worship is not genuine worship, the life is not genuine life; all is perverted, and a factitious, morbid, unsound condition of thought and life exists, utterly opposed to real Christian virtue. This is what is meant by the image being sixty cubits high and six cubits in breadth. What a perversion of gold, that glorious metal, it was to make it into such an image, and an instrument for debasing and corrupting mankind. But still worse, infinitely worse is it, to use the gold of piety, of a profession of devotion to the Most High, to construct a system by which the liberty of mind and heart bestowed by the Creator on His rational creatures should be paralyzed, and they be trained not to be thoughtful disciples of the truth which makes a man free, but slavish bondsmen, the devotees of a system which manacles the soul, makes each rank of men slaves of other men, as a staff in the hand of its master, as a dead body to be galvanized by the ruling magician. Such a system may appear imposing, but it is only an image, hollow and helpless, albeit gaudy and meretricious.

They who submit to the fettering of the soul implied in worshipping the idol, the system of priestly rule, instead of embracing the government of truth and goodness, become debased, contemptible, weak, mentally blind and dark, the enthralled intellect avenges itself by leaving the passions unchecked, the affections impaired, and the life immoral. Then, too, the hour of judgment soon gives its warning in the distance. Justice may seem to come slowly, but it comes surely. Every system that comes between the soul of man and God, is doomed to perish. It emasculates, withers, and blights the noblest instincts of God-given humanity, and produces such intolerable evils in men and nations, such decay, tyranny, and vileness, that at last its victims rise and sound its knell. Its doom comes, and it disappears amidst the cry of emancipated nations: Babylon the great is fallen, is fallen, and is become the habitation of devils, the hold of every foul spirit, and the cage of every unclean and hateful bird.

But true men avoid its condemnation, and its sorrow, by never bowing down to it, or suffering anything to come between their souls and their God. They never forfeit their glorious heritage, their heavenly birthright to seek the truth, to follow the truth, by truth to come to goodness, to blessedness. They know the truth, they feel its power, and it makes them free. They become free, for the truth has burst their bonds, the bonds of their own errors and self-indulgences. They walk in the truth, live in the truth, conquer themselves by truth again and again, until truth leads them to high and holy love, and fills them with spiritual beauty. They will not bow down to any image that Nebuchadnezzar, king of Babylon, may set up; they serve the living God. In vain, for these and such as these, the charms of music, or art, or any manner of seduction, may invite them to bow down to the golden image. They hear the sound of the cornet, flute, harp, sackbut, psaltery, dulcimer, and all kinds of music, but, like Shadrach, Meshach, and Abednego, it will ever be reported of them, "There are certain Jews whom thou hast set over the affairs of the province of Babylon: these men, O king, have not regarded thee, they serve not thy gods, nor worship the golden image thou hast set up." Let us ever imitate this noble example. Let us bow down to no ecclesiastical, political, fashionable, or individual idols, however allured by sweet persuasions, but ever love and abide in the Lord Jesus. Let Him be our Teacher, our Saviour, and our ever-present and Eternal Friend. Let His light be our beacon, His love our blessing. If we follow His voice, our path will be safe. We shall hear a voice behind us, saying, "This is the way, walk ye in it," and at death we shall hear a voice above us, saying, "Well done, good and faithful servants, ye have been faithful over a few things, I will make you ruler of many things; enter ye into the joy of your Lord."

SERMON XLIX.

THE THREE FAITHFUL ONES IN THE FIERY FURNACE.

"Shadrach, Meshach, and Abednego answered, and said to the king, O Nebuchadnezzar, we are not careful to answer thee in this matter. If it be so, our God whom we serve is able to deliver us from the burning fiery furnace, and he will deliver us out of thine hand, O king. But if not, be it known unto thee, O king, that we will not serve thy gods, nor worship the golden image which thou hast set up."—DANIEL iii. 16-18.

THERE is something so manly, clear, and admirable in the noble reply of the three faithful companions of Daniel to the persecuting demand of the king of Babylon, that it has been the lesson of true courage for martyrs in almost every subsequent age. It was an assertion of faith and bravery of soul really sublime. They were in the midst of hostile multitudes. They had previously been elevated to great dignities, with their honours, emoluments, and comforts, from which they would now be degraded.

The decree threatening the fiery furnace was no vain outburst of violent words. Being cast alive into fierce furnaces was a cruelty often practised in the terrible ages of ancient fury, and has indeed been continued in some places even to periods coming near to our own time. The three faithful ones were not only reported to the king, but brought into his presence, when he was in a towering rage. He had forgotten his own conviction, miraculously brought about, and therefore only transitory, that the God they worshipped was God of gods, and Lord of kings, and now he said, "If ye worship not" (the golden image which I have set up), "ye shall be cast the same hour into the midst of a burning fiery furnace; and who is that God who shall deliver you out of my hands?"

Neither the presence of the king, nor his rage, nor the multitude of his surrounding courtiers and chief officers, with fierce countenances, taking their cue from the enraged monarch, dismayed the three brave servants of the living God. They answered modestly and quietly, but firmly, "O Nebuchadnezzar, we are not careful to answer thee in this matter." They had no misgivings, nor any disposition to take second thoughts. They at once declined the king's authority in the question of whom they should worship. They would render unto Cæsar the things that are Cæsar's, and to God only the things that are God's. With what noble simplicity they uttered their determination! How happy it is to be without double thoughts in the path of duty! Do right, and have no further care: this is the path which leads to constant progress.

The grounds of their quiet, self-sustained confidence were twofold. They believed the Lord would deliver them from peril if he saw that best. They were familiar with the history of their nation. They knew well how often in the most terrible straits and afflictions God had delivered their fathers. They were men of prayer, who believed in a Living God watching over them, as He had watched over all past ages, and whose tender mercies are over all His works. They were doubtless in the habit daily, probably three times a day, as was Daniel's custom, of laying their whole affairs, their joys and their sorrows, before the Lord, and entreating His counsel and benediction. They were confident of His love and of His power. If His wisdom saw it good that they should be delivered, not a hair of their heads would be injured. This is the quiet, reposing trust of true faith. It relies on the omnipresence and the omnipotence of the God it loves, at all times. It feels that our affairs are in His hand, with heaven and earth at His control, and all is sure to be well. His Providence enters into every moment, and every particular of our lives. Providence is particular, and therefore universal.

But they had a second ground for their trustful faith. They were assured that this life is only a temporary training-place for the life to come. There is another and a better world. The fiery furnace might be a sharp passage, but it would be a short one. The dross would be burned off, and they would speedily be at home. If the earthly house of this tabernacle were dissolved, they had a building of God, the spiritual body, that no earthly flames could touch, and in which they would continue to live eternally in the heavens (2 Cor. v. 1). They had, therefore, no fear of death. Death with them was the door, with a short step, to a higher life. To their feelings and conceptions there was no death. They acted on the truth afterwards uttered by the Lord Jesus, " Whosoever liveth and believeth in me shall never die." Hence they stood to their convictions. Whether they were to live here a little longer or not was a small matter.

They would live on if the providence of their loving Heavenly Father deemed it best, but if not, they would abide by the truth. For with truth there was salvation and heaven, but without truth there was soul-darkness, depravity, decrepitude, and spiritual death. Hence, said these noble ones, and after them the spiritual heroes, the salt of the earth, of many succeeding generations, IF NOT, if our good Almighty Father sees it best for us to die, we will not worship thy image, O king; we will not forsake the truth.

The king was filled with fury at the patient and determined piety of these noble confessors. He commanded that the furnace should be heated seven times hotter than it was wont to be heated, and the servants of God were cast in. Bound in their clothes, the noble three fell into the midst of the burning fiery furnace, now so fierce that the men who threw them in, perished by the ardency of the devouring flames. They were cast in, and it was thought all was over. Nothing could live there. The king, however, was disturbed and uneasy in his mind, evidently impressed by one of those strange feelings of disquietude and uncontrollable power which strangely affect human minds, and which they must follow. He went to look into the furnace, and lo! the valiant victims of his fury were not dead, not even hurt, but walking in the midst of the fire. Instead of three, however, there were FOUR; an angel was there, a companion and guardian. He who gives His angels charge over us to keep us in all our ways, had not only defended the three from the flames, but opened the spiritual sight of the king, that he might know that the angel of the Lord encampeth round about them that fear Him, and delivereth them.

The aspect of the angel was celestial. The king was deeply moved, and humbled. He exclaimed, "Lo, I see four men loose, walking in the midst of the fire, and they have no hurt; and the form of the fourth is like a son of the gods." He cried out further, "Ye servants of the Living God come forth, and come hither." The spiritual sight of the king seems then to have been closed again, for Shadrach, Meshach, and Abednego came forth from the furnace alone, but unhurt: their very clothes had suffered no harm. The king, subdued, once more convinced, and bowed down again for a short time, uttered the memorable words, "Blessed be the God of Shadrach, Meshach, and Abednego, who hath sent His angel and delivered His servants that trusted in Him, and have changed the king's word, and yielded their bodies that they might not serve or worship any god except their own God. Therefore, I make a decree, that every people, nation, and language which speaketh anything amiss against the God of Shadrach, Meshach, and Abednego shall be cut in pieces, and their houses shall be made a dunghill, because there is no other God that can deliver after this sort."

In this decree we see the vain-glorious idolator still. He speaks of the Lord only as the God of Shadrach, Meshach, and Abednego. He had evidently the notion of family gods, and national gods, and he was determined to patronize this powerful God, as he conceived he had found Him to be, and he would now cut in pieces and destroy the homes of any who would gainsay this new God, whose worship he would set up. The love of rule, the lust of spiritual dominion, comes forth again in a new form. His purpose was modified, but evidently he had still the fixed idea that he had the prerogative of fixing the faith of his subjects, notwithstanding he was only just convinced he had been egregiously wrong, and whosoever would not conform to his new decree must be cut in pieces, and their houses be made a dunghill. How slow have monarchs and authorities been to learn that in matters of faith there should be no compulsion. Force may make hypocrites, but never sincere believers. The limbs may be fettered, and the body be destroyed, but the soul, possessed of inner freedom, defies all entrance into its secret mansions, the understanding and the heart, of any sentiments which are not welcome there. Persecution, though always cruel, is always in vain, and always fails if met by Christian firmness. A persecuting spirit must be a proud spirit, and therefore be in the very worst condition for perceiving the truth, for pride and truth are opposites, and antagonistic to each other. They come from opposing sides, and cannot blend. A persecutor, therefore, must be wrong, and cannot himself come into the perception of truth until he abases his pride by repentance, and in the spirit of meekness seeks for wisdom. "The meek He will guide in judgment; to the meek He will teach His way."

If rulers were generally good men, if they were always patterns of all that is excellent, having the same liabilities to error that is the common lot, and having absorbing cares in their important duties as guardians of the state, they have less time even than others for the calm investigations which are required for the discovery of truth; and therefore they have certainly more than the usual amount of hindrances against its acquisition, and hence should especially abstain from prostituting the power of the state for the enforcement of their own opinions. To follow the religion of the ruler of the state simply because it is the religion of the ruler, is not to be religious, but to seek to attain selfish aims in the name of religion. It is self-seeking in a sanctimonious guise. But sovereigns are often exceedingly immoral. Persecuting sovereigns have probably all been so. Philip II. of Spain, and Henry VIII. of England, both bitter persecutors, and notoriously bad men, are only specimens of the tribe. They, therefore, who in religion abase themselves before the rulers of the state, are certainly in the greatest likelihood of enthroning error where Jesus alone, the King of kings, has the right to rule. Fashion, however, has often a deep influence over superficial and weak minds, even in religion. To follow the multitude, and especially the respectable in the world's estimation, as to the creed we adopt and the worship we attend, is to many an attraction they are unable to resist, yet this also is a serious detriment to our spiritual progress. What is the chaff to the wheat?

Evils in our hearts and in our habits can only be subdued by truth, received in the love of truth. This is the sword of the two edges coming out of the mouth of the Lord. Truth only can introduce order, and promote the diffusion of love to the Lord and charity to our neighbour, and impart spiritual beauty to the soul. ..Truth is the light, the glory, the defence of man's eternal interests. Truth illuminates the path of life, is a Divine lighthouse when our passage is stormy, cheers the hours of sickness, and, when our journey of life is finished, takes us by the hand, ushers us to those circles of the blessed who are waiting for us, charged by their Adorable Master to welcome us to heaven. These invaluable benefits only attend truth when it is followed, received, and loved for its own sake. The goodly pearls are only found by the spiritual merchant who seeks them. The pearl of great price only rewards him who has sold all he had, his selfish fancies, his preference for fashion over principle, his truckling to power and gain; and sought by hungering and thirsting after righteousness to be filled with the virtue, the brightness, and the bliss of the kingdom of heaven.

Such evidently were the grounds of the decisions of the three faithful ones. They would not truckle to the crowd of courtiers, the demands of the king, or the fiery furnace. If the God they served would preserve them alive in the world, in the path of duty, they would live; but if not, they would still be true to

Him who was everything to them. The king, enraged at their opposition to his will, commanded that the furnace should be made seven times hotter than before, and they cast in. Happily Divine Providence has already produced an immense change in the general condition of the world, and there are so many checks to the wild frenzy of the spiritual rage of Babylon in our days, that it cannot torture men's bodies, to the extent to which in the olden time it was wont to go. But the glow of rage in the soul when the lust of dominion is thwarted, is in every age the same. From the fury that strove to exterminate the Albigenses, that devastated and almost destroyed the German nation, that wasted the valleys, and stained the snow-clad mountains of Savoy, and slaughtered the followers of Garibaldi on the field of Mentana, the grim savagery of the lust of spiritual power is ever the same. Make the furnace seven times hotter, it incessantly says, so that neither Jew, nor Moor, nor Protestant, nor anything that will not bow down to the golden image that we have set up, may breathe. Such is the spirit of Babylon. It was the spirit of Babylon of old. It is the spirit of the modern Babylon, but happily the system is withering at its root, and is already in such decay before the new lights of religion and science, that the sincere and peaceful of these days may pass it unheeded by. It is an old giant, toothless, fangless, and forlorn.

The three faithful ones were cast into the furnace with their garments, their coats, their hosen, and their hats. The soul has its garments as well as the body. The turban or hat corresponds to the highest doctrines, those which clothe the head of the soul. On the tiara of the high priest was written on a golden plate, holiness to the Lord. The coat which protects the chest and middle of the body, corresponds to the doctrines of charity to the neighbour, while the hose and shoes correspond to the precepts of daily duty and common life; so that casting the men into the furnace with their garments spiritually signifies the rejection with spiritual hatred of true believers, not only as to their great leading principles of love, faith, and virtue, signified by the faithful three, but all the doctrines of genuine religion, the garments of salvation, the robes of righteousness, the wedding garment, in fact all that makes them beautiful. Instead of glorious truth there is mummery, formality, and mental slavery.

When, however, mental despotism is firmly met, its power is broken. Let the righteous possess their souls in patience, and they will take no harm. The slaves of despotism hurt themselves, they do not hurt the good. Those who threw the men into the fire were destroyed by the fire of their own furnace. The witnesses for truth were unhurt. "The Lord had given his angels charge concerning them, to keep them in all their ways." O rich immunity to brave souls! O glorious safeguard! Let men be true to their principles, and they can come to no real harm. No weapon that is formed against thee shall prosper; and every one that shall rise against thee thou shalt condemn. This is the heritage of the servant of the Lord, and their righteousness is of Me, saith the Lord.

Why should any one seek to compel others to adopt his particular views, when they cannot see them to be true? It is truth seen and understood which is of value to a man, and it is of value because it purifies the heart, and betters the life of its receiver. To explain the truth in a spirit of love, at becoming seasons, is doubtless commendable, but to worry others, in season and out of season, with our special dogmas, which they do not see, and cannot admit, is rather the eagerness of proselytism than earnestness for truth. The Lord's precious gift is truth to be as seed, from which, if understood and loved, will come harvests of virtue and blessing. If our views be true, and we see and understand them to be true, we can explain them to others, and if they are in the love of truth, they will receive them for the same reasons which have commended them to us; and when they are thus received in light, and for their own sakes, they will impart spiritual freedom, they will give strength in the hour of temptation, and consolation in sorrow. But if we have intruded the truth violently and unseasonably, we shall have roused opposition where we needed good will, and we shall have defeated our own aims. We shall be like a physician who has offered good medicine, but introduced it scalding hot. Truth should be introduced like dew, or the gentle shower on thirsty land. It should come as a courteous and delicate friend, sincere and gentle, not as our property, but as the Lord's own treasure, the blessed gift of Infinite Love, to introduce happiness upon earth, the happiness which comes from enlightened, pure, and loving souls, ministering in all the ways of integrity and virtue, useful to increase the real kingdom of the Lord on earth, and for heaven.

The over-eager zealot should remember also that his views may possibly be erroneous, as Nebuchadnezzar's were, and that therefore to attempt to enforce them violently upon others, may only be diffusing the blight of error over the fair field of human knowledge, which will certainly vanish in due time, but which can only in the meantime do mischief in the world. Whether, therefore, our views be true or false, the attempt to force them upon others against their convictions, is harmful and blameworthy—it is the spirit of Babylon. Truth will commend itself by the fruit it bears, the light it yields, and the blessings it diffuses. It disclaims all other aid. "Let your light so shine before men that they may see your good works, and glorify your Father, Who is in heaven." The nations of them that are saved shall walk in the light of the holy city, and they shall bring their glory and honour into it. They will there see wisdom as the eye sees objects, and do good as the joy of their life, and they will have a blessed anticipation of an eternal home.

The seed of all divine blessings is the Word of God. Let us boldly be faithful to it always, like the faithful three at Babylon. If any would challenge our right in this respect, let us reply: "We are not careful to answer thee in this matter. Our God whom we serve is able to deliver us from the burning fiery furnace, and He will deliver us out of thine hand, O king. But, if not, be it known unto thee, O king, we will not serve thy gods, nor worship the golden image which thou hast set up." Let us ever diligently guard the Word, and our freedom fearlessly to study and to follow it.

O may we diligently preserve this seed of all that is noble in humanity and in progress, the seed of angelic virtues, of victory over every evil, the seed of the kingdom of heaven.

> On, spirit of liberty, on,
> O bless every valley and hill;
> Thy brightness each heart shall enthrone;
> And glow with thy loveliness still.
> On, on, till each nation, all over the world,
> Shall see thy blest banner, for ever unfurled.

SERMON L.

NEBUCHADNEZZAR'S VISION OF THE GREAT TREE.

"He cried aloud, and said thus, Hew down the tree, and cut off his branches, shake off his leaves, and scatter his fruit: let the beasts get away from under it, and the fowls from his branches: nevertheless, leave the stump of his roots in the earth, even with a band of iron and brass, in the tender grass of the field; and let it be wet with the dew of heaven, and let his portion be with the beasts in the grass of the earth: let his heart be changed from man's, and let a beast's heart be given unto him; and let seven times pass over him."—DAN. iv. 14-16.

THE experience of human life brings before us very wonderful vicissitudes. The rise and the fall of individuals and of empires alike exhibit the instability of human affairs, and how uncertain is the possession of those treasures of wealth and power for which ambition pants. Multitudes struggle for the splendours of earth, and a few attain them; for a time they seem the favoured children of fortune, their splendour dazzles mankind, and they stand on the summit of human greatness. The superficial envy them, the fumes of flattery swell their pride, their smiles are courted by those who surround them as gracious tokens of the favour of superior beings. But the tide turns, adversity sets in, shock after shock comes until all is is wrecked, prosperity, fame, health, sanity all gone, and the former idol of multitudes, the petted favourite of fortune, has sunk so low, that scarcely one remains to do poor service of all those who formerly watched and waited on his nod.

History has never failed to afford such instances of the rise and fall of human beings, but certainly few have been so complete as that furnished in this chapter, and which was foreshadowed to king Nebuchadnezzar in his astonishing dream; a dream which portrayed to him his greatness, his fall and his restoration. He stood in the midst of the earth, a potentate, the mightiest among men; his arms had vanquished all who had resisted him, and he had so extended and embellished his capital, that it not only far exceeded the magnificence of any other city, but also owed so much to him that he might be regarded as a second founder.

While, however, he was at the very summit of his brilliant career, the awful dream was given him, which he felt also was more than a dream. He feared it was a vision of coming events. Anxious and troubled, he sought for its exact interpretation, and at length obtained it from the fearless and faithful Daniel. The terrible fulfilment of this, no doubt, divinely appointed dream took place twelve months afterwards, when every particular was realized. In the midst of his greatness, the king lost his reason, had a mania for acting as a beast, a mania well known to physicians, until his humiliation was complete; when his reason returned, his counsellors and lords sought him once more, his kingdom was re-established, and he issued a decree containing the account of the whole matter, and closing with the grand lesson, which the whole of these wonderful events had impressed upon him, "Now I Nebuchadnezzar, praise, and extol, and honour the king of heaven, all whose works are truth, and His ways judgment, and those that walk in pride, He is able to abase." Never, perhaps, has this lesson been taught with greater force, never proclaimed with greater clearness. No condition is beyond the reach of change. The greater the height, and the greater the fall. Earthly riches find wings and fly away. How important, therefore, it is that we look for our stability in eternal things, our riches in that inner wealth which supplies the heart with heavenly graces, and the mind with those gems of spiritual wisdom which shine brighter in adversity, and will gleam with angelic radiance for ever. Give me neither poverty nor riches is the prayer of the truly wise, but give me, O Lord, the grace of contentment with my lot, whatever it may honestly be, and the love of being useful in the righteous performance of the duties of my station. Let us pray for such a daily cultivation of the graces of heaven, as may enable us in humble thankfulness to respond when the cry is raised "The bridegroom cometh," "Our lamps are ever burning, Lord, Thy servants are ever ready."

Let us turn now from the individual application of this wonderful history to its wider bearing, in the disclosures it makes, of that Babylonish state of the Church of which it was at once the warning and the symbol. Jerusalem had become a prey to Babylon, and Babylon had attained a pitch of astounding greatness, pomp, and power. The inflated phantasy of the possessor of this seemingly impregnable position of grandeur assumed, that it was fixed, and beyond all danger of disturbance. We learn, however, that at the very acme of their glory, and in the very hour of their fullest triumph, the stroke would come which would break down the power of Babylon; which would hew down the tree, cut off its branches, shake off its leaves, and scatter its flower. Nebuchadnezzar's own name signified *the anguish of judgment.*. The Babylonish spirit is the spirit of pride united to religion. It is self-love masquerading in saintliness.

Self-love appears in myriad forms, from the fawning whine of the street beggar, who will cringe and cajole, but who loves his lazy indolence too much to give himself to steady work, to the despot who to deck HIMSELF with fame and grandeur will waste whole kingdoms, will send the wail of widows through thousands of cottages, fill the air with the orphan's cry, and maim and slaughter hundreds of thousands of human beings. Self-love appears sometimes as the polite but over-reaching tradesman, sometimes as the pilfering cheat, sometimes as the marauding midnight ruffian, or the enraged assassin, but the character in which it becomes most appallingly extravagant, most exacting, most baleful, most intensely cruel, is when it comes forth in the garb of religion. It then transfers to itself the awful attributes of the Almighty, issues its fiats as infallible decrees, and assumes to inflict eternal as well as temporal miseries, upon those who are not submissive to its will.

This is the true and terrible Babylon, of which the other was the shadow going before. The word Babel means confusion. And, certainly, it is impossible to conceive of greater confusion than is introduced into Christianity, when instead of its meek spirit of serving and ministering to others, of self-denial, of loving deference to others, and taking the lowest seat; of returning good for evil; of seeking to spread light and truth around as God's universal gifts to train all men to happiness and to heaven, we are introduced to gaudy grandees with high sounding titles, claiming to lord it over all the world, to apostles of darkness and mystery who pretend to dispense with the teaching of science and common sense, and to have their decrees admitted on pain of destruction here if they can inflict it, and of everlasting ruin which they claim to be able to bestow. This spirit of Babylon is abundantly described both in the Old and the New Testaments. Thus, we read in Isaiah respecting Babylon, "And, thou saidst, I shall be a lady for ever, so that thou didst not lay these things to thy heart, neither didst remember the latter end of it. Therefore, hear now, this, thou that art given to pleasures, that dwellest carelessly, that sayest

The first living thoughts on the subject of religion which grow up in the soul, green and vigorous, from well-supplied heavenly knowledge, are the leaves of this tree. The leaves of the spiritual tree are charming, and they are for medicine (Rev. xxii.). The flowers, are the still higher beauties of spiritual thought; the spiritual sense of the Word affords abundance of heavenly flowers, and the fruits are all the virtues of an upright life, duties done, integrity maintained, every rightful claim of position and employment cheerfully adopted and obeyed. When religion has developed itself to become such a tree, then society flourishes in blessed security, then an individual so circumstanced will be prosperous and happy. The beasts of the field, the natural affections, the fowls of heaven, all soaring rational thoughts, will dwell under its principles, like grand boughs covering and protecting everything, and there is spiritual food for all.

But ambition is Babylonish, when it seizes these grand things, and renders them subservient to its arrogant self-seeking; substituting man and a vain-glorious hierarchy for God and true principles, seeking self-glory, self-merit, and selfish power, instead of regeneration and growth in heavenly love and wisdom. This is Babylon, and great as its influence and power may seem when it has attained its height, and enmeshed everything in its swelling pride, at the summit of its power the Divine Judge provides for its overthrow. The stroke on the bell of Providence soon sounds when blasphemy is full. So was it with Nebuchadnezzar. In the hour of his haughtiest self-inflation the fiat of judgment came. "The king spake and said, Is not this great Babylon that I have made for the house of the kingdom, by the might of my power, and for the honour of my majesty. While the word was in the king's mouth, there fell a voice from heaven, saying, O king Nebuchadnezzar, to thee it is spoken; the kingdom is departed from thee" (ver. 30, 31).

When Christian Babylon attained its most audacious state of arrogancy, which had been swelling with pride for three hundred years, from the time of Hildebrand to that of Boniface VIII., whose time was almost wholly taken up with virulent quarrels for supremacy with the most powerful government of his epoch; just after he had made the most monstrous assertion of his power over kings and governments, he was seized and imprisoned by the objects of his wrath, and was so stung with the violence of his passion that he lost his reason, and died by his own violence. It was the divine decree, hew down the tree and cut off his branches. When Leo X. again imagined the time had come to make the grandest building in the world, as the magnificent symbol of papal greatness, then came the REFORMATION, and the strongest portions of Christendom were lost to Christian Babylon; again, the decree went forth, "Hew down the tree and cut off its branches; shake off his leaves and scatter his flower, let the beasts get away from under it, and the fowls from its branches."

Again, in our own time, we have seen the same preposterous claims to stop the progress of science, to arrest the diffusion of the Bible, and to claim personal infallibility for the head of Christian Babylon, but no sooner was this done than the temporal power and state for which there had been so much cursing and excommunications, and so much slaughter, was entirely lost. It was again the decree going forth, "Hew down the tree and cut off its branches; shake off his leaves, and scatter his flower." But a great system, which has been diffused through many ages and interwoven with the entire life of many kingdoms and myriads of people, cannot at one stroke be altogether destroyed and removed. It has spread, and it has lived by an accommodation to the weaknesses, the errors, the prejudices, and the barbarism of the times, and was itself a semi-barbarism. It must continue, though with greatly reduced power, and only gradually die away. It has also much good, much piety, and much charity and virtue enclosed within it, though chiefly among its humbler members. For their sakes it must live on and even to some extent revive again, though with humbler claims, and purified through suffering.

Hence, we read, "Leave the stump of his roots in the earth;" that is, let the Babylonish persuasion remain in the Church, there are vast numbers who yet cannot bear to have it altogether rooted up. Let it be made firm "with a band of iron and brass." Iron is the symbol of the truth of the letter of the Word, and brass or copper of a good life in the external virtues of religion. This binding and strengthening by the inculcation of the duties of a pious life, is the same as Moses pronounced respecting Asher—"Let Asher be blessed with children: let him be acceptable to his brethren, and let him dip his foot in oil. Thy shoes shall be iron and brass; and as thy days, so shall thy strength be" (Deut. xxxiii. 24, 25). The shoes are of iron and brass when the rule of life is true and good. Divine Mercy watches over such, in whatever church they may be, and as their days, whether stormy or fair, cold or warm, so their strength shall be. They shall be shod with the gospel of the preparation of peace (Eph. vi. 15). Let it be comforted "in the tender grass of the field," and be wet with the dew of heaven.

The tender grass of the field corresponds to the tender promises and comforts of religion. The obedient servant of the Lord can feed in the rich meadows of the Holy Word, and be cheered and strengthened by the tender grass of the field. The dew of heaven too will come quietly down upon such. Calm, holy meditations will diffuse peaceful wisdom throughout their minds, "their heavens will drop down dew." The Lord Himself will be a dew to them, as He said, "I will be as a dew unto Israel, and he shall grow as the lily" (Hosea xiv. 5). They cannot have a man's heart, for that is a heart that freely learns and rationally investigates, freely weighs, and freely follows the truth. This cannot be given in Babylon, but an obedient heart can, like that of an ox that knoweth his owner, and the ass his master's crib (Isa. i. 3). Let this spirit of obedience be given him, until he is fully weaned from the insanities of spiritual pride, and he has learned that all power and all merit belong to the Most High, and man in himself is utter evil, and a mass of corruption. When trials and reflection have brought about this conviction, and made it lasting, their work has been accomplished, seven times will have passed over the man who has gone through this tribulation, his reason will be restored, and he will be well. All this happened to king Nebuchadnezzar, king of Babylon, and he sent out his decree proclaiming the result in the memorable words, "Now I Nebuchadnezzar praise, and extol, and honour the King of heaven, all whose works are truth, and His ways judgment: and those that walk in pride He is able to abase." All this has happened to the spiritual Babylon, which has been crushed, and then again restored, and done useful works among those portions of society who are not firm-minded enough to rise above superstition, and walk by the light of clear heavenly truth rationally understood. The Most High is ruling among the children of men, and giving the kingdom to whomsoever He will, for His will is perfect goodness, guided by perfect wisdom. Let us never forget also, that every Christian needs to guard himself against the spirit of Babylon. There are many little popes, in pulpit and in pew, who cannot bear with others or suffer their infallibility to be questioned, without bitter anger being excited. This is also the essence of Babylon. "Blessed are the poor in spirit: for theirs is the kingdom of heaven."

SERMON LI.

BELSHAZZAR'S FEAST AND DEATH.

"Belshazzar the king made a great feast to a thousand of his lords, and drank wine before the thousand. Belshazzar, whiles he tasted the wine, commanded to bring the golden and silver vessels which his father Nebuchadnezzar had taken out of the temple which was in Jerusalem; that the king and his princes, his wives and his concubines, might drink therein."—DAN. v. 1, 2.

WHEN we attempt to realize the gorgeous and infatuated scene at Babylon, on the fatal night to which this chapter of the Divine Word relates, we cannot but be amazed at the extent to which human folly will go.

We learn from ancient historians, that the Babylonian host had been defeated by the Medes and Persians, under the virtuous Cyrus and his uncle Darius, and retreated into Babylon; by the defence of whose strong walls, and the succour of the magazines of the city, they hoped to be enabled to defy the army by which they were pursued and beleaguered.

Had the people been virtuous, and the monarch a true king of men, they would probably have been secure, and ultimately victorious, but the nation had long been seduced by wealth and luxury, it was effeminate and corrupt; the king, a weak, profligate, luxurious and vain tyrant, dainty in his guilt, seeking curious modes of mocking heaven, and parading his contempt for virtue. They were thus a mass of gilded rottenness; an impious band of satyrs, dancing on a volcano. On the other hand, the armies around the city were led by chiefs, modest, sober, assiduous, skilful in war, and ready to take advantage of any negligence in the disorderly host they had driven into the city, and held in what had been intended for safety, but which had become a huge net, which they were not strong enough to defend, and from which they could not escape.

The city, as is well known, was built on the two shores of the Euphrates. The river, two hundred yards wide, flowed through the midst of it. There were immense walls along the sides of the river, with huge gates of brass, similar to the defences on the land sides, and so strong, that with proper care and watchfulness, no armed boats could endanger its safety. But Cyrus, who had continued the siege of the city for many months, had caused to be dug a canal, from a bend above the city to a place below, that he might divert the river, and so leave its bed fordable. All was ready, so that advantage could be taken of an approaching festival to be kept in Babylon, when the revels would be continued all night, and riotous indulgence make the defenders careless, and besotted, exposed to be attacked and surprised, and little able to resist.

All was in reality prepared for taking the city that very night; and on that very night, the debauched king bethought him of the sacred vessels, brought by his ancestor Nebuchadnezzar from the captured Jerusalem, and he conceived it would be something unusually delightful to his polluted mind, to insult the Jews, and the God of heaven, by profaning the sacred vessels.

The banquet was at its height, the music, the lights, the liberal flow of wine, the uproar of a thousand nobles, imparted a wild madness to the scene, and caused the enemy outside to be forgotten, and even the brazen gates, the security of the city from the river, were left carelessly open, so completely had insane recklessness taken possession of monarch and people. But the end was near. No sooner had the haughty and besotted king carried out his profanity, and passed the sacred vessels, already desecrated by himself, to his princes, his wives, and his concubines, and they had also profaned them, than a mysterious hand appeared busy on the wall. The king saw it, and saw it had left a strange writing there. He felt he had gone too far, and a painful dread of something awful to come, changed his countenance, made his whole frame shake with terror, and he cried out wildly for his astrologers, Chaldeans, and soothsayers, to be brought in to explain these dread characters. He promised great rewards to those who could read the writing, and dissipate his fears. His wise men were appealed to in vain. His nobles shared his terrors, but could render no assistance.

The alarming reports of this terrible occurrence had filled the palace, and reached the queen-mother, who hastened to her son. She remembered the extraordinary things which had happened in the days of Nebuchadnezzar, her husband's father, in which Daniel had so worthily figured. Perhaps she was still a protectress of Daniel, and familiar with him, although it was the custom in Babylon, when a monarch died, to dismiss his wise men from the court, and to surround the successor with new soothsayers, as well as new counsellors.

At the queen's advice Daniel was called in. He stood before the terrified monarch venerable in age, in wisdom, and in fearless majesty, a true messenger of heaven. He undertook to decipher the writing, which being probably in the ancient Hebrew letters, would constitute no difficulty to him, and give the interpretation. First, however, he presented before the king a view of himself, such as monarchs too seldom hear. He detailed the Lord's dealings with his ancestor, Nebuchadnezzar. He depicted how Divine Providence had cast down the mighty monarch from his state, and after his repentance and chastening, raised and restored him again. And then the prophet continued, in words which must have penetrated to the inmost conscience of the king, "And thou, his son, O Belshazzar, hast not humbled thine heart, though thou knewest all this: but hast lifted up thyself against the King of heaven; and they have brought the vessels of his house before thee, and thou and thy lords, and thy wives and thy concubines, have drunk wine in them; and thou hast praised the gods of silver and gold, of brass, iron, wood, and stone, which see not, nor hear, nor know; and the God, in whose hand thy breath is, and whose are all thy ways, hast thou not glorified."

Not a word of defence had the cowed and guilty king to say. Silently he awaited the interpretation, as the utterance of a judge's doom, which indeed it was.

The words written on the plaster were, Mene, Mene, Tekel, Upharsin. The meaning being, Numbered, Numbered, Weighed, To the Persians. He explained the inscribed characters in language which, to the criminal king, must have sounded like the utterances of God Himself. MENE: God hath numbered thy kingdom and finished it. TEKEL: Thou art weighed in the balances, and found wanting. PERES, which is only another form of Pharsin: Thy kingdom is divided and given to the Medes and Persians.

The king, notwithstanding the terrible announcements he had heard, was true to his promise, and ordered Daniel to be fully rewarded, perhaps in the hope of thus deferring, or turning aside, the judgments. But it was too late. While these striking events were occurring in the banqueting hall, the water of the river was being turned into its new channel. Cyrus divided his army into two large bodies, one to march along the bed of the river, already fordable, from above; and the other from below the city. The gates having been negligently left open and unguarded, there was no resistance of any importance, and in the brief and terrible terms of the text, "In that night was Belshazzar the king of the Chaldeans slain. The Babylonian empire was ended, and the Persians, first under Cyrus, in conjunction with Darius the Median, and afterwards alone, succeeded to the government of the whole region; and Babylon received the first great blow towards that utter decay, by which, step by step, it sunk, to become mere heaps of earth, the habitation of owls and hideous creatures; its very name lost, except in history; and marsh and mound, the abode of the bittern and the wild beast, covering the ground where stood the city which had been the glory of kingdoms, the beauty of the Chaldee's excellency.

How impressive an example does this dreadful lesson yield, that in every case, to the mightiest monarch as to the meanest peasant, the wages of sin is death. To nations as to men the divine laws are ever the same. "Keep therefore and do" (the Lord's commandments), "for this is your wisdom, and your understanding in the sight of the nations which shall hear all these statutes, and say, Surely this great nation is a wise and understanding people. And it shall be if thou do at all forget the Lord thy God, and walk after other gods, and serve them and worship them, I testify against you this day, that ye shall surely perish."

Interesting and instructive, however, as the death of king Belshazzar and the downfall of Babylon are, as illustrations of the unerring character of Divine laws for all men, they are specifically intended, in the spiritual sense, to be a prophecy of the career and the downfall of spiritual Babylon,—of that state of perversion of the Christian Church in which the lust of domination has taken the place of love to the Saviour, and a complete state of insane self-seeking prevalent in the Church, to the extent of phrensied delight in claiming divine honours, and using religion for purposes of gain and vain-glorious pride.

The feast made to a thousand lords would represent the ecstasy spread throughout the fallen Church, and manifest in its conclaves, at the success of the Babylonish spirit. The wine which Belshazzar drank before his lords represented the delirious phantasy, that the Lord had committed His power on earth to men, to Peter and his successors, and that priests consequently are greater than other men, and the chief-priests greater than emperors and kings; and the mightiest among men should kiss their feet. They drink in the fancy that they can suspend God's laws, forgive sins, and open heaven to those they favour, and curse and excommunicate those who do not obey them. The false dreams, which are caught at with avidity by souls animated by the thirst of being greatest, constitute the wine which is drunk, and which intoxicates those who partake of it, until the most insane ravings fill the atmosphere with infatuated nonsense where there ought to be the sound lessons of a lowly, virtuous, and heavenly life. They can make wafers into God, they can make ground holy, holy water which shall scare away evil spirits, they can make holy dolls, holy images, holy oil, holy bells, queens of heaven, and sanctify men, by bits of wood and bones, and any amount of fraud and folly. These phantasies, and the spirit which is in them of substituting external mummery for change of heart and real religion,—the religion of loving the Lord, and showing that love by truly keeping His commandments in all we do, is the wine by which Babylon has made the nations drunk. The subtle reasoning which encourages the infatuated desire to become the greatest, which swelled itself up in the Christian Church until it far surpassed all the dreams of merely earthly ambition, is the wine of her fornication, by which the inhabitants of the earth have been made drunk (Rev. xvii. 2); for all nations have drunk of the wine of the wrath of her fornication (Rev. xviii. 3).

Under the influence of this delirious wine, the fiercest wars, the most terrific persecutions, the foulest abominations have been originated, and continued, and even yet, the Church instead of being the tamer of human passions, and the subduer of self, fully sustains and sanctions the dreadful readiness with which nations go to war. She blesses their banners, and sends them out to break all God's commandments, to devastate and destroy. To secure her own ambitious views, all the principles of religion were by Babylon made mysterious. Upon her forehead was a name written, MYSTERY, BABYLON THE GREAT, THE MOTHER OF HARLOTS, AND ABOMINATIONS OF THE EARTH. Because, when the understandings of men were enslaved by being paralysed before these so-called mysteries, they could be led at pleasure by a self-loving priesthood.

The golden and silver vessels derived from Jerusalem represent portions of the letter of the Word, which could be made subservient to the ambitious aims of the priesthood; portions of the Jewish ritual, and prophecies concerning the Divine

Priest and King, the Lord Jesus Christ, in all things sensualized. These, in their proper use are vessels to contain the heavenly wine of spiritual wisdom, but in the hands of the king and lords of Babylon, they contain the intoxicating wine of phantasy, the wild dreams of lordship and dominion. They praised the gods of gold and silver, of brass and iron, wood and stone. Idols of the six kinds of material named represent false doctrines; concerning the Lord, gold and silver idols; concerning the neighbour, brass (or copper) and iron; and concerning the religious life; wood and stone. On all these subjects there are divine laws, full of love and wisdom, which are not of our making, and which we should obey. When, however, we make artificial doctrines and rules, putting men, and human schemes and contrivances, instead of the Lord Jesus, love itself and wisdom itself embodied, and His laws of justice and judgment, we have the selfish vindictive god of ambitious priests, instead of the universal Lord, our Saviour. Instead of the true charity of doing unto others what we would have them do to us, we have love only for those of our sect, and hatred to those we call heretics. Instead of doing justly in every act and situation of life, we have the petty observances which are called laws of the Church, and the regulations which set forth artificial poverty, the unnatural life of celibacy, absurd self-inflictions, and minute specifications about meat and drink, not necessary for purposes of health, and we laud these. We are then praising the idols of gold and silver, brass and iron, wood and stone. But in the midst of our delirious phrensy, there appears on the plaster of the wall the fingers of a man's hand; and a mysterious and terrible writing is seen written over against the candlestick, MENE, MENE, TEKEL, UPHARSIN.

The apostle said to Christians, "Ye are our epistles written in our hearts, and read of all men" (2 Cor. iii. 2). The principles of their religion were manifest in their characters and conduct. The Lord Jesus said of him that overcometh, "I will write upon him my new name" (Rev. iii. 12).

The true principles of Christianity flowing out from renewed hearts and minds, manifest solid virtues in all things that are accordant with integrity, truthfulness, lovingkindness, and in the varied ministrations which fill and adorn life with beauty and use. But in the artificial conduct which Babylon enjoins, which is a plaster covering, and not a natural outgrowth, whenever a time of crisis and judgment comes, it is palpable in the abuses, the monstrosities, the vilenesses which burst forth on all sides, what a terrible hell has been hidden within. Read the account of any epoch of trial, in a Babylonish nation, such as the French Revolution, and you will see from the awful manifestations of spirit, both with priests and people, that under the smooth plaster of a tame and decorous life, have been hidden fiendish lusts and awful passions. This is then made manifest to the intellect of those who retain the power of discernment; for the intellect of man is the candlestick of the Lord, intended to hold up the light of heaven in the world. The writing was over against the candlestick, to intimate that the will of the Divine Providence is that men should reflect upon this awful manifestation, and understand that in such a system there has been no regeneration, no change of heart and mind, and therefore self remains unsubdued, and indeed exists in its most insidious and destructive form. Whited sepulchres are there, appearing fair without, but inwardly full of dead men's bones, and all uncleanness. The astrologers, the Chaldeans, and soothsayers cannot tell the meaning of this. They represent the teachers of the Babylonish system. They have always extolled it as divine, and the perfection of wisdom, and cannot in the least explain how it is that its issues are so calamitous.

The queen-mother advises that Daniel should be sent for; that is, those who are in the affection for goodness and truth, advise that such as love the Word of God should be consulted. They are the true Daniel; they will speak kindly but fearlessly. They testify at once, that the source of all the misery and all the terror, is, that Babylon is an external religion, with an unchanged heart. "Thou, O Belshazzar, hast not humbled thine heart; but hast lifted up thyself against the Lord of heaven." "The God in whose hand thy breath is, and whose are all thy ways, hast thou not glorified."

Here the finger is laid on the centre of the plague. Babylon is a system of religion without regeneration, external form without internal purity, superstition instead of light, the decrees of man instead of the Word of God. Such a system must perish. Mene, Mene. It is numbered and found false in relation to God, and false in relation to man. Its good is hollow and superficial. Its virtues are of little value, and the idea of merit defiles them all. They are weighed in the balances of true righteousness, and found wanting. The kingdom is divided, and given to the Medes and Persians. Babylon will cease to be a church. It will remain only as a carcase, a superstition. The Church will be given for a time to those who are somewhat divided among themselves but are united in this, that they exalt and spread the Word of God. There is the divine seed out of which a pure church will come, but not yet. The soldiers who have overcome Babylon will take the kingdom. The reformers, heroic souls, who could no longer bear the iniquities of Babylon, such as it was at its worst, who struggled against papal abominations, when it was danger to protest, and death to defy, these are the spiritual Medes and Persians. They renounced and broke down Babylon, and with them the Church would be, because with them the Word would be; the Church not in entirety or thorough purity, but as much as mankind could bear, and until the period when the New Jerusalem would come down from the Lord out of heaven. In that night was Belshazzar, the king of the Chaldeans slain. Belshazzar signifies *Master of secret treasures*. And his being slain in that night teaches that the state of the papal Babylon, in which she was master of the treasures of the Divine Word, which she kept hidden from the people, was brought to an end. The same thing is taught by the ten horns, who are ten kings, who hate Babylon the great, and make her desolate and naked, and eat her flesh, and burn her with fire (Rev. xvii. 16).

They repudiate, condemn, and renounce the cumbrous system of spiritual despotism, the substitution of man and his mystery for God and His Word, but they are not for a time able to accept the central truth of the New Jerusalem, that the Lamb, the Lord Jesus Christ, in whom are Father, Son, and Holy Spirit, the whole fulness of the Godhead bodily, is King of kings and Lord of lords. The Lamb will in due time overcome them; not to harm them, but to save them. They will yield their homage to Him, and join those who with Him are called elect and faithful.

The Babylon of the ancients, though once a benevolent rule, became a fearful oppression, and when she fell the world breathed more freely. Mankind said, "How hath the oppressor ceased; the golden city ceased! The Lord hath broken the staff of the wicked, and the sceptre of the rulers. The whole earth is at rest, and are quiet; they break forth into singing" (Isa. xiv. 4, 5, 7). But oh! far more happy was it when the power of papal Babylon was broken, and the Word of God set free. Since then, spiritual liberty has led the way to liberty of every kind, political, social, and scientific. Man, with the Word in his hand, walks abroad in the domains of Him who is his loving Father and Saviour, and gathers truth everywhere. A free Bible ultimately makes everything else free. If the truth shall make you free, ye shall be free indeed.

SERMON LII.

THE RESTORATION OF JERUSALEM.

"'So shall ye know that I am the Lord your God dwelling in Zion, my holy mountain; then shall Jerusalem be holy, and there shall no strangers pass through her any more."—JOEL iii. 17.

THE careful reader of the Divine Word will notice that in the Old Testament a large part of Scripture is occupied with two captivities of the people of Israel, the captivity in Egypt and the captivity in Babylon. The first bondage to which they had been reduced under Pharaoh, and from which the Lord redeemed them by the hand of Moses, was the emblem as Christian divines have always taught, of that slavery to worldliness and sin, which is forsaken when a soul truly turns to the Lord, made spiritually free by truth from Him, and enters on the spiritual journey of regeneration. The journey of Israel led to the possession of Canaan, and was crowned by the constitution of Jerusalem as the capital of the country, the grand seat of their greatest ceremonies, and the centre of their worship and their church. At Jerusalem was the temple, and to Jerusalem three times in the year must every Jew go up. It was the centre of their instruction, of their hopes and their love. It was to them "the City of God, the mountain of holiness; beautiful for situation, the joy of the whole earth, the city of the Great King." It was, however much more than this, it was the symbol of the Lord's Church when the Blessed Redeemer, Jehovah in the flesh, would open it to all nations, replacing the sacrifice of lambs, sheep, bulls and goats, by the purer worship, the offerings of the affections and thoughts, the spirit and truth of His children.

The earthly Jerusalem was the type of the spiritual Jerusalem, the Christian Church; and the law was the shadow of good things to come (Heb. x. 1). Its priests were the type of Christians, who were to be a royal priesthood, a holy nation, to offer up spiritual sacrifices, and shew forth the praises of Him who had called them out of darkness into His marvellous light (1 Pet.

ii. 5, 9). Thus, the apostles frequently portray both the Jews and Jerusalem. "He is not a Jew," Paul said, "who is one outwardly, neither is that circumcision which is outward in the flesh, but he is a Jew who is one inwardly, and circumcision is that of the heart in the spirit, and not in the letter" (Rom. ii. 28, 29). Jerusalem that now is, is in bondage with her children; but Jerusalem which is above is free, and is the mother of us all (Gal. iv. 25, 26). Still more markedly does the Apostle speak in the epistle to the Hebrews, "Ye are come unto mount Zion and unto the city of the living God, THE HEAVENLY JERUSALEM, and to an innumerable company of angels; to the general assembly and CHURCH of the first-born, which are written in heaven" (Heb. xii. 22, 23).

That Jerusalem was the type of the Christian Church then does not admit of question. Its very name illustrates this, for it signifies THE SIGHT OF PEACE. What a beautiful ideal of a church is enclosed in that exquisite appellation, the sight of peace. For when we have a sight of the Lord Jesus, we behold the Prince of peace and the Source of peace. The principles of true Christianity are the principles of peace. Truth, charity, mutual love, doing unto others as we would they should do unto us, are the very essence and rules of peace. And above all, the glorious kingdom for which the Christian lives, and to which his hopes and aims aspire, is emphatically the kingdom of peace. The peace of a virtuous life, the peace of a soul abiding by faith and love in the Saviour, and the peace of the golden world of order, love, and joy; these are the very constituents of the Church, the heavenly Jerusalem, of which the earthly capital of Judea was the beautiful but transitory type, which would give place to the grander reality when the Prince of Peace appeared and opened His spiritual kingdom.

We thus have a most satisfactory reason why so large a portion of the Divine Word is taken up with the history, the events, and the loveliness of Jerusalem. The bondage the Israelites fled from, their coming into Canaan, and their being made citizens of their magnificent metropolis, were all typical of Christians rescued from the fetters of evil lusts and corrupt habits, and then being constituted into a Jerusalem, not confined to Judea, but wide as the world, embracing citizens whose renewed hearts and minds were knitted together by diviner things, than earthly Solyma ever knew, things of heavenly wisdom, living faith, devoted love to a Divine and loving Saviour, and self-sacrifice in doing His holy will. But earthly Jerusalem, after some glorious centuries, became corrupt and faithless, disobedient and perverse. Where the living God had filled His house with glory, and shone forth with His responses from between the cherubim, there idols became multiplied, and the covenant broken. The people committed two evils; they forsook the Fountain of Living Waters, and hewed out for themselves cisterns, broken cisterns, that could hold no water (Jer. ii. 13). They burned incense to other gods, and worshipped the work of their own hands (Jer. i. 16).

They courted intercourse with Assyria, and with Babylon, until they became Babylonish themselves, and then the greater Babylon devoured them. The remains of the nation were kept in captivity seventy years, and they then were restored, and formed a second Jerusalem. This restoration of Jerusalem from Babylon, this second return from captivity, occupies almost as prominent a place in the prophetical writings as the return from Egypt does in the books of Moses. We shall not be astonished at the captivity of the Jewish nation in Babylon, and their return to their own land, being so often the theme of the prophets, if we bear in mind the extreme misery and degradation they sustained, and the deeply rooted patriotism of the Jew. The awful way in which Babylon strove to trample the nation out, is intimated in Jeremiah, "Moreover, I will take from them the voice of mirth, and the voice of gladness, the voice of the bridegroom, and the voice of the bride, the sound of the millstones, and the light of the candle. And this whole land shall be a desolation, and an astonishment; and these nations shall serve the king of Babylon seventy years" (xxv. 10, 11).

The astonishing fixity and the wondrous depth of Jewish love of nation and country, has no parallel. Other peoples, after two or three generations, are unaffected by the remembrance of a land their ancestors have quitted. They become entirely contented denizens of their new homes, and mostly enthusiastic admirers of the new lands, now their own. But Jewish home-love has endured nearly two thousand years of absence, and burns with wonderful energy still. When, therefore, they were defeated, dispersed, almost destroyed as a nation, the temple burnt, their capital uninhabitable, and its remaining people carried away apparently never to return, settled as outcasts, and derided as slaves by the rivers of Babylon and the neighbouring lands, we may well enter into the spirit of the most pathetic of all the Psalms, and feel as though it were composed of the anguish and tears of the captives—" By the rivers of Babylon, there we sat down; yea, we wept when we remembered Zion. We hanged our harps upon the willows, in the midst thereof. For there they that carried us away required of us a song; and they that wasted us required of us mirth, saying, Sing us one of the songs of Zion. How shall we sing the Lord's song in a strange land? If I forget thee, O Jerusalem, let my right hand forget her cunning. If I do not remember thee, let my tongue cleave to the roof of my mouth; if I prefer not Jerusalem above my chief joy" (cxxxvii.).

With all their love of home, and all the misery of absence, combined with the accumulated sorrows of captivity and slavery, we may well conceive how joyous their return would be. How glad they would learn the decree of Cyrus! How exultantly they would commence their return home. How they would kiss the dear spot from which they had so long been absent, and with what energy they would strive to rebuild the city and the temple, and once more have the faith that they were under the protection and blessing of the Lord their God. This feeling is portrayed in another Psalm—" When the Lord turned again the captivity of Zion, we were like them that dream. Then was our mouth filled with laughter, and our tongue with singing: then said they among the heathen, The Lord hath done great things for them. The Lord hath done great things for us, whereof we are glad" (cxxvi.). Bearing these considerations in mind, we may readily perceive why so much is said, and in terms of such joyous exultation, of the return to their own land, of Jerusalem being built again, of its being established with abounding prosperity to abide for ever. This latter phrase, however, strictly rendered, is for an age, or dispensation.

The prophecies of this return were all given either before the captivity, as in the instances of Isaiah and Jeremiah, or during the captivity, as in the cases of Ezekiel, Daniel, Haggai, and Zechariah. The restoration of the nation of Jerusalem after the misery of the Babylonish bondage fulfilled all those prophecies respecting the return of the Jews to their own land, so far as their literal application is concerned, and there is nothing in Scripture to warrant the anticipation of A THIRD RETURN. They have accomplished their use as a separate nation—the use of preserving the Word, and the great doctrines of the Unity and Fatherhood of God; and now that Christians are learning to be Christian to the Jews, and to rise to a Christianity of real love and goodness, the Jews will gradually rise above their narrow and isolating forms, and learn, we doubt not, in time to be Christian too. They will then rejoice in Jehovah, the God of their fathers, not less dear or less glorious, because He is also Jesus the Saviour of all men in every land, the Deliverer from all sin, from all selfishness, and therefore from all sorrow. This would be to come into a Jerusalem far more magnificent and more happy than any earthly city; a city indeed of the living God, a city whose light is the glory of God, whose streets are of transparent gold, whose atmosphere inspires only thoughts of purity, peace, and joy; and whose inhabitants are all of the great family of the good and the true, of innumerable varieties of mind and body, but all united by the blessed girdle of love to God and love to man.

We have already said that the only literal return of the Jews to their own land, contemplated by the prophecies, was the return from Babylon THE SECOND TIME, as it is denominated in Isaiah; and these prophecies were literally fulfilled in the period of the literal dispensation which closed with the resurrection of our Lord. After that, the new spiritual dispensation of Christianity began, a dispensation of which the Redeemer Himself said, "Woman, believe me, the hour cometh, when ye shall neither in this mountain, nor yet at Jerusalem, worship the Father. Ye worship ye know not what: we know what we worship: for salvation is of the Jews. But the hour cometh, and NOW IS, when the true worshippers shall worship the Father in spirit and in truth: for THE FATHER SEEKETH SUCH TO WORSHIP HIM. God is a Spirit: and they that worship Him, must worship Him in spirit and in truth" (John iv. 21-24).

We have already said that the return from Babylon is the only return referred to in the prophetic writings, so far as their literal application goes; and, therefore, the expectation of many at the present day that the Jews are to return to Palestine again, is an error, gathered chiefly from the prophetic declarations which speak of the return of the Jews from Babylon to their own land, and the restoration of Jerusalem, WHICH WERE FULFILLED five hundred years before our Lord came into the world.

Let us notice a few of these declarations. "And it shall come to pass in that day, that the Lord shall set His hand again, A SECOND TIME, to recover the remnant of His people, which shall be left, from Assyria, and from Egypt, and from Pathros, and from Cush, and from Elam (Media), and from

Shinar (Babylon), and Hamath, and the isles of the sea" (Isa. xi. 11). Again, "Go ye forth of Babylon, flee ye from the Chaldeans, with a voice of singing declare ye, tell this, utter it even to the end of the earth; say ye, The Lord hath redeemed His servant Jacob" (Isa. xlviii. 20). In Jeremiah also the language is equally clear. "Like these good figs, so will I acknowledge them that are carried away captive of Judah into the land of the Chaldeans, for their good. For I will set mine eyes upon them for good, and I will bring them again to this land: and I will build them, and not pull them down; and I will plant them, and not pluck them up. And I will give them a heart to know me, that I am the Lord: and they shall be my people, and I will be their God: for they shall return unto me with their whole heart" (Jer. xxiv. 5-7).

The resurrection of dry bones was a vision to the prophet Ezekiel, in the land of the Babylonians, where his countrymen were then prisoners, to represent the approaching end of the captivity, and the restoration of Israel; the resurrection of the nation, then politically dead, to their beloved country once more. "Then, he said unto me, Son of man, these bones are the whole house of Israel: behold they say, Our bones are dried, and our hope is lost: we are cut off for our parts. Therefore, prophesy, and say unto them, Thus saith the Lord God: Behold, O my people, I will open your graves, and cause you to come up out of your graves, and bring you into THE LAND OF ISRAEL. And shall put my spirit in you, and ye shall live, and I shall place you IN YOUR OWN LAND: then shall ye know that I the Lord have spoken it, and performed it, saith the Lord" (Ezek. xxxvii. 11, 12, 14).

One other declaration we will cite, and we conceive it will be abundantly evident that the return of the Israelitish people and the restoration of Jerusalem, to which the prophets refer, were the return from Babylon, with the permission to rebuild Jerusalem, with its temple, after that restoration of the nation. "For I, saith the Lord, will be unto her a wall of fire round about, and will be the glory in the midst of her. Ho, ho, come forth and flee from the land of the north, saith the Lord, for I have spread you abroad, as the four winds of the heaven, saith the Lord. Deliver thyself, O Zion, that dwellest with the DAUGHTER OF BABYLON. For thus saith the Lord of hosts, After the glory, hath he sent me unto the nations which spoiled you: for he that toucheth you, toucheth the apple of His eye" (Zech. ii. 5-8).

It is perfectly evident, we trust, that the great captivity from which the Israelites were to be brought, when they were restored to their own land, was the seventy years' exile in Babylon, and no other return is even hinted at in the sacred oracles, and consequently the expectation of those who imagine that a restoration of the nation to its ancient glory in Palestine is yet to be expected, is a mistake. It is a mistake of those who have not yet learned the grand lesson of Christianity, upon which all progress and happiness rest,. "The kingdom of God is not lo here or lo there, but the kingdom of God is within you."

They who change their hearts from unselfish states by the power of truth from the Lord Jesus, who grow in love and unselfishness, who seek to do away with all prejudices in themselves, and rejoice in doing the Lord's will on earth as it is done in heaven, who shun all evils as sins against Him, and abhor all idea of merit or self-righteousness, these will enter the New Jerusalem, the new city of truth, the holy mountain, for Christian and for Jew alike, for Catholic and Protestant, black and white, bond and free. "And the Lord shall be king over all the earth: in that day shall there be one Lord, and His name one".(Zech. xiv. 9).

We have seen that Jerusalem was the type of the Christian Church, and this is admitted by the teachers of all portions of Christendom; the redemption from Egypt was a type of deliverance from the bondage of sin, by which alone a man becomes really a Christian. So far so good. What then, after centuries of glorious existence, would the captivity of Jerusalem to Babylon mean? Does it not clearly foreshadow that the spiritual, the Christian Jerusalem, would gradually succumb to Babylon, and be fully degraded, and trodden under foot, by the ambitious lust of rule? And has not this been fulfilled? From what, have the divisions and struggles that have rent the Christian Church for twelve hundred years arisen but from the struggles as to who should be greatest? This is the very essence of Babylon. Let any one read the sweet and simple pages of the gospel, and then observe the gaudy decorations, the meretricious pomp and splendour, the high-sounding names which have been foisted upon Christianity in many lands, and ask himself is that Christian purity, or Babylonish pride?

With the struggle to be greatest in religion comes contempt for others, animosity, hate, persecution, sectional heart-burnings, and sectarian virulence. These are all signs of Babylonish ambition, not of Christian meekness. When they prevail, Israel is in captivity to Babylon. But, blessed be the name of the Most High, Israel will be brought out of Babylon. Jerusalem will be restored to freedom, and be a city of light,—a city of love. The Lord our God, as our text declares, will dwell in Zion, His holy mountain. The mountain of the Lord's house shall be at the top of the mountains, and above all the hills (Isa. ii. 2). Or in other words, Love to the Lord Jesus shall be above all other affections. In the grand solemn silences of the heart, in its holiest sympathies, which like great mountains lift themselves up to heaven, this one shall reign supreme, Jesus is all in all. He is the First and the Last. His will, of perfect love, in all things, must be done.

In this inmostly holy sentiment the Lord Himself will dwell. From the Lord within an impulse will constantly flow forth in harmony with His Word, and our ears shall hear a word behind us saying, This is the way, walk ye in it, when ye turn to the right hand and when ye turn to the left. Then shall Jerusalem be holy. Jerusalem shall be, and be called, a city of truth (Zech. viii. 3). Her inhabitants shall delight in truth, be sanctified by the truth, the Word, which is truth, shall open its glorious streams within her, and all shall know that "there is a river, the streams whereof shall make glad the city of God, the holy place of the tabernacles of the Most High. God is in the midst of her, she shall not be moved. God shall help her and that right early." There shall no strangers pass through her any more. A stranger is one foreign to the spirit of the place, and a stranger to the spiritual Jerusalem would be one strange to goodness and truth. Too many strangers have gone through the Old Jerusalem, defiled her palaces, and made her inhabitants wretched, but no stranger shall pass through the New Jerusalem. Strangers repel the city from them, or themselves from the city. When the ambitious or impure strive to enter, they miss the way and get to Egypt or to Sodom instead.

Blessed are the pure in heart, for they shall see God; they shall behold also the city of God, and the glory of God shall enlighten them. They shall eat of the bread of life, and drink of the living water. They shall have an inward heaven, and increase in interior loveliness, until they are called at last to the realms of eternal joy and peace.

"So shall ye know that I am the Lord your God dwelling in Zion, my holy mountain; then shall Jerusalem be holy, **and there shall no strangers pass through her any more.**"

www.ingramcontent.com/pod-product-compliance
Lightning Source LLC
Chambersburg PA
CBHW030603300426
44111CB00009B/1085